Clandestine Political Violence

This volume compares four types of clandestine political violence: left-wing (in Italy and Germany), right-wing (in Italy), ethnonationalist (in Spain), and religious fundamentalist (in Islamist clandestine organizations). Donatella della Porta develops her own definition of clandestine political violence that is oriented toward theory building. Building on the most recent developments in social movement studies, della Porta proposes an original interpretative model. Using a unique research design, she singles out some common causal mechanisms at the onset, during the persistence, and at the demise of clandestine political violence. The development of the phenomenon is located within the interactions among social movements, countermovements, and the state. She pays particular attention to the ways in which the different actors cognitively construct the reality they act on. The internal dynamics of the clandestine political organizations are given special attention. Based on original empirical research as well as existing research in many languages, this book is rich in empirical evidence on some of the most crucial cases of clandestine political violence.

Donatella della Porta is a professor of sociology at the European University Institute (EUI) and a professor of political science at the Istituto Italiano di Scienze Umane. She was the 2011 recipient of the Mattei Dogan Prize for distinguished achievements in the field of political sociology. She directs both the Centre on Social Movement Studies at the EUI and the Mobilizing for Democracy project with funding from the European Research Council. She is coeditor of *European Political Science Review*. Her previous publications with Cambridge University Press include *Meeting Democracy* (edited with Dieter Rucht, 2012); *Approaches and Methodologies in the Social Sciences* (edited with Michael Keating, 2008); and *Social Movements, Political Violence, and the State* (1995).

T0382282

Cambridge Studies in Contentious Politics

Editors

Mark Beissinger *Princeton University*
Jack A. Goldstone *George Mason University*
Michael Hanagan *Vassar College*
Doug McAdam *Stanford University and Center for Advanced Study in the
Behavioral Sciences*
Sarah A. Soule *Stanford University*
Suzanne Staggenborg *University of Pittsburgh*
Sidney Tarrow *Cornell University*
Charles Tilly (d. 2008) *Columbia University*
Elisabeth J. Wood *Yale University*
Deborah Yashar *Princeton University*

Continued after the index

Clandestine Political Violence

DONATELLA DELLA PORTA

European University Institute

CAMBRIDGE
UNIVERSITY PRESS

CAMBRIDGE
UNIVERSITY PRESS

University Printing House, Cambridge CB2 8BS, United Kingdom

One Liberty Plaza, 20th Floor, New York, NY 10006, USA

477 Williamstown Road, Port Melbourne, VIC 3207, Australia

314-321, 3rd Floor, Plot 3, Splendor Forum, Jasola District Centre, New Delhi - 110025, India

79 Anson Road, #06-04/06, Singapore 079906

Cambridge University Press is part of the University of Cambridge.

It furthers the University's mission by disseminating knowledge in the pursuit of education, learning and research at the highest international levels of excellence.

www.cambridge.org
Information on this title: www.cambridge.org/9780521195744

© Donatella della Porta 2013

This publication is in copyright. Subject to statutory exception and to the provisions of relevant collective licensing agreements, no reproduction of any part may take place without the written permission of Cambridge University Press.

First published 2013

A catalogue record for this publication is available from the British Library

Library of Congress Cataloging in Publication data
Della Porta, Donatella, 1956–
Clandestine political violence / Donatella Della Porta.
    pages   cm. – (Cambridge studies in contentious politics)
Includes bibliographical references and index.
ISBN 978-0-521-19574-4 (hardback) – ISBN 978-0-521-14616-6 (paperback)
1. Political violence.   2. Violence.   I. Title.
JC328.6.D445   2013
332.4´2–dc23   2012035664

ISBN 978-0-521-19574-4 Hardback
ISBN 978-0-521-14616-6 Paperback

Cambridge University Press has no responsibility for the persistence or accuracy of URLs for external or third-party internet websites referred to in this publication, and does not guarantee that any content on such websites is, or will remain, accurate or appropriate.

To Herbert

Contents

Acknowledgments

If every book is a journey, this voyage started a long, long time ago. I first became interested in political violence before starting my PhD, back in the early 1980s. That interest was driven by social and scientific concerns. As regards the social domain, in the 1970s in Italy and other countries of the world, very high levels of political violence had challenged not only the state but also social movements' capacity to mobilize. In the scientific domain, although much had been written on terrorism, it had been mainly treated as an isolated pathology, whereas political violence had rarely been addressed within social movement studies. My work on Italy, carried out during my PhD studies at the European University Institute, indicated that left-wing political violence could instead be better understood if located within the escalation of social conflicts, during long-lasting interactions among movements, countermovements, and the state. If that case study provided "thick" knowledge and theoretical suggestions, it also challenged me to consult further works to assess my analyses' capacity to travel beyond the Italian case.

A first step in this process was a binary comparison of Italy and Germany, two cases similar in several respects. The Wissenschaftszentrum Berlin für soziale Forschung, the Harry Frank Guggenheim Foundation, and the Alexander von Humboldt Stiftung offered me material and intellectual support during this period. My work continued in the same direction through a broader comparison of the same type of political violence in the form of a coauthored work (with Pat Steinhoff and Gilda Zwerman) comparing left-wing violence in Italy, Germany, Japan, and the United States.

As social movements became more peaceful, I shifted attention away from radical forms of collective action, until, especially after the events of September 11, 2001, I was stimulated again to look at political violence by a social concern that soon brought about a scientific puzzle. In the beginning of this new wave of attention to radical politics, I tended to decline invitations to comment on religiously inspired violence, which I considered very different from the left-wing phenomenon I had studied in the past. I am grateful, however, to the colleagues who insisted on calling on me, as it was particularly other scholars' references to my work on social movements, in attempts to understand its most recent forms, that convinced me of the potential comparability of these different cases.

Over the last decade, I had several welcome occasions to explore broader comparisons. First, at EUI, in 2007–8, the Robert Schuman Center for Advanced Studies asked my historian colleague Gerhard Haupt and me to lead a yearlong European forum, hosting postdoctoral Fellows from various disciplines. Many highly stimulating debates have thereby nurtured my work. For those, I am grateful to Gerhard and our fellow researchers, Giulia Albanese, Lorenzo Bosi, Chares Demetriou, Julia Eckert, Daniel Monterescu, Mate Tokic, and Claudia Verhoven, as well as to the dozens of PhD students who have participated in seminars and conferences. So successful was that year's experience that we continued to offer cross-disciplinary courses on political violence for several years thereafter.

Another occasion to reflect on cross-type comparison came from a research project on the radical Right (VETO, or violent, extremist, terrorist organizations) that I directed within the START consortium at the University of Maryland. For this opportunity, I am grateful to Gary Lafree and Clark McCauley, who trusted my work, and to Manuela Caiani and Claudius Wagemann, who collaborated on it.

Other stimuli came from opportunities to organize conferences, edit special journal issues, and cooperate on various writing projects. In 2011, the ZIF-Center for Interdisciplinary Research at Bielefeld University asked me to collaborate on the organization of a large international conference on radicalization and de-radicalization, based on which I coedited a special issue of the *International Journal of Conflict and Violence*. At the same time, with Lasse Lindekilde, I coedited a special issue on de-radicalization policies for the *European Journal on Criminal Policy and Research*. I also continued to learn from the several articles I wrote with Lorenzo Bosi on political violence, with Bernard Gbikpi on riots, and with Herbert Reiter on the policing of protest. Although the list of colleagues who offered comments during conferences, seminars, and lectures is too long to be recorded here, I want to express my gratitude to three friends and colleagues – Lorenzo Bosi, Stefan Malthaner, and Sidney Tarrow – who had the loyalty to read and comment on the penultimate draft of this work. Even though the responsibility for errors or omissions remains mine, the final result was much improved by their suggestions.

The same can be said for the constructive comments I have received from the anonymous referees for Cambridge University Press. At the Press, I am also grateful to Lew Bateman, who has supported this project since its very early stages. For this volume, as for many others, Sarah Tarrow has been much more than an editor-in-chief, contributing her high level of commitment and her skills to make my English more readable.

For the last ten years, the Department of Sociology and Political Science at the European University Institute has been a most wonderful place to be. I have enjoyed innumerable stimuli and much support from colleagues, PhD students, and postdoctoral mentees. In the last year of preparation of this manuscript, I had the privilege to be given by the European Research Council (ERC) an advanced grant, entitled "Mobilizing for Democracy," that has helped me in reflecting on the interaction among violence, social movements, and quality of democracy. I also worked on part of the research while a visiting scholar at the Wissenschaftszentrum fuer soziale Forschung in Berlin and at Humboldt University. I thank my colleagues Dieter Rucht, Michael Zürn, and Klaus Eder for their support there. Although neither the ERC nor the European Commission of the European Union is responsible for what I report in this volume, their contribution to the research is gratefully acknowledged.

Some ideas presented here have been developed from my previous work, which is reported in the following publications: "Unwanted Children: Political Violence and the Cycle of Protest in Italy, 1966–1973" (coauthored with Sidney Tarrow), in *European Journal of Political Research* 14 (1986); *Il terrorismo di sinistra* (Il Mulino, 1990); *Social Movements, Political Violence and the State* (Cambridge University Press, 1995); *Policing Protest: The Control of Mass Demonstrations in Western Democracies* (edited with Herbert Reiter; University of Minnesota Press, 1998); *Social Movements: An Introduction* (coauthored with Mario Diani; Blackwell, 2006); "Research on Social Movements and Political Violence," in *Qualitative Sociology* 31 (2008); "Leaving Left-Wing Terrorism in Italy: A Sociological Analysis," in Tore Bjørgo and John Horgan, eds., *Leaving Terrorism Behind* (Routledge, 2008); and "Micro-Mobilization into Armed Groups: The Ideological, Instrumental and Solidaristic Paths" (coauthored with Lorenzo Bosi), in *Qualitative Sociology* 35 (2012).

To Herbert Reiter, who has patiently *sopportato* and *supportato* me for more than twenty-five years now, I dedicate what he has humorously called my "opus magnum."

Acronyms

AI	Amnesty International
AN	Avanguardia Nazionale (National Vanguard)
AQ	al-Qaeda
AQAP	al-Qaeda in the Arabian Peninsula
B2J	Bewegung 2 Juni (June 2nd Movement)
BR	Brigate Rosse
CCOOs	*comisiones obreras*
CPO	Collettivo Politico Operaio
EE	Euskadiko Ezkerra (Patriotic Left)
EIA	Euskal Iraultzarako Alderia (Basque Revolutionary Party)
ETA	Euskadi Ta Askatasuna (Basquen-land and Freedom)
ETA-M	ETA military
ETA-PM	ETA politico-military
FCC	Formazioni Comuniste Combattenti (Fighting Communist Formations)
FGCI	Federazione Giovani Comunisti Italiani (Italian Communist Youth Federation)
FIS	Front Islamic de Salut
FLNQ	Front de Libération National du Quebec
GAL	Grupos Antiterroristas de Liberacion
GIA	Groupe Islamique Armé
HB	Herri Batasuna
KAS	Koordinadora Abertzale Socializta (Socialist Patriotic Coordinator Committee)
LAB	Langile Abertzale Batzordeak (Patriotic Workers' Committee)
LC	Lotta Continua (Continuous Struggle)
MB(s)	Muslim Brotherhood, or Muslim Brothers
MNLV	Movimento de Liberacion Nationale Vasco (Basque Movement of National Liberation)
MSI	Movimento Sociale Italiano
MWL	Muslim World League
NAP	Nuclei Armati Proletari

NAR	Nuclei Armati Rivoluzionari (Revolutionary Armed Nuclei)
ON	Ordine Nuovo (New Order)
P2	Masonic Lodge Propaganda 2
PAC	Proletari Armati per il Comunismo
PCI	Partito Comunista Italiano (Communist Italian Party)
PCIml	Partito Comunista Italiano Marxista Leninista
PL	Prima Linea (Front Line)
PLO	Palestine Liberation Organization
PNV	National Basque Party
PO	Potere Operaio (Worker's Power)
PSOE	Partido Socialista Obrero Espanol (Spanish Socialist Workers' Party)
RAF	Rote Armee Fraktion (Red Army Fraction)
RZ	Rote Zellen (Red Cells)
SDS	Social Democratic Students
SID	Servizio Informazioni Difesa (secret services)
SIFAR	Servizio Informazioni Forze Armate (military intelligence)
SMOs	social movement organizations
SPD	Sozialdemokratische Partei Deutschlands (Social Democratic Party of Germany)
UCC	Unità Comuniste Combattenti (Communist Fighting Units)
UGT	Union General de Trabajadores (General Workers' Union)

I

Political Violence and Social Movements

An Introduction

11 September 2001:

The September 11 attacks, often referred to as September 11th or 9/11 (pronounced "nine eleven"), were a series of coordinated suicide attacks by al-Qaeda upon the United States. That morning, nineteen al-Qaeda terrorists hijacked four commercial passenger jet airliners. The hijackers intentionally crashed two of the jets into the Twin Towers of the World Trade Center in New York City, killing everyone on board and many others working in the buildings. Both towers collapsed within two hours, destroying nearby buildings and damaging others. A third airliner was flown into the Pentagon in Arlington, Virginia, just outside Washington, D.C. The fourth plane crashed in a field in rural Pennsylvania after some of its passengers and flight crew attempted to retake control of the plane, which the hijackers had redirected to target either the Capitol Building or the White House. There were no survivors from any of the flights. Nearly three thousand victims died in the attacks, along with the nineteen hijackers. (Wikipedia, http://en.wikipedia.org/wiki/September_11_attacks, accessed 15 February 2012)

5 September 2010:

Armed Basque separatist group Eta says it will not carry out "armed actions" in its campaign for independence. In a video obtained exclusively by the BBC, the group said it took the decision several months ago "to put in motion a democratic process." The Basque interior minister called the statement "insufficient." Madrid has previously insisted that Eta renounce violence and disarm before any talks. Eta's violent campaign has led to more than 820 deaths over the past 40 years. It has called two ceasefires in the past, but abandoned them both. This latest announcement comes after the arrests of numerous Eta leaders and during an unprecedented period of debate within the Basque nationalist community over the future direction of policy. (BBC News Europe, http://www.bbc.co.uk/news/world-europe-11191395, accessed 3 April 2011)

31 December 2010:

Italy has reacted with fury to the Brazilian president's decision on his last day in office not to extradite an Italian former left-wing militant. The Italian foreign ministry recalled its ambassador to Brazil, while the defence minister said Luiz Inacio Lula da Silva had shown a "lack of courage." But Brazil's government said the move was not an "affront" to another state. Cesare Battisti has been convicted in absentia of murdering four people in Italy between 1978 and 1979. The 56-year-old has maintained his innocence, saying he is the victim of political persecution in Italy and that he risks being killed if extradited. "I am guilty, as I have often said, of having participated in an armed group with a subversive aim and of having carried weapons. But I never shot anyone," he wrote in a book published in 2006. Battisti has been on the run since escaping from an Italian jail in 1981 while awaiting trial. He spent the intervening years in France – where he started a career as a novelist – Mexico and finally Brazil. (BBC News Latin America and Caribbean, http://www.bbc.co.uk/news/world-latin-america-1209847, accessed 3 April 2011)

2011:

The second decade of the twenty-first century began with some most dramatic instances of right-wing, racist violence. On 22 July, a militant from the extreme Right killed eight people in the bombing of governmental buildings in Oslo and shot another sixty-nine, mostly teenagers who were participating in a camp run by the Labour Party Workers' Youth League (AUF) on the island of Utøya. In November 2011, German authorities found evidence that a right-wing, clandestine cell was responsible for the killing of nine migrants (eight from Turkey and one from Greece) and a policewoman; all of these crimes had been committed in the last thirteen years. On 13 December 2011, a member of the extreme right-wing group Casa Pound shot and killed two Senegalese street vendors and wounded another three in two crowded markets in Florence. Two German right-wing militants as well as an Italian were found dead by police, apparently having committed suicide.

What do these episodes have in common? Of course, they all refer to political violence in one of its most extreme forms: the perpetration of killings by small, underground groups (or even single individuals) oriented to (more or less clearly stated) political aims. I refer to this phenomenon as *clandestine political violence*. Yet there are of course many differences among these instances. September 11th is the most dramatic episode of what has come to be known as religious fundamentalism. The actions by Cesare Battisti belong to the story of a left-wing, ideological violence, which was particularly aggressive in Italy in the 1970s but has since disappeared. The right-wing radical who killed two migrants in Florence was part of a long-standing Italian fascist tradition. Finally, the cease-fire in Spain is not the first proclaimed by Euskadi Ta Askatasuna (Basquen-land and Freedom [ETA]), one of the longer-lasting and most active ethnonationalist clandestine organizations in Europe.

Furthermore, these episodes refer to the activities of clandestine organizations of varying size (from a couple of militants to a few hundred people), life duration, structure (from hierarchical structures to loose networks), and degree of clandestinity of structures and activists, as well as to organizations with very different motives and ideologies. The groups in question employed political violence of very different intensities, with 9/11 representing the most deadly case. In addition, their choice of targets was widely different, as was the context – national and/or international – in which they operated.

In fact, the phenomena to which these four episodes refer have been studied in the social sciences using very different approaches, and within different sub-disciplines. The separatist political violence of the ETA has been addressed especially by scholars of nationalism, with a focus on the dynamics of the long history of (tense) relations between the center and the periphery in Spain. Left-wing political violence has also been located within long-standing conflicts, but in this case it is commonly – or, at least, more often than it is the case for other types of violence – addressed within a social movement approach looking at the political and social transformations that affect class cleavages. Although the use of violent means has often been stigmatized and considered as ultimately ineffective, research on both left-wing and nationalist forms has tended to stress their links with legitimate (even if escalated) conflicts. In contrast, the radical Right has been analyzed more often as an (irrational) reaction to the breakdown of existing social ties and/or normative systems. Similarly, contemporary religious fundamentalism has been seen mainly as a consequence of failed attempts at modernization.

Furthermore, political violence by Islamic fundamentalists has been considered as distinctive in several ways:

- New, religious forms of terrorism are considered not only more lethal but also more indiscriminate, evil, and cruel. They use the most lethal means (e.g., suicide bombers or weapons of mass destruction – not only nuclear but also chemical, biological, or radiological weapons).
- Its loose, networked (rather than hierarchical) structures and the use of new communication technologies make this "new terrorism" more dangerous (Simon and Benjamin 2000). Goals are absolute and not negotiable. According to David Rapoport, "the transcendent source of holy terrorism is its most critical distinguishing characteristic: the deity is perceived as being directly involved in the determination of ends and means" (2012: 19). The assumed radicality of religious beliefs has been seen as responsible for some assumed characteristics of the "new terrorism." Samuel Huntington (1996) infamously stressed the particular tendency of conflicts involving Muslims to turn violent.
- Because of their focus on the destruction of the adversary – Western civilization (M. J. Morgan 2004: 30) – Islamic fundamentalists are said to use not only radical but also global strategies. The weakening of state sponsors is in fact seen as implying fewer constraints on violence (Simon and Benjamin 2000).
- New, "religious" terrorists have been attributed motivations such as fanaticism, rage, sadism, and paranoia (Laqueur 2003), as religious ideas are seen as based on different value systems from those of the West and as not dependent on other people for their legitimation (Hoffman 1999).

How the aims of these fundamentalists should be assessed and the extent
to which their aims determine the form of their organizations are, however,
topics that should be addressed empirically, and many of the aforementioned
statements about the new forms of terrorism have been contested.

First, some have questioned the assumption of increasing lethality. The
consequences of terrorist attacks tend to be small: only a few have exceeded
100 deaths, and still fewer have exceeded 50 (Guelke 2006). In addition, past
incidents vary in focus and range: the massacres in Madrid in 2004 (191 deaths)
and London in 2005 (52 deaths) are not so different from previous attacks; take,
for example, attacks by the radical Right such as the bombing in the Bologna
railway station in 1980, which involved about 100 victims. Additionally, there
are illustrations of strategic discrimination by fundamentalist Islamic groups.
For instance, Islamic underground organizations have made no use of weapons
of mass destruction (chemical or biological): the sarin gas used in Tokyo in
March 1995 was the work of the Japanese cult Aum Shinrikyo (ibid.). Of the
twenty most lethal attacks, only nine are classified as exclusively religious
(Crenshaw 2011). Religion is, in fact, not always the explanation for suicide
terrorism. As Pape (2005) recalls, of the Lebanese suicide bombers he studied,
only 21 percent were Islamist, whereas 71 percent were communist or socialist
and 8 percent were Christian.

Regarding organizational decentralization, the development of a loose global
network (also known as "franchising") has been mentioned only in the case of
al-Qaeda (AQ), and this structure has been in place only for part of its history;
the group started with a quite centralized organizational structure. Scholars have
also recalled that older clandestine organizations have been far from homogeneous. Anarchist groups, for instance, have also promoted loose networks of
autonomous cells. As for the aims of these new terrorist groups, the very
definition of their actions as religious is contested. In general, "religion is a
problematic label because it implies a monocausal explanation that does not
do justice to rich practices of terrorist activity" (Duyvesteyn 2012: 34). What is
understood as religious (and nonreligious) varies in time and space: the actual
construction of a myth of religious violence helps in creating a stigmatized
religious other (Cavanaugh 2009). Even though the language of these groups
might be archaic, their rationale tends to be secular: because Middle Eastern
regimes (such as Saudi Arabia and Egypt) cannot be overthrown by force,
al-Qaeda turns to the far enemy (Gerges 2005). Based on an in-depth empirical
analysis, Pape stated that "there is little connection between suicide terrorism
and Islamic fundamentalism" (2005: 4), as suicide terrorist campaigns are
"directed towards a strategic objective. From Lebanon to Israel to Sri Lanka
[the secular, Marxist-oriented Tamil Tigers – or LTTE – of Sri Lanka are
responsible for the greatest number of suicide attacks] to Kashmir to
Chechnya, the sponsors of every campaign have been terrorist groups trying
to establish or maintain political self-determination by compelling a democratic
power to withdraw from the territories they claim" (ibid.). Suicide terrorism is

used when perceived as the only successful weapon, as Americans are seen as weak, frail, and cowardly (ibid.: 123). In fact, the overwhelming majority of suicide bombers come from the Muslim countries where US combat troops are located (ibid.: 125).[1] Recent forms of political violence, just like older ones, have local roots. In the beginning, al-Qaeda stated that its aim was to expel the American military forces from Muslim territory, citing Vietnam or Lebanon as examples (Crenshaw 2011).

Given the very different interpretations that dominate studies on different types of political violence, research that compares various types of clandestine organizations is needed to identify similarities and differences. But does the problematization of such statements regarding the inherent peculiarity of Islamic violence and the search for comparative knowledge take us too far? Are we, metaphorically, comparing apples with oranges? Does this endeavor push us to look for too high a level of generalization, neglecting historical developments? Does it bring about conceptual stretching?

This chapter introduces the potential advantages and challenges of a cross-type, global comparison of a specific form of political violence: in this case, clandestine political violence. It first conceptualizes the phenomenon I address in this volume, explaining why I prefer this term to the more widely used term "terrorism." I suggest that the concept of clandestine political violence has the analytic advantage of singling out a more specifically sociological phenomenon, pointing toward the implication of the choice to go underground. I then develop some ideas about how to approach it. The chapter continues with a critical assessment of social science literature in the field of studies of clandestine political violence. Some contributions from social movement studies are then presented as particularly valuable not only for addressing the meso (organizational) level, which is considered to be of fundamental relevance, but also for linking it with the macro and micro levels. After developing these considerations, the chapter presents the main characteristics of the proposed approach, as follows:

- Relational: It locates political violence in the radicalization of conflicts that involve the interactions of various actors, both institutional and noninstitutional.
- Constructivist: It takes into account not only the external opportunities and constraints but also the social construction of experiential reality by the various actors participating in social and political conflicts.
- Emergent: It recognizes that violence develops in action, and it aims at reconstructing the causal mechanisms that link the macrosystem in which clandestine political violence develops, the mesosystem formed by radical organizations, and the microsystem of the symbolic interactions within militant networks.

---

[1] According to Pape (2005), this form of altruistic suicide is based on (1) a response to occupation in which the occupied people suffer from a (2) conventional inferiority of power, against (3) an enemy vulnerable to coercive pressure and in a situation in which the group receives support from the population (social approval).

A subsequent methodological section then justifies the use of historical comparative analysis, as well as addressing some more specific choices in the research design of this study. It presents the empirical studies to which I refer in the rest of this volume, discussing the use of in-depth interviews and organizational documents and judicial sources, as well as secondary analysis of historical and sociological studies. The chapter closes with an introduction to what follows.

CLANDESTINE POLITICAL VIOLENCE: CONCEPTUALIZING THE OBJECT OF STUDY

Conceptualizing clandestine (oppositional) political violence is no easy task. Not only is the operationalization of political violence complicated, but the empirical phenomena that are placed under the label of political violence are so broad that they jeopardize the very search for causal explanations. In this section, I define my concept, pointing at the relevant expected consequences of the choice to use repertoires of harsh violence and clandestine organizational forms.

Political violence consists of those repertoires of collective action that involve great physical force and cause damage to an adversary to achieve political aims. The classical social science definition of violence refers to "behavior designed to inflict physical injury on people or damage to property" (Graham and Gurr 1969: XVII), or "any observable interaction in the course of which persons or objects are seized or physically damaged in spite of resistance" (Tilly 1978: 176). *Political* violence, then, is the use of physical force to damage a political adversary. If we leave aside state or state-sponsored violence, oppositional political violence therefore consists of "collective attacks within a political community against a political regime" (Gurr 1970: 3–4).

This definition is far from easy to operationalize, however, as the understanding of both "great" and "damage" is highly subjective as well as historically bound (della Porta 2002). A certain degree of physical force may be involved in forms of collective action that are usually not considered violent per se; moreover, all collective action seeks to damage a more or less visible adversary. We can add that political violence is generally understood as behavior that violates the prevailing definition of legitimate political action, but the degree of legitimacy is not easy to assess empirically.

Operationally, however, there is certain agreement that, at least in contemporary democratic countries, violent forms of collective action include attacks on property, rioting, violent confrontations between ethnic or political groups, clashes with police, physical attacks directed against specific targets, random bombings, armed seizure of places or people (including armed trespassing), holdups, and hijacking. In all of these forms of action, the main objective is to display a high degree of physical force.

If we accept this broad operationalization, however, we need typologies that help us to identify sociologically homogeneous sets of phenomena. Various types of political violence can be distinguished: for instance, lethal versus nonlethal, indiscriminate versus targeted, and high-scale versus low-scale violence are some relevant dimensions. In a comparative research study on Germany and Italy between the 1960s and 1980s (della Porta 1995), I suggested the following dimensions as most relevant for a typology: (1) the intensity of violence (low-level violence, usually not enacted against people, versus high-level violence, including political assassinations) and (2) the organizational form of violence (open versus underground). On the basis of these two variables, I formulated a fourfold typology including the following: (1) *unspecialized violence* – low-level, less-organized violence; (2) *semi-military violence* – violence that is also low-level but is more organized; (3) *autonomous violence* – violence used by loosely organized groups that emphasize a "spontaneous" recourse to high-level violence; and (4) *clandestine violence* – the extreme violence of groups that organize underground for the explicit purpose of engaging in the most radical forms of collective action.

I consider the concept of clandestine political violence as particularly useful because the choice of clandestinity brings about quite specific sets of constraints. The very choice to go underground of a relatively small group of activists is heuristically relevant, as it triggers a spiral of radicalization, transforming political organizations into military sects. Therefore, in this volume, I focus especially on clandestine violence – a form of violence that has often been considered under the label of terrorism.

Although I refer to the literature on terrorism, for several reasons I prefer not to use the term "terrorism," as I believe it too plagued by conceptual stretching to be kept as a social science concept. "Terrorism" is a much-contested term. Definitions of the phenomenon have variously addressed means, aims, and effects. Attempts at producing a shared definition have taken different paths, focusing on the amount of violence (high), the characteristics of the victims (civilians), the characteristics of the actors (clandestine), and the purpose and effects of the action (terrorizing) (Buijs 2001: 9; della Porta 1995). The many social science definitions of terrorism have indeed stressed elements such as

its often symbolic character, its often indiscriminate nature, its typical focus on civilian and non-combatant targets, its sometimes provocative and retributive aims, the disruption of public order and endangering of public security, the creation of a climate of fear to influence an audience wider than the direct victims as well as its disregard of the rules of war and the rules of punishment. Some key elements of many definitions also refer to the fact that terrorism is usually an instrument through which its perpetrators, lacking mass support, attempt to realize a political or religious project. It also generally involves a series of punctuated acts of demonstrative public violence, followed by threats of continuation in order to impress, intimidate and/or coerce target audiences. (Expert Group on Violent Radicalisation 2008: 6)

Although various attempts have been made to build some common definitional ground, they are, I think, not sufficient to delimit a useful sociological concept.

Based on an expert survey, Schmid and Jongman have proposed a definition that
bridges what they identified as the sixteen most recurrent defining elements.
According to their analysis, the most frequently quoted elements are violence
or force (present in 83.5 percent of the definitions); political goals (65 percent);
fear or terror (51 percent); threats (47 percent); psychological effects (41.5 percent);
victim-target differentiation (37.5 percent); purposive, planned, systematic, organized action (32 percent); method of combat, strategy, and tactics (30.5 percent);
extranormality, in breach of accepted rules, without humanitarian constraints
(30 percent); and coercion, extortion, and induction of compliance (28 percent)
(2005: 5–6). Combining these aspects, they suggested that

> terrorism is an anxiety-inspiring method of repeated violent actions employed by (semi-)
> clandestine individual, group, or state actors, for idiosyncratic, criminal or political
> reasons, whereby – in contrast to assassination – the direct targets of violence are not
> the main targets. The immediate human victims of violence are generally chosen ran-
> domly (targets of opportunity) or selectively (representative or symbolic targets) from a
> target population, and serve as message generators. Threat- and violence-based commu-
> nication processes between terrorist (organization), (imperiled) victims, and main targets
> are used to manipulate the main target (audience(s)), turning it into a target of terror, a
> target of demands, or a target of attention, depending on whether intimidation, coercion,
> or propaganda is primarily sought. (ibid.: 28)

Although a useful exercise in the sociology of knowledge, this catchall definition
risks mixing up definitional elements that belong to different conceptualizations.
Aspects such as the "anxiety-inspiring method" are also debatable because, as
admitted in the very definition that is suggested, violent repertoires, like
nonviolent ones, aim at producing many different emotions in various audiences.

Employing a similar aim but a different methodology, Leonard Weinberg,
Ami Pedahzur, and Sican Hirsch-Hoefler proposed a definition that is based
instead on the lowest common denominator found in seventy-three definitions
collected from some of the main journals in the field. They eventually suggested
that "terrorism is a politically motivated tactic involving the threat or use
of force or violence in which the pursuit of publicity plays a significant role."
(2004: 786) This definition, however, seems to underconceptualize terrorism, as
most violent forms of protest aim at publicity.

Furthermore, as has often been mentioned, a shared definition of terrorism
becomes all the more difficult as the term "terrorist" is increasingly used to
stigmatize an adversary. This is especially true during waves of political violence,
when the discussion of terrorism is instrumentalized to justify restrictive security
policies, and securitizing actors overemphasize the risks of terrorism to push for
"securitizing moves" (Buzan, Wæver, and de Wilde 1998). According to a judge
of the International Court of Justice (ICJ), "terrorism is a term without any legal
significance. It is merely a convenient way of alluding to activities, whether of
States or of individuals, widely disapproved of and in which either the methods
used are unlawful, or the target protected, or both" (Higgins 1997: 28).

It has also been noted that political violence, even when we focus on its "terrorist" forms, is an abstract concept, including very different empirical types. Jenkins warned, in fact, "not to think of terrorism or terrorists as monolithic. Terrorism is a generalized construct derived from our concepts of morality, law, and the rules of war, whereas actual terrorists are shaped by culture, ideology and politics – specific, inchoate factors and notions that motivate diverse actions" (2006: 117). Most fundamentally, there is a risk of reifying terrorism (and terrorists) based on the use of some forms of collective action. Even when means are easily definable as terrorist, it is tricky to talk of a terrorist organization, as this would hypostatize the use of one type of means over other types that the organization in question will very likely be using as well (Crenshaw 2011; Tilly 2004).

What is more, the multiplicity of forms included in the definition produces risks of conceptual stretching. As Tilly reminded us, with specific reference to political violence, in the social sciences the value of a concept is linked to its capacity to "point to detectable phenomenon that exhibit some degree of causal coherence" (2004: 8). Tilly therefore refused to use the term "terrorist" to describe actors that are actually characterized by complex repertoires of action – highlighting the need to investigate types of events that can in fact be included in the same social science category.

With these caveats in mind, I have operationalized clandestine violence with a view to specific forms, targets, and aims as well as organizational structures.

First, clandestine violence defines quite drastic forms of violence. These forms include the intention to cause death or serious physical harm to civilians with the purpose of intimidating and thwarting them, and the use of extranormal means – that is, means that go beyond societal norms. As mentioned in the report of independent experts:

While there are grey zones and borderline cases of what is and what is not acceptable in certain political contexts, there are certain forms of peacetime political violence and wartime activities which are widely seen as totally unacceptable. These include unprovoked attacks on civilians and the taking of hostages and other forms of willful killings. Terrorism is considered extra-normal because the violence is usually one-sided, the victims cannot save their lives through surrender and unarmed civilians are often terrorism's main targets. (Expert Group on Violent Radicalisation 2008)

To distinguish clandestine violence from armed resistance, I also consider the characteristics of the targets, which include noncombatants. International legal definitions often include references to attacks against civilians. This aspect has also been used to try to focus the definition of terrorism for legal purposes. To cite just one illustration, in the European Union's Framework Decision on Combating Terrorism of 2002, terrorism is referred to as an intentional act that may "seriously damage a country or an international organisation where committed with the aim of seriously intimidating a population, or unduly compelling a Government or international organisation to perform or abstain from performing any act, or seriously destabilizing or destroying fundamental political, constitutional, economic or social structures of a country or an international organization." Actions that are deemed as terrorist offenses include attacks on a person's life, attacks on the physical integrity of a person, kidnapping, hostage taking, seizure of aircraft or ships, or the manufacture, possession, or transport of weapons or explosives.

In contrast to civil wars or revolutions, clandestine political violence has a strong and prevalent communicative, *symbolic aspect*. It has often been noted that "terrorists want a lot of people watching, not a lot of people dead" (Jenkins 1975: 4). Similarly, according to my conceptualization of clandestine political violence, communication is addressed to different groups to elicit fear in some of them and support in others. In fact, in general, the psychological effects include fear and horror, but also sympathy and admiration, as "terrorism is primarily an extremism of means, not one of ends" (Bjørgo 2005: 2).

Last but not least, the specific characteristics of political violence are linked to the actors that perpetrate them. Secrecy is included in some definitions of terrorism – for example, in Neil Smelser's recent one, terrorism consists of "intended, irregular acts of violence or disruption (or the threat of them) carried out in secret with the effect of generating anxiety in a group, and with the further aim, via that effect, of exciting political responses or political change" (2007: 242). As aforementioned, in my analysis, clandestinity acquires high heuristic value. Based on my previous work, I expect that, especially in democratic regimes, the very choice of going underground will bring about specific dynamics, allowing us to talk of a particular class of events. Clandestinity is in fact linked with a lack of territorial control, which many scholars identify as a particularly discriminating factor in the determination of the dynamics of specific forms of violence; that is, it distinguishes clandestine violence from civil wars (de la Calle and Sánchez-Cuenca 2012). I focus on relatively small groups, those with limited military capacity and little or no control of territory. Although I draw from some of the interpretations developed to explain them, this work does not deal with civil wars, armed resistance, or revolutions.

Throughout my examination of political violence by small, clandestine groups, however, I also compare different types. Ideology has been a main criterion in classifying clandestine oppositional groups. Among others, Vasilenko (2004) has distinguished underground political groups, which struggle for political power; separatist groups, which aim at territorial secession; nationalist groups, which aim at excluding people of other nationalities and ethnic groups from political, economic, and cultural activities; religious groups, which aim at affirming the leading role of their own religion; and criminal groups, which are oriented toward material profit. Similarly, within the category of insurgent terrorism, Reinares (2005: 224) differentiated among sociorevolutionary, right-wing, religious, nationalist, and single-issue types. It has been suggested that these types tend to come in waves, with the religious type characterizing the most recent wave of clandestine violence. In this book I cover the left-wing, right-wing, ethnonationalist, and religious types.

As discussed in the following section, within each of these different types I look for causal mechanisms present at their onset, during their persistence, and at their demise.

EXPLAINING CLANDESTINE POLITICAL VIOLENCE: SELECTING AN APPROACH

Research on clandestine political violence has been located mainly within two different fields of analysis that have only rarely overlapped: terrorism studies and social movement studies. In this section, I review their general respective merits and limits, before proposing my own approach.

Terrorism Studies and Their Limits

Political violence by small, clandestine groups has often been addressed within so-called terrorist studies. Publications in this field have been numerous, with periodic peaks related to moments of increased political violence. The years between 1990 and 2007 saw a rise in research funds, as well as in the number of books published with "terrorism" in their titles (from about 50 in the 1990s to more than 3,000 in the 2000s), conferences and courses, dedicated journals, and journal articles. After 9/11 a new book on terrorism was published every six hours, whereas scientific articles on the topic tripled between 2001 and 2002. Between 1971 and 2002, 14,000 articles were published, about 6,000 of which were peer reviewed; 54 percent of these articles occurred between 2001 and 2002 (Ranstorp 2009). Attention also remained high later on. According to PsicINFO, which reports information on about 2,000 social science journals, as many as 556 journal articles on the topic were published in 2007 alone (Silke 2009).

However, it has been quite widely observed that, despite the production of some valuable knowledge, the large quantity of research in the field of terrorism has not been accompanied by scientific quality and has experienced limited empirical investigation. According to Andrew Silke, "a review of recent research works found that only about 20 percent of published articles on terrorism are providing substantially new knowledge on the subject" (2003: xvii). Far-reaching generalizations have been proposed based on sporadic evidence (Schmid and Jongman 2005). Also criticized is the ahistoricity of the field (Breen Smyth 2007: 260), as well as the lack of collaborative research (Silke 2009).

Research on extreme forms of political violence has been episodic, with some peaks in periods of high visibility of terrorist attacks but little accumulation of results. For instance, before 2003, there had been very little scholarly attention paid to Muslim extremism. In 2000 and 2001 only 7 of the 102 articles published in two major journals (*Terrorism and Political Violence* and *Studies in Conflict and Terrorism*) dealt with Muslim radicalism or the Middle East; in contrast, these topics are the focus of half (39 out of 80) of the articles published in 2007 in the same two journals (see Silke 2006, 2009: 41–3).

Many have made note of the selectivity of the sources used in such publications, which contain repetitive mentions of US government assertions but little use of independent evidence: "Most important key experts simply replicate official US government analysis. This replication is facilitated primarily through a sustained and uncritical reliance on *selective* US governmental sources, combined with the frequent use of *unsubstantiated assertions*" (Raphael 2009: 51, emphasis in the original). This explains the lack of critical scrutiny on US counterterrorism – which itself often made use of illicit, terrorist means.

Indeed, terrorist studies have clearly been influenced by practical policy concerns, multiplying in times of crisis and being characterized by lower scientific standards than those of other subdisciplines (Crenshaw 2011). In particular, some areas of terrorist studies have been criticized as being not only event driven and policy driven but also deeply enmeshed in the actual practices of counterterrorism (R. Jackson 2007a: 245). Much of this writing has been seen as oriented toward justifying "morally disturbing counterterrorism" (R. Jackson, Breen Smyth, and Gunning 2009). Some terrorism experts have been described as belonging to an epistemic community with notable influence on and frequent contacts with (and contracts from) the CIA and governments, spreading "a cabala of virulent myths and half truths" (Silke 2004: 20).

This issue is also linked to the fact that terrorism studies has its roots in security studies, a field focused at least in part on counterinsurgency or, as critically noted, on "counterinsurgence masquerading as political science" (Schmid and Jongman 1988: 182). This approach has been considered as oriented more toward developing antiterrorist policies than toward gaining a social science understanding of the phenomenon. In fact, "many who have written about terrorism have been directly or indirectly involved in the business of counterterrorism, and their vision has been narrowed and distorted by the search for effective responses to terrorism, often very loosely defined" (Goodwin 2004: 260). Some scholars suggest that "terrorology is intellectually sterile, if not bankrupt, because the construct of 'terror' employed by terrorologists was not developed in response to honest puzzlement about the real world, but rather in response to ideological pressure" (George 1991: 92). One study on the field highlighted several stories of dubious consultants, bogus interviews, faked affiliations, charlatans and self-proclaimed experts, a lack of ethical codes, contradictory testimonies in court, and collusion with governments and civil servants (Ranstorp 2009: 25ff.). In many of the works listed as "terrorist studies," critics say, terrorism is considered not only as illegitimate, nonstate political violence, at best sponsored by rogue states, but also as posing a significant and existential threat by fanatics linked by formidable global networks (R. Jackson 2009). An "orthodox terrorism theory" has been identified as "a discourse designed and employed to legitimize the violence used by the incumbent power center to enforce its political will whilst simultaneously delegitimizing the use of political violence by opposition movements or organizations against the state" (Franks 2006: 193).

At times, policy prescriptions have even been stigmatized as legitimizing aggressive external interventions and the use of violence against civilians by the United States and its allies (e.g., aid to anti-Sandinistas, military help to authoritarian and violent regimes, support for Israel against Palestinians) (Raphael 2009). In some cases, even unorthodox methods – including torture and targeted assassinations (R. Jackson 2007b) – have been presented as appropriate responses in the "war on terrorism." Critical scholars have observed that "when virtually the entire academic field collectively adopts state priorities and aims, and when it tailors its research towards assisting state agencies in fighting terrorism (as defined by state institutions), it means that terrorism studies function ideologically as an intellectual arm of the state and is aligned with its broader hegemonic project" (R. Jackson 2009: 78). In fact, several terrorism specialists are seen as distancing themselves from the field, which they criticize as being politically biased and scientifically shallow (Ranstorp 2009: 24), and populated by opportunists (Horgan 2008: 58).

Still, in mentioning these weaknesses, I do not mean to say that nothing good has come from the scholarly research usually classified as belonging to terrorist studies. In fact, good scholarship has developed in research that uses the concept of terrorism and is cataloged as belonging to the field of terrorism studies. The very criticisms developed by scholars in the field, which I have just mentioned, testify to the presence of critical thinkers dedicated to developing a valid and reliable knowledge base on clandestine political violence.

First of all, there are several very instructive case studies on individual underground organizations or waves of political violence, often written by area specialists or contemporary historians, that provide rich information on important cases such as those in the Basque countries (Clark 1984), Northern Ireland (White 1993), Cyper (Demetriou 2007), Argentina (Gillespie 1982; Moyano 1995), Saudi Arabia (Hegghammer 2010), Egypt (Malthaner 2011), and Palestine (Gunning 2007). Large-N studies have been helpful, especially in excluding the impact of some specific contextual characteristics as robust explanations for the development of violence. Second, often with a focus on specific types of political violence, scholars have developed comparative knowledge on the origins and evolution such types of violence (see, for example, Bjørgo 2005; Bjørgo and Horgan 2009; Gambetta 2005). Third, in various disciplines, serious efforts have been made to develop broader theories to explain specific forms of political violence, drawing on international relations, criminology, and sociology (e.g., Crenshaw 2011; Horgan 2005a, 2005b). More specifically, the Welsh (or Aberystwyth) school of critical security studies has recently challenged the prevailing hegemonic security discourse, stressing the influence of contextual values on the perception of risks and the choice of solutions.[2] It has also stressed

---

[2] By extending attention from national security to securing humans, not as individuals but as people embedded in groups (Booth 1991), this approach has broadened the security agenda to incorporate nonmilitary issues and interventions from below (e.g., the potential of nonstate actors to contribute to security).

the importance of contextualizing terrorism by looking at its temporal historical location, the life of the group prior to violence, the embedding of violence within broader practices, and the evolution of violent tactics and their combination with other, nonviolent ones.

Thus, some research on extreme forms of political violence has been able to trace processes of conflict escalation through the detailed examination of historical cases.

Social Movement Studies and Violence: The Traditional Agenda

Building on this knowledge, as well as on my previous work in the field, I hope to contribute to the research and understanding of clandestine political violence in two ways: first, by developing an explanatory model that is inspired by social movement studies and, second, by empirically comparing different types of clandestine political violence.

My choice to develop an understanding of clandestine political violence by building on social movement studies has various rationales. First and foremost, previous research has indicated that clandestine political violence often spreads during waves of protest. It also often develops inside social movements – and is indeed one of the most visible (although infrequent) by-products of social movements. Most clandestine organizations have their roots in splits within social movement organizations, and most of the militants of underground organizations have previous experiences in social movement organizations (della Porta 1995).

Social movements are networks of individuals and organizations that have common identities and conflictual aims and that use unconventional means (della Porta and Diani 2006: chap. 1). Although they only very rarely advocate violence, they do use disruptive forms of protest that sometimes give way to escalation. Especially since the 1970s, new forms of political participation have become increasingly widespread (Norris 2002), including marches, boycotts, petitions, occupations, and roadblocks. Although they are not violent per se, many forms of protest break up everyday routines, and they often challenge law and order. Violence might therefore ensue from interactions in the streets between protesters and the police forces that are called on to restore public order. Additionally, in specific historical contexts, some forms of protest, including extensive use of forms of physical force that are stigmatized as illegitimate in the dominant culture, are considered as violent per se (della Porta 1995: chap. 1).

The link between social movements and political violence has not gone unnoticed. A few social movement scholars have in fact focused attention on the processes of radicalization in social movements, linking them to the interactions between these movements and the state (della Porta 1995), the "inversion" of collective actors (Wieviorka 1988), and the construction of exclusive identities (Goodwin 2004). Social movement studies are being cited with increasing frequency by scholars of clandestine political violence in the

Middle East (Gunning 2009; Karagiannis 2011; Wiktorowicz 2004). In particular, the above-mentioned school of "critical terrorism studies" brought about an interest in the application of social movement theories in international relations and area studies. Social movement theories have been praised for their potential to de-exceptionalize violence, by locating it within broader contexts and complex processes.

However, there is much room for development, as it is still true that "social movement scholars, with very few exceptions, have said little about terrorism" (Goodwin 2004: 260). According to data presented by Jeroen Gunning (2009), a keyword search for "social movements" within 1,569 articles in two of the core terrorism studies journals gives only 17 articles; a search of the IBSS database for "terrorism-terrorist" under the heading "social movements" yields 81 articles, most of them published after 2000.

Past and recent developments in the field of social movements might help to address some limits in the existing knowledge on political violence, offering concepts and hypotheses for theoretically oriented research. Although social movement scholars may have paid little attention to violence, preferring the study of more widespread (and accepted) forms of protest, some explanation of violence can be derived from their research on *repertoires of protest* – defined as limited sets of forms that are either learned from previous waves of protest at the national level or adopted and adapted cross-nationally (Tilly 1978). Within the dominant paradigm of social movement studies, political violence can be explained as an outcome of the interactions between social movements and their opponents. In this field, during the 1970s and 1980s, much attention was paid to the impact of political opportunities and organizational resources, as well as framing, on forms of action (della Porta and Diani 2006). The dominant model can be synthesized as shown in Figure 1.1.

Social movements are often defined by their use of unconventional forms of action. In social movement studies, the term "protest" is widely used to refer to *nonroutinized* ways of affecting political, social, and cultural processes. Usually,

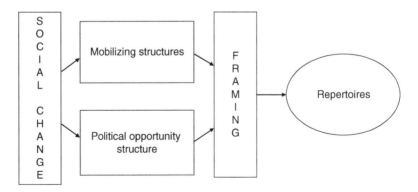

FIGURE 1.1. The classical social movement agenda.

"social movements employ methods of persuasion and coercion which are, more often than not, novel, unorthodox, dramatic, and of questionable legitimacy" (Wilson 1973: 227). Protests are, in fact, "sites of contestation in which bodies, symbols, identities, practices, and discourses are used to pursue or prevent changes in institutionalized power relations" (Taylor and van Dyke 2004: 268).

Social movement studies have observed that different forms of protest have different degrees of disruptiveness and, most importantly, follow different types of logic. How and why is one form of protest chosen over another?

To answer this question, we can begin by examining the complexity and multiplicity of the objectives protest is meant to achieve. An important characteristic of protest is the use of indirect channels to influence decision makers. As Michael Lipsky noted, as a political resource of the powerless, "protest is successful to the extent that other parties are activated to political involvement" (1965: 1). Protest thus sets in motion a process of indirect persuasion mediated by mass media and powerful actors: "Protest leaders must nurture and sustain *an organization* comprised of people with whom they may or may not share common values. They must *articulate goals and choose strategies* to maximize their *public exposure* through communications media. They must *maximize the impact of third parties* in the political conflict. Finally, they must try to *maximize chances of success among those capable of granting goals*" (ibid.: 163, emphasis in the original). Additionally, protest action has an important internal function: creating a sense of collective identity, which is a condition for action toward a common goal (Pizzorno 1993).[3]

As actions need to cover a plurality of sometimes contradictory objectives, the leaders of social movement organizations find themselves faced with a series of strategic dilemmas in choosing the form that protest should take (on strategic dilemmas, see Jasper 2004, 2006). First, forms of action – such as violent ones – that are more likely to attract media attention are also those that are more likely to be stigmatized by potential allies. In addition, those actions that are more apt to produce internal solidarity might not encounter public approval. Although leaders must often favor more radical actions to maintain rank-and-file support, these are precisely the kinds of actions that risk alienating potential allies.

Choices are influenced, then, by the resources available to particular groups. Social movement organizations need to mobilize resources in their environment and then invest them in various organizational tasks. The availability of some material and symbolic resources might push rational actors to use political violence. In a pivotal study on protest strategies, William Gamson (1975) observes that the use of violence increases the probability of success of the challengers. In a similar vein, in their well-known study on poor people's movements, Frances Fox Piven and Richard A. Cloward (1977) suggest that

---

[3] In fact, "movement strategists are fully aware that at least some of their tactics must widen the pool of activists and develop 'solidarities,' rather than 'merely' having an impact on politicians" (Rochon 1998: 159).

the existence of "radical flack" facilitates mobilization, insofar as the use of violence is a substitute for other resources.

However, organizational resources are not only material in nature. Forms of action are culturally constrained. The repertoire of action that defines citizens' known choices when they want to resist or promote changes is finite, constrained in both time and space. The "technology" of protest evolves slowly, limited by the traditions handed down from one generation of activists to the next, which are crystallized in institutions (Tilly 1986). Rooted in the shared subculture of the activists, repertoires contain the options considered practicable, while excluding others: "These varieties of action constitute a repertoire in something like the theatrical or musical sense of the word; but the repertoire in question resembles that of *commedia dell'arte* or jazz more than that of a strictly classical ensemble: people know the general rules of performance more or less well and vary the performance to meet the purpose at hand" (Tilly 1986: 390). In addition to what is known, choices of forms of action are also constrained by what is considered to be right: that is, there are normative limits. Some forms of action are not even assessed in terms of their efficacy, as their moral implications are considered dubious or plainly wrong.

Radicalism or moderation is also influenced by the available structure of political opportunities, which define the environmental responses, the reactions of authorities, and the strength and postures of potential allies and opponents (McAdam 1982; Tarrow 1989; Tilly 1978). Violence tends to develop especially in periods of social transformation, which exacerbate political conflicts. In his influential model of collective action, Charles Tilly (1978: 52–5, 172–88) linked the use of violence to the emergence of new social groups, as violent actions tend to increase when new challengers fight their way into the polity and when old polity members refuse to leave. Stable formal characteristics of a political system such as the degree of functional and territorial centralization, and particularly past inter-actions with political and social opponents, are expected to have an impact on the development of political violence. The same can be said of more contingent political opportunities, such as those provided by the strength and strategies of allies and opponents. One dimension mirrors the traditional comparison between consensual and majoritarian democracy, stressing centralization versus decentral-ization of power (Kitschelt 1986: 61–4; Kriesi 1996; Rucht 1994: 303–12). Regarding the functional separation of powers, scholars believe that the greater the division of tasks among the legislature, executive, and judiciary, the more open the political opportunities. Another set of hypotheses concerns territorial decen-tralization; the basic suggestion is that the more that power is distributed to the periphery (local or regional government or component states within a federal structure), the greater the possibility that social movements will access the decision-making process and therefore will be less likely to use radical means.

Social movement strategies have also been compared cross-nationally with reference to the relatively stable characteristics of national political cultures (Kitschelt 1985: 302–3). Countries with a strategy of exclusion (that is, repression of conflict) are expected to experience polarization of conflict with opponents, whereas a strategy of inclusion (co-optation of emergent demands) would produce moderation of conflicts – or at least of their forms (Kriesi et al. 1995). In the same vein, social movement research has addressed the influence of a country's democratic history, noting that past authoritarianism often reemerges in times of turmoil. Young democracies tend to fear political protest and to have police forces that remain steeped in the authoritarian values of the preceding regime, with ensuing risks of radicalization (Flam 1994: 348; on Italy, see della Porta and Reiter 2004; Reiter 1998).

Organizational resources and contextual opportunities are not just given; they exert their effects especially according to how they are framed by social movement actors. In social movement studies, the concept of framing has been used to address the way in which social movement actors make sense of their external reality. Frames are schemata of interpretation that enable individuals "to locate, perceive, identify and label" what happens within their life space and in the world at large (Snow et al. 1986: 464). Frame analysis focuses on the attribution of the meaning that lies behind the evolution of social movements by looking at the recognition of certain facts as social problems, of the strategies to address them, and of the motivations for action. Snow and Byrd (2007) have recently observed with reference to Islamic terrorism that ideology is too monolithic a concept to address the ideological variations among Islamic groups and does not possess the flexibility required to link ideas, actions, and events. Different collective actors might give different meanings to the same conditions; this observation can perhaps help us to understand why similar contextual conditions are met with different reactions by different actors. The particular subcultures to which movements refer contribute to the creation of distinctive repertoires.

Developing a Dynamic Approach

Social movement studies provides a tool kit for building relevant innovations in the research on political violence, but the practice requires some adaptations. First, scholars who take this approach have tended to stress structure over agency, at the same time overemphasizing instrumental reasoning (see della Porta and Diani 2006 for a review). Explanations based on the political opportunities approach, in particular, have looked at the way in which contextual structures affect social movements by strongly limiting if not totally determining their extent, forms, and potential success. In addition to an emphasis on the dependency on external support of social movement organizations, resource mobilization has also stressed rational reasoning, downplaying normative concerns or at least considering them as exogenous to protest. Even framing approaches have been accused of adhering too closely to an instrumental logic.

Additionally, social movement studies have focused on specific social movements in a specific geographical area and historical era: that is, left-wing movements in the contemporary world. Ethnic and religious movements, as well as right-wing and even labor movements (past and present), have only rarely been addressed within this field. Assuming mature democracy as a precondition for protest, social movement studies have very infrequently analyzed social movements in authoritarian regimes or during transitions to democracy.

These general problems are all the more relevant for research on clandestine political violence. First of all, small radical groups do react differently from more moderate organizations to the same broader contextual opportunities. As we will see, the extent to which clandestine political organizations act instrumentally is at least an open question that should be addressed empirically. Moreover, much political violence develops in authoritarian regimes, or at least in imperfect democracies.

In this volume, I suggest that, to address the aforementioned challenges, the use of social movement categories for research on political violence must be accompanied by some reflection on the relational, constructivist, and emergent aspects of its development.

Relational Violence

Tilly has suggested categorizing the scholars working on political violence as idea people, who look at ideologies; behavior people, who stress human genetic heritage; and relational people, who "make transactions among persons and groups much more central than do ideas or behavior people" (2003: 5). Relational people, he continues, focus their attention "on interpersonal processes that promote, inhibit, or channel collective violence and connect it with non-violent politics" (ibid.: 20; see also McAdam, Tarrow, and Tilly 2001: 22–4).

Following a relational perspective, I suggest that forms of action emerge, and are transformed, in the course of physical and symbolic interactions among social movements and not only their opponents but also their potential allies. Changes take place in encounters between social movements and authorities, in a series of reciprocal adjustments. Clandestine political violence is rarely adopted overnight or consciously. Rather, its emergence follows a (more or less gradual) process, defined as "actions of some kind associated with other actions and reactions, often expressed in some sort of reciprocal relationship" (Taylor and Horgan 2012: 130). Repeated clashes with police and political adversaries gradually, and almost imperceptibly, heighten radicalism, leading to a justification for ever more violent forms of action. In parallel, clandestine groups interact with a supportive environment, in which they find logistical help as well as symbolic rewards (Malthaner 2011). Indeed, violence has a relational component that derives from interchanges between people; interpersonal processes "promote, inhibit or channel collective violence and connect it with nonviolent politics" (Tilly 2003: 20).

Constructed Violence

Violence is produced through and also produces cognitive and affective processes. Cultural processes are particularly important for research on radical organizations, because political violence is mainly symbolic. Political violence develops in contexts in which some cultural resources are available. It produces heated debates on violence itself, and it aims at producing emotional effects more than material damages. Beyond the instrumental dimension of increased visibility, another important consequence of direct action on the protestors in the innermost circles is that it strengthens their motivations through the development of feelings of solidarity and belonging. Although emotions as explanations for behavior had long been viewed with suspicion (in not only social movement studies but also political sociology and political science at large), attention to their role has recently (re)emerged. Scholars have begun to emphasize the emotional intensity of participation in protest events as passionate politics (Aminzade and McAdam 2001; Goodwin, Jaspers, and Polletta 2001), together with the role of subversive "counter-emotions" in cementing collective identities (Eyerman 2005).[4] Recent evolution in research on social movements also helps to address symbolic processes through an analysis of the specific narratives that accompany the development of political violence. The role of dramaturgy, rhetoric, and rituals in intensifying commitment has been investigated for protest events in general (as the effect of an "emotional liberation"; see Flam 2005) as well as for specific critical emotional events. All of these elements are particularly relevant for understanding the emotionally intense experiences and specific cognitive processes in clandestine oppositional organizations.

Emergent Violence

Violence also has an emergent character that cannot be accounted for by a causal model. The choice to use violence develops in action. As Kalyvas observed, "almost every macrohistorical account of civil war points to the importance of preexisting popular allegiances for the war's outcome, yet almost every microhistorical account points to a host of endogenous mechanisms, whereby allegiances and identities tend to result from the war or are radically transformed by it" (Kalyvas 2006: 3). New cleavages, identities, and interests are created, weakened, or strengthened during the struggle. Motivations also change in action, as "often civil wars politicize innocuous or non-violent prewar cleavages" (ibid.: 79). Violence therefore acquires a logic of its own, producing the very same polarization that then fuels it. In Kalyvas's words, "the advent of war transforms individual preferences, choices, behaviour, and identities – and the main way in which civil war exercises its transformative function is through violence.... Collective and individual preferences, strategies, values and identities are continuously shaped and reshaped in the course of the war" (ibid.: 389). Similarly, in guerrilla movements, as Elisabeth Wood (2003: 19) has observed, "political culture – the values, norms, practices, beliefs, and collective identity of

---

[4] Research has highlighted the mobilizing capacity of "good" emotions (such as hope, pride, or indignation) and the movements' work on potentially dangerous emotions (such as fear or shame) (Flam 2005). Reciprocal emotions (such as love and loyalty, but also jealousy, rivalry, or resentment) have especially important effects on movement dynamics.

the insurgents – was not fixed but evolved in response to the experiences of the conflict itself, namely, previous rebellious actions, repression and the ongoing interpretation of events by the participants themselves." I expect that the same happens for clandestine political violence, which in fact creates and re-creates the conditions of its own development.

This type of approach is helpful in bridging the macro, meso, and micro levels. Explanations of clandestine political violence tend to focus on either macro-systemic causes, meso-organizational characteristics, or microindividual motivations, with little communication among different levels of analysis (della Porta 1995). They address one of three questions: In what type of society is political violence most likely to develop – that is, what environmental conditions foster political violence? Which groups are most likely to use violent repertoires – that is, which characteristics of political organizations eventually lead them to adopt the most extreme forms of political violence? Which individuals are most likely to resort to political violence?

Although the existing macro-, meso-, and microanalyses have generated interesting knowledge about the environmental preconditions for violence, the characteristics of violent groups, and individual commitment to violence, none provides a global explanation for the complex phenomenon of political violence. Macroanalyses fail to consider the intermediate processes between general structures and individual behavior,[5] mesoanalyses give us a voluntaristic interpretation of violence as a strategic choice carried out by single groups or organizations, and microanalyses tend to attribute this political phenomenon to purely psychological factors.

In my explanatory model, I aim at linking the contextual, organizational, and interpersonal perspectives – in other words, environmental conditions, group dynamics, and individual motivations. For although clandestine political violence, as a political phenomenon, is certainly influenced by the conditions of the political system from which it emerges, it is a phenomenon involving fairly small organizations whose dynamics inevitably influence its very development. Moreover, like other forms of deviant behavior, political violence generates changes in individuals' value systems and perceptions of external reality that in turn affect the organization as a whole. As I discuss subsequently, in the social movement field, this attention to causal mechanisms linking different analytic levels entered the agenda with the "contentious politics" turn, bridging research on social movements with work on revolutions, civil wars, and so on.

METHODOLOGICAL CHOICES

From these theoretical assumptions, some methodological choices followed. In particular, building on my previous work on a specific type of clandestine

---

[5] James Coleman (1986) has stressed the need to identify the micromechanisms that explain the relationships among macrophenomena in terms of individual behavior.

political violence, I decided to look for common causal mechanisms within very different cases.

A Global Comparison

From the methodological point of view, research on political violence has taken two main courses. On the one hand, macro (large-N) studies adopted a strategy of comparison by variables, looking for general laws about the causal conditions that would explain the phenomenon. These studies faced some major methodological challenges, such as doubts regarding the reliability of indicators of the dependent variable (various forms of violence), the validity of the indicators chosen as proxies for the independent variables (given the limited choices), the assumption of independence of units (in a context ripe with cross-national diffusion and international effects), and the assumption of unit homogeneity (resulting from fuzzy conceptualizations).

On the other hand, case studies and small-N (often binary) comparisons adopted in-depth, case-oriented comparative strategies to understand the emergence and development of specific instances of clandestine political violence. This type of study also encountered some methodological challenges, such as, first and foremost, uncertainty regarding the generalizability of knowledge beyond specific places and times. Another challenge is related to the idiosyncratic effects of the dominant paradigms in the different subdisciplines in which specific types of political violence have been studied. So, as aforementioned, left-wing political violence was often explained as an escalation of broader (class) conflicts, right-wing and racist violence as effects of relative deprivation (and scapegoating), ethnonationalism via the long histories of specific center-periphery conflicts, and religious fundamentalism as a product of the crisis of modernization. Additionally, research on each type of political violence remained rooted in specific (geographical) area studies, inheriting the specific explanatory preferences (or biases) of these studies.

This volume experiments with global comparison as a third strategy. The aim is to compare a limited number of cases across types to assess the generalizability of explanations on specific forms of clandestine political violence. It is based on a small-N comparison of very different cases in view of identified common mechanisms. In this sense, using the language of Mahoney and Goertz (2006), the aim is not to provide a complete causal explanation of clandestine political violence (by identifying the causes of an effect) but rather to investigate the effects of some specific mechanisms, which I see as being at work in the evolution of the various types of clandestine political violence analyzed in this text.

Methodologically, I aim to go beyond most of the previously mentioned case studies and small-N comparisons of similar forms of terrorism. I consider it important at this stage in comparative research to move beyond the analyses that trace dissimilarities between similar types and to look instead for similarities in the way in which different types have developed. Building on my in-depth comparison of two country cases of left-wing political violence in Italy and Germany, in this volume I compare them with other types that are very different from one another (that is, using a most-different-case research design; see the following discussion). In particular, following McAdam, Tarrow, and Tilly's *Dynamics of Contention* (2001) as well as della Porta and Keating's *Approaches and Methods in the Social Sciences* (2008), I compare different types of political violence, looking at left-wing, right-wing, ethnic-autonomist, and religiously motivated forms.

On the one hand, this might help provide a better understanding of religious violence by introducing new concepts and potential explanations, because "whereas the majority of studies of Islamic activism tend to assume that a particular set of grievances, translated into religious idioms and symbols, engenders mobilization, various generations of social movement theory and concomitant debates have demonstrated that other factors are inextricably linked to mobilization processes, including resource availability framing resonance and shifts in opportunity" (Wiktorowicz 2004: 4). On the other hand, it might also usefully challenge social movement studies, addressing the question of how useful concepts and hypotheses developed in social movement studies may be for the analysis of social movements that social movement scholars have rarely addressed. In fact, "social movement theory has largely been generated in conversation with movements that scholars support" (Kurzman 2004: 294), and "the Muslim world has yet to be fully integrated into social movement theory" (Wiktorowicz 2004: 4).

Although I map the differences among various forms of political violence, my main aim is to identify robust causal mechanisms that played a role in the onset, persistence, and demise of clandestine political violence. Within a most-different-case research design, I look especially for similarities in different types of political violence: revolutionary left-wing violence in Italy and Germany, right-wing violence in Italy, ethnonationalist political violence in the Basque countries, and religious violence in Islamic groups.

Causal Mechanisms

Because I am making global comparisons, I am not interested in discovering general laws and invariant causes that could explain all the cases at hand. As we will see, the historical context of the selected cases varies, as do the characteristics of the selected organizations. Rather than searching for invariant determinants, I want to identify some common processes that are present in the evolution of these different cases of radicalization. For this purpose, I use the concept of causal mechanisms.

In recent years, the language of mechanisms has become fashionable in the social sciences, signaling dissatisfaction with correlational analysis (Mahoney 2003). Mechanisms should allow us to build general causal explanations: "A mechanism is a precise, abstract and action-based explanation which shows how the occurring of triggering events regularly generate the type of outcome to be explained" (Hedström and Swedberg 1998: 6).

There are, however, differing definitions of causal mechanisms. I would suggest that the various views tend to cluster around two main conceptualizations:

1. Mechanisms are (historical) paths that involve a search for events, which are observable and context dependent.
2. Mechanisms are micro-level explanations that involve a search for variables at the individual level, aiming at universal, law-like causal explanations.

In macroanalyses, causal mechanisms (of type 1) have been linked to systematic process tracing (Hall 2003) through a "causal reconstruction" that "seeks to explain a given social phenomenon – a given event, structure or development – by identifying the process through which it is generated" (Mayntz 2004: 238). Mechanisms refer, therefore, to intermediary steps between conditions and outcomes.

In micro-level explanations (type 2), the attention is instead focused on individual agency. According to Hedström and Bearman (2009), "analytical sociology explains by detailing mechanisms through which social facts are brought about, and these mechanisms invariably refer to individuals' actions and the relations that link actors to one another" (ibid.: 4).

Distinguishing as many as nine ways to define a mechanism, Gerring (2007) proposes a minimal common denominator in the search for the means through which a cause produces an effect. Thus he sees the core meaning of mechanism as "the pathway or process by which an effect is produced or a purpose is accomplished" (ibid.: 178). In contrast with Gerring, who is looking for a common core, Mahoney (2003) suggests a definition of mechanisms as "unobserved entities, processes or structures through which an independent variable exerts an effect on a dependent variable" (ibid.: 1). They generate outcomes but do not themselves require explanation, as they are "hypothetical ultimate causes" that explain "why a causal variable exerts an effect on a given outcome variable" (ibid.: 1–2). Identifying mechanisms with general approaches, he distinguishes three main mechanisms: rational choice (the micro level), structural functionalism (the macro level), and the power of collective actors (the meso level).

Combining insights from Gerring and Mahoney, I propose a third conceptualization:

3. Mechanisms are chains of interaction that filter structural conditions and produce effects.

I would not restrict capacity of action to individuals; thus instead I include collective actors. Adapting Renate Mayntz's definition (2004: 241), I understand mechanisms as a concatenation of generative events linking macro causes (such as contextual transformation) to aggregated effects (e.g., cycles of protest) through individual and/or organizational agents. In this way, I believe that the search for mechanisms helps in combining attention to structure and to agency. Following Tilly (2001), I conceptualize mechanisms as relatively abstract

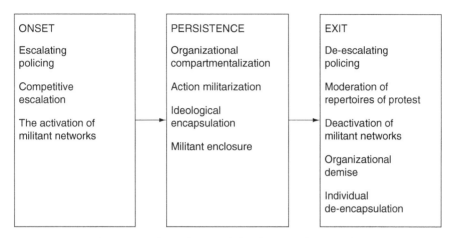

FIGURE 1.2. Mechanisms in the evolution of clandestine political violence.

patterns of action that can travel from one episode to the next, explaining how a cause creates a consequence in a given context.

Throughout the volume, I therefore look at certain mechanisms that initiate chains of interaction, and I single out these mechanisms as contributing to the onset, persistence, and demise of clandestine political violence (see Figure 1.2). In regard to the onset of violence, I present escalating policing, competitive escalation, and the activation of militant networks. The persistence of clandestine organizations, and also their transformation, is linked to mechanisms of organizational compartmentalization, action militarization, and ideological encapsulation at the organizational level, as well as militant enclosure at the interpersonal level. Finally, with regard to the termination of clandestine political violence, I address the contributions of mechanisms of de-escalating policing, moderation of repertoires of protest, deactivation of militant networks, organizational demise, and individual de-encapsulation.

Case Selections and Sources

As aforementioned, my research design is based on a small-N comparison within a most-different-case comparative strategy. Tarrow (2010) has listed several advantages of paired comparisons, among them their capacity to extend the range of generalizability of some observations. He has also pointed at some challenges, which I try to address in my small-N comparison. Most-different research designs risk decontextualization (and frustrating results) if they aim at identifying macro causes. It is all too obvious that the economic, social, political, and cultural macro conditions vary enormously between Italy in the 1960s, Spain in the 1970s, and the Middle East in the 1990s. Therefore, I do not aim at an exhaustive explanation of clandestine political violence. My more modest goal is to look instead at some specific causal mechanisms that are at work in all four types of clandestine violence. I see this global comparison as analytically challenging, especially because in the social sciences the narrative of a "new terrorism" has suggested that religiously motivated violence is incomparable with previous historical forms of the phenomenon (for a critique, see Crenshaw 2011), a statement I challenge in this work.

In my analysis, I build on my previous research on some of the most relevant cases of political violence in Europe. In this process, the presentation of the results will reflect the unequal amount of research I have done on the different cases, as well as the unequal attention the different forms of clandestine political violence have received in the social sciences in general, especially concerning the specific aspects I want to address. Of the cases examined in this text, I have conducted the most in-depth fieldwork on the Italian case, followed by that of Germany and Spain. For all three countries, I have updated my previous research through an analysis of secondary sources. Even with these disparities, the focus on these cases allowed me to build on my previous knowledge, which I consider to be extremely important for case-oriented comparison (della Porta 2008c). In particular, I rely on my empirical analysis of the following:

- Left-wing underground organizations in Italy and Germany in the 1970s and early 1980s (della Porta 1995)
- Right-wing underground organizations in Italy in the 1970s and early 1980s (ibid.)
- Ethnic violence in the Basque Country from the 1960s to the 1990s (della Porta and Mattina 1985)

For all these cases, I have triangulated my data by combining interviews with activists and observers, as well as biographical sources, with documents from the involved organizations and judicial materials. As aforementioned, my previous fieldwork on some of these cases is a resource I did not want to neglect.

Additionally, I made use of the increasing number of recent contributions to the analysis of Islamic fundamentalism that refer to social movement literature. Secondary literature on other cases of left-wing, right-wing, and ethnic clandestine political violence is also used to improve the interpretation of the empirical results of my own research.

I selected these cases for multiple reasons. In a problem-oriented manner, Tarrow (2010) links the application of most-different research design to the social and political relevance of some cases. This consideration also led my case selection: the cases I chose not only represent the four different types of clandestine violence I wanted to address but are also among the most relevant historical examples.

Focusing first on the European cases, the example of Italy in the 1960s and 1970s represents the most significant growth of left-wing and right-wing types of political violence (Germany is second for left-wing conflicts). Ireland and Spain exemplify the escalation of ethnic (or ethnonationalist) violence. In these countries we find the highest number of terrorist attacks and victims of clandestine political violence, as well as the longest-lasting clandestine organizations. The United Kingdom (mainly Northern Ireland) was home to as many as 54 percent of the victims of acts of clandestine political violence in Western Europe between 1950 and 1995 (a total of 2,777 people); Spain and Italy follow, with 23.4 percent and 10.7 percent respectively, and Germany occupies the fifth place with 3.5 percent (Engene 2004: 107). In Spain, 32 terrorist groups have been identified, 24 in Italy, and 10 in Germany; among these organizations, respectively 18, 15, and 6 groups were responsible for at least one lethal attack (ibid.: 111). In the same period, the ETA was accused of having killed 481 people in 439 attacks (ibid.: 129), whereas in Italy, left-wing clandestine groups killed 60 people in 71 attacks, and right-wing clandestine groups killed 120 in 27 attacks (ibid.: 136).

Italy and Germany therefore provide paradigmatic cases of the left-wing (and, in the case of Italy, also right-wing) clandestine violence that developed in Europe in the 1960s and 1970s. The choice of the ETA as a case study of clandestine ethnic political violence is based on its historical relevance and also on the fact that my previous research on the Basque Country offered me not only specific information on the political violence there but also a more general historical knowledge of that case. Additionally, if we look at social science literature on nationalism, the Basque case is considered – in several respects – as a paradigmatic case of radicalization in center-periphery relations, featuring construction of a territorial identity based on a (developing) definition of the specificity of the regional language and history, without the influence of religious issues, as in the Irish case. As for al-Qaeda, the group is not only the most dramatic recent challenge but also the most researched case of clandestine violence of a religious type (even though the quality of the research is, at best, uneven). This consideration has pushed me to move beyond the European context and to include a case of clandestine political violence that had its roots in the Middle East, however global it eventually became.

The triangulation of sources was designed to balance the shortcomings of each type. Some official sources had the advantage of providing a "thick" description of violent events and actors, as public prosecutors' offices and judiciary police must collect large amounts of information on the evolution of violent events, from their planning to their consequences. However, they have significant potential biases. As Becker (1970: 43) observed, law enforcement records tell us more about the institutions that produce them than about the criminals and their actions. Because they reflect the investigators' strategic decisions about how much to invest in a specific field, official statistics are misleading from the quantitative point of view as well as being qualitatively biased: they deal mainly with the "criminal" side of radical organizations and their members, and they tend to present images of radical organizations that fit some of the requisites established by law for certain types of crime – for instance, they aim at demonstrating the existence of very structured groups or "conspiratorial" actions when these are requisites for the application of particular laws.

To address this bias, I have also used materials from inside the radical organizations I have analyzed. Given the limited amount of written internal sources, biographical material is all the more important. Of course, even this information must be handled with care, for, as historians rightly stress, the reliability of information coming from oral history is disputable (della Porta 2010). In biographical recollections, the selection of information follows – consciously or unconsciously – psychological needs (such as providing a coherent image of one's own life), as well as aesthetic considerations (such as creating a beautiful narrative). For my research purposes, however, this limitation was, in a way, an advantage. The biographical reconstructions, which emphasize the subjective side of events, allow us to observe the way in which history forms the individual consciousness, how public events intervene in private life, and how perceptions shape behavior. They in fact helped to reconstruct the movement milieus, the militants' perceptions of their external worlds, their definition of the costs and benefits of participation, their political socialization, and the dynamic of producing and sustaining a collective identity. By locating political activities inside the broader individual existence, these biographical reconstructions provided subjective explanations for the choice of adhesion to a radical organization as well as the maintenance of commitment. The emphasis on the subjective side helps, therefore, to reconstruct one aspect that I consider highly relevant: the militants' image of external reality.

I have therefore used both types of sources in my research. I had already collected a massive set of data on left-wing terrorism in Italy (della Porta 1990). For Germany, access to documents collected in a series of studies on political violence sponsored by the Federal Ministry of Home Affairs offered a good point of departure. For both countries, I supplemented this material with additional information derived from empirical research, which focused respectively on the environment in which protest developed, the movements' organizational structure, and the individual activists. In my comparative analysis of environmental factors, I used a combination of written and oral sources. My main sources for information about clandestine political organizations and their militants were trial records, archives, and interviews with former activists.

More specifically, on left-wing clandestine organizations in Italy I drew on court and police records (a total of about 100 references to trials for "political" crimes), documents produced by the radical organizations (a total of about 50 documents), and biographical accounts by political militants (a total of about 40 oral life histories and 100 written biographies). The information collected refers to 30 organizations, 1,600 violent events, and 1,400 members of radical groups. I filed some data using structured codebooks; the databases so constructed include each violent event and each militant of radical organizations, and schemes for the life histories of the radicals and stories of the radical organizations (della Porta 1995: chap. 1).

On the violent events I collected information referring mainly to the organization involved, the form of action, and its target. For the most radical

TABLE I.I. *Case Selection*

Type of Organization	Situations That Developed into Clandestine Political Violence
Left-wing	Radical Left, Italy 1970s and 1980s
	Radical Left, Germany 1970s and 1980s
Right-wing	Radical Right, Italy 1970s and 1980s
Ethnonationalist	Basque ethnonationalism, 1970s and 1980s
Religious	Al-Qaeda

Note: Cases on which I have done fieldwork in the past are in bold.

organizations, my data address organizational structure, actions, and ideologies. The quantitative information on the militants refers to social background, friendship networks, political experiences in legal organizations, and experiences in the clandestine organization. Because much information was missing in my Italian dataset, I used a simplified scheme for the German case.

For the collection of the Italian life histories I utilized an outline developed during a research project of the Istituto Carlo Cattaneo. The scheme included questions about each individual's family and its environment; his or her subjective perception of the primary socialization; his or her involvement in the clandestine organization, including how he or she was recruited; the characteristics of the group; the individual's everyday life outside as well as inside the terrorist group; and the end of his or her experience in the clandestine group (della Porta 1995).

On right-wing clandestine violence, I used both secondary literature and primary readings of ten life histories of radicals, collected within the Carlo Cattaneo project. I was also able to consult trial records.

On the ETA, I used the two months of fieldwork I completed in 1983, including interviews with activists and experts as well as reading of published trial records and organizational documents.

THE STRUCTURE OF THE VOLUME

This volume is organized around some main mechanisms in the development of clandestine political organizations. Although in the description of all mechanisms I tried to integrate data at various levels (macro, meso, and micro), some of the mechanisms tend to be more driven by the context of the clandestine groups, others by their own organizational dynamics, and still others by interpersonal, small-group interactions. I present these main mechanisms while looking at the onset, persistence, and demise of clandestine political violence.

The following three chapters look at some mechanisms that activate polarization processes, by studying in particular escalating protest policing (Chapter 2), competitive escalation during protest cycles (Chapter 3), and the activation of militant networks (Chapter 4).

Following social movement studies, a process of radicalization is identified, first of all, in the evolution of (more or less intense) protest cycles. During intense political and social conflicts, forms of action escalate following internal competition as well as encounters with the state. In *escalating policing*, violence develops as a reaction to hard and indiscriminate repression, which is considered by the challengers as brutal and deeply unjust. In processes of reciprocal interactions, violence and "counterviolence" spiral around each other. Transformative events of increased radicalism not only create martyrs and myths but also push forward the development of structures and norms that reproduce violence, building pathways into clandestine political violence.

I use the term *competitive escalation* to indicate a causal mechanism that links the radicalization of forms of action to the interactions within and among social movement organizations, social movements, social movement families, and social movement sectors. Violence is used in these situations in part to outbid the competitor and in part as an unplanned consequence of experimentations with new tactics during frequent interactions that include physical fights. Activists are thus slowly socialized to the use of radical means of action. Protest, which challenges public order, often brings about encounters between protestors and police, which tend to become the most visible face of the state.

I then look at the *activation of militant networks* that sustain high-risk activism, fueling small-group pathways toward clandestine forms of violence. Affective and cognitive dynamics lie at the bases of recruitment processes within close networks of friends-comrades.

The four chapters that follow focus more on the mechanisms of development of underground organizations. In particular, clandestine political organizations are transformed through mechanisms of *organizational compartmentalization* (Chapter 5), *action militarization* (Chapter 6), and *ideological encapsulation* (Chapter 7).

Organizational structures in clandestinity vary, in an unequal mix of hierarchical and network-like components. Clandestine groups try to adapt to a more or less hostile environment, often attempting a precarious balance in which some structures are open to sympathizers and others are more secretive. A mechanism of organizational compartmentalization tends, however, to push the groups toward increasing isolation. As state repression produces arrests and deaths among their ranks and as support shrinks, the clandestine groups tend to opt for increasingly compartmentalized, isolated structures.

A similar mechanism is visible in the action strategy of these organizations. Although violence is initially used sporadically and low-intensity forms tend to prevail, over time there is an *action militarization*, with a preference for spectacular and deadly forms of action. The more isolated the groups, the more they lose hope of persuading potential supporters through political propaganda, and the more they use (often indiscriminate) killing and assassinations, engaging in a sort of war with the state and its apparatuses.

In parallel to these transformations, the narratives developed by the clandestine organizations change as well. A mechanism of *ideological encapsulation* defines the evolution toward an increasingly elitist definition of the self, a Manichean vision of those outside of the organization as absolute evil, and an essentialization of violence.

The following chapter addresses the development of freedom fighter identities at a more micro level through the mechanism of *militant enclosure* (Chapter 8). Although grievances and motivations surely count in the sequences of individual choices toward the underground, these choices are rarely made by isolated militants. Rather, grievances and motifs are nurtured within special milieus that support the maintenance of commitments in the underground. Through militant enclosure, militants move more and more deeply into a closed ghetto. While relations outside of the organizations become – logistically and psychologically – increasingly limited, the clandestine organization remains the only target of affective focusing as well as, at the same time, the only source of information. While the affective life focuses on the other members of the clandestine group, imprisoned or dead fellow militants, in particular, become the object of revenge and emulation. At the same time, cognitive closure toward the outside discourages the acknowledgment of defeats and mistakes, and the perception of alternative ways.

By emphasizing these mechanisms I do not mean to imply that escalation is unavoidable and endless. Focusing especially on the Italian cases, Chapter 9 looks at how groups and/or their members exit from the underground. Using the language of the rest of the volume, I look at how mechanisms of escalation are reversed. The moderation of repertoires of protest, de-escalating policing, organizational demise, deactivation of militant networks, and affective and cognitive openings are all mechanisms that, although with tension and difficulty, lead to micro-, meso-, and macroprocesses of disengagement from violence.

In Chapter 10, I summarize the functioning of the mentioned mechanisms and discuss the generalizability of the results.

2

Escalating Policing

In the Middle East, movements initially aiming at reform radicalized following repression by the state. In Egypt, support for violence was heightened by the military occupation of entire communities. In the mid-1980s,

a milieu had formed in Ayn Shams which identified with and supported the Islamist movement, including their political criticism against the Egyptian government – a milieu to which, at that time, a considerable part of the area's residents seemed to belong. Their support for the Islamist groups included protests against the police operation, which was regarded as unjustified repression against all Islamist groups and against the entire neighborhood. People in Ayn Shams, another resident emphasized, never informed the police about members of the Islamic groups, and nobody cooperated with the police, with the exception of criminals and drug traffickers who had been paid for their cooperation. People even provided refuge to members of the Islamic groups when members were pursued by the police. The Islamist groups, Ahmad's father emphasized, were just the young people from the neighborhood, and they did nothing wrong. They had just defended themselves against the arbitrary attacks by the police: "And because of what happened, the arrests [...] and the torture, and the suffering, and they were humiliated and tortured to death – it turned into some kind of revenge between the victims' families and their friends [and the police]." He added that: "I myself don't regard what has happened as terrorism because the word terrorism was an invention of the police. The events started in the form of revenge." (Malthaner 2011: 135–6)

Street battles involved, in addition to members of various Islamic groups, "teenagers, and, as witnesses recounted, many ordinary residents, including elderly women throwing stones at the police from their balconies." New riots followed police intervention after the assassination of a police officer, again with mass arrests (of about 300 people) and several killings. Additionally, the area was put under curfew, and the Adam Mosque remained closed for more than a year. As Malthaner recalls, in several interviews with residents of Ayn Shams, even 15 years after the incidents, anger and indignation against the government and the behavior of police remained very strong. Ahmad's father, a retired school-bus driver, told the stories of several neighbors who were arrested in 1988 and had never returned. Another of his accounts was of a young sheikh at a local mosque who had been taken away, tortured, and returned from prison a blind man. The perception expressed in these interviews was that the police had attacked not only the Islamic groups but also the entire neighborhood, without reason or justification, and had used violence far out of proportion to the alleged offenses. The clashes, they said, were between police and all the people of Ayn Shams, who also suffered under the effects of the curfew and the closure of the market....

... As one officer explained, the main problem for the police was that the people in Mallawi and the surrounding villages did not cooperate: "People here are very negative. [...] We wish they would tell us about the hideouts of the militants." (2011: 241)

Escalation continued, fueled by people's mistrust in the state, which in turn favored indiscriminate police repression. As Malthaner recalls, in the 1990s,

police operations also took the form of collective punishment against the militants' families and the general population in alleged strongholds. After violent incidents, any male person wearing a beard was arrested, houses of alleged al-Jamaa members were destroyed, and, according to human rights organizations, their parents, sisters, or wives were detained in order to force fugitives to surrender.... This policy of "collective punishments" ... was clearly designed to terrorize the local population into stopping their support of al-Jamaa. Yet, reports and statements indicate that these measures, initially, had rather the opposite effect, following the same pattern observed in other areas. They increased sympathies with the Islamists and produced anger and indignation at the police, whom many people accused of "starting the terrorism, which prevented cooperation with the security forces rather than furthering it." (2011: 237)

As in the Egyptian example, political violence throughout the world is intertwined with state responses to social movements in a sort of macabre dance. A mechanism of *escalating policing* can be identified at the onset of clandestine political violence in both democratic and authoritarian regimes. In the cases analyzed in this text, a reciprocal adaptation brought about an escalation of protest forms and approaches to policing. Policing was in fact perceived as tough and, especially, indiscriminate and unjust; transformative repressive events contributed to justifying violence and pushing militant groups toward clandestinity.

In social movement studies, explanations for protest strategies have been found first and foremost in the political opportunities available for social movements. As mentioned in Chapter 1, the degree of institutional openness to challengers is influenced by some stable features, such as functional differentiation and territorial decentralization of power, as well as by more contingent conditions, such as the availability of allies or the instability of coalitions in power.

Looking at the exogenous determinants of the protest repertoire, social movement scholars have stressed the roles of both stable institutions and contingent developments. As for the first, more centralized political power is seen as leading to political institutions that are less accessible from below and thus to more violent protest. Additionally, radicalization has been considered as more likely when historically rooted cultural elements about the proper ways to deal with opponents orient authorities toward exclusive strategies. Scholars also mention less durable political contingencies, such as the lack of availability and influence of political allies, which close windows of opportunity for protestors, often producing escalation (for a review, see della Porta and Diani 2006: chap. 8).

Some scholars have linked low levels of freedom and democracy to domestic terrorism in Western Europe (Engene 2004), and less proportional electoral systems to ethnic violence (Skiolberg 2000, in Crenshaw 2011). The weaknesses of democracy, civil liberties, human rights, the rule of law, and so on are often considered as root causes for terrorism. When normal channels of access to the political system are blocked, activists perceive terrorism as necessary, as there is "no other way out" (Goodwin 2004).

Another political precondition identified as explaining high levels of political violence is the weakness of the state in terms of repressive capacity and even territorial control. The resulting power vacuum can be occupied by violent groups that find safe havens for training and socialization into violence. As Huntington (1968) suggested long ago, the corruption of those in government might justify violence by reducing not only their legitimacy but also the hope of achieving change through nonviolent channels. This is all the more true if powerful foreign actors are seen as supporting corrupt regimes. On the other hand, well-established democracies have also been targets of clandestine violence that has been defined as attacking and at the same time exploiting the very liberty that democracies provide to their citizens. In these situations, political violence is the result of incomplete democratization processes. Political violence in Italy has been explained, for instance, by a blocked political system, in which the Left was considered antisystemic and unfit to govern (della Porta 1990; Zwerman, Steinhoff, and della Porta 2000). Radicalization on the right has also been seen as more likely when some opinions do not find party expression (Heitmeyer 2005: 146).

In addition, scholars have mentioned that blockages in international relations can push superpowers to use terrorism as a way to fight surrogate wars. During the Cold War, for example, clandestine attacks as well as civil wars acted as proxy wars between the two superpowers, who fueled but also controlled the conflicts. The end of the Cold War has in fact seen an increase in civil wars, as new groups and interests became mobilized in systems not yet endowed with democratic structures (APSA 2007).

Conditions of occupation by foreign powers have also been seen as triggering the temptation to use clandestine violence as a cheap form of opposition, when it is impossible to address and mobilize large groups of the population. At the same time, repression by a colonial power tends to exacerbate demands for independence and fuel feelings of injustice. Thus, foreign occupations (Garrison 2004) have been said to fuel humiliation and, subsequently, high levels of political violence.[1]

However, the reference to political opportunities (or lack thereof) as explanations for the radicalization of political groups meets with some concern. First, it has been observed that, to be acted on, opportunities and constraints must be perceived by social movement activists. In this sense, the important point is not the political institutions or distribution of power per se but how they are framed (Gamson and Meyer 1996) – or, as McAdam, Tarrow, and Tilly (2001) put it, the attribution of opportunities and threats. A main caveat in this regard is the need to consider the various actors' perceptions of similar contextual characteristics – that is, how they are socially constructed. Looking at activists' construction of the external reality is especially relevant because radical groups are usually tiny minorities reacting with extreme forms of violence to situations that are assessed differently by most of their fellow social movement activists.

A second problem with the concept of political opportunities is that it is static. It tends to imply a direction of causality from contextual structures to actors' choices. Radicalization is instead a process that develops relationally. Opportunities and constraints for specific groups are created in the course of frequent interactions with the state. A good portion of the explanation of radicalization is in fact not in the political preconditions but rather in the process.

Both reflections bring a third caveat into evidence. The concept of political opportunities has become broader and broader over time, as new aspects are continuously added and as it is used to address an increasingly complex set of stable or contingent contextual characteristics that, however, tend to be quite distant from the actor's appreciation. The functional division of power and the degree of decentralization have analytic power for scholars, but it is questionable to what extent such characteristics are evaluated by activists in their choices of forms of protest. I would suggest in this chapter that activists react especially to a more proximate dimension: the policing of protest, that is, the police handling of protest events – what protestors usually refer to as "repression" and the state characterizes as "law and order." Protest policing has a direct impact on social movements, being a sort of barometer for the available political opportunities but also, given some mutable degree of discretion, directly affecting protest repertoires. In addition, it tends to vary for different actors, and to develop relationally. The analysis of protest policing allows for an understanding of the interactive processes that fuel violent escalation. Protestors and police and social movements and the state influence each other according to the strategic choices they make, in a process involving innovation and adaptation on both sides (see also McAdam 1983). In fact, tough protest policing has characterized many cases in which political violence has developed (della Porta 2008d).

---

[1] Sobek and Braithwaite (2004; see also Crenshaw 2011) have shown that the level of US dominance abroad is correlated with the level of terrorist attacks against American targets.

The policing of protest is a central factor in the radicalization of protest. Social movements do challenge the power of the state, establishing a (temporary) counterpower. Taking to the streets and often forcing their presence beyond legal limits to get their voices heard, members of social movements interact directly with police forces, which are supposed to defend law and order. The intervention of the police in cases of violations, however, is not automatic: indeed, many minor violations of public order are tolerated to avoid major disorder. Although the government sometimes sends specific orders (or, at least, signals) about the type of intervention required (or desired) at political demonstrations, police officers at various hierarchical levels enjoy broad margins of discretion, as most decisions are made on the ground and are determined by the assessment of the specific situation as well as by interactive dynamics.

For many years a neglected issue in the social science literature, the policing of protest started to attract attention in the 1990s. The collection entitled *Policing Protest: The Control of Mass Demonstration in Western Democracies* (della Porta and Reiter 1998b) introduced the concept of protest policing, which was subsequently used in a range of case studies as well as small-N and large-N comparisons.[2] As this work suggests, styles of policing vary, and repression does not happen only in the street. Police strategies have been distinguished in terms of the following:

- Coercive strategies: the use of coercive force and/or arms to control or disperse a demonstration
- Persuasive strategies: all attempts to control protest through contacts with activists and organizers
- Information strategies: the diffuse gathering of information as a preventive element in the control of protest, as well as the targeted gathering of information (including the use of audiovisual technology) to identify those who break the law without having to intervene directly

Although it may occur selectively and with frequent inversions, the policing of protest in democratic regimes has been characterized by some trends toward a growing publicity, nationalization, and demilitarization. In parallel, especially since the 1980s, research on the policing of protest in European democracies and the United States has identified a reduction of strategies of control based on an escalation of force (that is, hard forms of power) – which are characterized by a low priority given to the right to demonstrate, low tolerance for emerging forms of protest, limited negotiation between police and protestors, and frequent use of

---

[2] Quantitative research, based mainly on large-N, cross-national designs, addressed its causes (Davenport 1995; Poe and Tate 1994; Poe, Tate, and Camp Keith 1999) and effects (Francisco 1996; Gupta, Singh, and Sprague 1993; Lichbach 1987; Moore 1998; Opp and Roehl 1990). At the same time, ethnographic approaches and case studies contributed to the analysis of police behavior in public order intervention (Critcher and D. Waddington 1996; D. Waddington and Critcher 2000; P. A. J. Waddington 1994).

(even illegal) means of coercion. Instead, there was a shift toward soft forms of power based on negotiated control, with recognition of the right to demonstrate, tolerance for (even disruptive) forms of protest, frequent communication between protestors and police to ensure a peaceful evolution of events, and limited use of coercion (della Porta and Fillieule 2004; McPhail, Schweingruber, and McCarthy 1998: 51–4).[3]

Social science research has linked the style of police intervention to some characteristics of the external environment. First, police have been said to be sensitive to perceived threats but also to the expected demands of authorities and public opinion. Research on police units has stressed that their organizational imperative is keeping control over situations, rather than enforcing the law (Bittner 1967; Rubinstein 1980; Skolnick 1966). If police officers enjoy a certain degree of discretion in their encounters with citizens, they must also maintain (to varying extents) the support of authorities and the public. Research on the policing of social movements has identified a tendency to use harsher styles of protest policing against social and political groups that are perceived as larger threats to political elites, given that they are more ideologically driven or more radical in their aims (see Davenport 1995, 2000; della Porta and Fillieule 2004; Earl 2003). Additionally, police repression is more likely to be directed against groups that are poorer in material resources as well as in political connections (della Porta 1998; Earl, Soule, and McCarthy 2003).

In addition, the forms taken by state power have a clear impact on the policing of protest. In countries such as Italy and post-Franco Spain, authoritarian legacies were reflected in delayed and contradictory trends toward the more inclusive forms of policing that developed in the 1970s. In authoritarian regimes such as Franco's Spain, Egypt, or Algeria, repression of political opposition was brutal. If repression is always much more brutal in authoritarian than in democratic regimes (e.g., Sheptycki 2005, on Latin America; Uysal 2005, on Turkey), even authoritarian regimes vary in the amount, forms, and types of actors of protest they are willing to tolerate, as well as in the forms in which they police the opposition (Boudreau 2004). Moreover, variations also exist in democratic regimes, with some countries considered as traditionally more consensual and others as more repressive.

In both types of regime, the police's strategies in addressing the demonstrations reflect some more general characteristics of the police force, including its organizational resources and professional culture. The degree of militarization

---

[3] However, it should be noted that the advent of negotiated management did not signify the disappearance of coercive intervention. Research has frequently stressed the selectivity of police intervention and the survival of harsh modes of protest policing in the 1980s and 1990s (della Porta 1998; Fillieule and Jobard 1998), as well as a revival of coercive tactics in the 2000s (della Porta, Peterson, and Reiter 2006). Antagonistic interventions with a show-of-force attitude and a massive, highly visible police presence were generally reserved for small extremist groups – in this period of demobilization that was not connected with a broader movement – or for universally stigmatized phenomena like football hooliganism.

of the structure and equipment, legal competences, and degree of professionalization all influence police officers' strategic choices. In addition, police tactics in the control of protest follow some general conceptions of the role of the police (Noakes and Gillham 2006). Intelligence-led policing is certainly facilitated by the expansion of police preventive powers (e.g., in the case of control of football stadiums) or by the frequent use of phone tapping and video camera surveillance (which were originally used against organized crime and terrorism).

As for the effects of protest policing, the way in which the government and police use their power to repress protest has relevant impacts on protest (Francisco 1996; Gupta, Singh, and Sprague 1993; Lichbach 1987; Moore 1998; Opp and Roehl 1990). Because it increases the costs of protesting, repression might reduce an individual's availability to participate. However, the sense of injustice as well as the creation of intense feelings of identification and solidarity can strengthen the motivation to oppose an unjust and brutal regime (Davenport 2005; della Porta and Piazza 2008; Francisco 2005). So, especially when the protest is widespread and well supported, repression can backfire because of outrage about police disrespect for citizens' rights at the national as well as the transnational level (Davenport 2005; Francisco 2005). Protest policing might also influence the organizational forms used by social movements, for instance, by spreading a sense of mutual mistrust through the use of infiltration (e.g., Fernandez 2008). Repression has also been said to play a major role in social movements in authoritarian regimes, as "violence is only one of myriad possibilities in repertoires of contention and becomes most likely where regimes attempt to crush Islamic activism through broad repressive measures that leave few alternatives" (Hafez and Wiktorowicz 2004: 62). Authoritarian regimes (Fuller 2002) have been said to fuel humiliation and, then, political violence.

Conversely, protest has an impact on police forces and strategies. The policing of protest is a key feature in the development and self-definition of the police as an institution and as a profession (J. Morgan 1987). In contemporary democratic societies, the way in which a police force addresses protest is a significant aspect of its self-image (Winter 1998).

In this way, police control tends to impact the repertoires of protest through a reciprocal adaptation (or, sometimes, escalation) of police and demonstrators' tactics (della Porta 1995). In fact, protest and its policing "is a dance between those who challenge authority, speak true to power, and hope for a more just world and those who wish to extend their privilege and power" (Fernandez 2008: 171). Cross-nationally and transnationally, social movement and police strategies interact with each other in a process of double diffusion (della Porta and Tarrow 2012).

As I shall suggest in what follows, escalating policing has been an important causal mechanism at the onset of clandestine political violence. In democracies as well as authoritarian regimes, activists perceive the policing of protest as not only tough but also indiscriminate and unjust. Police and protestors escalate their repertoires of action and reaction in a pattern of reciprocal adaptation. Repressive transformative events therefore produce martyrs and myths; this process justifies violence and pushes militant groups underground.

I look at the policing of protest in the four types of clandestine political violence discussed in this text. Because, in the Italian case, the policing of the radical Left and of the radical Right were clearly intertwined, I address them together in the next section, which will be followed by an analysis of the Basque case and then of the policing of political Islamism, with particular attention to the three paradigmatic cases of Egypt, Palestine, and Saudi Arabia.

ESCALATING POLICING OF LEFT-WING AND RIGHT-WING PROTEST

Tough, escalating forms of policing of the Left and the labor movement had characterized postwar Italian history. Throughout the 1950s, protest policing involved hard repression of several political groups and forms of collective action, with frequent "use of firearms by policemen against protestors, strikers, peasants who occupied land" (Canosa 1976: 181). As many as sixty-two demonstrators died between 1948 and 1950, and thirty-three died between 1951 and 1962 (Canosa 1976: chaps. 2 and 3). The laws on public order, a legacy of the fascist regime, gave great power to the police. As members of a militarized body, policemen were not allowed to form or join a trade union; they received no special preparation in crime control, and what training they received was primarily physical and military, oriented to the repression of mass disorder. The style of policing reflected closed political opportunities for the main social movement of the time, the labor movement, and its political allies in the Old Left.

On the right, the threat to outlaw neofascist parties never materialized, although a feeling of isolation and persecution spread after the end of the fascist regime. The first decades after World War II saw a formal exclusion but also an informal tolerance of the radical Right. The policing of the (mainly small) right-wing demonstrations never took dramatic turns, in a period in which a sort of internal cold war was addressed especially toward the largest communist party in the Western world (Reiter 1998). Although the lack of a true purge had kept many fascist leaders in place in the public administration, after the end of the war, former fascists were also recruited in the struggle against the communists and in the repression of an increasing class conflict. As Franco Ferraresi wrote, "this is why the many neo-fascist groups and the organizations which had proliferated already in the first months after the war found little to no hostility on the part of the state. These groups usually had short and turbulent lives marked by confused programs, rivalry and fights between the leaders, and frequent scissions, re-compositions, dissolutions and re-foundations" (1995: 44). However, they also performed quite violent actions, such as attacks against the headquarters of political parties or monuments in honor of Jews or partisans, with limited repression.

Political opportunities for the left-wing movements started to open up during the center-left governmental coalition that took power in 1962, with the participation of the Socialist Party. Its effect was to make the policing of protest softer, even though no actual police reform took place. Additionally, the policing of the student protests and the other actors that mobilized beginning in the second half of the 1960s was inconsistent, mixing initial tolerance with increasing repression when protest polarized the political system (see Canosa 1976: chap. 4). In 1968, three people were killed during marches organized by the trade unions, and another three died in demonstrations in 1969.

When the student movements emerged in the 1960s, the governing elites felt particularly endangered. The late 1960s saw a closure of political opportunities for the left-libertarian social movements, with the end of the center-left governmental experiences and a turn to the right, which brought about the development of a so-called tension strategy – that is, the use of radical Right violence to justify an authoritarian turn of the state. The repression was perceived as directed in general against the Left; so, at first, the trade unions and the Partito Comunista Italiano (Italian Communist Party [PCI]) sided with the social movements in denouncing state repression and fascist aggression (della Porta 1995).

Right-wing radicals acted underground, with planned coups d'état and, apparently, the massacre in Milan on 12 December 1969. Rumors spread of involvement of secret services in both. Already in 1964, the head of the military intelligence (Servizio Informazioni Forze Armate [SIFAR]), General De Lorenzo, had to resign, accused of planning a coup. In the 1970s, "disclosures about the intelligence service (SIFAR) included the fact that it had kept dossiers on many of the country's political leaders, leftists in particular, and had provided covered funds for a number of patriotic organizations, including veteran groups and, most disturbing, the New Order and National Vanguard" (Weinberg and Eubank 1987: 39).

Collaboration between secret services and neofascist groups also emerged during investigations of attempted coups d'état. In one of them, in December 1970, groups from the Avanguardia Nazionale (National Vanguard [AN]), the Ordine Nuovo (New Order [ON]), and the National Front gathered near major state buildings, waiting for an order by Junio Valerio Borghese, a former military general. In 1974, judicial investigations led to arrests among police and military officers for complicity in the attempt. Later, there would be rumors of the involvement of the reformed secret services (Servizio Informazioni Difesa [SID]) and of the Masonic Lodge Propaganda 2 (P2) in the protection of the extreme Right. Vito Miceli, former head of SID, was arrested in 1975, and the P2 was involved in investigations of a federation of neofascist groups organized to subvert the democratic system – the so-called Rosa dei Venti. Claims that the secret service protected the radical Right were particularly frequent in the period of the *stragismo*, the "strategy" of massacres perpetrated by right-wing terrorism. In the late 1960s and the beginning of the following decade, *deviati* parts of the secret services (that is, a clandestine group within the organization that did illegal things) were accused of having offered support to the extreme Right.

In the first half of the 1970s, state responses to social movements were characterized by some reforms but also increasingly harsh handling of large protest groups. Protest events (even from the extreme Right) were sometimes prohibited for fear of counterreaction, and right-wing activists sometimes fought with police. On the right, as on the left, there were complaints that a so-called strategy of the opposite extremisms was used by the state to limit freedom of expression on both sides. The list of (mainly left-wing) protestors who lost their lives during police charges with jeeps and tear gas bullets (Canosa 1976: 274–85) grew in the early 1970s: between 1970 and 1975, policemen killed seven protestors and passersby during interventions at political gatherings (ibid.).

Tough policing was a vivid memory for the Italian left-wing activists. Activists recalled fights with the police: "I still have a rain coat, I've always kept it, with a hole of a tear gas bullet" (Life History no. 21: 310); "furious clashes until 2pm, from 5 am to 2 pm" (Life History no. 5: 86); "a policeman who aimed his gun at my belly" (Life History no. 21: 31); "my burned hand, when I tried to throw back a squat candle" (Life History no. 3: 19). These encounters aroused intense emotion, strengthening commitment to radical politics. Some emotions were negative ones. A militant remembers his fear: "In the marches, the demonstrations that degenerated into clashes, the moment in which tension spreads and the clashes are more and more near, when the charge by the police is in the air, those were the moments I felt fear about" (Life History no. 9: 244). But, together with fear, repression also fueled more positive emotions; thus a future member of a clandestine left-wing organization described his first demonstration, in Milan in the late 1960s, as follows:

We were looking for other classmates, quietly walking in the street, when pandemonium broke out: tear gas, cries, blows, people running everywhere. In the beginning, we did not realize what was happening. We had our share of tear gas and we tried to run away.... We wandered around in the city center, looking for the march, following the smoke and the cries. We saw a squad of policemen in combat gear. It was all very spectacular: tricolour bands, the trumpets to start the charges. I saw Milan in a way I would never have imagined, with the smoke of the tear gas, and a really ghostly scene: torn placards, broken road-signs, and people wounded in the street.... I arrived home very late. My eyes were red from the smoke of the tear gas, my clothes were torn. But I was so happy and excited, because something very important had happened, and I had been there. (Life History no. 12: 10–11)

Left-wing activists also remembered the fear of a coup d'état: an activist described "periods when I had my backpack already prepared under my bed" (cited in Novelli and Tranfaglia 1988: 122); another wondered, "How many people – I do not refer only to the comrades of the extra-parliamentary left – did not sleep at home; how many eyes were focused on the barracks" (ibid.: 204). The "paranoia of a coup d'état" brought about "a conspiratorial identity" (Life

History no. 18: 47); "*What to do when there is a coup d'état* was the classic book that all the comrades had hidden on their bookshelves," added another (Life History no. 6: 19).

Events such as the massacre in Piazza Fontana had a high emotional impact and were considered by the left-wing activists as a sort of "lost innocence" (Grispigni 2012). As a militant recalls,

of course, interest rose after the fascist massacre of Piazza Fontana, on December 12, 1969. For the first time, there was a strike. We did not go to classes, but went to the funeral in Piazza Duomo. There was a huge public march and the Mass. I remember that, with a lot of effort because it was packed with people, I entered the Duomo. There were all these biers. (Life History no. 12: 10)

The mobilization after the massacre and the death of an anarchist, Giuseppe Pinelli, while he was being interrogated by police during the investigation, represented very intense experiences for many activists: "Although [we were] not yet involved in the student movement, a classmate and I thought that we wanted to see this march. We went to the central building of the University. I remember it as a wonderful feeling. I had never seen so many people all of my age, all with the same interests as mine" (ibid.).

State repression – as "suffered violence" – justified radical responses. As a left-wing activist explained,

It is first of all a problem of suffered violence. The first images are linked to the police charges. The first, strong signs of an unsustainable situation, a situation which really had to be changed, comes those years from Avola and Battipaglia. They came from those demonstrations, by the way not student ones, that were hit and repressed, with the death of people who had demonstrated ... the first demonstrations in which there were clashes.... I did not remember them as having been planned. (Life History no. 9: 243)

At the same time, the perception of the involvement of state institutions in massacres and coups d'état (see subsequently) increased mistrust in the democratic quality of the existing system. At perceived critical junctures, an exceptional moment is seen as requiring exceptional commitment. Again in the words of an Italian militant,

this is the period just after the military coup in Chile. We started to feel the need to defend ourselves. This argument was for me absolutely convincing. I was certain that any mass struggle that was to approach power could never reach it without a very violent fight. The massacre of Piazza Fontana testified to it. While Vietnam was for me very far away, I had felt the experience of the Popular Front in Chile as very near to the Italian one. Consider, too, that there was very widespread paranoia about an imminent fascist coup. (Life History no. 12: 17)

Also, on the right, these years were certainly intense, as hidden supports by the secret services raised suspicions of a possible turn toward an authoritarian regime. Contacts with the secret services were in fact admitted from inside the radical Right. In an interview, the radical Right leader Pino Rauti assigned the responsibility of the Piazza Fontana massacre to the secret service and the strategy of tension, admitting that his organization, the ON, "had collaborated with the state in the name of a common enemy" (Cento Bull 2007: 115). He declared that the extreme Right had in fact "collaborated more or less under the counter, and at some moments especially under the counter," with "the secret services. The links with the military." At one point, he stated, "The idea of a coup ... circulated among the extreme right. As a shortcut to achieve power. Faced with a communist threat," and he pointed out that "the fact of growing up with the conviction that there existed a communist threat prevented us from being ourselves, in the fullness of the program" (cited in ibid.). Another right-wing leader, Giorgio Pisanò, expressed his belief that the bombs in Piazza Fontana had been planted by "the Ministry of the Interior. The Office of Classified Affairs within the Ministry of the Interior" (cited in ibid.: 116), also confirming the collaboration of the extreme Right with the secret services. In a climate of fear and witch-hunting, according to yet another right-winger,

the preferred scheme was that after the Second World War, in order to face the communist danger, Italian sectors within the armed forces and among the industrialists, which in turn were controlled by the CIA, recruited some veterans of the Social Republic, who were viscerally anti-communist and trained them as sappers and guerrillas.... Obviously for the people who came from the experience of the Social Republic the memory of the purges and systematic executions was still alive and vivid, with the *foibe* in the region Venezia-Giulia and the massacres, the mass killing in the Emilia triangle. (ibid.: 117)[4]

Repression became even tougher in the second half of the 1970s. Throughout the decade, as right-wing and left-wing radicals engaged daily in brutal – sometimes deadly – fights, police strategies were unable to avoid escalation, using mass charges that hit peaceful protestors as well as agents provocateurs. On a few occasions in 1977, the army was mobilized to curtail prohibited marches by the extreme Left, and firearms were used by both sides. Political opportunities were perceived as extremely closed by the New Left. In these "years of emergency," the PCI proposed a "historic compromise" – that is, a collaboration between "Catholic and communist masses" – and, in 1978 and 1979, supported (from outside) the national governments led by the Christian Democrats. The PCI thus gave up its role as defender of citizens' rights, and laws changed in an illiberal direction (Corso 1979; Grevi 1984).

In the mid-1970s, political opportunities (and perceptions thereof) closed down, even for the neofascists. The dissolution, by ministerial decree, of the ON in 1973 and its sister organization (AN) in 1976 marked this shift. In 1973, a Roman court recognized the ON as responsible for the reconstruction of the Fascist Party, and, in application of a statute law from 1952, the interior minister signed a decree that

---

[4] Another militant, Delle Chiaie, admitted to having supported the failed coup d'état led by Prince Junio Valerio (Cento Bull 2007: 135).

dissolved the organization. Some ON leaders then flew into exile in Franco's Spain, while others went underground, founding the group Ordine Nero (Weinberg and Eubank 1987: 45), which counted at least seven territorial units and was responsible for at least forty-five bombings. The AN was dissolved on the same grounds in 1976. In 1974, a reform of the secret services, especially their "*deviati*" components, followed international developments that saw the breakdown of authoritarian regimes in Southern Europe as well as some changes in US foreign policy (Guerrieri 2008). In 1974, paramilitary camps were raided by the police, and there were many arrests of neofascists (Weinberg and Eubank 1987: 45). The radical Right's reaction to the perceived increase in repression was the 1976 assassination of Vittorio Occorsio, the judge who had investigated the ON.

On the left, deadly fights with police or political adversaries became transformative events, signaling new turns in the spiral of escalation. High emotions were aroused by the memory of the "April days" of 1975, when neofascists shot dead the left-wing activist Claudio Varalli. During the violent protests that followed, a police van killed another militant, Giovanni Zibecchi, in Milan; a private policeman killed another, Tonino Miccichè, in Turin during a house occupation, and a policeman in plainclothes killed yet another, Rodolfo Boschi, in Florence (Scavino 2012: 196–7). The militants often recalled those "three days of fighting" (cited in Novelli and Tranfaglia 1988: 163). These "were the moments when rage and the desire to rebel came to possess us all.... Those deaths gave us a strange feeling, almost as if it were not possible to go back anymore" (cited in ibid.: 206). In the second half of the 1970s, the list of left-wing activists killed by police during protests or after arrests grew, and with it the highly emotional moments of the victims.

Similarly, on the right, memories of friends who died at the hands of the police or political adversaries are frequently recounted in the context of incidents such as the January 1978 events in Acca Larentia, in Rome, when three right-wing militants lost their lives in an attack by radical leftists of the Nuclei Armati per il Contropotere Territoriale against the MSI headquarters in via Acca Larentia. Two of the activists were killed by political adversaries, and one by police officers who had intervened to quell the fights. As an activist in the underground Nuclei Armati Rivoluzionari (Revolutionary Armed Nuclei [NAR]), Francesca Mambro, recalled, "at Acca Larentia ... for the first time, and for three days, the fascists will fire at the police. And this was obviously a no-return turning point" (Ferraresi 1995: 293). Also in this period, a young Movimento Sociale Italiano (MSI) activist, Alberto Giaquinto, was killed by police officers during an attack against a Democrazia Cristiana (Christian Democracy [DC]) section. Waves of repression are in fact cited as motivating Terza Posizione activists to join the NAR (Cento Bull 2007: 143).

Compared to the Italian case, protest policing in Germany was in general more selective and (relatively) easier, even if prior to the student movement the police had "an image of any gathering of people as potentially destructive, an irrational 'formation of a mob,' from which a danger to the state order could rapidly develop" (Busch et al. 1988: 319). Whereas in the early 1950s police had charged marches against rearmament and on labor issues, killing two protestors (on 11 May 1952 and 1 May 1953), later on, force was rarely used in the handling of industrial conflicts, reflecting the general institutional inclusion of the labor unions and the Sozialdemokratische Partei Deutschlands (Social Democratic Party of Germany [SPD]). The Kommunistische Partei Deutchlands (KPD), its related organizations, and some right-wing groups were, however, declared "enemies of the constitution" (Grässle-Münschen 1991: chap. 3).

As in Italy, police reactions to the student movement in Germany included a mixture of harder and softer tactics. Particularly significant was the June 1967 killing by a Berlin policeman of a student, Benno Ohnesorg, during a protest against the visit of the Shah of Iran. In what was defined "an exercise for an emergency," the police used hard repressive tactics (Sack 1984). In addition, the attack against student leader Rudy Dutschke became proof that "the state was ready to do anything and that its fascist face appeared as soon as it felt in danger for whatever reason" (Baumann 1976: 81). These events were considered by the activists as the culmination of exclusive attitudes toward the student movement. During the demonstration that followed the attack against Dutschke, "the street lit by torches and the shout Rudi Dutschke meant to me: this bullet was directed against you too. For the first time, they fired at you" (ibid.: 2).

On these occasions, recollections of the end of the Weimar Republic were often quoted in the press, and the students' "breaking of the rules" was compared to the political violence that preceded the rise of Nazism. The social democratic SPD, governing in alliance with the Christian Democratic Union (CDU) and pushed by both its coalition partners and its search for legitimation, initially took a fairly negative attitude toward the student movement. However, the shock of the death of Benno Ohnesorg led the social democratic mayor of Berlin to resign and intensified the internal conflicts among the SPD and even among the police, while "the ways and forms of reciprocal behaviour of the state powers and the protestors became a theme of great relevance in the public discussion. The marches and their control by the police became a political issue" (Busch et al. 1988: 318).

German activists also mentioned other episodes of repression as transformative events. For example, one activist remembered a police "orgy of clubs. I threw myself in the battle. Two minutes later I found myself in an ambulance" (Klein 1980: 199). Another memory involved "three policemen who were beating a girl" (ibid.: 57). Rote Armee Fraktion (Red Army Fraction [RAF]) member and student movement defense lawyer Horst Mahler explained that police repression of the movement had dramatically undermined his confidence in the state: "We marched in the streets against the genocide in Vietnam with the belief that we were doing the best thing in the world. Then, there was the massive aggression of the state apparatus, and there was one death" (quoted in Baum and Mahler 1979: 39).[5]

---

[5] Mahler later experienced repression directly, as he was sentenced to ten months in prison and was found guilty in a civil trial; he had to pay a quarter of a million marks in damages to Springer after a protest against the right-wing attempt on the life of Rudi Dutschke in 1968 (Mahler 1977: 78).

In contrast to Italy, however, the policing of protest in Germany became more tolerant by the 1970s, when

in the administration of justice the opinion tended to prevail that demonstrations should not only be tolerated, but that, as active citizen rights, they must take priority over concerns about executive order. The intervention of the police – until now oriented to fight violent troublemakers with closed units – had to be rethought according to the "principle of the flexible reaction" and through an intervention suitable to the specific situation, designed to avoid the escalation of conflict and violence. (Busch et al. 1988: 320)

To avoid escalation, authorities experimented with negotiation strategies: for instance, the Berlin and Munich police created the *Diskussionkommando*, composed of small groups of policemen, in uniform but without arms, charged with the task of talking with the activists during demonstrations and discouraging violence (Hübner 1979: 212; Malpricht 1984: 83–5).

This tolerant turn in protest policing coincided with the SPD–Freie Demokratische Partei (Free Democratic Party [FDP]) governments, inaugurated in 1969, and some liberal reforms in demonstration rights; however, it was followed by the Radicalenerlaß (January 1972), which was designated to homogenize the various procedures developed by the various German states, blocking access to the civil service to individuals with "anticonstitutional" attitudes. Although actual exclusions were rare (only 430 people of the more than 500,000 investigated were excluded from public services), the symbolic effect of this law was quite strong. Additionally, in the second half of the 1970s, the handling of the antinuclear protests – often involving the occupation of sites where nuclear plants were to be built – included moments of escalation around selected sites with extensive preventive police action.

Moreover, the counterterrorist policies themselves produced occasions for further radicalization. Criticism of the state's authoritarianism intensified when the imprisoned terrorists staged hunger strikes to call attention to harsh living conditions in the high-security units. Antiterrorist laws also increased the activists' mistrust in political elites, and militants killed by police became heroes. German militants in fact often linked their radicalization to the memory of several young RAF militants killed in shoot-outs with police (among them are twenty-year-old Petra Schelm in July 1971, twenty-four-year-old George von Rauch in December 1971, and twenty-three-year-old Thomas Weißbecker in March 1972) or to the isolation treatment, beginning in 1973, of RAF prisoners. Similarly, a German activist remembers the death of an RAF prisoner in a hunger strike: "The day came when Holger Meins died.... For us this death was a key experience.... The death of Holger Meins and the decision to take arms were one and the same decision. Reflection was not possible anymore" (Speitel 1980a: 41). And another added, "If all I needed for not only promoting the armed struggle, but also for taking it up myself was the right kick, then Holger Meins was this kick" (Klein 1980: 256).

Feelings of discrimination, moreover, went beyond the actions of state and police. The existing ways in which the past history of a state is framed contribute to the dramatization of some events. As former RAF member Klaus Jünschke noted, "the acceptance of special prison units also legitimates all other means aiming at the same goal: constriction therapies, brain surgery, genetic manipulation. The [state's] inadequate reflection on German history from 1933 to 1945 corresponds to this lack of sensitivity toward the complete control of human beings, towards total dominion over human beings" (1988: 131). In 1977, the deaths of three RAF militants in the Stammheim prison were taken as a "confirmation that fascism had now exploded in an open way" (Neuhauser 1978: 84). The Federal Republic of Germany thus came to be identified with the Nazi state. In an interview, Mahler observed:

How could young people, enthusiastic about the universal good, feel OK in a state that had already shown itself as a murderous Leviathan, as the institutionalized crime against humanity? ... It was not a lack of reverence or a presumed evil of the young people that prevented their identification with the German state and the German people. It was instead the traumatic memories of fascist cruelty, the absence of an antifascist revolution in West Germany, and the continuity of state involvement in imperialism. (1980: 26–7)

When we compare the two cases, however, we see that the policing of protest was softer and more selective in Germany than in Italy. Germany's more inclusive approach might be linked to the federal asset, which allowed the SPD *Laender* to experiment with de-escalation techniques, the demilitarized and unionized police, and the neocorporatist model of industrial relations, with early integration of the labor movement and left-wing parties and a stronger rule of law and accountability. The deep reform of the police in Germany after World War II found no parallel in the Italian police force, in which the first reforms arrived in the early 1980s and the fascist laws on public order remained in power even longer. However, growing public stigmatization of police repression played a role in increasing moderation. Also, in general, protest policing was more tolerant when the Left was in government, whereas conservative governments were inclined to use harder tactics.

In addition, the position of the Old Left had a relevant impact, increasing the influence of a civil rights coalition it joined. In contrast, repression took harsher forms when the Old Left abandoned that coalition (della Porta 1995: 192). In the latter case, the hard line of protest policing tended to prevail, as happened in both countries in the second half of the seventies. The mere presence of the Old Left, however, did not guarantee that the civil rights coalition would gain influence over actual policing. If the Old Left were in a marginal position in the party system – as was the case in both countries in the fifties and in Italy until the eighties – the hard line tended to prevail. When the Left was gaining power but was not yet in government, dirty forms of protest policing could predominate, as occurred in Italy in the early 1970s.

In general, more tolerant, selective, and softer police behavior favored the diffusion of protest; repressive, diffuse, and hard techniques of policing tended to discourage mass and peaceful protest while at the same time fueling the most radical fringes. There was indeed a reciprocal adaptation of police and protestors' tactics. In the 1980s, both countries saw more tolerant police attitudes and a deradicalization of protest repertoires. Public order policies then became more tolerant, more selective, more oriented toward prevention, more respectful of democratic procedures, and softer – although this evolution was hardly linear, as both countries experienced relapses when political conflicts escalated into violent forms.

ESCALATING POLICING AND ETHNIC PROTEST

The policing of protest also played an important role in the Basque Country, both during Francoism and afterward. Repression of ethnonationalists in this region has historically been particularly virulent. During the military rebellion against the Spanish republic, the Basque Country had in fact sided with the republic, which, in 1936, had recognized the autonomy of the Basque provinces. By June 1937, however, the Basque Country was occupied by the rebels, led by Franco. Heavy and indiscriminate repression continued after the end of the civil war, in the spring of 1939, with mass executions, concentration camps, and forced labor; this period was sadly known as "times of silence" (Richards 1998). The Basque provinces of Biscay and Guipuzkoa were declared traitor provinces, the Basque flag (the *ikurrina*) was banned, and Basque nationalism was confined to the private sphere (Muro 2008: chap. 4). About 150,000 Basques then left Spain (11.5 percent of the inhabitants of the Basque provinces of Alava, Biscay, and Guipuzkoa), about 1,000 died in the aftermath of the civil war, and 16,000 were arrested as suspected nationalists.

Repression remained intense later on. As Jaime-Jiménez and Reinares (1998: 168) summarized, "post-war repression was severe and, in many cases, indiscriminate. Between 1939 and 1944, nearly two hundred thousand people were executed because of political reasons." After the end of the war, the supporters of the republic hoped for an intervention by Allied forces; their hopes were disappointed, however, and the US rapprochement to Franco's Spain was perceived as a betrayal of democracy by those who had trusted the Western powers as potential allies. When it became clear that no external help could be expected to reestablish the Republican legality against the *golpistas* in government, many of the Spanish opposition went into exile or disbanded.

After Franco's victory, the police forces were reorganized: the Policia Armada, largely made up of veterans who had fought against the republic, was created. Together with the Guardia Civil, which was a militarized force, the new police force had the main task of fighting any political opposition. All public protest was prohibited. In 1959, the Public Order Law established procedures to repress public demonstrations, whereas some units of the Policia Armada were trained in anti-riot intervention. In 1969, the Compania de Reserva General was created with the same purpose and the same militarized organization and culture, and the Guardia Civil was endowed with anti-riot equipment (Jaime-Jiménez and Reinares 1998: 170). In fact, throughout the 1960s and up to the 1970s, "the number of deaths caused by the police at demonstrations remained very high" (ibid.: 170).

During Franco's regime, laws against terrorism were issued and applied to all critics of the regime. On 2 March 1943, a law was passed codifying the repression of armed opposition, which was further sharpened by a decree regarding repression of banditry and terrorism in 1947, a military justice code issued in 1945, and a decree on military rebellion, banditry, and terrorism in 1960. Crimes of military rebellion included dissemination of false or tendentious information to cause disturbance in the public order, international conflicts, or decline in the prestige of the state; meetings; strikes; and so on. Penalties for terrorist acts – broadly defined as attacks on public security – were severe and included death if the action resulted in the demise of a person (even if it was unplanned). Jurisdiction over such crimes was assigned first to a military tribunal, later to the tribunals for public order, and then back again to the military. In 1975, preventive detention of suspected terrorists was authorized, defense rights were further hampered, and trials were conducted in secret. No extenuating circumstances were considered and no appeals allowed.

This legal structure paved the way for tough repression of all opposition, resulting in mass arrests, high numbers of political prisoners, and high penalties, including death sentences. States of exception were declared twelve times from 1956 to 1975; these included temporary abrogation of the privacy of mail, of habeas corpus, and of freedom of movement and freedom from arbitrary house arrests: "Persons could be arrested and held at any location for any length of time without anyone being informed of their whereabouts or even of the fact that they had been arrested" (Clark 1984: 240). As Pérez-Agote (2006: 115) observed,

the state of exception gave inhabitants a sense of shared purpose. That is, because they were singled out for state violence, the inhabitants felt communally and collectively under assault ... imprisonment or exile ceased to be degrading, rather the stigma was transferred to the state, especially the security forces ... at the same time, state oppression reinforced the network that converted this violence into one subject of interpersonal communication.

This also bolstered emotional support for the ETA, as many people had *etarras* in the family or knew someone who had been arrested or sent into exile (ibid.).

Because its citizens were very active in labor protests, the Basque Country was particularly hard hit by the virulent repression that followed the strikes of 1947, 1951, and 1956. Repression culminated in December 1970 in Burgos, when sixteen ETA members were tried by a military tribunal for crimes of terrorism and banditry. The trial ended with six death sentences (three of them double), which, under strong international pressure, were transformed to thirty years in prison. Later, however, in 1975, ETA members Juan Paredes Manot ("Txiki") and Angel Otaegi were executed after a dubious trial before a military tribunal; two dozen other ETA members had already been killed in various ways by the Spanish state (Muro 2008: 107).

Torture was common during the Franco dictatorship. In 1975, Amnesty International (AI) published evidence of mass arrests, including 1,000 detainees in the two Basque provinces, 500 of whom were held for more than seventy-two hours without notification (Clark 1984). Re-arrests were often ordered by civil governors, after detainees had been released by the judges. AI also reported clear evidence of forty-five cases of torture and credible indications of an additional 250. These included severe and systematic beatings, burning by cigarettes, near drowning by submersion in water, enforced sleeplessness, fake executions, and various threats to obtain information but also to produce general intimidation.

The use of the Basque language was completely prohibited, not only in public but also in the private sphere, as was the use of any Basque symbol (Pérez-Agote 2006: 80). In fact, "nationalism took refuge in those areas of life that the state found more difficult to penetrate: the family, inter pares groups, private associations, friendship groups, and the Catholic Church" (ibid.: xxii). After Franco's coup d'état,

> the Basque language and culture went through the most critical period in their history. Although these two elements "did not lose the war" as it were, the political group – that is the Basque nationalist party – that upheld them, did and, as a result of defeat, so did the entire cultural movement behind the party. The linguistic and cultural repression was ferocious. The Basque language, both written and spoken, was prohibited in public and in private, and its use punished even in the environment of the family. All folklore or cultural demonstrations (dancing, music, literature, etc.), however insignificant, were suppressed. In short, any identity with anything other than the Spanish language was denied. (Jauregui Bereciartu 1986: 589)

In the late 1930s, official documents defined as unhealthy provocation the practice of giving children names such as Inaki that "were not only written in a language different from the official Spanish, but contain a meaning contrary to the Unity of the Fatherland ... betray an unquestionable separatist meaning" (Pérez-Agote 2006: 82). Basque nationalists bitterly remembered the "humiliation I received when the teacher laughed at the way I talked Spanish…. Basque was completely ridiculed" (ibid.: 81).

Repression hit the lower clergy as well. Traditionally a refuge for the Basque language, the lower clergy had organized a sort of resistance against Franco's repression of Basque culture and had engaged in a critique of the Catholic hierarchy, writing (from 1940 to 1960) various collective letters and even a clandestine journal. In 1964, priests were arrested after the celebration of the first Aberri Eguna, the day of the Basque fatherland. In August 1968, after eight priests had been placed in detention and the tribunals for public order had asked the bishop of Biscaye for permission to proceed against another sixty-six, forty priests occupied the palace of the bishop and stayed until the authorization was refused (Itcaina 2007: 129). A few months later, sixty priests were targeted by strong repression after they locked themselves in the Derio Seminary in Bilbao, asking for the resignation of their bishop. Five of them were sentenced to serve between ten and twelve years in jail, and the others were sent to special jails for priests. Also, later on, numerous priests were arrested for alleged support of the ETA. This radicalized part of the lower clergy had provided the ETA with safe spaces, in churches and convents, to meet and hide weapons, as well as recruits and ideas deriving from liberation theology.

Experience of repression was widespread. In Pérez-Agote's assessment,

Practically all those that came from a Basque nationalist background had some experience with state violence, either personally though a death, imprisonment, persecution or exile or through the physical harm of someone close to them. Moreover, they all had unforgettable memories of the ... state of exception. The social experience of this repression permeates both their individual and collective lives (collective memory). Politics and violence belonged to everyday life, constituting the subject matter in interpersonal communication and associative relations and was consequently expressed in the context of the multitudinous popular demonstrations that grew more frequent after 1970. (2006: 99)

Furthermore, "the large number of political prisoners in a society as small as the Basque ones meant that the repression (in different ways and to different extents) was a generalized personal experience" (ibid.: 94).

Violent repression during Franco's regime and immediately after his death was often a direct memory for ETA militants, especially as it was linked to important symbols of the Basque nation. As one of them recalled, "I was arrested.... I went with a girl to dance, in a dancing place, where they played songs in *euskera*.... Suddenly, the *guardia civil* entered and charged. They charged although there was no demonstration of any type. And they entered in the *sala de fiesta* with ten jeeps" (Reinares 2001: 133). Particularly intense are the memories of torture once in the hands of the police: "I remember ... it was 1976 and the day of *euskera*. I have it written in my memory. Our group of people, we did not sleep. They did not let us sleep. We stayed for six days without sleeping. And there were constant threats. The pistol in your head ..." (ibid.: 139). Another recalled, "I was in prison for ten days. They hit me. We just wanted to be independent" (ibid.: 154).

Franco's dictatorship thus justified a violence that was considered as necessary, in the face of an authoritarian regime. Franco's repression "legitimated, to the regime's regret, Basque nationalist sentiments and social concerns.... Basque nationalist consciousness during this period did not need to refer to some mythical age, given that repressed social life itself was experienced as foundational, as a founding myth" (Pérez-Agote 2006: xxi). The brutality of the regime was seen as justifying violence, as, in the words of a Basque activist, "it was they who used violence. It is in a situation of dictatorship, like francoism. Its form of relations with us was violence" (Reinares 2001: 89). Revenge became legitimized as a normal reaction to the violence of the other: "When I'm tired of getting them, I have to give them, no?" (ibid.: 137). In fact, there was a widespread perception that "of course you had to recur to violence. Given that the regime, who is repressing you, is a violent regime. Of course, they are recurring to violence continuously; clear, they put you in prison, they torture you" (ibid.: 87). At the same time, repression by the center reduced the legitimacy of Spain as a nation: for the Basque militants, in the words of one of them, "Franco represented Spain" (ibid.: 163), and "Spain? Repression. Spain was the police" (ibid.: 166). Consequently, the ETA gained credibility as the most effective group under highly repressive circumstances. The choice to engage in a clandestine and violent organization thus started to appear quite normal; one activist remembered, "To enter in ETA? No, in some way, I did not ask myself. That is, my problem is that it was the only way of doing politics to attack a regime violently, because there was no other way of doing politics" (ibid.: 87).

While memories of past repression remained alive, the opening of political opportunities during the transition did not moderate political violence; it instead increased. After Franco's death, the pacted transition was led by center-right Adolfo Suarez who, even if apparently committed to democracy, proceeded very cautiously and with as few breaks as possible with the past regime. In 1981, the attempted coup d'état increased insecurity about the young Spanish democracy, which consolidated in the following years. In the period between 1976 and 1978, the democracy enacted several policy steps, including the abrogation of fourteen articles of the 1975 law on the prevention of terrorism, that appeared conciliatory. The jurisdiction of the tribunal for public order (TPO) was abolished in 1976, even though military tribunals remained in charge of attacks against the army.

On 25 November 1975, King Juan Carlos released almost all of the political prisoners: 1,000 were freed immediately; about 500 others were released in July 1976. Of the remaining 150 Basque detainees, 50 were released on a case-by-case base. A third amnesty in 1977 established the rehearing of all cases defined by the TPO. There were also proposals of freedom and exile for the remaining few dozen; the proposals for 23 prisoners were approved, whereas 5 remained in prison. In October 1977, the parliament almost unanimously approved a total amnesty for all political prisoners. However, the number of ETA prisoners started to increase again, rapidly reaching a few hundred.

The process of de-escalation was slow, and at times inconsistent. There was a new repressive turn in 1976, after the left-wing clandestine organization GRAPO (Grupo Revolucionario Antifascista Primero de Octubre, that is, Revolutionary Anti-Fascist Group First of October) kidnapped a top political advisor of Juan Carlos, asking for the release of political prisoners. Political demonstrations were then temporarily banned, and the police were given power to detain suspects for up to ten days without charges, to search without warrants, and to intercept mail and phone calls. Following the assassination of the journalist José Maria Portell, antiterrorist laws were passed in 1978,

notwithstanding the criticism of Basque politicians. The government reintro-
duced police detention (although it was subject to judicial approval) and the
right to intercept mail, and it denied amnesty in the case of terrorist crimes.
Repression of protest continued, culminating, in March 1976, in the assassination of five Basque workers during a demonstration. The fight against the ETA
continued to fuel restrictive legislation. Law 56/1978 and decree law 3/1979,
which were further developed in 1980, permitted authorities to detain suspects
incommunicado for up to ten days, as well as preventive detention. Terrorism
continued to be defined very broadly, and reports of torture, facilitated by the
new antiterrorist laws, continued to divide public opinion.

The struggle against repression became emotionally intense, in particular
through transformative events that remained in the activists' memories.
Among the triggering points of their politicization, the Basque militants remembered the Burgos trials, which involved the last death penalties before Franco's
death, and the Marcha por la Libertad of July 1977, a request for amnesty and
self-government. An activist recalled the climate during the protest for amnesty
during the democratic transition as follows:

I was very, very marked by the March for freedoms. I was fifteen. The March of freedoms
was a march that went through all Euskadi with four columns that converged in Iruna.
And, in fact, you went in the march when it went through your village. And you shared
your food, and they slept in peoples' places.... And so I started to know people who were
not of my village, who were from Guiputzca, had a brother or a friend in prison, to people
who had another brother or friend in exile. And for me it was very strong, because I lived
it with much intensity. (Reinares 2001: 78)

Even if, after the death of Franco, Prime Minister Suarez's politics was oriented
toward compromise, it remained particularly ambivalent toward Basque nationalism. Weak support for the legalization of Basque symbols (such as the *ikurrina*
flag) and the exclusion of ETA prisoners from pardons in 1975 and 1976 in turn
reduced support for the Constitution in the Basque Country. However, a statute of
autonomy (approved in December 1979 by the Parliament) recognized the competences of the Basque government and parliament (except those of Navarra) in
matters of police, culture, education and health care, and industrial and agricul-
tural policies; gave autonomous institutions the capacity to collect taxes; recognized Euskera as an official language; and created a Basque radio and TV station.

However, for many years, the policing of protest generally remained tough. The
Public Order Law was not amended until 1991, and "the antiriot units continued to
respond to breach of the public order in almost the same way as before: between
1975 and 1979, the police caused the deaths of thirty-six people in street confrontations. Not even the approval of the new democratic Constitution in 1978 proved
a definite turning point" (Jaime-Jiménez and Reinares 1998: 170). Tensions
remained high, as "the elites of the Franco regime continued to play an important
role in the political decision making of the state" (ibid.: 173). The army and the
police forces were in need of reform to democratize their structures and especially to

intervene in their military ethos and main focus on the repression of the opposition; however, fear of reactions from inside delayed these reforms. Although the 1977 Moncloa Pacts included vague references to police reform, "almost the entire structure and personnel remained" (ibid.: 176).

Only in the 1980s, with the demobilization of social conflict that followed the formation of the Partido Socialista Obrero Espanol (Spanish Socialist Workers' Party [PSOE]) government, were there some reforms in protest policing. In 1986, the new state police law created a fully civil police body, and, in 1992, the Francoist Public Order Law was abolished. Along with a generational change, a more tolerant policing of public order developed, especially in cases of labor unrest (Jaime-Jiménez and Reinares 1998: 181ff.).

In the Basque Country, the pacted transition was therefore not sufficient to legitimize the Spanish state, which was accused of following the Fascist tradition, established during the long-standing Francoist regime, of resorting to torture against Basque patriots. In 1980, AI denounced Spain's deterioration of rights and increase in maltreatment, including torture, with methods very similar to the ones described in its 1975 report (Clark 1984: 262). A parliamentary committee was even denied access to installations of the ministry of the interior. Franco's death produced many expectations that were ultimately frustrated, at least in the short term. In the words of an activist, "we all thought that, when Franco died, we were going to have a reunified Euskadi, *euskaldun* [Basque speaking], independent, socialist" (ibid.: 102). After Franco's death and during the democratic transition, the lack of purges was considered a sign of continuity with the former regime; as an activist recalled, "Franco died and everything went on ..." (ibid.: 123).

During transition and consolidation, the continuation of repression and military presence in the Basque Country was felt as an attack against the community. In this period, the Basque Country remained the most militarized region in Spain. In the 1980s, as many as 17 percent of the Spanish troops were deployed in an area that covered only 3.5 percent of Spanish territory. Repression was perceived as permeating everyday life, as in an occupied land. An ETA militant recalled,

Well, at the level of the environment, in the streets, you could not go quietly with your friends. Because a jeep arrived or two guardia civil, and they asked for your documents with bad manners, throwing you against the wall. It was an environment of absolute repression. Everything was repression.... I remembered that three or four buses of the guardia civil arrived and at least 40 jeeps. They came here and took the village. They took it militarily. They entered in the houses. (Clark 1984: 134)

Feelings of injustice increased the identification with a repressed community; for example, another Basque activist remembered, "I saw a guardia civil hitting a pregnant woman because she spoke euskera ... the guardia civil asked the pregnant woman why she was speaking euskera. He told her, it was the language of the terrorists, and that she had to speak Spanish as we were in Spain" (Reinares 2001: 130).

Transition to democracy is remembered by militants as, at best, a disappointment. Because "from 1970 onward, [dissatisfaction with the government] took more and more to the street," it became difficult to accept a political delegation proposed as democracy (Pérez-Agote 2006: 102). As a member of the nationalist Left lamented, "the entrance of political parties to the scene has implied that they are now the only channel through which to participate. It's very difficult for people to participate in parties. Furthermore, participation cannot terminate in the parties. These have become bureaucratized. The consequence is an even greater disillusionment, because one realizes that this channel is insufficient" (ibid.: 140). Thus, there was a widespread impression that popular energy was "shut up" (ibid: 143). In the words of a former ETA militant, "things changed, yes, a lot, but not substantially ... everyday people don't even demonstrate anymore. Nobody participates now ... because it is not that the people aren't interested, it's just that it's not worth anything" (ibid.: 142). In particular, a shared negative view of police violence – as the "same as always" (ibid.: 146 – caused many people to "endorse ETA action with their heart" (ibid.: 149).

Direct and indirect memories of repression are often quoted as reasons to rebel. A Basque militant recalls that "well, those who entered ETA, more than for an ideology, it was because their heart told them to" (Reinares 2001: 158). Violence became justified as self-defense of a community: "Much more than the social and nationalist aspects, it was the intensity with which I lived the repression of our country.... It was not that I was especially mistreated.... It was that they killed us, fired at us, or at the very least they did not allow us to be minimally free, right? At least, I felt it this way. I thought it was an expression of rage, of response to repression, but more as self defence" (ibid.: 129).

There remained widespread suspicions of secret collaboration between security forces and extreme Right groups that used clandestine violence to attack and kill ETA members, especially in France. In total, since 1975, these clandestine nationalist groups were responsible for 509 attacks and 41 killings. In 1979, right-wing assaults increased, with 11 assassinations, 37 people injured, and 4 kidnappings. Even worse was the situation in 1980, with 21 people killed, 55 wounded, and 2 kidnapped. Among the clandestine nationalist groups responsible for these crimes were Alianza Apostolic Anticomunista (Clark 1984: 256) and the Grupos Antiterroristas de Liberacion (GAL), which organized shootings, bombings, and kidnappings in the French Basque Country. Between 1983 and 1987, GAL killed twenty-seven people, whom they accused (often mistakenly) of having relations with the ETA. Including these people and the victims of the other groups, the total number of deaths brought about by these anti-ETA gangs was sixty-one.

These groups were often formed by Francoists who had connections in the internal security apparatus, but judicial investigations also indicated that, under the PSOE, the Spanish state had secretly funded the GAL, which was composed of security officers and contracted gunmen. Links were found to

senior government officials, including Minister of the Interior José Barrionuevo
(Muro 2008: 139). Awareness of this government involvement emerged after the
GAL commandos had, in 1983, "mistakenly kidnapped and abused a French
salesman whom they incorrectly believed to be an ETA activist." When the
victim filed suit against the Spanish government, the Supreme Court "found
several high-level government officials guilty of illegally hiring hit-men to attack
political opponents and sentenced a former minister of interior to ten years in
prison" (Zirakzadeh 2002: 82).

   Throughout the years, strong emotions developed at the ritual funerals of
patriots killed by those violent anti-ETA groups. An ETA member remembered,
"With this friend, we went to the funeral of someone who had been killed by
the GAL. I was sixteen ... it was a very small village. All the people went to the
funeral. There was then a demonstration. And we saw the Guardia civil on the
mountain. On all the mountains" (Reinares 2001: 79).

   Etarras – that is, ETA fighters – (and suspected *etarras*) in prison also
continued to be motivations for frequent and emotionally intense mobilizations.
Whereas in 1975 5,000 Basque residents were arrested for terrorism, in 1985,
940 were arrested for crimes related to terrorism (Zirakzadeh 2002: 81).
According to official statistics, 714 people were detained in 1981, vis-à-vis a
yearly average of 222 (Sánchez-Cuenca 2009: 21). Arrested *etarras* (or suspects)
were often moved from one prison to the next, without notification, and were
kept in special prisons. Protests, often led by the relatives of the imprisoned
militants, continued to ask for amnesty.

   In addition, nonviolent marches frequently organized by the Movimento de
Liberacion Nationale Vasco (Basque Movement of National Liberation
[MNLV]) – a platform of various radical Basque nationalist organizations –
had a highly ritualistic character that contributed to identification with the
movement, as well as providing occasions for the strengthening of radical
identity. The typical nationalist demonstration of the 1990s and 2000s has
been described by Casquette:

The Basque flag, the *ikurriña*, was the most widely represented symbol at every demonstration covered in this study. Apart from the countless *ikurriñak* evenly scattered throughout
the demonstration, invariably a huge one held by Basque dancers (*dantzariak*), by relatives
of ETA prisoners, or simply by anonymous militants opens the march. Singing is another
symbolic element with plenty of significance: It is not hard to hear a classic Basque song that
goes "Come, come home boy" ("Hator, hator mutil etxera"), in open reference to prisoners.
Occasionally, the "Basque Soldier's Hymn" (*Eusko gudariak*) concludes the demonstration.
Apart from the flag and songs, a third kind of symbolic element present at every demonstration is the portraits of ETA prisoners, around 400–500 in the years covered here. These
portraits are carried by relatives, who always occupy a preferential place. Banners demanding either prisoners' amnesty or that they fulfill their sentences in prisons located in the
Basque Country are also present. "Long life to the ETA" (*Gora ETA*), "Independence"
(*Independentzia*), and cries in support of ETA prisoners can also be heard. Songs, cries, and
placards are exclusively in the Basque language, in spite of the fact that many demonstrators

have no good command of it, or no command at all (according to the last sociolinguistic survey conducted in 1996, only 25.2% of the population was fluent in the Basque language, though language proficiency no doubt is more likely among nationalists in general, and even more so among radical nationalists). (Casquette 2003: 27–8)

All of these memories of interactions between state and activists created mistrust and hampered the potential for de-escalation.

In conclusion, although we cannot speak of closed opportunities in general, during transition and consolidation, "ETA is caught in the grip of forces that are created by insurgent violence itself and that tend to make violence self-sustaining, almost apart from the wishes of the participants or the objective conditions that led to the insurgency" (Clark 1984: 278). Although its organizational resources and action capacity declined, it remained a main concern for the Spanish democratic state. Even during democratization, inconsistent de-escalation policies, as well as path dependency from past habits, contributed to the long survival of clandestine political violence.

ESCALATING POLICING AND RELIGIOUS PROTEST

In the case of Islamic fundamentalism, repertoires of action have also been sensitive to changing (opening and closing) windows of opportunity. Whereas for the previously addressed types of violence we could focus on the national political context, to understand today's Islamic violence we have to look at the interaction of different national contexts and transnational phenomena. In particular, Muslim rebellion has been linked to reactive and indiscriminate repression in several local conflicts in the Middle East and North Africa and to civil wars in Afghanistan or Bosnia, as well as to political and institutional exclusion in the West.

The heavy repression of Islamist (and other) protests by authoritarian regimes in the Middle East played an important and dramatic role in the radicalization of Islamic movements. As Hafez observed, repression was particularly relevant in these regions, as "movements under a repressive environment accumulate material and organizational resources slowly and must be careful not to lose them to state repression. To overcome this problem, movement organizations must find ways to absorb the inevitable blows of state repression without suffering disintegration" (2004: 40). Moreover, in the West, the "war on terrorism" – which can be read as the war on Islam – contributed to the spread of frames of injustice and the politicization of religious identities. In both situations, repression tended to be perceived as aggression against pious religious communities, which resulted in politicization and radicalization of religious identities.

In Egypt, the repression of the Islamic movement brought about its radicalization. Violence erupted when, at the end of the 1980s, the regime closed down other channels of institutional access and peaceful opposition that had slowly opened up at the end of the 1970s. It was in the first half of the 1980s that violence escalated; the number of deaths increased from 120 between 1970 and 1989 to 1,442 between 1992 and 1997 (Hafez and Wiktorowicz 2004: 71). There, indeed, "the cycle of violence began largely in response to a broad crackdown on the Islamic movement that ensnared moderates, radicals, and a number of tangential bystanders. The crackdown included arrests, hostage taking, torture, executions and other forms of state violence" (ibid.: 62). Torture as well as shoot-to-kill policies became widespread, along with the storming of mosques, mass arrests, and executions. Repression was not only brutal but also indiscriminate, hitting the militants of the violent organizations as well as their families, and even "anyone wearing a beard with a trimmed mustache" (ibid.: 78). Indiscriminate forms of repression especially "antagonized hitherto inactive supporters and sympathizers and intensified the moral outrage of the activists" (ibid.: 70).

Political repression produced, first, a politicization of the Muslim Brotherhood (MB), which typically oscillated between comprehensive efforts at cultural renaissance, charity activities, and more political action. Already in the 1940s, some radicalization had occurred following the government's repression of Islamists, who were growing in number and becoming more oppositional. In the early 1950s, after some initial cooperation with President Nasser, a wave of repression followed a presumed plan to assassinate the president. This brought about mass arrests in 1954, and a further turn toward radicalization. With the end of the liberalization period, which had allowed for the growth of the MB and the election of representatives of the MB in parliament as well as its increasing influence in the civil society, the repression by the Nasser regime radicalized elements of the Brotherhood and led individuals to transform the ideology of modernist Islamists into a "rejectionist call to arms" (Esposito 2002).

In the following decades, splinter groups from the Muslim Brothers emerged. Al-Jamaa was strengthened by the repression of the MB, as activists, frustrated by the lack of results of peaceful protest, chose more radical forms of action, eventually founding clandestine organizations. As a militant jihadist declared, "what is astonishing is that every time the Muslim Brotherhood rushes to issue their statements of moral condemnation, denunciation, and disavowal of all that is jihad – they call it terrorism – the more the government redoubles its constraints against them" (cited in Hafez and Wiktorowicz 2004: 75). In the 1970s, confrontations with state institutions accompanied and fueled the quickly rising influence of Islamist groups in the universities.

In the early 1980s, the government reacted to sectarian clashes by arresting 1,500 opponents and dissolving thirteen organizations (Malthaner 2011: 74ff.). The assassination of President Sadat was the radicals' response to those arrests, and the execution of the death penalty against four Islamists fueled further repression. As Malthaner writes,

while they appreciated martyrdom, the attackers also rationalized the assassination in political terms, as an act to punish Sadat for the harm he had done to Muslims and for the preceding crackdown against the Islamist movement. They hoped to 'give a lesson' to his successor and that their deed would be a step towards an Islamic order: "... they thought that now the sharia would come." (ibid.: 74)

Later, President Mubarak alternated tolerance with repression. In the 1980s, al-Jamaa had been allowed not only to form bands to repress "immoral" behavior in Upper Egypt but also to organize welfare services (from food distribution to clothing and school supplies for the poor) and "mediation" institutions to peacefully solve local disputes (Hafez and Wiktorowicz 2004). A new escalation occurred, however, in 1987 and 1988, with frequent confrontations during police interventions at the university campuses in Assiut and in some neighborhoods (Malthaner 2011). Again, repression did not halt the conflict but instead escalated it. Between 1992 and 1997, al-Jamaa was responsible for about 1,300 fatalities targeting police and government officials, as well as intellectuals, artists, tourists, and Coptic Christians. In turn, the violence increased repression.

One characteristic of protest policing that facilitated escalation was not only its brutality (including shoot-to-kill policies and torture) but also its indiscriminate nature. Since the mid-1990s, the authorities had intervened by "moving ruthlessly against the militant groups and arresting tens of thousands of alleged members and supporters" (Malthaner 2011: 80). Furthermore, certain events played a transformative role. In 1990, the violent death of al-Jamaa leader Ala Mohieddin was perceived by the activists as "the threshold to all-out confrontation, to which they responded by assassinating the speaker of parliament two months later. It marked the beginning of a violent insurgency which would torment Egypt for the next eight years" (ibid.: 80).

Research on the Egyptian case – recalled in the incipit to this chapter – also shows how radicalization developed at the local level, involving Muslim activists in violent clashes with police. In August 1988, such clashes occurred after police interrupted worship in several mosques in Ayn Shams; they "interrupted sermons, and arbitrarily arrested young men wearing a beard and *galabiyya*" (Malthaner 2011: 80). In one of these events, activists built barricades and threw stones at the police officers, who responded by killing five people, wounding dozens, and arresting more than a hundred.

In the early 1990s, in addition to the imposition of curfews and police occupations of entire villages (such as Imbaba, Dairut, and Mallawi), repression hit family members of suspected Islamists and, especially after violent confrontations, males wearing a beard. During curfews, "hundreds of residents were arrested, houses of alleged members of al-Jamaa were destroyed, and their families were taken into custody. With electricity cut off, markets dissolved, and sugar cane fields were eradicated because militants used them to hide during ambushes. Economic activities in the villages were almost brought to a standstill" (Malthaner 2011: 240).

Repression in the form of collective punishment produced waves of solidarity with those who were perceived as defending the community. As in the Basque

Country, the state responded to disturbances by militarizing the territory of the suspected community. Again, according to Malthaner's reconstruction,

the Egyptian security forces' repressive and violent reaction severely affected living conditions and put towns and village communities under enormous pressure. From the early 1990s on, Egyptian police deployed a large number of forces in Upper Egypt and carried out brutal and arbitrary arrest operations against alleged strongholds in a manner which resembled, as one observer remarked, punitive expeditions in the tradition of Cairo's semi-colonial rule over its southern provinces. Suspects could be held without trial under emergency law, and in the mid-1990s human rights organizations put the number of political prisoners in Egypt at an estimated 20,000 to 30,000, most of them alleged Islamist activists. Military courts handed out a large number of death sentences (more than 80) and several hundred alleged al-Jamaa members were killed during arrest operations by the police. (2011: 167–8)

The events in Palestine, specifically the evolution of a spiral of repression and radicalization, are similar in many ways to the Basque case. The very emergence of a Palestinian nationalism as well as Islamism is interpreted as a reaction to the defeat of Arab nationalism in the Six-Day War of 1967 (Gunning 2007: 28–9), as well as, more directly, to the Israeli repression of the Gaza insurrection in the early 1970s. The Likud-led deportment and imprisonment of nationalists and the relative tolerance of Muslim Brothers (MBs) helped the growth of the latter (ibid.: 33). As Eitan Alimi observed, before the first intifada, "the Palestinians in the occupied territories faced oppression on two levels. First, the Israeli political arena was completely closed to any form of individual or collective Palestinian participation. Palestinians interested in exerting political influence on the Israeli political system faced a 'blocked opportunity' situation…. Second, political life in the occupied territories was systematically scrutinized and circumscribed" (2007: 35). No municipal elections were held, trade unions were banned, freedom of movement was restrained, and administrative detention for a (renewable) period of up to six months was used even without charges or trial (ibid.: 39). Between 1979 and 1983, thirty-six Palestinians were killed by Israeli military forces, most of whom were shot during demonstrations; Palestinians were subject to seventy attacks by Israeli settlers (ibid.: 36). By 1981, Defense Minister Sharon had tried to "eliminate the PLO presence in the territories and, as it turned out, in the region altogether," through the removal of local mayors, frequent curfews, closures of universities, and increased censorship (ibid.: 64). Further radicalization followed Israeli so-called iron fist policies in 1982 and 1985, with the formation of networks of support for what developed into the first intifada.

However, this did not stop protest. Mass arrests (25,000 people served sentences prior to the intifada) fueled mass participation in the intifada, as in prison those arrested became more politicized but also more knowledgeable about Israeli society. Moral outrage resonates with everyday experiences of discrimination. As Khalidi observed, the quintessential Palestinian experience, which illustrates some of the most basic issues raised by Palestinian identity, takes place at the borders: an airport, a checkpoint: in short, at any one of those many modern barriers where identities are checked and verified. What happens to Palestinians at these crossing points brings home to them how much they share in common as a people. Because it is at these borders and barriers that the six million Palestinians are singled out for "special treatment" and forcefully reminded of their identity. (1997: 147)

These policies radicalized Palestinian organizations, as well as forcing several activities to go underground. In fact, "the restrictions imposed by Israel on political activities in the occupied territories, together with the daily misery of life, had a considerable impact on Palestinians' mode of organization, forcing them to adapt their activity to the available space of action and the ongoing threat they experienced" (ibid.: 55). The first intifada nevertheless represented an attempt to exploit potential alliances inside Israeli society. As a Palestinian activist declared, "we realized that if we used deadly weapons we will fail to cause a divide inside your society, we wanted to keep the momentum of fights and conflict inside Israeli and not to cause you to reunite by using guns" (quoted in Alimi 2007: 109, also 111).

If the Palestinians had shown some (strategic) restraint, this was not true of their counterpart: between 1988 and 1991, only 14 Israeli soldiers were killed, as compared to the 798 Palestinians killed by Israeli security forces (Alimi 2007: 125). In 1989 alone, 26,820 Palestinians were injured by live ammunition, beatings, and plastic and rubber bullets; 34,000 were injured in 1990, and 46,000 in 1991 (ibid.: 130). Collective punishment was also used through curfews and land confiscation (ibid.: 131). In addition, Israeli settlers and other civilians were responsible for assassinations (thirteen between December 1987 and December 1988; twenty-two in 1989) and other attacks on Palestinian civilians (ibid.: 151).

In 1996, the birth of the radical branch of the Tanzim within Fatah interacted with exclusive policies by the Israeli state. Netanyahu's decision to open the Jewish holy site at the Western Wall Tunnel brought about five days of massive protests, which resulted in the deaths of sixteen Israeli soldiers and police officers and about seventy Palestinians. As Alimi recalled,

signs of such a shift were also evident between state forces from both sides, leading Palestinian security forces to aim weapons at their Israeli counterparts during joint patrols as part of the joint security initiative established following the Oslo Accord of 1993 (i.e., Defense Coordination Offices – DCO). Later on, in the al-Naqba commemoration day on May 15, 2000 massive demonstrations initiated by the Tanzim took place with stone throwing and Molotov cocktails and, this time, shootings incidents throughout the territories. The confrontations lasted for several days, as a result of which eight Palestinians died and hundreds of Palestinians and approximately 30 Israelis were injured. (2011: 109)

After the Israeli withdrawal from Lebanon, Israeli armed forces heavily repressed the Palestinian intifada; this conflict was initially expressed through public demonstrations and the throwing of stones and Molotov cocktails, until the Tanzims joined in and began shooting. Again, according to Alimi's reconstruction,

this critical step toward radicalization on the part of the Tanzim was countered by an even heavier Israeli crackdown consisting of bombing of buildings and the tactic of "land clearing," and the use of war equipment such as helicopter gunships, tanks, cannons, etc. The increase in Palestinian casualties resulted in a further radicalization of their mode of action. This time, Palestinian shootings concentrated on the main roads leading to Jewish settlements while other shootings took place from within Palestinian houses, all of which resulted in an even heavier Israeli response. This was the first sign of a clear revert to the guerilla-like armed struggle ideology, which was marked by the decision to form the "al-Aqsa Martyrs Brigades," the armed wing of the Tanzim. (ibid.: 110)

The death of Muhammad al-Durah, a young boy caught with his father in the crossfire, at the hands of Israeli forces on 30 September 2000 had transformative power, as it triggered six days of harsh protest in the territories. Israeli liquidation policy, introduced between the end of 2000 and the beginning of 2001, contributed to the dramatic escalation of the second intifada. These deaths and humiliations, as well as selected killings of Fatah leaders, increased anger and indignation; these sentiments exploded in the second intifada, which began in 2000 and featured much more brutal forms of actions than in the first intifada. Spirals of escalation developed with suicide bombings, to which Israel responded with targeted killings. During the second intifada, "Israel's decision to assassinate Hamas' political leadership only served to increase the organisation's popular appeal, as mass funerals increased Hamas' visibility and public anger led to an increase in volunteers and political support" (Gunning 2009: 50).

In Saudi Arabia, the policing of dissent favored a (more limited) escalation. Thomas Hegghammer described it as a mix of complacency and oppression that proceeded in spirals with increasing oppositional violence. In particular, a wave of repression followed the Riyadh bombs in 1995, which "prompted the government to crack down with an iron fist on veterans of the Afghan and Bosnian jihad, the very people who only a few years previously had gone out to fight with the state's blessing" (2010: 74). The government overreacted, ordering indiscriminate arrests of about 200 people: "Lacking a clear trial of investigation, the authorities proceeded to mass arrests and harsh interrogations in the hope of identifying the culprits" (ibid.). In the following three years, new waves of arrests followed violent attacks. Two thousand people, especially Shiites, were arrested following a bombing in Khobar in 1996. Massive arrests of Saudi jihad veterans (totaling at first about 800, followed by an additional 300) also followed the discovery of a plan to attack a US consulate in 1998 and 1999. In all these cases, there are reliable accounts of torture, as well as of the holding of detainees without trials (ibid.: 74–5). The effect of repression, perceived as indiscriminate, was to increase the acceptance of attacks on the Saudi territory among the Islamic activists, together with al-Qaeda recruits. Acts of revenge – such as the assassination of alleged torturers in the state security bodies – followed.

In the late 1990s, the policing of Islamist activism became more tolerant, thanks to both a general liberalization and a specific tension within the regime between its chosen image as defender of Islam and the repression of Islamists at home, as well as to some sympathies for jihad in the Saudi police forces. This opening, however, meant that "the torture of the mid-1990s radicalized a generation of militants who were subsequently given considerable room for maneuver" (Hegghammer 2010: 78). Freed and left unsupervised, former prisoners sometimes joined al-Qaeda in the Arabian Peninsula (AQAP), whereas the authorities were afraid to confront hostile acts, as the public opinion had mobilized in solidarity with Muslims after 9/11.

In 2002, a new turn toward harder policing of jihadist activities led to new arrests, shoot-to-kill policies, and exchanges of gunshots during arrests. As Hegghammer synthesized, "these early confrontations broke barriers on the use of violence in the kingdom, strengthened the internal cohesion of the nascent QAP and gave the project of 'jihad on the Arabian Peninsula' a sense of urgency within the jihad community" (2010: 157). Heavy repression, which followed discovery of plans for violence and American pressures, in fact strengthened a sense of victimization. The escalation also followed hard police intervention at some protest events, the ensuing decisions by activists to carry arms, and a spiral of confrontations and arrests, as well as the banning from preaching of radical scholars.

Arrests and mistreatment had heavy effects in terms of mistrust toward state authorities, who were perceived as having betrayed their own commitment. As a militant explained,

we went out to Bosnia to defend our brothers with the encouragement of the [Saudi] television and its *ulama*. So we went there and came back, only to find prison and torture. I personally stayed in a cell for a year and three months for no reason whatsoever, except that I had gone to Bosnia. Many of the brothers were imprisoned ... and they were tortured systematically. (Hegghammer 2010: 75)

In fact, "the shock of the maltreatment was amplified by the fact that the detainees had perceived their activities abroad as entirely legitimate and even encouraged by the state. A common theme in the Saudi jihadist literature is the profound bitterness about the state ingratitude towards the sacrifice of the jihadists" (ibid.). This also explains why arrests and torture had such a traumatizing effect on activists: by extorting confessions about the prisoners' opinions of the authorities as infidels, they "actually created the very phenomenon they were trying to counter" (ibid.).

Examples of this interactive diffusion of protest and policing in the Arab countries are many. The mid-1990s saw escalation in Bahrain, as the police reacted to peaceful protest with arrests, often without legal charges (Lawson 2004: 99). Any increase in protest was followed by restriction of freedom, through bans on demonstration and arrests as well as collective punishment of Shiite districts – with periodic shutoffs of water and electricity – and of universities – with cancellations of examination sessions (ibid.: 102, 104).

As in Egypt, and with more brutality, the massacres perpetrated by the GIA (Groupe Islamique Armé [Algerian Armed Islamic]) (Kalyvas 1999) spiraled with state repression, which had created a political environment permeated by brutality (Hafez 2004). After a period of liberalization that had opened up in 1989, in 1991 the authorities reacted to rising support for the FIS (Front Islamic de Salut) and its probable victory with a coup d'état, holding thousands of Islamic activists (estimates range from 6,000 to 30,000 people), including members of local governments; reintroducing special courts; banning FIS-like organizations; destroying unofficial mosques; and sentencing 166 Islamists to death, as well as killing many others during arrests. Whereas the opening of political opportunities in Algeria before 1992 had allowed "for the formation of inclusive Islamist organizations that marginalized radicals and accommodated the state regime through institutional participation," later on,

the closure of the political system in 1992, combined with indiscriminate state repression of Islamists, made possible the expansion of the radical wing. The radicals organized in exclusive movement organizations largely to shield themselves from counterinsurgency measures, solidify the cohesion of their members, and minimize deflections. The anti-system frames promoted by these groups gained empirical credibility in the context of state repression and provided a rationale for the expansion of violence that included anyone supporting the regime and its legitimacy. (ibid.: 53)

In 1996, political prisoners numbered almost 50,000; torture and disappearances were frequent. In this period, "the political exclusion and indiscriminate repression of the FIS resulted in the migration of many FIS activists toward radical organizations.... Hitherto small and marginal groups began to win over hundreds of FIS supporters in the months following the military coup" (ibid.: 46), which then converged in the GIA.

The emergence and evolution of al-Qaeda was influenced by the interactions of these paths of escalation of national struggles with the development of the conflict in Afghanistan. Together with socialization to violence, mass migration (as well as inter-Arabic migration) resulted in an increasing number of stateless people; this phenomenon was also as a consequence of restrictive citizenship regimes in Iran, Egypt, South Arabia, and Kuwait. Interacting with old and new migration in Europe, this produced a growing deterritorialization of Islam that contributed to export radicalization processes in other regions, where antiterrorist policies contributed to further radicalization.

Although the conflict in these regions started from an already greatly escalated conflict and a high degree of acceptance of violence, a gradual radicalization process also took place. The end of the civil war in Afghanistan, the US occupation of Iraq and US presence in Saudi Arabia, and Usama bin Laden's expulsion from Saudi Arabia and relocation in Sudan are all important events in explaining al-Qaeda's choice to directly attack US targets, first in the Middle East and Africa and then in America. Islamist mobilizations in the Balkans, Kashmir, Chechnya, and the Philippines, and their repression, also represented escalating moments, providing military skills as well as justifications for violence. In 1996, the expulsion of bin Laden from Sudan, as a result of pressure from the United States, and his relocation in Afghanistan ended in a call for violent jihad against the Americans in the same year and the foundation of the International Islamic Front for Jihad against Jews and Crusaders in 1998, which led to more attacks on American targets. As Alimi observed,

we now know that it was only after the increased "heat" by the Clinton Administration, resolutely reacting to the 1998 bombings of US embassies, exerting pressure on the Taliban regime, and launching cruise missile strikes against an al-Qaeda camp in Afghanistan in an attempt to hit bin Laden, that al-Qaeda's jihad campaign was redirected against US forces on US soil. (2011: 111)

The attacks on September 11, and the US reactions to it, have in turn reinvigorated a declining movement by shifting strategies from the traditional focus of religious nationalism against the autocrats in the Muslim world, sometimes accompanied by refusal of violence tout court (Karagiannis and McCauley 2006), to global war (Gerges 2005; also Kepel 2002). In Iraq, the story of Marwan Abu Ubeida, a twenty-year-old suicide bomber from a privileged family, is instructive. Sunni and deeply religious, he was pushed to join the insurgents by "the killing of twelve demonstrators by US soldiers near a school in Falluja in April 2004. Abu Ubeida was among the protestors, but he was not armed. However, the apparent excessiveness of the shooting caused him to join others in small-scale operation against coalition forces" (Hafez 2007: 45).

Violence related to Islam (such as the actions of the Egyptian Islamic Jihad) has been said to be decreasing in the Middle East, after a process of institutionalization and integration of excluded social groups. In parallel, conservative Islam (characterized by the veiling of women and other traditional practices) has also grown, but with a dimension of privatization and state deconstruction. Islamist groups also proved sensitive to the opening of opportunities. This has been the case, for instance, with Hamas, which tended to become more moderate when support for the peace process increased, justifying this turn with Islamic concepts such as patience and truce (Wiktorowicz 2004: 15).

Thus, all of these (in part interrelated) radicalized conflicts in the Middle East as well as in other countries with large Muslim populations had effects on Islamic mobilization in the West. Especially after 9/11, in the West, Arab and Muslim peoples have been viewed with suspicion and disdain (Spalek and Lambert 2008). Harsh imprisonment as well as torture has stimulated rather than tempered violence (English 2009: 134).

Targeting and suspicion of Muslims as a community has been particularly well documented in the UK, where Tony Blair's antiterrorist policies have been accused of contributing to the criminalization of nonviolent activities through detentions without trial or shoot-to-kill policies (Guelke 2006). Especially after the 7/7 attacks in London in 2005, the Muslim population has been particularly targeted by "increasing anti-terrorist measures, greater policing powers, racial and ethnic profiling in the criminal justice system, civil society debates around culture that place South Asian Muslims at its heart, although never explicitly, and questions around the apparent unassimilability of Muslims, with a focus on 'community cohesion'" (Abbas 2007: 291). Already in 2001, the Antiterrorism, Crime and Security Act gave the police the power to hold without charges foreigners suspected of involvement in terrorism. Arrest records give evidence that this law is being used discriminatorily: significantly, of the more than 500 Muslims arrested under terrorist charges between 2001 and 2004, only 2 were convicted (Poynting and Mason 2006: 374).

Accusation of deviations from respect for freedoms and for defendants' rights also abound. Sixteen arrested Muslims were held without charges for three years in the high-security prison of Belmarsh. Stops and searches increased disproportionally for the Muslim population, which comprised 45 percent of those stopped and searched (Poynting and Mason 2006: 374). The brutality of arrests (e.g., two brothers were arrested during a raid on their houses by 250 police officers and were then released without being charged) and the shoot-to-kill policy (which led to the assassination of the innocent Jean Charles de Menezes) have also been denounced. The accusation that MI5, Britain's special forces, colluded in the torture of Muslim prisoners further increased fear of discrimination.

Read as an attack on Western civilization, the bombings in London brought about anti-Muslim rhetoric as well as Islamophobic attacks, including vandalism and physical aggression against Muslim citizens: the number of religious hate crimes increased from 40 incidents in 2004 to 269 the next year, after the 7/7 attack (Poynting and Mason 2006). As in Northern Ireland, the targeting of Muslim neighborhoods for intense surveillance and the outlawing of associations that were involved in Muslim issues increased the sense of isolation from the broader society of these suspect communities and intensified feelings of discrimination (Pantazis and Pemberton 2009; Spalek 2010, Vertigans 2010). In sum, "policies like indefinite and extended pre-charge detention, deportation, weakened standards on torture, new speech offences and ill-treatment have harmed race and community relations and diminished the prospects of Muslims being willing to cooperate with police and security services" (Vertigans 2010: 32). Similar trends have been noted in Australia (Poynting and Mason 2006), Germany (Schiffauer 2008), and the United States (Huq 2010). In the US War on Terror, "the newly constructed enemy was a total enemy, inherently evil, one that could not be reasoned with, and therefore the new common sense held that it had to be destroyed" (Croft 2006: 117).

In all these cases, the fear of being stigmatized for praying in some mosques or supporting some associations considered by the state to be suspect indicators of radicalization has changed "the marginal costs of certain forms of religious behaviors and thereby can create a disincentive to communal or individual forms of faith" (Huq 2010: 35; see also della Porta and Lindekilde 2012).

In the Middle East and in the West, escalating policing has therefore contributed to the spread of feelings of injustice that have justified calls for revenge.

ESCALATING POLICING: CONCLUSIONS

In this chapter, I have suggested building reflection on the impact of political opportunities on protest repertoires in two ways. First, as in my previous work (della Porta 1995; della Porta and Reiter 1998a, 1998b), I have focused attention on the policing of protest, considered as an influential barometer of the attitudes of the elites toward the challengers. Second, I propose a relational, constructed, and emergent view of escalating policing.

Research on the policing of protest has grown since the 1990s; during this period, scholars have developed typologies of control of public demonstration and have singled out trends and determinants of policing styles. Large-N studies have addressed the explanation of police choices. Much reflection has also developed on the effects of policing, looking at the forms and amount of repression that are more likely to curb protest. In this chapter, I have focused especially on the mechanism of escalating policing. How does tough policing produce radicalization? Notwithstanding the differences in the analyzed contexts, militants' recollections point at some similar mechanisms.

I have observed that the tougher the police strategies, the less they seem able to stop the radicalization of protestors. First, repression tends to discourage the moderates, pushing them to return to private life and leaving room in the protest arena for the more radical wings (see, e.g., Tarrow 1989). Second, repression might also radicalize the moderates. In particular, indiscriminate repression seemed to be the most counterproductive, as it enlarged the circles of victims and therefore the feelings of injustice. The cases of Franco's Spain, Egypt, and Saudi Arabia showed that the militarization of territory as well as the torture of arrested activists seemed to fuel protestors' anger and their use of increasingly violent means. In contrast, the comparison between the policing of left-wing groups in Italy and Germany indicated that, in the latter, police moderation was reflected in de-escalation on the part of demonstrators.

However, political violence from the opposition was not the only factor that interacted with brutal and indiscriminate repression: in these cases we also observed the effects of inconsistent repression. The Italian extreme Right committed its most brutal massacres when it was supported by part of the state, and this protection gave neofascists not only the expectation of impunity but also the potential to achieve their aims of establishing an authoritarian state.[6]

This was also in part true for the anti-ETA vigilantes in Spain, who committed their crimes as they enjoyed the tacit indifference or even active help of some Spanish institutional apparatuses. Even in the authoritarian regimes in the Middle East, inconsistency has characterized state attitudes toward the Islamic

---

[6] Scholars also suggest that the American radical Right has developed within broader movements (farmers' associations and pro-gun groups) as a reaction to the militarization of state responses (including gun control; the authorities' actions during the conflict in Waco, Texas, in 1993; and so on) (Wright 2007).

movements, which have been tolerated or even supported – as allies against the Left and/or nationalist movements – in some periods and heavily repressed in others. Inconsistency in the attitudes toward the fighters in Afghanistan – who were praised and financed when rebelling against the Soviet troops but heavily stigmatized later on – has often been recalled.

In the case of long-lasting processes, we noted a reciprocal adaptation of tactics. That is, proceeding through reciprocal diffusion (della Porta and Tarrow 2012), escalation was relational. From the point of view of practices of violence, there was a reciprocal influence, with brutal behavior on one side producing and reproducing brutal actions on the other. Stones, sticks, and Molotov cocktails are used to protect the protestors from police baton charges; barricades are constructed to stop police tracks; and even firearms can be used to respond to police shooting at demonstrators.

Escalation develops, then, in action. During the policing of protest, transformative events take place. In Italy, after it was proven that the Italian intelligence service had helped protect the assassins responsible for the neofascist massacre at Piazza Fontana (1969), the state became the "state of the massacre," which made it "right, there in Italy, to use mass violence against those responsible for the 'massacre perpetrated by the state'" (Life History no. 12: 10).

Emotionally charged events – such as the deaths of comrades at the hands of the police – also favor radicalization, through processes of identification. Research on religiously motivated violence has stressed the importance of the emotions aroused by dead heroes. These motivations are usually presented as linked to the Muslim story of suffering, with some episodes acquiring mythical status: for example, the story of twelve-year-old Mohammed al-Dura, killed in Gaza in crossfire between Palestinian snipers and Israeli defense forces, achieved great significance. Similar effects were seen after the death of Benno Ohnesorg in Germany, the deaths of three neofascist activists in Acca Larentia (a street in Rome) for the Italian radical Right, the "April Days" for the Left in Italy, or the killings of demonstrators in Spain.

Escalating policing produced cognitive effects, as the everyday experiences of fights with police supported the construction of an image of the state as unfair. In all of these cases, direct experiences of state repression produced radicalization processes. Beyond the immediate experience of the fights, its construction was also important. A state that was "firing at me," or at my community, was perceived as unjust. As Hafez (2004: 53) noted, antisystem, radical frames "gained empirical credibility in the context of state repression and provided a rationale for the expansion of violence that included anyone supporting the regime and its legitimacy." When read as a part of the history of repression (Boudreau 2004), policing styles strongly affected protest tactics, although not often in the intended direction.

Repression also increases the perception that there is no other way out, as it is read as proof of the need to take up arms to resist an authoritarian state. In fact, the more exclusionary a regime, the more it tends to incubate violent action, as "those who specialize in it tend to prosper, because they come to be viewed by many people as more realistic and potentially effective than political moderates, who themselves come to be viewed as hopelessly ineffective" (Goodwin 1997: 18).

Along with the perception that there was no other way out, activists also remembered high expectations of change. Several activists in fact mentioned the impression of living in an historical moment. A Neapolitan activist recalled that, talking about a revolution, "we asked ourselves ... 'how many years would be necessary?,' 'boh, I think only a few. Probably ten'" (Life History no. 2: 388).

Although the closure of opportunities is observed in older and more recent cases of radicalization, this is not always the case. In Spain, radicalization happened during transition, in part as a reaction to its inconsistencies and in part as a way to put pressure on changing institutions. Even though explanations of radicalization are generally focused on at the national level, the Islamic cases demonstrate the importance of transnational conflicts. In these situations we see, in fact, the interaction of multiple conflicts in different states in the development of a global jihad. True, Egyptian Islamists were reacting to the specific characteristics of repression under Nasser, then Sadat, and then Mubarak. Additionally, in Saudi Arabia, Islamic activists felt the specific inconsistency of a regime that had supported their participation in the jihad in Afghanistan but did not allow for any challenge inside. But, as is discussed in greater detail in the following chapters, these specific national conflicts interacted with each other as well as with conflicts in Bosnia or Chechnya and with the dissatisfaction of the new generations of Muslims in Europe or the United States. It was from these interactions, more than from a specific repressive strategy in one country or another, that the radicalization of a transnational movement emerged.

3

Competitive Escalation

Militants who joined the underground were socialized to violence during harsh social conflicts that involved competitive relations not only with outsiders but also within the social movement family. Socialization to violence happened in action, especially around specific geographical areas, through the radicalization of specific forms of action.

In Italy, in the 1970s, competition between traditional unions and new, emerging rank-and-file ones led to escalating industrial conflicts at some factories. For example, a former militant remembers that before entering an underground organization he had already burned the cars of some bosses of the big Pirelli factory – where he worked and was a delegate to the factory council (Life History no. 3). Another militant also took part in actions of sabotage, which he described as actions "linked to the working class knowledge of the production" (Life History no. 9: 260). Yet another remembers "popular processes against the bosses, some of whom were acquitted, others expelled from the factory" (Life History no. 29: 24). Activists went to the headquarters of the Magneti Marelli and took files containing personal information on the workers (ibid.: 25).

Spirals of revenge also developed in the fights between movements and countermovements. On the left-wing side, there was "an atmosphere [that encouraged the] lynching of fascists. 'If you see black, shoot at once,' this was the slogan, ... there was a man-hunt, without any pity, it was a hunt against the fascists that then had repercussions for us, because there was a spiral of revenge" (Life History no. 6: 29). As many left-wingers remembered, "Milan had a large bunch of funerals that were a continuous plea, over the deaths, those killed by the fascists, a continuous plea to revenge, and then when you take revenge, well it is not traumatic" (Life History no. 3: 65).

As a response to such violence – in particular, the increasingly bloody physical conflicts with neofascists – by the first half of the 1970s, organizations began to create *servizi d'ordine* (marshal departments). Piero, with the Gruppo Comunista Garbatella, participated in "a marshal body, a group of comrades that addresses the problem of the self defence of its part of the march and of its presence on the street in an aggressive way, let's say in a way proportionate with the level of the fight" (Life History no. 9: 297).

In the mid-1970s, *servizi d'ordine* also contributed to organizing "proletarian expropriations," or "political" robberies in big stores. As a militant recalls, "I thought that the military action had to be done by proletarians. We did proletarian expropriations, well organized: with the servizio d'ordine and the squads.... These actions were done by working class families, fifty of them, not a few" (Life History no. 16: 201); "'today you do not pay' and you go out without paying" (Life History no. 12: 345).

Violence often develops in situations of competition over the control of specific spaces. Fights with the police often escalated around the "defense of a territory," such as squatted houses or sites for nuclear plants. There, battles became ritualized: "Every morning I left home, I went to fight the police in the street battles, I came back home for lunch, and went back to fight in the afternoon and until night. It was a Londonderry, I mean a series of battles carried out with Molotov cocktails and stones to conquer five meters of land" (Life History no. 27: 26). Another militant talked of the political isolation he experienced when he and his fellow militants went to defend the squatted houses and had to fight with the marshal body of the PCI, which intervened on the side of the police (Life History no. 27: 433).

In all these cases, participation in violent action had relevant effects in terms of socialization. In the words of an Italian militant, "every day you talked about the use of physical force and every day you practiced it" (Life History no. 8: 35).

All of these memories describe the relevant impact of practices of violence within harsh political conflicts on the political socialization of those who ended up in the underground. This happened through the radicalization of forms of action during competitive interactions not only with political adversaries but also with potential allies and within the movement family itself; I call this phenomenon *competitive escalation*. As we will see, Italian left-wingers were not unique in this regard: in right-wing, ethnonationalist, and religious forms as well, involvement in violence during intense waves of protest most often preceded recruitment to clandestine organizations. Explanations of political violence have often looked at environmental conditions, distinguishing (structural) root causes, (dynamic) facilitator causes, and (contingent) precipitating events. In this chapter, after reviewing some of these explanations, I look at works on protest cycles and violence, focusing on competitive escalation as a causal mechanism in violent developments.

Looking at the macro, contextual level, research on extreme forms of violence has addressed *preconditions* (or root causes), which represent the contextual opportunities; *facilitator causes*, such as grievances, which make extreme forms of political violence possible or attractive; and *precipitating events*, which trigger violent reactions (Crenshaw 1981). At the socioeconomic level, there has long been debate on the impact of poverty on political violence. Although there is no proof of an effect of economic indicators (at either the macro or the micro level), it has been suggested that rapid modernization and urbanization could lead to some types of violence. The idea is that sudden social changes (e.g., rapid economic development in oil-rich countries) challenge traditional social arrangements in the absence of an alternative social and political system. Right-wing violence is said to be the effect of the social disintegration induced by some specific paths of modernization (Heitmeyer 2005: 146). Islamist violence has often been discussed in the frame of failed, delayed, or incomplete modernization.

The link between poverty and violence is considered even more likely in cases of relatively unequally distributed income (Engene 2004; Weinberg 2005) and, especially, in ethnically or religiously divided societies in which some groups experience deep-rooted feelings of discrimination. In these regions, differential access to economic resources among specific groups of the population is considered particularly conducive to violence. In parallel, political violence has been said to grow during economic crises, when entire generations or specific class groups fear worsening conditions and see no future for themselves. Research on civil wars has also pointed at some material – even geographic – conditions, such as the presence of mountainous terrains in which guerrillas can more easily hide (e.g., Fearon and Laitin 2003),[1] or of extractable resources that influence the structure of incentives for guerrilla recruits (Weinstein 2007).

Assumptions about social preconditions are also related to those about cultural preconditions. The search for identity, which can be unsettled by rapid processes of modernization, is expected to lead to identification with radical ideologies. At the cultural level, historical antecedents of political violence, perpetrated by the state (a dictatorship or foreign occupation) or other opponents, are seen as facilitating the acceptance of armed struggle. Socialization into a cultural narrative of revenge and martyrdom has been said to be conducive to new waves of terrorism. It has also been observed that civic types of nationalist ideologies tend toward moderation and accommodation, whereas ethnic, exclusive ones are more prone to radicalization, as they often incorporate traditions of violence (Reinares 2005). An historical presence of pan-Islamic nationalism has been seen as legitimizing participation in conflict abroad (Hegghammer 2010).

All of these explanations provide some leverage for the understanding of political violence. The search for common causes at the contextual level has been criticized, however, under various perspectives. First of all, some have questioned the choice of variables and indicators in much of the large-N

---

[1] For instance, Fearon and Laitin have considered rural-based insurgency to be more likely when "the economy is poor, population is high, there is large mountainous terrain, there is non-contiguous territory and political life is fragile" (2003: 79–82).

research. According to the American Political Science Association's Task Force on Radicalization,

there are two problems with existing literature which prompt us to be somewhat skeptical of the results and to look for insights elsewhere. First, the causal determinants within existing models don't change at all (e.g., the percent of the country that is mountainous), they change very slowly (e.g., per capita GDP) or they change rarely (e.g., the degree of political democracy). Second, the same variables are employed to operationalize diverse theoretical explanations and thus different arguments claim support from the same statistically significant variables. (APSA 2007)

Additionally, it seems problematic to link the behavior of very small groups to conditions that affect the population at large (Crenshaw 2011). And although long-standing conditions provide limited explanatory power for sudden outbursts of violence, reference to precipitating events offers only a partial way out, as it often risks being too ad hoc.

This might explain the inconsistency of the results of research on macrodimensions. Whereas some scholars have noted an association between economic strains and political violence (Blomberg, Hess, and Weerapana 2004), others have reached contrasting results (e.g., research on the support for armed attacks on Israeli civilians in the West Bank and Gaza Strip; see Krueger and Malečková 2003). Even more relevant, the search for invariant causes risks hiding specific historical circumstances. Historical antecedents for violence are present sometimes, but not always. Political violence can take different paths, developing under very different circumstances. In fact, violence-conducive contextual characteristics vary in time and place. As we have seen, repression can produce escalation or can be effective in silencing dissent. Ethnic divisions or social inequalities may or may not precede violence.

Large-N causal analyses also risk missing the importance of processes over time, isolating violence from the complex evolution of political and social conflicts. It is usually during long-lasting protest waves that escalation occurs. Summarizing the debate on the "root conditions" for violence, Tore Bjørgo observed that terrorism is not caused by poverty, terrorists are not insane or irrational, suicide bombing is not caused by religion, and state sponsorship is not a root cause. Rather, "terrorism tends to be the product of a *long process* of radicalization that prepares a group of people for such extreme action" (2005: 3, emphasis added). In a recent volume, Neil Smelser pointed to the existence of

long fuelling process, with the possibility that the accumulating sequence of conditions and causes will produce other kinds of outcomes all along the line … first, a wide range of conditions that come to be regarded as dispossessing or depriving; next, a transition to how these conditions are regarded by affected groups; a focusing of these dissatisfactions into an ideology, which becomes the basis for channeling individual motivations by recruiting and mobilizing groups; next a series of structural conditions and short term situations that simultaneously constitute blockages to certain kinds of political expression and opportunity structures for the expression of others, including collective violence;

next the availability of publicity, financial means, and weapons and technologies as resources; and finally the vulnerabilities of target societies, which constitute a final set of opportunities. (2007: 52)

Various forms of extreme political violence often represent steps in long-lasting escalation processes, as noted in regard to the escalation of lower-level conflict into civil war, in which the degree of violence prior to civil war is seen as one of its most important causes (Kalyvas 2006).

What is more, structural explanations do not take into account the role of agency. The passage from structural causes to effects is not automatic: "Even when violence is clearly rooted in preexisting conflicts, it should not be treated as a natural, self-explanatory outgrowth of such conflicts, something that occurs automatically when the conflict reaches a certain intensity" (Brubaker and Laitin 1998: 426). When scholars see on the one hand the causes and on the other the effects, they do not recognize the relational and interactive nature of the phenomenon, which often features long causal chains in which the identification of dependent and independent variables is as misleading as it is fictitious.

By allowing us to look at processes and agency, one of the main analytical advantages in using social movement studies to understand political violence is in their capacity to locate violence within broader conflicts, of which violence is only one form, as well as within the complex networks – or organizational fields – within which actors using violence interact. As I argue in what follows, one main observation coming from social movement studies is that causal mechanisms for radicalization are activated not only by interactions between movement activists and opponents but also by competition inside social movement families during cycles of protest – that is, moments of intensified protest mobilized by many and different actors. Social movement studies have suggested the term "movement families" to identify "a set of coexisting movements, which, regardless of their specific goals, have similar basic values and organizational overlaps, and sometimes may even join for common campaigns" (della Porta and Rucht 1995: 4). Movement families are located within a social movement sector, that is, "the configuration of social movements, the structure of antagonistic, competing and/or cooperating movements which in turn is part of a larger structure of action (political action in a very broad sense)" (Garner and Zald 1985: 120; see also McCarthy and Zald 1977: 1220).

Competition increases during protest cycles. Looking at interactions in these intense moments helps in overcoming some of the limitations of a static analysis of causes and effects. I look in particular at the *competitive escalation* that develops during cycles of protest. This also helps me to introduce references to the social movements in which violence developed.

Research on protest cycles indicates that violence is driven less by strategic concerns than by relational dynamics developing during moments of intense mobilization. The concepts of cycles, waves, or campaigns all attempt to describe and explain periods of intensified protest. The analysis of protest cycles is particularly useful for an understanding of the development of political violence, which is frequently one of the (though neither the only nor the most important) outcomes of protest. Tarrow has defined cycles of protest as

a phase of heightened conflict across the social system, with rapid diffusion of collective action from more mobilized to less mobilized sectors, a rapid pace of innovation in the forms of contention employed, the creation of new or transformed collective action frames, a combination of organized and unorganized participation, and sequences of intensified information flow and interaction between challengers and authorities. (2011: 199).

He has in fact identified a recurrent dynamic of ebb and flow in collective mobilization, as in culture and the economy, that proceeds "from institutional conflict to enthusiastic peak to ultimate collapse" (1994: 168).

Cycles have their own dynamics. Cycles evolve through different stages: expansion through diffusion, radicalization/institutionalization, exhaustion, and restabilization (Tarrow 2011). Diffusion happens at the beginning of a cycle, as the first movements to emerge lower the cost of collective action for other actors, by demonstrating the vulnerability of the authorities. In addition, the victories of the early risers undermine the previous order of things, provoking countermobilization. Civil rights coalitions emerge to push for increasing recognition of the right to demonstrate. Repeatedly, spin-off movements contribute to the mobilization of other groups, inventing new forms of action, enlarging the protest claims, and winning some concessions, but also pushing elites and countermovements to form law-and-order coalitions (della Porta 1998). When elites reorganize, often adopting a mix of repression and concessions, mass protest tends to decline in intensity: radicalization, and also institutionalization, might ensue.

During cycles, the repertoires of collective action tend to change. In the initial stages of protest, the most disruptive forms often come to the fore (della Porta and Tarrow 1986). New actors invent new tactics, as emerging collective identities require radical action (Pizzorno 1978). As the cycle of protest extends, the reactions of the authorities produce not only a proportional increase in radical forms of action but also a simultaneous moderation of protest forms, with a reduction of disruptive action. Both processes, for different reasons, bring about the demise of the cycle.

Radicalization is activated by competition between movement activists and opponents, in the form of, in particular, escalating policing (see Chapter 2) but also of competitive escalation within the social movement sector, as well as within social movement families. Competitive dynamics tend to intensify during cycles of protest, as social movement organizations multiply and then split over the best strategies to adopt, some of them choosing more radical ones. Looking at violence as an escalation of the protest repertoire during cycles of protest points to the fluid borders between different strategies, as well as the reciprocal adaptation and learning processes between social movements and external actors, mainly police and other adversaries. However, social movements are also often divided on which tactics to pursue. In this sense, different groups not only adapt to environmental conditions but also exercise agency: they discuss strategies, experiment with them, and divide over them. As Alimi recently observed,

> one of the most basic features of opposition movements is that they consist of various actors and groups who, based on common interest and beliefs, interact informally with one another and mutually affect each other's strategy. These actors do not necessarily hold the same ideology, strategy, or preferable modes of action and goals. The mechanism "competition for power" between movement actors is about how challengers sometimes complement and sometimes undercut each other's strategies. This occurs as they struggle over whose strategy and tactics will dominate the goals, resource flow, translation of the struggle to specific gains, and the support of yet uncommitted adherents and allies. (2011: 99)

In these various steps, organizations, movements, and countermovements interact, gaining and losing weight and power in intense relations of cooperation and competition. Protest tends to develop from splinter groups coming from within groups of traditional actors. The peak of contention sees the mobilization of social movement organizations that actively sponsor the diffusion of protest. When the momentum is over, political parties and other more traditional actors regain control, taking advantage of the disruption of previous assets and negotiating new agreements. Radicalization is also produced by the uneven pace of demobilization. Whereas those at the periphery, who are also more moderate, tend to drop out earlier, the core activists, who are also more radical, tend to remain mobilized. Thus "unequal rates of defection between the center and the periphery shift the balance from moderate to radical claims and from peaceful to violent protest" (Tarrow 2011: 206).

In what follows, I focus on this competitive escalation, which I define as the causal mechanism that locates the escalation of protest repertoires within an organizational competition. Focusing on the onset of clandestine political violence, I look at competitive escalation in left-wing, right-wing, ethnic, and religious types of conflicts.

COMPETITIVE ESCALATION AND LEFT-WING VIOLENCE

In the Italian cycle of protest of the late 1960s and early 1970s, violence developed from the intensity of the conflict, with a growing number of social and political actors interacting with one another: the forms of action were initially disruptive but peaceful, and the aims were moderate – mainly calls for the reform of existing institutions. Although they remained mainly nonviolent, protest repertoires radicalized at the margins, especially during street battles with adversaries and the police. In particular, escalating police strategies contributed to radicalization. Throughout a very long process, students and workers paved the way for the mobilization of other actors. New collective identities were formed on issues of gender equality or urban structures, while groupings of different sizes, forms, and ideas enriched the left-libertarian social movement family, combining Old Left social rights concerns with emerging visions of liberty.

In his analysis of the Italian case, Tarrow (1989) observed that the forms of political violence used tend to vary according to the stages of the cycle. At the outset of protest, violent action was usually limited in its presence, small in scope, and unplanned. Typically, in this phase it occurred as an unforeseen result of direct action such as sit-ins or occupations. As protest developed, violent forms of action initially spread more slowly than nonviolent ones, frequently taking the shape of clashes between demonstrators and police or counter-demonstrators. Starting out as occasional and unplanned outbursts, such episodes nonetheless tended to be repeated and to take on a ritual quality. During this evolution small groups began to specialize in increasingly extreme tactics, to build up an armory for such action, and occasionally to go underground. Their very presence accelerated the moderate exodus from the movement, contributing to demobilization. This author and Sidney Tarrow thus summarized the results of a large-N study on repertoires in the Italian cycle of protest:

Violence tends to appear from the very beginning of a protest cycle. In this phase, it is usually represented by less purposive forms of action and it is used by large groups of protesters. Clashes with adversaries or police during mass actions are the more widely diffused types of political violence during the height of the cycle and decline at its end. In the last phase, aggression carried out by small groups of militants and direct attacks on persons become more frequent. The more dramatic forms of violence rise when the mass phase of the protest cycle declines. To put it differently, as mass mobilization winds down, political violence rises in magnitude and intensity. (della Porta and Tarrow 1986: 620)

Generalizing from the Italian case, Tarrow suggested that the final stages of a cycle of protest tend to see both a process of institutionalization and a growing number of violent actions:

When disruptive forms are first employed, they frighten antagonists with their potential cost, shock onlookers and worry elites concerned with public order. But newspapers gradually begin to give less and less space to protests that would have merited banner headlines when they first appeared on the streets. Repeating the same form of collective action over and over reduces uncertainty and is greeted with a smile or a yawn. Participants, at first enthused and invigorated by their solidarity and ability to challenge authorities, become jaded or disillusioned. Authorities, instead of calling out the troops or allowing the police to wade into a crowd, infiltrate dissenting groups and separate leaders from followers. Routinisation follows hard upon disruption. (1994: 112)

The analysis of the evolution of violent forms of action during that cycle has in fact shown the specific relations between cycles of protest and violence (see Figure 3.1). In a joint article, this author and Sidney Tarrow concluded:

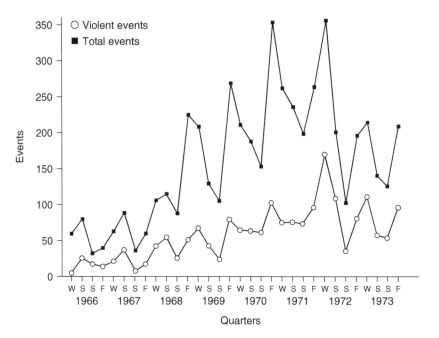

FIGURE 3.1. The number of protest and violent events per year in Italy. *Source*: della Porta and Tarrow 1986: 616.

The incidence of political violence is strictly connected with collective action in at least two ways. First, it grew in total numbers during the whole cycle. Second, its percentage weight was average in the beginning, low during the upswing, and high in the declining period of the protest wave. Violent forms were, therefore, part of the protest repertoire from the very beginning and their presence tended to grow in total numbers during the whole cycle. But it was when the wave of collective action declined that their percentage distribution increased. (della Porta and Tarrow 1986: 616)

In his analysis of the Italian cycle of protest, Tarrow pointed at the role of internal competition in its evolution:

During the upward curve of the cycle, as mass participation increases, there is creative experimentation and a testing of the limits of mass participation. As established groups, such as trade unions, parties and interest associations, enter the movement sectors, they monopolize conventional mass forms of action, producing incentives for others to use more disruptive forms of mass action to outflank them. But as participation declines later in the cycle, the mass base for both moderate and confrontational mass actions begins to shrink. New groups who try to enter the movement sector can only gain space there by adopting more radical forms of action that do not depend on a mass base. Through this essentially political process, the social movements sector evolves, divides internally, incites repression and eventually declines. This differentiation, competition and radicalization of the social movement sector are the central processes that give the cycle a dynamic character. (1989: 19)

The spread of protest was triggered by a demonstration effect: early risers showed the possibility and potential success of contention. There was, however, also competition: within the social movement sector, victories by those mobilizing challenged existing rights and interests, and within the social movement family, organizations competed over the best strategies to adopt. As Tarrow observed, "competition may arise from ideological conflict, from competition for space in a static organizational sphere, or from personal conflicts for power between leaders. Whatever its source, a common outcome of competition is radicalization: a shift of ideological commitments toward the extremes and/or the adoption of more disruptive and violent forms of contention" (2011: 207).

Competition increased with the pace of mobilization as large numbers of social movement organizations were created during the protest – in fact, "the growth in popular participation in the upward phase of the cycle invites organizational proliferation, and these new organizations compete for space with each other and with earlier risers" (Tarrow 2011: 208). Competition interacted with repression, as "when elites sense that the mass base for the collective action is in decline, they can re-knit the fabric of hegemony by repression, by press campaigns against violence, as well as by selective reform" (Tarrow 1989: 343). In this way, state responses contributed – often consciously but sometimes not – to the division of the movement into good and bad activists, trying to co-opt the former and repress the latter.

In fact, radicalization in Italy in the 1970s grew in dense organizational fields, from intense interactions among social movement organizations that cooperated and conflicted with one another on the use of violence (among other issues). My research has shown that underground organizations have evolved within and then broken away from larger, nonviolent social movement organizations. In the late 1960s, the decline of the student mobilization, and the consequent reduction in available resources, increased competition among the several (formal and informal) networks that constituted the so-called left-libertarian families. After having created semiclandestine marshal bodies, the organizations then tended to split on the issue of violence (della Porta 1995: chap. 4). Exploiting environmental conditions conducive to militancy, these splinter groups underwent further radicalization and eventually created new resources and opportunities for violence.

During the cycle of protest of the late 1960s to early 1970s, a myriad of new groups emerged at the school, university, or factory level. Most developed from, but also challenged, previously existing social movement organizations such as major trade unions, student unions, Catholic organizations, and left-wing political parties. With the evolution of protest, various sites of coordination developed; these sites were at first often territorial and issue based, but some also had a strong political and ideological basis. Competition and cooperation gave rise to the foundation, in 1968 and 1969, of the main organizations of the Italian New Left: the Union of the Italian Communists (Marxist-Leninist) (Unione dei Comunisti Italiani-ML), the Workers' Vanguard (Avanguardia Operaia [AO]), the Worker's Power (Potere Operaio [PO]), Il Manifesto, the Student Movement (Movimento Studentesco [MS]), and the Continuous Struggle (Lotta Continua [LC]). The coordination of local protests, which often involved weekly meetings of representatives of different organizations, was, for instance, the basis of the LC, which was at first just a group of comrades who mobilized around the strikes in the large factories in Northern Italy, often through *Assemblee operai studenti* (workers' and students' assemblies). In this dense environment, various groups formed, with internal ideological differences that reflected past organizational and strategic debates on the left. For instance, in the beginning, the LC was not much more than an "umbrella term for a loose coalition of extreme left groups and radical workers who met everyday in the bar" (Tarrow 1989: 268).

In time, the groups that emerged from the coordination of the thousands of small collectives that operated at the local level not only became more central-ized at the national level but also acquired a more exclusive structure, moving from a movement identity to a strong organizational identity. In 1972, with about 150 chapters all around the country, the LC discussed overcoming the limits of spontaneity to "return to the patrimony of militancy, discipline, and seriousness typical of the working class" (Bobbio 1988: 129). From this, the assumption developed that "there are not only many groups, ... there are many political lines. Among them, *only one is correct*, because it contributes to unify-ing and strengthening the working class; the others are wrong because they weaken the working class" (quoted in Bobbio 1988: 97).

Typical of most of the mentioned groups of the New Left was the creation of specialized semimilitary units or "marshals" to provide "self-defense" for move-ment activities and militant actions, sometimes even in physical fights with one another. A member of a left-wing underground group recalls that "thanks to the activities in the marshal, I had no trouble in adapting myself to the more dramatic techniques of the armed struggle.... It was all familiar to me. One could say that I had substituted the gun for the monkey-wrench" (monkey wrenches were widely used as "arms" by the marshal bodies) (quoted in Novelli and Tranfaglia 1988: 247). Another activist remembers, "Our milieu is the one of the marshal body of Lotta Continua, the youth circles.... We lived in a very fluid relations, the most continuous, with our network of militants or legal sympathizers.... I remember some of them, they drove us crazy, because they run away to see their mom, their girlfriend" (Life History no. 29: 39, 40, 46).

Justification for violence developed in action, especially during conflicts with political opponents, in a sort of community polarization (for a review, see Zald and Useem 1987). An Italian left-wing militant recalls, for instance, that

at school, there was a very small group of fascists, a daily source of fights. They were few, but evil. Moreover, they had the external support of a military group, the Alpha Group, based in a residence hall ten meters away from my school. They were fanatics, really threatening; many of them ended by bombing trains. They came to the entrance of the school and made revenge attacks, they even knifed people. (Life History no. 12: 9)

In 1970, as a defense against the neofascists, his collective organized a marshal body, which he "joined with excitement, very glad to have been chosen" (Life History no. 12: 9). Activities

consisted of the fact that we met at six o'clock, or at very dreadful hours, and we patrolled all around the school with iron bars, to check if any fascist was there. Then, we garrisoned at the entrance, to be sure that all the students could enter the school quietly. After that, we went to class – at the second hour, of course, because we were members of the marshal, and this was appreciated even by our professors. (Life History no. 12: 10)

In these struggles, violence became increasingly brutal, leading to a reciprocal adaptation to increasingly dangerous weapons, from stones and sticks to monkey wrenches, heavy chains, and guns. In the Italian radical Left, because "the physical struggle with the political counterpart, I mean with the fascists, was a matter of almost every single day ... it was therefore inevitable that we would start to equip ourselves in a military way" (Life History no. 13: 29). These continuous battles justified violence as a needed defense – as an Italian militant recalled, "the problem of the fascist in Rome was big and then, there was little to ethically reflect upon: you needed to defend yourself" (Life History no. 16: 197).

In the second half of the 1970s, recruitment to the underground developed inside the "autonomous" collectives: "Squads of the underground organizations were built inside a legal collective. A militant of the organization got involved in the collective and convinced those who he thought were more conscious to start an intermediary structure" (Life History no. 12: 31). The life history of Marco, a militant of a clandestine violent organization, testifies to this escalation in the experiences with and justification of violence. He remembers the splits in the organization called Movimento Studentesco in 1973–4 as starting "this thing that I always hated, of the internal divisions on streams of different degrees of radicalism" (ibid.: 334). With the so-called autonomous groups (which advocated for an autonomous organization of workers), in 1974, he participated in burning the car of a school director and in a holdup in the house of an arms trader, where – he recalled – a sick girl was sleeping.

In the second half of the 1970s, experiences with violent forms of protest spread, peaking in the so-called 77 Movement – according to a militant, "a very violent movement that sedimented through the bad network of the previous stories and political class" (Life History no. 29: 41). In the words of another, "in these years, between 1974 and 1977, the radical autonomous collectives grew enormously; month after month, they multiplied their presence in the city, their bases, their guns" (Life History no. 12: 25). In the second half of the seventies, "From a 'trot' phase, in Milan the armed struggle started to ride at full gallop. There were armed actions every day, at every march, at every deadline, at every strike" (Life History no. 12: 23). As mentioned in the incipit, in this period violent practices developed around the defense of specific territories. A militant recalled that "the origins of this neighborhood group are linked to an insurrectional day ... an anti-imperialist demonstration that involves the whole neighborhood. For hours, there are clashes with the police, and this signals the possible use of violence as not just self-defence but also as an instrument of liberation" (Life History no. 9: 255). In particular, after a young activist was killed during the clashes in the Roman neighborhood of San Basilio, militants started to talk about the need for an underground organization. Later, the aforementioned militant remembers, "there is no complex political project, there is this need to re-unify the political and the military" (ibid.: 439).

The use of guns often predated an individual's entrance into an underground organization and contributed to the socialization to violence. As an Italian militant remembered, "we started to study the way in which a gun works, to take a gun in our hands, to assemble and disassemble it. We practiced firing, and I enrolled at a rifle-range" (Life History no. 12: 19). The use of guns was first noted during the occupation of San Basilio, in Rome, during a particularly intense incident on 8 September 1974, in which police fired at and killed a young worker of an autonomous committee, Fabrizio Ceruso. Later on, "guns in the streets had become as common as the sticks of the flags some time before, and guerrilla attacks that started with marches and then reverted to marches were an everyday practice" (cited in Novelli and Tranfaglia 1988: 294). In fact, guns were given to teenagers, and shooting practices were organized (Life History no. 9).

These practices were followed by discourses that legitimated violence. According to an activist's recollections,

the discussion in the workers' committees took for granted the use of violent means. The differences were between those who supported use of the armed struggle directly linked to some phases, moments and conditions, and those who began instead to conceive the armed struggle as a political fact per se, a process that becomes autonomous from the specific social conditions. (Life History no. 27: 27)

When he went underground, there was therefore no trauma, as he could still rely on "a solid social environment" (ibid.: 32). He observed, in fact, that "I know that the judges who interrogated the first repentants, they were shocked, because they did not expect at all that type of penetration in the social fabric" (ibid.: 34).

Violence also produced internal struggles when the projects failed to link public political activities and mass violence (Scavino 2012: 153). In the mid-1970s, a militant remembers the debate on violence, the "splitting in the group, and the spreading of the thousands of forms, also spontaneous, also not organized. You started to see what was going to take a definite form in 1976" (Life History no. 9: 264). This is seen as a testimony to "the possibility of a mass practice of violence, subversive and antagonist, that was going to be the 1977" (ibid.: 264). The acceptance of illegal forms of action was so widespread that "there were periods in which we intervened in a general meeting of the movement and, in front of 200, 300 or 500 people, we almost openly supported the strategy of the armed struggle" (Life History no. 12: 33). As a future Italian left-wing militant recalled, when he became responsible for the marshal body of the Potere Operaio (Worker's Power [PO]) in Rome, "I started to study the problems, how to say?, political-military, that is, I started to read all what was available. I think I have read everything: Lussu, Marx himself, that Polish there, von Clausewitz: I have read all was available" (Life History no. 16: 192). In fact, he spoke of "two levels. One was the marshal body: there they taught us little: Molotov cocktails, the use of explosives.... And then there was the school of Valerio ... I was his pupil for those two or three years. And I have learned everything he knew" (ibid.: 196).

Many militant groups took on the project of linking armed struggle with mass violence:

We wanted to solder the armed struggle to the mass violence of the workers who fought against the police at Pirelli, who destroyed the sleepers at the Alfa Romeo factory, who occupied the tollbooths of the highway and the railway stations; to solder the armed struggle and the violence of the squatters. For instance, in San Basilio ... the squatters fired their guns at the police. We wanted to be a link between the suggestive hypothesis of building the armed struggle and the mass movement. (Life History no. 12: 20)

Although it was extremely violent, the 77 Movement was very critical of the Red Brigades. In contrast to the members of the Brigate Rosse (BR), who were considered as "*compagni che sbagliano* [comrades who make mistakes], with their concept of a strategic use of the armed struggle," the new radicals aimed at "linking the use of force, forms of struggle, mass practice and realization of the objectives" (Life History no. 9: 263). The BR was instead considered to be "hostile to the movement. In '77 the BR did not exist, the '77 movement outlawed them. They were put at the margins by an armed and illegal practice that has a mass dimension and therefore excludes the formations such as the BR" (Life History no. 9: 265). The same activist remembers that "most of the Autonomia was against the kidnapping of Aldo Moro" (the president of the Christian Democratic Party, kidnapped and killed by the BR). In this moment, "the project was to revitalize the elements of the movement that were dispersed" (ibid.: 269). Similarly, Marco remembered that, at an assembly after the kidnapping of Aldo Moro, 90 percent of those who attended were against it: "For us, the Moro kidnapping, as it was developed and ended, is a clamorous failure from the political point of view. There is a restriction of the spaces we had opened in society and, at the human level, it was an image of violence, cold, that creates many problems" (Life History no. 12: 355).

It was in these radicalized milieus, however, that other clandestine organizations were founded. The second-largest and longest-lasting clandestine organization in Italy, the Prima Linea (Front Line [PL]) emerged, at the end of 1976, via a split within the Comitati Comunisti per il Potere Operaio (CCPO), when some members of the group faced legal prosecution after carrying out their first assassination. Whereas one wing condemned illegal actions, the "military structure" (which

included a former member of the BR) opted for organizational "compartmentalization" and the use of increasingly violent forms of action.

Similarly, in 1977, another relatively large clandestine organization, the
Fighting Communist Formations (Formazioni Comuniste Combattenti [FCC]),
emerged from a split in the collective that published the magazine *Rosso*. The
FCC was founded by militants of the Communist Brigades, a kind of marshal
body formed from the various groups close to *Rosso*. After a gradual increase in
the use of violent forms of action, the May 1977 assassination of a policeman
during a public march organized by the more radical groups in Milan produced a
split, with the majority in favor of pursuing mass actions and retaining legal
structures and the Communist Brigades instead choosing to go underground.

In the FCC, as in the PL, military skills increased when a former member of
the BR joined the group – as a militant recalled, "this guy arrived and, for
contingent and personal reasons, because he was a clandestine, he was much
more anxious to stress the logistical aspect.... He had a surprising, scientific
ability for robbing banks" (Life History no. 12: 24, 25). Similarly, previously
existing groupings with developed military skills were at the origins of other
underground groups. As a militant observed, "the real legacy of the armed
struggle was ... the [large] number of cadres [that were] able to build up an
armed structure from nothing" (ibid.: 24–5).

Research on various cases has observed that repertoires of action have
radicalized in much the same forms and according to much the same timing
during cycles of protest involving different political and social actors. Ruud
Koopmans (1995) looked at similar developments in two German waves of
protest, at the end of the 1960s and at the beginning of the 1980s; in both cases

the action repertoire was relatively radical in the initial periods of rapid expansions,
around 1968 and 1981. Subsequently, these radical forms declined, while the number of
demonstrative actions continued to increase, reaching their peak in, respectively, 1972
and 1983. After this period of moderation, the number of demonstrative actions
decreased, and simultaneously radical actions made a come-back, although in both
waves they did not reach the level of the first peak of disruption. (ibid.: 141)

Protest cycles started with symbolically innovative tactics and then shifted to
mass action, which sometimes escalated into violence. When mass mobilization
declined, many movement activists returned to more institutional forms,
whereas small groups resorted to more radical action.

As is always the case, however, comparative analyses have not only confirmed
but also challenged and specified the various components of this picture. For
instance, my comparison of the Italian and the German cases showed similar
dynamics, but also relevant differences (della Porta 1995). In both countries,
there was some radicalization of the student protest, with a shift from defensive
to organized violence. This radicalization involved only small groups within
much broader nonviolent movement milieus, fueled by conflicts with the police
and political opponents. In both countries, while the protest spread to various

social groups, semimilitary violence was criticized within the movement but contributed to the spread of some radical symbolic violence in small and loosely coordinated autonomous groups. The presence of clandestine organizations contributed to the radicalization of protest forms. Later on, in the 1980s, in both countries, the mobilization of the peace movement against the deployment of NATO missiles helped to spread nonviolent repertoires.

A main difference emerged, however, in the spread of violence. Whereas in Germany a consensual culture and neocorporatist agreements, together with members of the Left in government, tended to facilitate moderation, in Italy violence escalated during longer-lasting and more intense protests (see also Chapter 2). In particular, developing from the crisis of the New Left organizations, the Italian radical "autonomous" groups had a much broader base and were more highly structured than their German counterparts. The more exclusive attitudes of the Italian state toward challengers and the presence of a violent, neofascist countermovement, interacting with a larger acceptance of radical frames and forms of action in the social movement sector, help explain the higher degree of escalation in the Italian cycle.

COMPETITIVE ESCALATION AND RIGHT-WING VIOLENCE

Italian right-wing organizations also developed during harsh conflicts, in direct opposition to left-wing groups, but they were also fueled by strong criticism of the neofascist party Movimento Sociale Italiano (MSI). This is true for both periods that have been singled out by several scholars within the history of radical Right clandestine organizations in post–World War II Italy.

The presence of a strong neofascist movement has been considered a peculiarity of the Italian case. Looking for explanations for the high degree of clandestine political violence found in Italy in the 1960s and the 1970s, scholars have observed that "one of the most distinctive features of the Italian experience was the strength and intensity of the neo-fascist terrorism" (Weinberg and Eubank 1987: 3). The radicalizing effect of the presence of such a movement "was played in two ways, one passive and the other active." On the one hand, "the very presence of a large neo-fascist movement in Italian politics served as a provocation to leftist groups whose adherents' view of the world was shaped in no small measure by stories of the heroic struggle waged by the resistance against Fascist rule during World War II."[2] On the other hand, "mass protest produced a revitalization of neo-fascism.... If leftists saw the neo-fascist presence as a provocation, the neo-fascists themselves saw an opportunity. The opportunity was based on the exploitation of the popular fears of the mass protests going on in schools, universities and industrial plants all over Northern Italy" (ibid.: 17–18).

---

[2] This would contribute to explaining another peculiarity – the fact that Italy's left-wing revolutionary terrorists also differed from their peers (Weinberg and Eubank 1987).

The 1960s and 1970s were also decades of radicalization for the extreme Right, which felt excluded by the other political parties. In the 1960s, right-wing radical groups split from the neofascist party Movimento Sociale Italiano, the most important of which was the Ordine Nuovo (ON), which was founded as early as 1956, and the Avanguardia Nazionale (AN), which was a further split from the ON in 1960. Since they were born, they were in contact with other neofascist groups in Europe, and in the 1960s the ON and AN organized a long series of physical attacks against their left-wing adversaries. Whereas the European fascist regimes in Italy and Germany provided the ideological frames, the contemporary authoritarian regimes in Southern Europe (in Greece, Portugal, and Spain) offered some logistical protection, as did some members of the Italian secret services.

Clandestine violence in the late 1960s spread within existing institutions, including, in particular, the MSI, which housed many complex relations among violent splinter groups. The first period lasted from 1969 to 1975 and was allegedly oriented toward the preparation of a (failed) coups d'état. The radical Right generation active in this period had already been involved in the various attempts to fund a fascist party, often splitting from and reconverging in the MSI. In 1951, among the thirty-six people tried for founding the Fasci d'Azione Rivoluzionaria were the future leaders of this generation, such as Julius Evola, Clemente Graziani, and Pino Rauti. The Avanguardia Nazionale was founded in 1959 by Stefano Delle Chiaia, a former MSI leader, who planned a revolution stimulated by small basis groups. The Ordine Nuovo also emerged from the neofascist MSI, living a theoretically public but practically clandestine life until 1973, when it was sentenced for "reconstitution of the fascist party" and banned, at which point it became totally clandestine.

Quantitative research based on newspaper and police data indicated that 96.5 percent of the right-wing militants arrested for terrorism had previous membership in radical Right groups (Weinberg and Eubank 1987: 86), most of which were somehow affiliated with the MSI. In fact,

many neo-Fascists ... had been drawn from the ranks of the MSI. There were only a handful of individuals who made the long voyage from one side of the political spectrum to the other, and fewer still who drifted to the extremes from the political centre. In thinking about how these people became involved in violent groups, it is worth noting that a little over 12 percent (305 of the 2,490 persons about whom information was obtained) were related by family to other members of the group. (Weinberg and Eubank 1988: 544)

The theory that such groups had their roots inside the MSI is confirmed by the individual histories: "Almost all of the young people – barely over 20 – tried in 1973 and 1976 as members of ON and AN, had started their political path inside the youth movements of the MSI" (Minna 1984: 39). In 1968, Valerio Borghese, a fighter of the Republic of Salò (which had been formed by fascists who refused to comply with the armistice to end World War II) and former honorary president of the MSI, funded the Fronte Nazionale Rivoluzionario, which involved several former Salò fighters as well as militants of the AN and ON and members of the military hierarchies (ibid.: 47).

Especially for those who joined the radical neofascists in the 1960s, there is "a pattern of youthful participation in the MSI followed by disenchantment, withdrawal and affiliation with one of the more militant neo-fascist organizations, a form of youth rebellion well before the explosion of 1968" (Weinberg and Eubank 1987: 37). At the individual level, in fact, "constant to many of the analysed cases is the beginning of political activity in the legal right-wing party, the MSI, and the youth organizations linked to it (Giovane Italia, Fronte della Gioventù, Fuan)" (Pisetta 1990: 192). Some of the activists even came from families that had been involved in the Repubblica Sociale Italiana, the aforementioned Republic of Salò, which after the armistice continued to fight the Allies in loyalty to the regime (ibid.: 199; see also chap. 7). As aforementioned, the extreme Right organizations of the first generation had international links with fascist regimes in Spain and Greece (where, for example, a military camp was created in 1968), as well as contacts with the Italian secret services, SIFAR (ibid.; see chap. 3).

Links between the radical Right groups and the MSI still existed in the second half of the 1970s. In this period, the radical group Costruiamo l'Azione emerged from the so-called Tivoli group (the Circolo Europeo Drieu La Rochelle), which was linked to the Ordine Nuovo. Its leader, Paolo Signorelli, came from the MSI. In 1977, a group of young activists from the MSI section Monteverde in Rome founded the Nuclei Armati Rivoluzionari (NAR), which would be responsible for eight assassinations and more than 100 attacks before dissolving in 1980.

However, relations with the MSI grew increasingly tense.[3] Especially in the second half of the 1970s, criticism of the old generation took on a dramatic tune. In the radical Right journal *Quex*, the MSI was defined as "the party of betrayal and mediocrity": "deprived of a true strategy, deprived of political flexibility, sectarian, immovable, the organizations that vegetated for twenty years are now dead" (no. 2, 1979, cited in Guerrieri 2010). Even more explicitly, the MSI leaders were defined as "political frauds," "paid mercenaries," "*ducetti* of the lowest category," "lacking ideas and principles," "part and parcel, support of this putrefied system, and therefore to be fought against and destroyed, as all regime supporters" (*Quex*, no. 3, 1980: 3, cited in Guerrieri 2010).

In the eyes of another new radical Right group, Costruiamo l'Azione, the MSI had a reactionary face and was seen as having sold out for paltry public party

---

[3] Later on, research on the radical Right noted the difficult interaction between the two extreme right-wing areas: one "macho and chauvinist, with hooligan attitudes and consumptions linked especially to the characteristics of youth subcultures, and the politicized one, fascinated by the nazi- and Evola stereotype, linked to the tradition of the radical right, with militant attitudes. The Saturday night attacks, the rock concert, the passion for alcohol and soccer are expressions of the first soul; the political initiative, from marches to leafleting, from the meetings on negationism to workshops on anti mondialism, are expressions of the second" (Marchi 1994: 174).

financing. According to a former militant, "the MSI is sclerotic, it has a leadership which is incredible, a true gerontocracy.... There is a base that does not reason as the top, and the top does anything it can to constrain ... this juvenile exuberance" (interview with M.B.: 93–5, in Pisetta 1990: 195). As NAR activist Valerio Fioravanti declared regarding the street fight with police that followed the deaths of militants during the fight in front of the Roman MSI section of Acca Larentia: "In reality, our target was not the Carabinieri, our aim was to kill our treacherous father, in a mythological sense, to kill the MSI which had sold us out" (Cento Bull 2007: 148). Young people of the radical groups also felt instrumentalized by the MSI. A militant lamented that "it happened that when you glued the [MSI] posters during the electoral campaigns you thought you did something right, to defend an idea, but often those who asked you to do it only had an interest in occupying a chair" (interview with A.I.: 56, in Pisetta 1990: 196). A right-wing militant talked of a "very dramatic game played above our heads" (interview with M.M.: 120, in Pisetta 1990: 198). The MSI was accused of instrumentally using the young activists to promote disorder:

I cannot forgive them for sending kids of the Fronte della Gioventù in front of the schools where they knew they would be wounded with iron bars ... for us it was clear that the party needed deaths ... they hoped there were victims in front of the schools, to be able to show that violence was communist. (interview with A.d'I.: 57, in Pisetta 1990: 201).[4]

The MSI was not the only traitor; the same was said of "the leaders of those extraparliamentary organizations that in Italy had a relevant importance in a recent past, but whose revolutionary charge was invested in regime complots, in pseudo attempted coup d'état, letting themselves (voluntarily, we have to believe) be instrumentalized from the most reactionary and conservative forces of the system" (*Quex*, 1980, no. 3: 3, cited in Guerrieri 2010).

Throughout the 1970s, as protest became increasingly violent, radical Right activists started to kill and be killed, during both street fights with and individual aggression by radical Left activists. The killing of the two young sons of an MSI activist in Primavalle in 1973; of Mikis Mantakas, a militant of the FUAN (the MSI university students' association) in 1975; and of three other activists during an assault to the MSI section in via Acca Larentia in Rome in 1978 were very intense memories for the young activists in the second half of the 1970s. It was said that, during terrorist actions, one NAR militant, Franco Anselmi, brought with him a balaclava hat, dirty with the blood of his comrade Mikis Mantakas.[5] In September 1977, future NAR activists were involved in the assassination of Lotta Continua activist Walter Rossi, who was

---

[4] Another militant stressed that "the MSI had a responsibility because it got us involved, it pushed us into a logic that was a logic of hater, a logic of death. It ideologized people that were prone to be ideologized, that were 17 years old, like me" (interview with Roberto: 47, in Pisetta 1990: 196).
[5] Mikis Mantakas was a Greek student who died in 1975 during the fights between radical right-wing and left-wing activists in front of the justice palace, the location of the trial on the fire that had killed the two young sons of an MSI activist in Primavalle in 1973 (Guerrieri 2010).

shot dead while running away during street fights, as well as in the February 1978 assassination of left-wing activist Roberto Scialabba and the injuring of his brother. In June 1979, Francesco Cecchin, a young militant of the Fronte della Gioventù, died while escaping from political adversaries. As an act of revenge, radical right-wingers broke into a PCI section, wounding thirty-five people. In 1980, Valerio Verbanio, member of a left-wing collective, was killed in his apartment, in front of his mother, and Angelo Mancia of the MSI was killed by a Volante Rossa.

The context of continuous battles is also often mentioned as justifying the choice of violence on the right. One activist thus recalled fights at his high school: "[The leftist students] threw down desks and we tried to assault them" (quoted in Pisetta 1990: 200). Another mentioned, "We had to enter the school in a group.... If there were troubles, if there was tension in the air, we met before school in order to arrive at school together, because, you know, it is difficult to attack a group of ten people" (ibid.: 200). Still another recalled the 1970s as the years when "there were fights almost every day and I can assure you that we never shirted away from fighting" (ibid.: 134).

In these situations, violence started to be justified as defensive. A militant of Terza Posizione, Gabriele Adinolfi, stated that

the first person to be beaten with a bar in Italy, Spanò, was beaten by the [left] student movement, the first person to be killed by a bottle full of sand was Ermanno Venturini, in Genoa, and the first person to be shot dead was Mikis Mantakas in Rome. I believe that even the first person to be knifed was Falvella in Salerno. In other words, the escalation was always taking place from the left to the right ... the taste for civil war was developed by the extreme left ... the left developed a strategy of hatred. (quoted in Cento Bull 2007: 141)

He also remembered, however, that "the physical struggle for us was a test of strength" (ibid.), and "we went to conquer the streets" (ibid.: 142). And another militant explained, "Eventually the fascists were forced to go around carrying guns, and they had to use pistols, because they were attacked and *sprangati* [hit with bars]" (quoted in Pisetta 1990: 201).

A sort of battle spirit toward politics is particularly stressed by the militants of the second generation. A militant of Terza Posizione talked of "years of lead, of civil war, of daily clashes, years in which what mattered was to survive or to eliminate the enemy" (quoted in Catanzaro 1990: 141). Some also cite the need to defend their right to mobilize: "We deliberately decided to carry out military actions that would allow us to be politically active ... we carried out various successful military actions which wounded a great number of our enemies but lastly allowed us to engage in politics" (Cento Bull 2007: 122). One of the militants, talking about the mid-1970s, recalled: "At that point, in those years, political struggle became a territorial problem ... it was a climate of continuous violence" (Ferraresi 1995: 342). Similarly, another remembered, "Outside school, there were the externals, the external and the internals together, do you understand? So I had to go to school at 7:30, so they did not get me in the morning and leave at 2:30pm. It was like going to a battlefield" (ibid.).

Although it grew within a much smaller milieu than on the left, right-wing violence also developed in Italy within a broader movement, made up of several diverse organizations not only in cooperation but also in competition with one another. Notwithstanding formal and informal alliances with the Neofascist Party (the MSI), the radical groups also emerged from widespread critics of the party's moderation, and tensions developed among the organizations that had been founded in the 1960s and those that emerged in the 1970s from a challenge to the former.

COMPETITIVE ESCALATION AND ETHNIC VIOLENCE

In the Basque Country, radical nationalism developed during a very long conflict that saw cycles and waves of particularly intense protest. The emergence of Basque nationalism in the latter part of the nineteenth century (the National Basque Party [PNV] was founded in 1895) has been seen as a reaction of the urban middle class to migration and the first wave of industrialization in a context characterized by a fragmented social structure. It is not by chance that the ETA is particularly present in areas with a certain type of industrialization, such as Guipuzkoa and especially the Goierri region, which is a mountainous area that experienced a late but very fast growth of the manufacturing industry and has a high persistence of Basque language use (Clark 1984).[6]

Competitive escalation also happened in ethnonationalist types of violence. In an explanation of why violence had emerged in the Basque Country but not in Catalonia, Juan Medrano noted different degrees of organizational competition, which he assessed as higher in the Catalonia case. However, this interpretation has been challenged. Luis de la Calle Robles (2009) has noted that, since at least the civil war, Basque ethnonationalist organizations have been embedded in a very competitive environment.

Even before the civil war, the PNV was in strong competition with the Carlistas, who also had a traditionalist base but bridged traditionalism with "*espanolistas*" positions. In addition, the first wave of industrialization had brought about the spread of a class discourse and of related left-wing organizations, which competed with the nationalist narrative. During the Republic, the Basque electorate was in fact equally divided into three groups: Carlistas, nationalists, and Republicans (especially members of the PSOE, whose electoral strongholds remained stable after Francoism) (de la Calle Robles 2009).

---

[6] In fact, 85 percent of the victims of political violence are from the Basque region, especially in the provinces of Guipuzkoa and Biscay; the same trend can be seen in the background of ETA activists, of whom about half come from Guipuzkoa (0.25 out of every 1,000 inhabitants) and 40 percent (0.12) from Biscay.

The ethnic conflict radicalized in this environment. The ETA was born inside the PNV, contesting its alignment with the nonviolent opposition of the all-party government in exile and its confidence in a negotiated concession of autonomous status after the return of democracy. The strong reliance of the PNV on the support of Western democracies was bound to produce internal criticism after those countries recognized the Francoist regime, abandoning the Spanish democratic opposition. In the early 1950s disillusionment with the allegedly passive collaborationism of the traditional Basque nationalism, in particular of the PNV, pushed a small handful of students from the University of Deusto – all of whom belonged to the urban middle class – to create a discussion group called the Society of the Basque Student and to produce a newsletter, *Ekin*. It is not a coincidence that most of the ETA's founders came from a nationalist family background (Unzueta 1988).

In this period, the conception of ethnicity shifted from a racial to a linguistic definition. The Basque language, which had remained a marginal concern in the previous wave of ethnonationalist mobilization, became central, as the ETA advocated Euskera as a unique official language. In 1953, the group developed contacts and ultimately merged in 1956 with the PNV's youth organization, EGI – although it kept a critical stance toward the PNV, which was accused, among other things, of being too authoritarian in its internal life as well as promoting an exclusive conception of the Basque identity. In 1959, when the PNV expelled a member of the group, hundreds of others quit to follow him. On 31 July 1959 (the sixty-fourth anniversary of the foundation of the PNV), they founded the ETA, or Euskadi Ta Askatasuna (Basquen-land and Freedom) (Muro 2008).

Later, the ETA would also contribute to an ethnonationalist revival. Although less than 20 percent of those living in the region spoke Euskera, in the early 1970s, their self-identification as Basque was quite high (34 percent of the population felt Basque only, and 10 percent felt more Basque than Spanish; only 24 percent felt only Spanish, and 3 percent felt more Spanish than Basque). Furthermore, the percentage of those favoring independence doubled, from 6 to 12 percent following Franco's death, and then tripled to 36 percent in 1979 (Clark 1984: 171).

During its founding years, the ETA cooperated and competed with a fast-developing labor movement. Franco's dictatorship strongly repressed both the anarcho-syndicalist Confederacion Nacional del Trabajo (General Confederation of Labour [CNT]) and the socialist Union General de Trabajadores (General Workers' Union [UGT]), which had played an important role in the defense of the Republic. Thousands of unionists were killed, and many had to flee the country, while all unions were banned and strikes became illegal.

After World War II, however, the labor movement remobilized. The Manresa strike in 1946 ended with a compromise; in 1951 a streetcar strike in Barcelona spread to other sectors and was accompanied by public demonstrations. Along with the economic developments of the 1950s, strikes multiplied. In the late

1950s, in an attempt to legitimize itself internally and abroad, the regime began allowing collective bargaining as well as the election of delegates (*jurados*) at the factory level, changing labor relations. Workers on strike started to elect *comisiones obreras* (CCOOs), workers' committees that formed in relation to specific conflicts and were discontinued afterward. Largely communist-led, the CCOOs were declared illegal in 1967 (despite some opposition inside the official, vertical union, voiced by its leader José Solis). However, because they were already a strong organizational presence in the factories, they continued to be active, mixing an occasional visible presence with a clandestine, more stable one. With their movement-like character and hidden organized nuclei, the CCOOs were extremely successful in mobilizing workers into strikes, notwithstanding hard repression, imprisonments, and dismissals. The labor movement thus recovered its capacity to act collectively. As Fishman (1990: 16) summarized, "this politically divided labour movement would form one of the principal forces pushing to end authoritarian rule and return to democracy."

This form of labor protest, which challenged the authoritarian regime, found in the Basque country a particularly fertile soil. The second wave of industrialization in the 1950s and especially the economic crisis that hit the region with particular intensity in the 1970s and well into the 1980s brought about a radicalization of the Basque workers. Already in May 1947, a first general strike organized by the resistance committee involved 75 percent of the workers. Despite ending with 15,000 dismissals, it was considered a positive sign of resistance and was repeated in Bilbao in 1951. In April 1967, violent repression followed demonstrations during another strike in the Basque capital that coincided with the celebration of Aberri Eguna, the day of the Basque fatherland. In February and March 1969, strikes took place in Vizcaya. These events can be summarized as follows:

Partly because of the blue-collar workers' dissatisfaction with living and working conditions, wildcat-strikes, sympathy and general strikes constantly broke out during the late 1960s and early 1970s. More than 37 percent of all recorded strikes in Spain between 1967 and 1974 took place in the Basque region, even though it was home to only 11 percent of Spain's urban workers. Labor activists, belonging to more than a dozen underground Marxist, Christian and anarchist labor parties, established vast networks of militant shop-floor organizations. Hundreds of urban neighbors' associations also blossomed and, despite police surveillance, organized boycotts, marches, building occupations and petition drives to compel the government authorities to provide poorer residents with affordable housing, medical care, garbage collection and educational services for children. (Zirakzadeh 2002: 69)

The ETA's adoption of a Marxist discourse (see Chapter 7) was linked to its intervention in the industrial disputes and its orientation toward recruiting there; it also increased competition within the Left. Soon after its emergence, the ETA combined the traditional nationalist discourse with a class one, enjoying alliances both with traditional nationalist organizations and with the left-wing opposition and the labor movement. As Luis de la Calle Robles observed, "far from being empty, the boom of ETA in the early 1970s took place in a quite flourishing oppositional environment" (2009: 66).

In fact, workers continued to play an important role in the transition to democracy and afterward. Throughout the 1970s, industrial conflicts were frequent and widespread. The number of workers on strike went from about 500,000 (who together executed 10 million hours of strikes) in 1975 to more than 3.5 million (110 million hours) in 1976. Similar rates were measured in 1977 and 1978, and the figures increased to 5.8 million (170 million hours) in 1979, although they declined to below the 1976 level in 1980.

Notwithstanding the myth of the *transition pactada*, after the mid-1970s "there was an entire, very politicized country" (Reinares 2001: 69). As an *etarra* remembers,

everyday life was, in practice, demonstrations, barricades ... they went on the street, for a demonstration. To ask for a salary increase ... and the police arrived ... real fights, with guns and deaths ... that, everyday. Constantly ... , they made road controls ... they fired at you, killed you. And this after the death of Franco. (ibid.: 69)

In the words of another militant, "it was a period with many strikes. We lost many days of classes. There was a lot of political mobilization ... many days with police occupations of the Institute as well. It was the period of the transition ... we were young and we started to do many things" (ibid.).

The pacted transition developed under Suarez and his Union del Centro Democratico and culminated in the Moncloa Pacts in October 1977. Signed by the major parties, it divided the leadership of both CCOOs and the UGT, as well as disappointing many workers. The fear of weakening democracy as well as economic depression contributed to the demobilization of the workers, a development that was in part proactively pushed for from above. At the end of the 1970s, feelings of *desencanto* (disenchantment) followed the peak of participation in the mid-1970s. The attempted coup on 23 February 1981 scared activists and the Left, producing a decline in labor mobilization. Although organizationally they were very weak, the Spanish unions did show an astonishing capacity to mobilize workers in the late 1980s.

If the very emergence of the ETA reflected tensions in the Basque movement about the correct strategy to adopt, it also fueled those divisions. The great repression of 1969 favored the ETA because it was perceived as indiscriminate and as addressing the Basque-speaking population in particular, in contrast to what happened in Catalonia (see also Chapter 2). Additionally, local elites adopted a competitive (and exclusionary) stance (de la Calle Robles 2009). Especially after 1970 – with the Burgos trials against ETA militants and the ETA's assassination of Franco's designated successor, Carrero Blanco – the ETA became a symbolic point of reference for the Spanish anti-Franco opposition.

During and after the transition, the ETA developed through competition within the ethnonationalist front, and also with the Left and within the organization itself. During the transition, Basque nationalist forces tried to build a common front, with a view to the first general elections. Whereas the PNV favored participation, the two components into which the ETA had split in the mid-1970s took different positions. The ETA military (ETA-M) asked for an amnesty and the legalization of all political parties as a precondition for its support for democratization, whereas the ETA politico-military (ETA-PM) supported the left-wing party Euskadiko Ezkerra (EE) in exchange for the release of some prisoners (Sánchez-Cuenca 2009: 18). The division inside the nationalist front escalated on 8 September 1977, when the activists participating in two different marches in San Sebastian – one organized by the moderate ethnonationalists and the other by the radical ones – clashed with each other, using verbal insults as well as some physical violence (ibid.: 19). In the fall of 1977, the ETA-M intensified its violent attacks as an alternative strategy to the perceived failure of peaceful protest. As it explained in the sixty-ninth edition of its internal publication *Zutik*, "after the Freedom March and the latest demonstrations for amnesty, popular mobilizations plummeted and the masses shifted from actors to spectators in the parliamentary game" (cited in ibid.: 20). The ETA-M attacks in fact increased with the decline of the huge mobilizations for amnesty, after the Summer Freedom March, which, composed of various columns coming from different directions, converged in Pamplona following more than three weeks of demonstrations throughout the Basque Country. Other massive protests had also denounced heavy repression, including the killing of demonstrators (ibid.).

A study on the evolution of violence within the cycle of protest that accompanied the transition confirms that political killings increased as participation in demonstrations declined. Focusing on the 982 demonstrations that took place between May 1976 and December 1978, and on the 718 killings (214 of which resulted from state violence), Sánchez-Cuenca and Aguillar observed that "mass mobilization reaches its peak in the last quarter of 1977, after which there is a significant drop in the number of demonstrators. This drop is followed immediately by a rapid increase in the number of mortal victims. It would seem, therefore, that one cycle is replaced by the other" (2009: 15). In fact, intense protest accompanied the democratization period, between Franco's death in November 1975 and the victory of the PSOE in the 1982 elections (see Figures 3.2 and 3.3). Heavy protests were organized on topics such as regional autonomy (which comprised 38 percent of the total number of protest participants), economic issues (23 percent), and amnesty (8 percent). The protest declined, however, after 1977, in particular after the Moncloa Pacts were signed by the government, the opposition, trade unions, and the employers' association with the aim of addressing the economic crisis.

The Basque Country remained, however, a very contentious region. According to Casquette (2003: 17–19), data provided by the Basque police on the number of demonstrations during the late 1990s and the beginning of the years 2000 "unequivocally back the hypothesis of over-contention," with 4,000

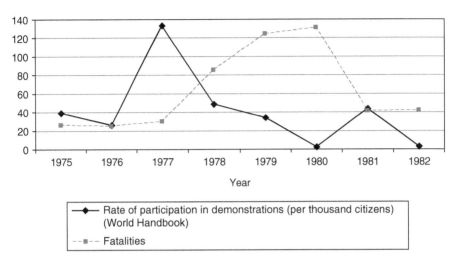

FIGURE 3.2. The cycles of demonstrations and terrorist violence in Spain. *Source*: Sánchez-Cuenca and Aguillar 2009: 27. Permission to reproduce gratefully acknowledged.

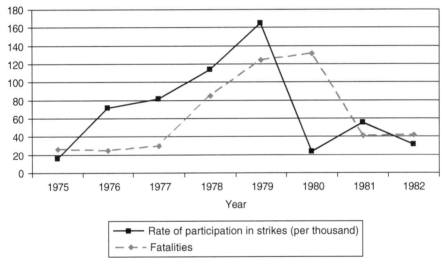

FIGURE 3.3. The cycles of strike activity and terrorist violence in Spain. *Source*: Sánchez-Cuenca and Aguillar 2009: 28. Permission to reproduce gratefully acknowledged.

demonstrations and public gatherings in the last ten months of 1998, 5,608 in 1999, 12,465 in 2000, and 8,730 in 2001 – as compared to an average of 9,515 demonstrations per year for the rest of Spain. In the same period, the number of demonstrations per thousand inhabitants was eighteen times higher in the Basque Country than in Spain. He concludes, "No question, then, that in social protest, at least, Bilbao occupies the world's leading position" (ibid.: 19). Data at the individual level confirms that opinion: according to a survey, in the Basque Country 54 percent of the population has attended lawful demonstrations, as compared to 27 percent in Spain.

The ETA did play a role in this contentious evolution. First of all, the union Langile Abertzale Batzordeak (Patriotic Workers' Committee [LAB]) and other organizations close to the ETA are quite strong in some localities, often in small- or medium-sized but not rural or isolated municipalities, and often, but not only, where there is a high presence of Basque-speaking persons (Beck 1999). Additionally, the ETA discourse conditioned new social movement activities, whether on women's rights or on environmental issues (Tejerina 2001: 51). In the 1990s, street violence was organized by organizations close to the ETA: about 300 incidents were counted in 1990 and in 1991; this number increased to about 500 in each of the following two years; peaked at about 1,000 in 1995, 1996, and 1997; and returned to about 500 in the following three years (de la Calle n.d.). These events aimed first at the moderate nationalists and Basque police and later broadened their targets to include national actors (de la Calle n.d.; see also van den Broek 2004).

In recent years, marches in Bilbao have been designed to perform a highly integrative function in the movement, through the development of intense emotions. This is evident in the routes of the marches, which are different from those of marches organized by other types of actors:

(a) It is somewhat longer, approximately 3 km, so that demonstrators enjoy more time to stick together and thus lengthen their liturgical performance, and (b) whereas the main route is completely flat, the two main streets along which the alternative route goes have a sloping topography, so that either from the front or from the back of the demonstration it is possible to enjoy an overall view of the marching crowd. In this way, those sympathizers unable to attend the demonstration have a chance to see the crowd the next day on the cover page of the *Gara* newspaper. The lengthy coverage of the event on the inside pages provides a detailed description of the event and is accompanied by a photographic report, as well as by interviews with anonymous, rank-and-file participants at the demonstration expressing their opinions and, more important, their feelings. (Casquette 2003: 30)

However, the intense protest culture in the Basque Country also testifies to some increasing tensions among different generations of Basque nationalism. Take, for example, the debate in the early 1980s about the *radikal rok basko* (radical Basque rock), which developed in the radical bar culture, shaping youth identity. A combination of British punk with ska and reggae that was employed by dozens of Basque punk bands, *radikal rok basko* was, in effect, the theme music of the radical youth (Kasmir 2002: 54). Notwithstanding its eventual endorsement by Herri Batasuna, it also divided the Basque scene. In fact, according to Kasmir,

today, 70% of the concerts that are organized in Euskadi, are organized in the orbit of [the nationalist radical party] HB. That is to say that there is a relationship between rock and roll, the milieu of HB, and a form of political thought, if you like. However, radical nationalists were not uniform in their acceptance of punk. Many saw it as a "foreign" expression that contaminated "authentic" Basque culture. Indeed, one HB supporter told me as we were having a drink in Bar Jai that punk "is not Basque; it's mass culture." ... He preferred to hear Basque folk in radical bars.... For their part, punk youths characterized these HB militants as "*cerrados*" ("closed minded"). Interestingly, there was particular tension between modernos and cerrados over the use of hashish. (2002: 56)

In conclusion, the ETA grew and radicalized during waves of protest, in cooperation and competition with other social movement organizations – within the nationalist social movement family and the workers' movement as well as, later on, within new social movements. Indeed, the ETA's presence conditioned the development of protest and the social movement sector in the Basque countries for at least half a century.

COMPETITIVE ESCALATION AND RELIGIOUS VIOLENCE

Religious networks are often safe spaces for activism against dictators, when given institutional legitimacy, or at least tolerance (Aminzade and Perry 2001: 159ff.). Religious spaces work as (relatively) free spaces, and this is one of the reasons why "religious groups have a unique institutional legitimacy that gives them distinctive advantages; it is harder to repress them; and they feel 'safer' to confront and discuss issues that no one else can" (ibid.: 159). Religious fundamentalism developed in these spaces, from a series of sectarian splits and within a religious revival.

As are all other religions, Islam is drastically divided internally. Only a very restricted Islamic religious milieu has played a role in socialization to violence, whereas most parts of Islam have opposed it from various perspectives. Oliver Roy (2004) pointed to the presence of different versions of Islam, all influenced by twin processes of individualism – Westernization and globalization. Among them, developing as a reaction to the institutionalization of Islamist parties, is neofundamentalism, defined as "a closed, scripturalist and conservative view of Islam that rejects the nationalist and statist dimension in favour of the ummah, the universal community of all Muslims, based on sharia (Islamic law)" (ibid.: 1). Its focus is not primarily political; it does not call for an Islamic state but instead targets society, stressing spiritual needs.

The concept of the neo-brotherhood and new age ideas are common to new religiosity in general, which is characterized by individualization, the quest for self-realization, deculturalization, and deterritorialization. Anti-intellectualism and emotional religiosity are linked to individualism, as in all religious revivals of the late twentieth century. As in Christianity, there is also the development of an increasing number of identity-oriented groups. Individualization is visible, for instance, in Islamic Web pages: "Islamic revivalism goes hand in hand with a modern trend: the culture of the self" (Roy 2004: 193).

The so-called shift from religion to religiosity implied complex processes of religious deterritorialization, as mass migrations reduce the territorial rootedness of specific religions. Islam is, therefore, presented as a universalistic discourse, linked neither to a territory nor to a specific culture, but is affected by the feelings of exclusion of youth from Muslim backgrounds, as well as by the Middle East crisis. In fact, Islam became also a Western religion, as a consequence of the rapid displacement of millions of people. At the structural level, a rebuilding of community and constriction of identity happens, for example, through local voluntary communities, mosques, and student associations. In many version of Islam, "an Islamic state should result from the re-Islamization of the *ummah*, not be a tool for this re-Islamization" (ibid.: 247). Furthermore, "in recent decades, jihad's primary Quranic religious or spiritual meanings, the struggle to follow God's path and to build a just society, became more multifaceted and contemporary in its application – for example, leading to a jihad to create a more just society or to engage in educational, community and social services" (Esposito 2006: 150).

Justification for political violence developed with the evolution of a neofundamentalist vision of Islam. According to Olivier Roy,

The early 1980s saw a dramatic change in patterns of Islam-related violence. Political violence, which till then was associated with Islamist movements, passed into the hands of neofundamentalist groups.... This shift began almost unnoticed, because in the previous two decades neofundamentalism had been seen by the United States, its Pakistani and Saudi allies, and many Arab regimes as a strategic tool for fighting communism, radical Shiism and even Arab leftist nationalism (from PLO to Baathism). (2004: 290)[7]

Although local concerns were dominant in the beginning, the neofundamentalist discourse increasingly stressed global concerns and became more and more exclusive in its vision of itself and the enemy.

Often considered a product of fanaticism or frustration, Islamic fundamentalism is also located within broader cycles of protest in which religious claims are intertwined with socioeconomic and nationalist ones. The nationalist dimension of religious clandestine violence has indeed been stressed. According to Esposito, "political Islam is in many ways the successor of failed nationalist ideologies and projects in the 1950s and 1960s, from Arab nationalism and socialism of North Africa and the Middle East to the Muslim nationalism of post-independence Pakistan" (2006: 146). Bin Laden's message has in fact been defined as primarily political (ibid.). Suicide terrorism itself has been presented as a strategy of nationalists fighting against occupation by democratic regimes, motivated by expectations of success, when other means are lacking.[8] Additionally, research has pointed to the role of social – especially class – conflicts in the development of

---

[7] In fact, neofundamentalism has been seen as using Muslim identity as a substitute for ethnic identity, with reference to Islamic culture as a set of anthropological paths and values that, however, do not exist as such, as indicated by the decline in fertility rates or the weakening of de facto monogamy (Roy 2004).

[8] According to Pape, "perhaps the most striking aspect of recent suicide terrorist campaigns is that they are associated with gains for the terrorists' political cause about half the time" (2005: 66).

Islamism (e.g., Gunning 2007; Ritter 2010). This means that the evolution of radical Islamist organizations has to be located not only within the dynamics of competition within Islamic movements, which always also involved nonviolent components, but also in waves of protest in which different types of organizations – religious, but also nationalist and class-oriented – interacted.

That religious, nationalist, and class motivations tend to interact is no new discovery. Under some conditions, the search for national independence takes a religious tone. As Pape observed, "under the circumstances of a foreign occupation, the relative importance of religious and linguistic differences normally reverses and religious difference can influence nationalist sentiments in ways that encourage mass support for martyrdom and suicide terrorism" (2005: 88). From this perspective, political violence is more likely when "the presence of a religious difference reduces room for compromise between the occupying power and the occupied community, because the conflict is seen as a zero sum game" (ibid.: 89).[9]

To understand the development of radical Islamism, it is therefore important to look at forms of internal competition. As Sadowski correctly reminded us, Muslims have internally diverse values, and this is also true of the so-called political Islam:

Studies of political Islam commonly begin from two faulty assumptions, guaranteeing that whatever questions are asked will generate misleading answers. The first assumption is that Muslims around the world share a common, relatively homogenous body of doctrine on a wide array of religious, social, and political matters. The second is that this doctrine is actually the primary determinant of Muslim behavior. (2006: 216)

Not only are there doctrinary differences between Sunni and Shia Muslims, but there are also rural-urban cleavages as well as cleavages related to the declination of Islam in specific national contexts (ibid.: 218). In addition, Islamic movements are divided over strategies, with pietistic movements aiming at personal transformation and political ones sharing a belief in the importance of political power.

Even political Islam is internally split: traditionalist groups tend to focus on local tradition and to privilege informal networks, whereas fundamentalist groups aim to purify Islam from local practices, often coalescing around clerics. Islamist groups, in turn, emerged from a critique of fundamentalism. As Sadowski summarized,

the Islamists, with their cosmopolitan backgrounds, introduced various tools they had borrowed from the West into their organizational arsenal. Ideologically, they drew on anti-modernist philosophies that embodied Western dissatisfaction with the consequences of industrialization and positivism: Spengler, Althusser, and Feyerabend supplied some of their favorite texts. They rearticulated Islam as a modern ideology in which

---

[9] The presence of American military forces for combat operations on homeland territory has a stronger explanatory capacity than does (Salafi) Islamic fundamentalism (Pape 2005: 103).

control of a totalistic Islamic state would permit the transformation of society in a manner that promoted not only piety but progress. Recruiting from the same intellectual groups through which Marxism penetrated the Muslim world – and often doing jail time in the same prisons as persecuted communists – they quickly learned the advantages of organizing into parties of disciplined cadres, organized into discrete cells, that could work to lay the foundations for revolution among wider groups. (2006: 221–2)

Conflicts between but also within these different versions of Islamism heavily influenced the evolution of Islamist clandestine organizations, in a context of increasing competition inside the Muslim world. Again according to Sadowski, "relations between Muslim communities have grown dramatically worse since the 1990s. Neo-fundamentalist groups such as the Salafis [Wahhabis who reject the authority of the traditional Saudi clerics] in Algeria and Syria, the Taliban in Afghanistan, the Jama'at-i Ulema-i Islam in Pakistan, and the Jaysh-i Muhammad in Kashmir are strikingly less tolerant than older Islamic movements" (2006: 228). In part a reaction to the increasing relevance of Shias in Iran and in Lebanon (through the Hezbollah), some Sunni Salafi groups have even denied that Shias belong to Islam, attacking Shia minority groups in Pakistan and Afghanistan, as well as the Iraqi security forces, which are dominated by Shia Muslims. In 2005, for instance, in the document "Why Do We Fight and Whom Do We Fight," the Islamic legal committee of AQ in Iraq stated that they wanted to "restore their rightly guided caliphate" and "reject rule by the Shia ... who have betrayed Muslims" (quoted in Hafez 2007: 73).

In fact, contextualized analyses of specific cases of radicalization during cycles of protest in the Middle East point at the importance, during cycles of protest, of internal competition between social movements and social movement organizations, often featuring interactions and competition among class, nationalist, and religiously oriented narratives. In the remainder of this chapter, I reconstruct the role of competitive escalation during cycles of protest in this type of political violence, referring especially to the work of Stefan Malthaner (2011) on Islamic groups in Egypt, Jeroen Gunning (2007) and Eitan Alimi (2011) on Palestine, and Thomas Hegghammer (2010) on the jihad in Saudi Arabia.

Competitive Escalation in Egypt

Founded at the end of the 1970s, the Egyptian radical groups al-Jamaa al-Islamiyya (the Islamic Group) and Tanzim al-Jihad (Jihad Organization) have grown inside a broader Islamist movement that – as Malthaner wrote (2011: 25) – radicalized in the political confrontations during the government of Anwar al-Sadat. Especially after the food riots in 1977, repression became particularly intense, affecting all members of the opposition, and culminating in 1981 (Esposito 2002: 88–9). Although both belonged to the radical Islamist wing, these two organizations differed from and competed with each other, investing much energy into internal fighting. Al-Jihad developed as a small and secret group; al-Jamaa al-Islamiyya, in contrast, was a large organization with a double organizational structure, including a grassroots level. After forming an alliance in the assassination of President Sadat in 1981, both groups suffered the heavy repression that followed but then reemerged during a wave of (also violent) protests in 1988 and 1989. Although violence initially took the form of clashes with the police, it radicalized in 1991, with attacks against police officers, politicians, intellectuals, Copts, and tourists. Whereas al-Jamaa participated in the protests, eventually being defeated by the Egyptian security forces, until its unilateral disbanding in 1998, al-Jihad was responsible for a few attacks between 1992 and 1993 but then renounced action in Egypt, instead joining the al-Qaeda network (Malthaner 2011).

The history of both groups can only be understood if we take into account their development within, and later competition with, the Muslim Brotherhood (MB) during broader waves of protest. Founded in 1928, the MB initially focused on educational and charitable activities at the local level as a way to form pious Muslims who could then create a new Islamic nation. Politicization evolved during confrontations with the Egyptian authorities but initially addressed topics such as opposition to the influence of foreign powers – in particular of Great Britain (which, even after Egypt became an independent state in 1936, still had troops on the Suez Canal) – as well as arguments against the Israeli state.

The later evolution of the MB was determined by competition with nonreligious nationalists. After some cooperation with President Nasser's government, which came to power after a coup d'état in 1952, strong tensions emerged, leading to repression and ensuing radicalization two years later. Islamists reorganized in the beginning of the 1970s, especially within the university system, which had been expanded by Nasser. Whereas left-wing and nationalist groups had been dominant in the late 1960s, addressing in particular social and economic issues, Islamic student groups initially focused on religious activities and then slowly extended their concerns to address political questions. Thus, in an interview with Stefan Malthaner, a student activist described this process as follows:

I think, first, the activity was mainly religious activity and did not focus on some political demand or quest. But through the activity increased the interest in political issues. [...] And the political issues then increased over time and it is also a symbol for the whole group, it is the disaster of 1967, this big defeat in the history of Egypt, that made up our minds that we are going in the wrong direction and we must have a new start and bring back the Islamic traditions. [...] But as students we were part of a big movement. [...] There was a big return at that time to Islamic prayers, Islamic regulations. (2011: 57)

The Islamist students thus came to perceive themselves as the vanguard of a broader movement, or a broad Islamic awakening: "They identified with the Muslim population and emphasized their strong bonds with their families, who approved of Islamic traditions and supported their struggle, rejecting notions of self-separation or challenging their parents' values 'because our religion makes this harmony in our life between what is right for a family and what is right for a person'" (ibid.: 61).

The Islamic student groups expanded rapidly: by the mid-1970s their several thousand members were distributed among all of the main universities (Kepel 1985: 144, cited in Malthaner 2011). Initially concerned mainly with providing services (such as lectures and teaching materials, or even clothes), they then started to put pressure on the administration to prohibit what they considered as anti-Islamic activities (such as concerts) (Malthaner 2011: 66–7). On these issues they even engaged in physical fights with other students and the university administration, as well as Sadat's government.

By the late 1970s the conflict had quickly escalated, involving different organizations and factions that then split over their reactions to state repression. In fact,

the Islamists rejected Sadat's policy of economic openness towards the West, and when the president began direct negotiations with Israel in 1979 and offered refuge to Shah Pahlavi after the Islamic revolution in Iran, campuses were blocked in protest and students clashed with the police. In reaction, police arrested numerous Islamic activists, the national student union was dissolved, and student activity was severely restricted. (Malthaner 2011: 62)

Whereas in Cairo and Northern Egypt some groups chose more moderate forms and claims, in Upper Egypt others – who later formed al-Jamaa al-Islamiyya – thought that an Islamist society had to be reached through a violent jihad that included attacks on property.

Radicalization in Egypt spiraled in 1981, after violence erupted in Cairo in June, followed by repression (including 1,500 arrests and the dissolution of thirteen organizations) and the assassination of President Sadat in October by a member of al-Jihad, the brother of an arrested al-Jamaa activist. In the following wave of repression under the presidency of Hosni Mubarak, most radical Islamist leaders were arrested, and four of them were executed, while the moderate Muslim Brothers wing grew under the unfavorable economic conditions determined by the declining oil price, which increased unemployment among university graduates and brought many migrants back from the Gulf states (Malthaner 2011: 73). While the moderate Islamist movement expanded,

the Muslim Brotherhood, reinvigorated by the influx of former student activists, became the most important oppositional political force, took over the leadership of most pro- fessional associations, and began to forge a coalition with other oppositional parties, such as the Labor Party. On the local level, a broad spectrum of religious associations spread "the call" and provided social services. Large Islamic charitable organizations operated hospitals and schools and, together with Islamic economic enterprises, formed a "parallel Islamic sector" rivaling or replacing the state as a provider of public services. (ibid.: 105)

In the competition with nationalist and communist organizations, the Islamists could exploit the increasing religiosity that was seen in the broader public, providing a basis of support for the activists. As Malthaner noted,

the militant Islamist groups emerged as the violent offspring, or the radical fringe, of a broader, oppositional but nonviolent, Islamist movement, and the Muslim Brotherhood and other (non-violent) Islamist groups remained al-Jamaa's main competitors. The conflict between the broader Islamist movement and the Egyptian state not only formed the origin of the militant groups, but also part of the environment within which they operated.... Protests, demonstrations, mass arrests, and police crackdowns were a regular occurrence in the late 1970s as well as during the 1980s. (2011: 115)

In the words of one of his interviewees,

there was already a change on the religious level of the people here, as many women wore the scarf, and many frequented the mosque to do their prayers. And also because of the harsh atmosphere of living, because of the rise of prices, the people found no shelter to protect them from the hard life but to get closer to God. [...] And they admired their bravery to voice something that the government doesn't want. (ibid.: 132)

In radical Islam, internal competition favored fractionalism. In fact,

the alliance between al-Jamaa al-Islamiyya and al-Jihad, forged to kill Sadat, collapsed after the arrests of 1981. The two groups split over an argument about leadership as well as over strategic issues and re-organized separately. Al-Jamaa al-Islamiyya re-emerged in the mid-1980s as an open movement on the local level, but confrontations escalated into a nation-wide conflict in the 1990s. Al-Jihad, on the other hand, after re-organizing abroad, planned to attack targets in Egypt. After their failure, they gradually joined the global terrorist project of al-Qaeda. (Malthaner 2011: 74–5)

In the mid-1980s, al-Jamaa created networks among small groups active in universities and neighborhoods, becoming gradually more centralized and developing a functional differentiation with separate branches, for example, one branch for open political work and proselytism, one for logistics and media, and one for military operations. Leadership was in the hands of al-Jamaa's "governing council" (*maglis alshura*), which comprised about 8–10 people and was until 1993 allegedly headed by Omar Adel Rahman, a blind al-Azhar sheikh who was also the group's "spiritual guide" (Malthaner 2011: 70). Gradually, however, decision making moved toward the military command, while the political leader was in exile. In the mid-1990s, a new wave of repression brought about a new decentralization.

As for al-Jihad, it increasingly went underground. In 1987 in particular, after an imprisoned leader failed in his attempt to relaunch the group, Ayman al-Zawahiri, who had been arrested and then released, founded a group called al-Jihad Organization. Based partly in Egypt and partly abroad, it recruited the remaining members of al-Jihad as well as some Egyptian Islamists in Peshawar and in training camps in Afghanistan and, together with Sayyed Imam, founded a new organization (Tanzim al-Jihad). In 1986, al-Zawahiri "came into contact with Usama bin Laden, and it was from their base in Afghanistan that al-Jihad began to establish a branch in Cairo" (Malthaner 2011: 74). Al-Jihad and al-Jamaa al-Islamiyya cooperated but also competed with each other:

Initially, the relationship between al-Jamaa al-Islamiyya and al-Jihad in Afghanistan was friendly, but became strained, not only due to personal animosities but also because of political and strategic differences, particularly in regard to their approach to the Muslim population. According to a former al-Jamaa leader who spent several years in Pakistan and Afghanistan in the early 1990s, his group regarded al-Jihad as isolated from the people and as "cowards," because they were reluctant to engage in a confrontation with the Egyptian government. At the same time, Zawahiri's group regarded al-Jamaa as "naive students" and accused them of rushing into confrontations with the Egyptian government without proper planning and thus "wasting" many of their young members in a hopeless war against a superior enemy. Al-Jihad, in contrast, favored an approach concentrating on carefully educating and training their members and forming a base of committed cadres. Al-Jihad's strategy of secretly preparing a coup d'etat – while refraining from direct involvement with the "masses" – certainly indicated a certain detachment from their constituencies and mistrust in popular support ("realism," in their words). In spite of that, it seems improbable that they considered the Muslim population unbelievers. (ibid.: 75)

The conflicts escalated again in the second half of the 1980s, after members of al-Jamaa al-Islamiyya were released from prison and mobilized again for the implementation of the sharia in an Islamic state, violently clashing with police (Malthaner 2011). In 1988, police interventions against mosques and Islamists produced a wave of riots in Ayn Shams, resulting in five people killed and hundreds wounded in August, the assassination of a policeman in December, and further rioting, deaths of activists, arrests, alleged torture of prisoners, and a curfew, which further polarized and radicalized the residents. These developments increased support for the organized Islamists, as the conflicts started to be perceived as an attack against the community.

In 1990, the assassination of the speaker of parliament followed the death of an al-Jamaa leader, triggering a wave of massive violence that lasted for eight years, along with attacks against policemen, government officials, and intellectuals. At the same time, sectarian tensions between Christian and Muslim communities increased, leading to spirals of reciprocal (physical and symbolic) attacks (Malthaner 2011: 113–14). Also in the 1990s, repression interacted with competitive escalation, as it increased support for (even violent) resistance to what was perceived as unjust behavior by the authorities.

Competitive Escalation in Palestine

Competitive escalation within and without the Islamist movement family can also be seen in the radicalization process in the Palestinian case, especially in the Gaza Strip and the West Bank. As in the aforementioned cases, competitive escalation in this region developed within broader waves of protest, which in their expansive moments gave birth to new groups but also triggered increasing competition in the low ebb of mobilization. Groups were created and split over the best strategy to use to resist repression.

In Palestine, the life of the Muslim Brothers (MBs) has been rich in internal splits on strategic issues. Created in 1987–8, Hamas has its roots in the long history of the MBs, particularly their cooperation and, above all, competition with other social movement families (class based and nationalist), but also in the internal competition within the Islamist movement. Hamas was in fact created as the paramilitary wing of the Palestinian MBs, which in turn developed as a branch of the Egyptian MBs. Involved in military actions against Israel, which provided the training ground for some future Fatah leaders, the Palestinian Brothers were heavily hit by Nasser's repression in the 1950s and decided to renounce armed resistance. Although they were revitalized after the Israeli victory in the Six-Day War in 1967 and the ensuing discrediting of traditional pan-Arabic nationalism, the MB had to compete with the nationalist Fatah and its capacity to mobilize the Palestinian diaspora and other Arabic countries' support, as well as with the nationalist- and Marxist-nationalist-dominated Palestine Liberation Organization (PLO) after 1969 (Gunning 2007: 29). In the 1980s, "the [right-wing party] Likud's decapitation policy … had resulted in the removal of the older PLO cadres, enabling a younger, more militant leadership to emerge, many of whom had been radicalised by the clashes between the nationalists and the Israeli army in the late 1970s and 1980s, and by their time spent in Israel (ibid.: 35–6). Nationalists and Islamists also competed with the revival of the Communist Party, which was favored by changing social conditions.

In this competitive environment, in the early 1970s the MBs in Palestine found their niche in charity activities. According to Gunning, "that the Brotherhood re-emerged as a modest charitable network, rather than a political faction, was a function of its relative weakness vis-à-vis the nationalists. Islamism was only just beginning to regain ground regionally" (2007: 30). As in Egypt, however, the massive enrollment of Palestinian students in Egyptian universities represented a turning point that overlapped with the oil price increase and related support for Islamist groups. In a climate of broader revival of religiosity, the MBs in Palestine also successfully competed with nationalists and communists for the control of professional, labor, and student unions, exploiting their higher appeals to the large percent of the student population coming from lower-class origins, small villages, and refugee camps, as well as discontent with Fatah's acceptance of a two-state option (ibid.: 33). In Gunning's account, "the Brotherhood, with its insistence on a one-state solution, a return to Islam and on meeting people's local social and communal needs, could capitalise on this discontent" (ibid.: 33). The repression of nationalist activists and the conflicts between the PLO and Jordan also gave a competitive advantage to the MBs, who had chosen a low profile in terms of repertoires of contention.

Internal competition in a very dense social movement sector also contributes to the explanation of the radicalization of the MBs, and the creation of Hamas as a semimilitary branch in 1987. Hamas emerged, in fact, from splits within the Palestinian Muslim Brotherhood (Gunning 2007), caused by long-lasting debates and fights among the various factions.

The economic recession of the early 1980s and the related frustration of the hopes of an increasingly educated population combined with the escalation of violent fights between PLO factions and the MB activists in the universities to increase internal demands for more radical actions within the Brotherhood. New generations of activists, radicalized by the Israeli "iron fist" repression in 1982 and 1985 in particular, replaced the old leadership in both the PLO and the MB and led the intifada after 1987 (Gunning 2007: 36). The MBs had already been challenged by the division of the group Islamic Jihad in the early 1980s, by a broader process of politicization and increasing support for armed struggle after the PLO's defeat in Lebanon, and by the development of an Islamist nationalism that had involved parts of the MB's membership (ibid.: 36–7). By the mid-1980s, this had brought about the construction of military cells inside the MBs.

After its creation, Hamas participated in the MB's internal struggles between the moderate leadership and the more radical younger component, pushing for not only more radical means but also a greater focus on Palestinian nationalism. As Gunning observed, "the establishment of Hamas had a profound impact on the evolution of the Islamic movement as a whole. Within years, Hamas had eclipsed the Muslim Brotherhood as the central Islamist political actor" (2007: 39), recruiting among those who were disappointed by Fatah's support for the peace process. Its increasing and increasingly heterogeneous membership, as well as growing repression, brought about an organizational restructuring. With the formation of the military Qassam Brigades, legal (social and political) activities were separated from activities focused on resistance, which were controlled by the (more radical) external leadership. The Qassam Brigades promised revenge through suicide bombings for the Hebron massacre, that is, the killing of twenty-nine Muslims in the Mosque of the Patriarch by a Jewish settler in 1994 (Esposito 2011: 142).

Competition within the religious groups also interacted with the struggles within other components of the Palestinian social movement sector. In particular, Fatah and the PLO were often divided on the peace process and the recognition of Israel. The Rejectionist Front led by George Habash was a mid-1970s reaction to Fatah's moderation. In the 1980s, grassroots groupings spread in the occupied territories, resisting Fatah's externally based attempts at control. Later on, "the Israeli authorities played a role in heightening the violent potential among the organizations, a potential that was inherent within the ideologies contending for influence among the Palestinians of the occupied territories. The framework of constraints and restrictions imposed by the military authorities was, to a large extent, designed as a strategy of divide and conquer"

(Esposito 2011: 63). Attempts at coordination within the social movement sector – such as the National Guidance Committee, founded in 1983 as an alliance between nationalists and communists – were hit particularly hard by Israeli repression (ibid.). Competition between communists and nationalists strengthened in the 1980s, along with PLO penetration among the workers. In the declining phase of the first intifada, divisions took dramatic forms inside the Unified/Coordinated Command of the Uprising (UNCU), particularly with regard to the units specializing in military defense against attacks by settlers. Competition between the MB and the PLO increased in the late 1980s, as the MBs increasingly profiled themselves as political actors by attacking Yasser Arafat for his UN declaration renouncing terrorism.

Later, in the early 1990s, repression had the perverse effect of bringing about a rapprochement between Hamas and the left wing of the PLO; this reconciliation originated in part in the Israeli prisons. The creation of the Palestinian Authority, with its strong control over previously autonomous civil society organizations, made Hamas's affiliated charities more attractive, as they appeared more independent (from both national and Western support). The fact that, beginning in 1993, the Qassam Brigades resorted to bombings (including suicide bombings, which were later imitated by Fatah's Martyrs' Brigades) as a way to jeopardize the peace process should be seen in the context of competition with the moderate nationalists – as should the second intifada, which contributed to decreasing support for Fatah and a new growth of Hamas. Israeli repression, including the assassinations of Hamas's leaders and the mass funerals that followed, furthered popular support for the organization, as did the internal conflicts, corruption, and authoritarian leadership in Fatah (Esposito 2011: 50).

Fatah's Tanzim paramilitary force also emerged from competition inside a dense movement network. As Alimi noted,

despite profound deprivation, ample incentives for violent outbursts, and preexisting violent-prone ideology, Fatah-Tanzim members' adoption of violent tactics was not a mere expression of the armed-struggle approach inspired by Hezbollah's mode of struggle, but rather a gradual development that took place in the context of an escalating action-counteraction dynamic with Israeli security forces and fierce competition for power among groups within the Palestinian movement. (2011: 97–8)

In fact, Tanzim's development in 1995 followed the creation of the Fatah-led Palestinian Authority and the increasing dissatisfaction of local activists with the takeover of power by Tunisian PLO leaders. The people's tense and ambivalent relations with Arafat can be explained by the attempts by the PLO leader to counterbalance the growing influence of religious Hamas with a radical but secular organization. A few years later, however, the Tanzim cooperated with Hamas in the riots on 15 May 2000 and then in the second intifada, among other actions (ibid.: 103).

Later, Hamas would also enter into competition with AQ. In January 2006, al-Zawahiri criticized Hamas's participation in the Palestinian Legislative Council elections:

The leadership of the Hamas movement has trampled on the rights of the Muslim *ummah* [community] by accepting what it calls – in a mockery of the intelligence and feelings of the Muslims – respect for international accords. It is with regret that I confront the Muslim *ummah* with the truth, and tell it: my condolences to you over the loss of the leadership of Hamas, for it has sunk in the swamp of surrender. (cited in Cragin 2007: 5)

Hamas responded by accusing al-Qaeda of indiscriminate attacks against innocent Muslims, stating,

the [Muslim] people loved al-Qaida because it declared war on the American enemy who supports the occupation of Palestine and is the occupier of Iraq and Afghanistan; however this love was taken out of people's chest when they hit the innocent. The victims of the Amman wedding and their families, of who we see and console them even today, are proof of the blind use of weapons which tainted al-Zawahiri and his group. (ibid.)

Competitive Escalation in Saudi Arabia

Saudi Arabia played an important role in the development of the recent wave of Islamist political violence, not only because of the attacks performed in the country but also because of the large number of Saudis who went to fight in Afghanistan and then joined al-Qaeda. Violent pan-Islamism has motivated many of the terrorist attacks in the country (in contrast to Egypt, where violence developed within a state-oriented sociorevolutionary Islam). According to Hegghammer's careful reconstruction, however (2010: 6), this is only one type of Islamic activism, which in Saudi Arabia took mainly nonviolent forms, including the state-oriented reformism of Sahwa, the *ummah*-oriented soft Islamism of the World Muslim League, and the morality-oriented pietism of al-Jama'a al-Salafiyya al-Muhtasiba (JSM). Locating AQ in a broader social movement family, in his periodization Hegghammer singles out three phases in the development of Islamism: the first phase (in the 1980s and first half of the 1990s) was characterized by a classical jihadist movement involved in national liberation struggles in Afghanistan, Bosnia, and Chechnya; the second phase (from the mid-1990s to 2001) saw the emergence of a more radical global jihad, featuring strong anti-Americanism and use of terrorism at the international level; and the third phase (2001–6) occurred when AQAP (al-Qaeda in the Arabian Peninsula) targeted the American presence in the country.

In the first phase, pan-Islamism was encouraged by the state in terms of both economic support and direct participation in distant conflicts. Thousands of Saudis "put their life at risk for people they had never met and for territories they could barely put on a map" to express pan-Islamic solidarity with Muslims in need (Hegghammer 2010: 16). The Saudi King Faisal had revived the pan-Islamic call, in part as a way to distract public opinion from domestic claims, promoting the emergence of the Mecca-based Muslim World League (MWL) in 1962 and the Organization of the Islamic Conference (OIC) some ten years later. The MWL, bolstered by heavy support from the state and a strong presence of Egyptian and Syrian MB members who had fled their countries to avoid repression, was involved in cultural and charity activities, nurturing in the 1980s a populist pan-Islamist movement for rank-and-file support to suffering Muslims all around the world.

Politicization followed, however, especially on the Palestinian cause, as "apolitical issues gave way to politically grounded suffering such as war, oppression and discrimination" (Hegghammer 2010: 19). Security issues became central. In the 1980s, with America's blessing, state support for pan-Islamism (particularly in Afghanistan) multiplied; at the same time, the oil crisis hit Saudi Arabia, jeopardizing the king's promises to grant employment to the growing student population. Internal opposition increased, nevertheless, especially within the moderate Islamist movement, when King Fahd allowed US intervention in the Holy Land after Saddam Hussein's invasion of Kuwait. As in Afghanistan, the conflict in Bosnia, where Islamists were no longer welcome, further contributed to the radicalization of the internal opposition, affecting not only the Saudis who went to fight those distant wars but also many of those who remained.

The radical global jihad developed in this climate, fueled by governmental repression of the moderate Islamist opposition and returning Saudi fighters in the mid-1990s. As Hegghammer recalls, "while it never turned violent, the Sahwa articulates a more explicit and biting critique of the Saudi system than the regime was willing to tolerate" (2010: 70). The repression that followed helped convince the activists of the need for violence and pushed remaining opponents into clandestinity. It is not by chance that a first terrorist attack in 1994 targeted a police interrogator and alleged torturer. The perpetrator, a former Afghan fighter, was criticized by other violent groups, but his death in prison produced a wave of outrage in the Islamist community and was avenged in 1995 by a car bomb in Riyadh killing seven people (among them five Americans) and a year later by a bombing at a US Air Force barracks (during which 19 people died and about 400 were wounded) (ibid.: 72). Different groups were responsible for the two attacks. Arrests (of about 2,000 people) and torture followed between 1996 and 1998, resulting in a further radicalization.

After the 9/11 attacks in 2001, the al-Qaeda branch in Saudi Arabia was strengthened by the revived pan-Islamism that followed the US-led wars on Afghanistan in the same year and on Iraq a few years later, as well as what was perceived as Muslim suffering in the Guantanamo prison, or in the Jenin's massacre in Palestine. Mass demonstrations testified to these sentiments.

Because it was linked to these waves of protest in Arabic nations, the evolution of al-Qaeda was also torn by internal conflicts. At its foundation, al-Qaeda was ideologically divided, with the Egyptians proposing a social-revolutionary discourse and others pursuing a classical jihad strategy against the infidel invaders. As we will see in Chapter 5, al-Qaeda in fact developed from the

service offices (*maktab al-khidamat*) that organized the fundraising, recruitment, and training of Arab support to the Afghan resistance against Soviet
occupation. Toward the end of the occupation, division emerged within the
maktab on the future activities of the Islamist volunteer network. Seeing as it was
closed to the Jordan MBs, "Azzam wanted the network activists – Mujahedeen –
to operate as an Islamic 'rapid reaction force,' available to intervene wherever
Muslims were perceived to be threatened," whereas bin Laden, who was influenced by the Egyptian Islamic Jihad, believed that the al-Qaeda activists should
"dispatch to their home countries to try to topple secular, pro-Western Arab
leaders, such as President Hosni Mubarak of Egypt and Saudi Arabia's royal
family" (Katzman 2005: 2). The internal struggle led to the exclusion of Azzam
from al-Qaeda in 1988 and, later on, to his assassination in November 1989
(Alimi 2011: 104). Whereas Abdullah Yusuf Azzam was focused on construct-
ing an Islamist state in Afghanistan and keeping AQ as an organized force for
quick intervention, bin Laden aimed at the creation of centralized and secret
organizations to bring about global jihad. Even though AQ's declaration of war
on the far enemy temporarily placated the internal conflicts, the tensions
between those who wanted to target the far enemy through global jihad and
those who, instead, targeted the near enemy via local aims remained a central
source of tension.

Within the broader Salafi community, which advocated return to the purity of
original religious practices, al-Qaeda had to fight with those who opposed
waging war against Muslim rulers and attacking Muslim people. Quintan
Wiktorowicz (2004) has described the intramovement framing struggle among
members of AQ over the permissibility of certain forms of violence. Although
there was little criticism about the need to support Muslims who suffered in
Afghanistan, Bosnia, or Palestine,

> this consensus, however, began to erode as "Arab Afghans" returned from the front and
> organized violence in their home states. Salafi Jihadis continued to support the use of
> violence while "reformists" emphasized the necessity of individual spiritual transformation,
> propagation, and advice to the rulers and umma (Muslim community). During the 1980s
> and 1990s as al-Qaeda developed, the initial debate between violent and non-violent salafis
> was over *takfir* – declaring a Muslim an apostate. (ibid.: 160)

Whereas the nonviolent groups stated that it was not possible to declare a ruler
apostata without knowing his beliefs, AQ preachers stated that one could
declare a ruler an apostate based on his actions. Later, a discursive struggle
developed on the means that should be used in the global jihad, with some Salafis
supporting a violent solution and others focusing instead on reform. In fact, to
persuade the Muslim population, AQ invested resources and energies into
framing its message by vilifying the popular intellectuals, especially religious
scholars, who supported the moderate position: they challenged their credibility,
accusing them of being not only emotional and ill-informed but also "the
scholars of power," "palace lackeys," and "corrupt *ulamas*" (ibid.: 171).

COMPETITIVE ESCALATION: CONCLUSIONS

Explanations of clandestine political violence have often looked at structural causes, considering the economic, social, political, and cultural conditions that are more conducive to radicalization and addressing both deeply rooted causes and contingent precipitating events. Attempts to formulate a general explanation for political violence have been frustrated, however, by the challenges created by the differences among phenomena considered as forms of political violence – and, therefore, by the risk of conceptual stretching. At the same time, evidence of multiple paths of causation, with clandestine political violence developing under very different social and political conditions, pushes toward more attention to processes rather than (only) causes, and agency rather than (just) structures.

I have considered the embedding of political violence within broader social and political conflicts as an important contribution from social movement studies to the understanding of the causes of violence. In particular, in this chapter, I have referred to the concept of the protest cycle as a main analytical contribution to the understanding of political violence. I have suggested that political violence has to be understood as one of the outcomes of intense interactions developing during moments of heightened conflict. The concept of cycles of protest also allows us to see the multiplicity of actors and forms of action at work in these moments.

According to Tarrow's theorization, which built on the analysis of the Italian case, different forms of violence were linked to different stages in the cycle. Further research in part confirmed the general value of those observations but also pointed at cases in which cycles of protest had not produced violence. Although more systematic research is necessary to identify when protest cycles end in radicalization and when they do not, my aim in this chapter has been to contribute to answering the question from the point of view of the operation of a specific mechanism of radicalization: competitive escalation. Even though I do not mean to suggest that competitive escalation operated as the unique trigger of clandestine political violence, I would nevertheless stress that, in all of the four very different cases, competition between and within social movement families contributed to escalation of the repertoires of contention.

In the Italian case, competition between social movement families mainly involved left-wing movements and right-wing countermovements, which revived long-lasting hostilities and built on a tradition of harsh conflicts. Within both social movement families, on the left as well as on the right, radical movements also grew in competition with the existing Old Left and neofascist traditions, respectively. Multiple conflicts – and readings of such conflicts – were also present in the Basque countries. There, nationalist and class narratives grew within atmospheres of reciprocal tension, with cooperation but also competition. The brutal repression of Franco's dictatorship and the slow and uncertain pace of the democratization process also contributed to debates and divisions over the best action strategies. Cleavages existed, within both the left-libertarian and nationalist social movement families. In the Middle East, nationalist and class- and religious-oriented movements competed within a broader opposition, with some general trends and events favoring the religious groups. The religious awakening, together with some moments of regime liberalization, contributed to the strengthening of the traditional MBs, but also of more radical groups, which often emerged from criticism of the MB's moderation. In Egypt and Saudi Arabia, authoritarian regimes contributed to competitive escalation, as did the Israeli occupying forces in Palestine.

Whereas the protest cycles intensified the production of social movement organizations, the radicalization of repertoires of action was, in some moments, a competitive asset in intermovement relations. Even within the same social movement family, however, different organizations competed for followers, adopting different frames and repertoires of action. In organizationally dense environments, different groups specialized in different tactics, but they also influenced one another, using processes of imitation and outbidding.

During protest cycles, practices of violence developed in moments of intense relations, and activists were socialized to these practices. Many social movement activists had participated in proletarian expropriations, armed marches, car burning, and break-ins or intifadas even before they entered clandestine organizations. In fact, through emergent processes during periods of "thickened history" (Beissinger 2002), violence emerges from violence.

The most radical tactics spread from one organization to the next, especially during periods of intense repression, with an ensuing increase in community solidarity. Escalation was helped, as Tarrow (1989) has observed, by the contemporary institutionalization of large parts of the movements that gave momentum to the ascending phase of the cycle. After becoming disillusioned by insufficient results or being co-opted into institutional politics, many activists left the protest scene, where, as a result, the radical fringes acquired increasing visibility and prominence.

4

The Activation of Militant Networks

ACTIVATION OF MILITANT NETWORKS: AN INTRODUCTION

Born in the "red" city of Reggio Emilia in 1950, Prospero Gallinari was one of the founders of the Red Brigades in 1970. The son of a peasant, he grew up in a family and community in which resistance against fascism and left-wing political activism was deeply rooted. In his autobiography, he remembers the relevance, in his adolescence, of the "old communists I had the good luck to meet. All people, neighbours or relatives, most of which had been partisans.... They were product of the resistance" (Gallinari 2006: 13). In this strongly politicized "red territorial culture" of the 1950s, his political career started when he was still in his early teens. He recalls:

I was twelve and, following the habits of the time, I started as a pioneer. I sold the "Milione," the little journal of the very young activists of the PCI, to then move up to distribute the "Unità" [the party daily]. I had just finished primary school when I started to meet with comrades, not just as friends or neighbours, but also as people I met at the party section or the Casa del Popolo. (ibid.: 14)

Socialization to left-wing values therefore happened during his childhood, especially while listening to his grandfather's tales not only of the antifascist struggle but also of rebellion as an expression of human dignity. He wrote in fact of his "family path" to politics, which began when he was just six years old, listening to stories of life experiences in 1919–20, "when the fascists started to become aggressive" (ibid.: 20–1), and also of the workers' struggles. The rebellious history of the red Reggio Emilia in fact plays a central role in Gallinari's narrative: it is a story of peasants' struggles, the building of workers' cooperatives, first experiences with socialism at the beginning of the twentieth century, and factories "occupied in 1920 by the workers under the motto 'Ag vol Lenin!' (We need Lenin), with the aim of creating a Soviet inside the factory" (ibid.: 25). The history of Reggio Emilia is therefore a history of contentious confrontation with the state in which the entire community participated.

The heavy repression of the labor movement – in particular, the five workers who were killed by the police during a peaceful demonstration in July 1960, making Reggio Emilia an important symbol of working-class resistance – is part of the direct experience of nine-year-old Prospero, who remembered,

That afternoon, I was in the fields ... when I saw several men and women nearing a big old nut tree.... It was a machinegun bullet that had penetrated the roots of the nut tree ... it was only two or three kilometers away from the center of the city, where the march was going on, against which the police was shooting.... Granddad came home to bring news. He came from the city center, and there were already news of many dead and wounded people. He had been to the hospital to donate his blood. (ibid.: 28)

In his autobiography, Gallinari recalled the intense emotion he experienced when, as a young child, he attended the funerals of the killed workers:

It was not the first time I went into the street, but I had never seen so many people. The city was too small to host the mass of the demonstrators. And what surprised me even more than the quantity of the people, was seeing them crying.... An anger and a suffering that will remain with me, in my cultural baggage, together with the resistance, and its epic symbols, the life and death of the Cervi brothers. (ibid.: 29)

Antonio Savasta was born in 1956 in Rome. His father was a police officer, and his mother was a housewife of working-class origins. Although his mother's family was of the left-wing tradition and his grandfather was a socialist who had refused to become a member of the Fascist Nationalist Party, politics was not discussed at home – as his father was of the opinion that "politics is dirty" (Life History no. 27: 416). Politics did not play a role in his first socialization. At sixteen, Savasta had "a limited experience of life, a limited consciousness of life, but a great taste for rebellion" (ibid.: 409). In fact, his very first (and superficial) contact with politics, while still in primary school, was with an extreme Right group, Europa e Civiltà, with whom he practiced sport and went leafleting (ibid.: 421). After moving into a "red" neighborhood, Centocelle, he began to get involved in left-wing politics. This was mainly a result of his participation in the youth subculture of the time:

I'm very interested in music, have long hair, and friends in the libertarian world of the hippies.... Obviously, the sense of freedom, liberation, and rebellion were couched in pacifist terms.... Vis-a-vis the traditional world and culture there was also a direct clash on issues such as drugs.... Drugs, hashish, marijuana was liberation, feeling good, overcoming an oppressive normality. (ibid.: 423)

He defined himself as an anarchist, like his brother, and as "young, long hair, hippy, libertarian, for free love and free drugs" (ibid.: 424).

His political commitment increased with the occupation of his school, and he became directly involved in the extraparliamentary New Left, as he perceived the PCI as "another world," "because [of] the way I was at that time, the long hair, the drugs, even if light drugs, hashish." Therefore, Savasta recalls that when his activism started "it had nothing to do with the Italian Communist Party, the

FGCI. I felt closer instead to Potere Operaio, Lotta Continua, because they dressed like us, they talked about the same things, we met at the same concerts, they were much more determined" (Life History no. 27: 424).

In the radicalized context of the early 1970s, politics involved an immediate experience of violence in the street battles with radical Right activists. Savasta recalls that, in his neighborhood, "there was this thing of anti-fascism, very strong" (Life History no. 27). He writes of being "punched by these people, just because I had long hair" and of having identified them as those who wanted to negate freedom, not only politically but also culturally. In 1972, he became a member of the militant organization Potere Operaio and had to change his external appearance: "For the first time, I had to wear different clothes. Before, I went around with the Eskimo and with long hair, I went to the assemblies with leather jackets à la Elvis Presley, long hair and shoes with high heels, tight jeans. Instead, I was told to wear good clothes, in order to avoid being stopped and searched" (ibid.: 428).

These excerpts from two life histories testify to differences in family characteristics and political socialization. As we will see in this chapter, notwithstanding some commonalities, they represent diverse paths in the underground, which tend to overlap with two generations of militants.

Various narratives on individual motivations can be found in different areas of research on political violence. In recent debates on suicide bombers, once clinical disorders are excluded, opinions tend to diverge. Some scholars have pointed to how the careful choreography of suicidal missions strengthens solidarity (e.g., Moghaddam 2005); some stress a moral logic (Atran 2006). Others have emphasized a strategic point of view, given the success of suicide missions in the past (Pape 2005). Similarly, researchers of revolutions have alternatively looked at the participation of *aggrieved individuals*, who suffer from socioeconomic dislocation (e.g., Goldstone 1991); *opportunists*, who seek personal gains; and *idealists*, who are ideologically committed to the movements.

The various interpretations are, however, not mutually exclusive. The Report of Independent Experts at the European Commission stated that "one of the most significant understandings gained from academic research over the recent years is that individuals who have been involved in terrorist activities exhibit a diversity of social backgrounds, underwent rather different processes of violent radicalization and have been influenced by various combinations of motivations." According to this report,

One particular type of radicalisation process characterises ideological activists who play leading roles in terrorist cells.... These individuals are often resourceful, educated, well integrated and are sometimes even considered as role models in their communities.... Another variety tends to embrace violent forms of militancy through a combination of loyalty to the leader and political activism.... For some youths the experience of belonging to a group and being accepted by peers or leaders is of primary value, sometimes overruling most other considerations.... The search for community and group solidarity plays an important role in attracting them to these groups.... Socially or politically frustrated youngsters may go through quite different paths of radicalisation into militancy and terrorism. Usually they personally experience discrimination, unfair competition with other groups over scarce resources or an absence of prospects for a good future. For some this feeling of rejection from society turns them into bitter enemies of their host society to which they no longer experience any meaningful form of bond. (Expert Group on Violent Radicalisation 2008: 12–13)

In a similar vein, Jocelyn S. Viterna (2006) has singled out three paths of women's participation in guerrilla armies: the politicized guerrillas, the reluctant guerrillas, and the recruited guerrillas. These three types display different motivations, the first one being attracted by ideological commitment (those who "were pulled into guerrilla participation by their strongly held beliefs in the political cause" [ibid.: 20]), the second by a perceived lack of alternatives (those who "were pushed into the guerrilla camps because a crisis left them with no other options" [ibid.: 24]), and the third by a search for adventure or retribution.

The different motivations I have mentioned can be easily summarized in the language of social movement studies as referring to instrumental, ideological, or solidarity incentives. As Bert Klandermans aptly synthesized, "a demand for change begins with dissatisfactions" (2004: 362) and is therefore linked with instrumental reasoning. Instrumentality is, however, not the only motivation to join: solidarity incentives are linked to the pleasure provided by belonging to a valued group. A third, ideological motivation to participate is "wanting to express one's views" (ibid.: 365).

Having admitted to the presence of different paths, in this chapter, I am interested in going beyond a classification of individual motivations, linking micro, meso, and macro levels of analysis to reflect on the ways in which (1) the context (the macro level) and (2) the organizational structure (the meso level) influence the types of individuals who are recruited.

In looking at insurgencies, in what he calls a "micropolitics of rebellion," Jeremy M. Weinstein (2007) has combined these three levels within a rational choice approach. Criticizing the lack of attention to the organizational dimension in research on civil wars, he explains the different (degrees and types of) uses of violence against the civil population by insurgents on the basis of the resources available to them and their effects on organizational strategy and types of membership. He argues, in fact, that "groups commit high levels of abuse not because of ethnic hatred or because it benefits them strategically but instead because the membership renders group leaders unable to discipline and restrain the use of force – and membership is determined in important ways by the endowments leaders have at their disposal at the start of the rebellion" (ibid.: 20). The assumption is that in resource-rich contexts, insurgent organizations tend to attract greedy individuals who aim at short-term (material) rewards; at the same time, they do not need popular support. Vice versa, in resource-poor contexts, insurgent organizations tend to attract idealists (through long-term rewards); also, they need the support of the population.

Similarly, Viterna's research (2006) establishes links between the types of recruits, the mobilized networks, and the characteristics of the external context. She demonstrates in particular that politicized guerrilla fighters exhibit family ties as well as previous memberships in political organizations. Biographical availability (especially young age) and location in the rebellious camps are instead particularly relevant for the recruited guerrillas. Whereas politicized guerrillas are more relevant in the founding phase, recruited guerrillas tend to arrive later on.

In the same vein, I look first at the different paths of militants who joined the underground, singling out the mobilization of militant networks as a mechanism of radicalization in the formation of specific milieus, in which radical practices are accompanied by cognitive radicalization as well as the development of strong affective ties in small groupings of friends-comrades.

The use of the term "paths" points at what criminologists studying deviant behavior have seen as trajectories, composed of sequences of incremental transitions (Taylor and Horgan 2012: 133). It implies that "involvement decisions are characteristically multistage and extend over substantial periods of time" (ibid.: 136)

Motivations are linked to various types of militant networks as well as to the timing of recruitment. I note that, in the cases examined here, the founders are mainly ideologically driven and more likely to show personal links with a history of resistance. Once contextual radicalization increases, younger individuals tend to join through personal networks, which could be either predominantly political or communitarian.

Although some basic causal mechanisms are common to all paths, the dominant individual motivations are different, as are the types of networks that are mobilized, the speed of the process, and its dynamics. Polarized environments as well as violent entrepreneurs affect social movement activists through relational, cognitive, and emergent processes. In this chapter, I focus on the activation of militant networks that sustain high-risk activism.

Militant networks play a significant role at all stages of the political careers of those who have, at one time or another, ended up in clandestinity. As we shall see, in Italy and Germany in the 1970s, the activists' acceptance of violence grew along with their emotional investment in politics, and their emotional investment grew with their experience of violence. Similar mechanisms are identified in the Basque case, in which participation in the radical nationalist milieu was facilitated by family and friendship ties and then escalated in daily experiences of violent confrontations with the police and militia groups. The relevance of informal religious networks has been stressed in various cases, from (Christian) antiabortion terrorism in the United States to Islamic fundamentalism (Juergensmeyer 2000).

Networks nevertheless varied, and their variety had relevant consequences at the meso and macro levels. In the incipit of this chapter I have illustrated two paths that, respectively, represent two generations of Italian left-wing radicals.[1] In the remainder of this chapter, we will see that both paths are present in all the different forms of clandestine violence, in different balances during different periods.

ACTIVATION OF MILITANT NETWORKS IN LEFT-WING ORGANIZATIONS

Activists who ended up in armed struggle often came with a long history of political engagement. For the Italian left-wing militants, in at least 843 cases of 1,214, those who decided to join an underground group had at least one friend who was also a member; moreover, in 74 percent of these cases, the new recruit had more than one friend, and in 42 percent more than seven (della Porta 1988: 158). These networks were made up not only of friends but also of fellow comrades. In Italy, of more than 1,000 militants analyzed, 38 percent had been involved in the New Left – especially in two radical groups, the Potere Operaio (Worker's Power) and the Lotta Continua (Continuous Struggle) – and as many as 84 percent in the small groups of the *autonomia* (ibid.: 161–2).

There were, nevertheless, different networks for different generations. In Italy, the paths of the founders of the BR show several similarities to that of Prospero Gallinari. A similar story of continuity with family tradition is told by Alberto Franceschini, another founder of the Red Brigades, who is also from Reggio Emilia. As he recalled, his grandfather was the son of poor, landless peasants. Originally an anarcho-syndicalist, he then became a socialist and, in 1921, at the Congress in Livorno, was among the founders of the Communist Party of Italy. During the fascist regime, he had been tried by the special tribunal for political crimes, sentenced, and sent into confinement on Ponza Island with other opposition leaders, including the future president of the Italian Republic Sandro Pertini. He remained there for about seven years, until he was released after an amnesty and sent to confinement in Southern Italy. After the armistice he returned to Reggio Emilia, where he was hunted by the fascists of the Salò Repubblica (who had not recognized the armistice) and joined the resistance. After the liberation, he became the housekeeper of the Camera del Lavoro (the Chamber of Labour), where his son's family also went to live, with young Alberto. Alberto's father, a worker at the Reggiane and then an employee of the Camera del Lavoro, had also participated in the resistance with the Squadre di Azione Partigiana. Like Prospero, Francesco remembered his very early socialization to politics: "At five, six years old, I was already involved in politics, I have several memories, still untouched, on dad's shoulders, during the Reggiane struggles, the jeep police that charged the demonstrators, the marches, the speeches.... At that time there was no kindergarten, it was the section of

---

[1] A similar analysis is developed in Bosi and della Porta 2012.

the Party that took over those functions" (Alberto Franceschini, quoted in Fasanella and Franceschini 2004: 20). And, like Prospero, he took part in the July 1960 demonstration to protest the police killings: "I was thirteen years old. For me, it was the confirmation that my granddad was right, that all his discourses on the resistance were right.... I knew very well one of those young people who had been killed." It was, he recalled, the beginning of "a debate, due to last for at least a decade, and that was to bring several of us to the armed struggle" (ibid.: 23).

Also similar to those of Prospero Gallinari and Alberto Franceschini are the life histories of another five *reggiani* among the founders of the Red Brigades: Roberto Ognibene, Attilio Casaletti, Tonino Loris Parioli, Lauro Azzolini, and Franco Bonisoli were "almost all from Communist families and all critical of the Party" (ibid.: 7). Comparable, too, are the stories of activists from the Collettivo di Borgomanero, who also joined in the very early phases of the Red Brigades. One of them, Alfredo Buonavita, came from a peasant and communist family with ten children that had emigrated to Piedmont from southern Avellino. A member of the Federazione Giovani Comunisti Italiani (Italian Communist Youth Federation [FGCI]), he was expelled because of activities in a Collettivo Operai Studenti. He also recalled antifascism as "something very strong, here, for us *brigatisti* of that specific time, especially in this area" (Life History no. 5: 102) as well as "a physical, ideal, ethical" continuity with the partisans (ibid.: 93).[2]

For all these militants, their partisan legacy was fundamental to their motivations to continue the revolutionary struggle. Common to activists in this path is in particular the presence of deeply rooted family traditions that make the passage to armed struggle appear as a sort of normal evolution. This was particularly so in communities in which class conflict had been strong and frequent, thus raising the possibility of younger family members being influenced by older relatives who had previously participated in the resistance and being raised in local environments that nurtured those memories.

In Reggio Emilia, the mythical metalworkers of the Reggiane factory played a particularly central role; this conflict, as Gallinari recalled, "exploded again after July 1943 [the liberation from Nazi occupation], declaring a struggle against the war and hunger, and paying for this the price of nine workers killed, among which a pregnant woman. Workers were killed by machine guns during a march against fascism and calling to 'stop the war'" (2006: 25). This history – so rooted in the consciousness of the city that, as Gallinari recalled, he "learned it face-to-face, before reading about it in books" – continued with the struggle and the occupations of the 1950s, which saw about 1,000 arrests per year and 500 sentences in two years for political crimes. In Gallinari's memories, "those

---

[2] In some cases, men in the underground took the nickname that had been used by their fathers during the resistance against fascism (Galfré 2012). In addition, one of the first armed groups in the Italian Republic, the Gruppo XXII Ottobre, was funded in Genoa by former activists of the PCI and the FGCI who had felt the need to "do things" (Serafino 2012: 371).

struggles also expressed a true counter-power. In the occupied factory, the workers continued to work and the city mobilized around them" (ibid.: 27). In his grandfather's account, the peasants had supported those struggles with voluntary donations of their produce, distributed through the cooperatives to the workers involved in the struggle and their families.

Gallinari's narrative involves continuity with this territorial culture, and a slow detachment from the Communist Party to which he had belonged. In his role as a member of the local directive committee of the youth organ of the party, the FGCI, Gallinari, along with other young activists, came to disagree with the party, which he accuses of having "betrayed the ideals, betrayed the hopes, betrayed the efforts that had cost so much" (2006: 36). Influenced by the protests in 1968 and 1969, the critical young activists within the party rented an apartment to meet with others to discuss the turbulent times. The party reacted strongly to this, threatening to expel those who frequented the apartment; although some obeyed, "for many, it was simply the acknowledgment of something that, in their hearts and minds, had already happened: the break" (ibid.: 57). After being expelled from the party, the group of young rebellious communists founded the Collettivo Politico Operai Studenti and then sought contacts with "the revolutionary forces in the neuralgic centres of the social struggle" (ibid.: 62). Through a member of the student collective in Trento, they entered into contact with other future founders of the Red Brigades and with them founded the Collettivo Politico Metropolitano – later to become, through fissions and scissions, the Sinistra Proletaria – and decided to move to Milan, as "the central place of the struggle is the metropolis" (ibid.: 64). With other members of the group, Gallinari then founded the Red Brigades.

In the BR, this path was particularly widespread among the founders. In fact, the context in which the armed group emerged was characterized by the institutionalization of previously existing movement organizations, which triggered feelings of betrayal. Successive moments of heightened conflict were then perceived as signals of a potentially revolutionary situation that would allow for the redressing of past mistakes and return the movement to the purity of its beginning.

At the meso level, such groups indeed showed ideological and organizational continuities with the organizational culture their activists learned from inside. Not only did the Red Brigades imitate the bureaucratic centralism of the PCI, but their aims were also framed within the traditional discourse of a class struggle (see also Chapter 7). In terms of recruitment, this implied a conception of individual selection of the armed vanguard, usually with an extended period of ideological indoctrination and progression of the recruits through various steps in their involvement in violent actions.

In contrast, the life histories of the Italian militants of the second generation resemble that of Savasta, even though they more often ended up in one of the many clandestine groups founded in the second half of the 1970s, rather than in the BR. These militants had less (or less visible) continuity with a family history of left-wing activism, and in fact their encounters with politics happened later and in a less linear way than did the encounters of those in the previous paths. Political violence was legitimized less by reference to ideology or political strategies than by identification with radicalized activist milieus. Experiences with political violence often predated entrance into an armed organization, developing in a radicalized environment through street battles with neofascists and police.

Savasta recalled that, in the Potere Operaio, he started justifying violence as "an active defense against the fascists.... Those were the days of hunting the fascists. The marches started to be self-defended against the fascists. The first arm is the stick, which you could transform into a red flag" (Life History no. 27: 426). Violence was also justified by the international symbols and myths of Che Guevara and the Vietcong, as well as by state repression. But violence was experienced in particular through intense emotions: "I was in the fifth row of the marshal body that was facing the police, with a terrible fear ... I saw the first Molotovs being thrown ... there was the fight ... and then we ran with the police behind us" (ibid.: 427). In various parts of the interview, Savasta emphasizes the "big emotional charge, the desire for change, against the widespread moral" and speaks of the "intensity of the relationship, in the sense that we talked really about everything" (ibid.).

In this emotionally charged atmosphere, radicalization happened around a symbolic, occupied territory: the squatted houses in San Basilio, where a young activist was killed by a policeman in September 1974. This served not only as the symbol of a struggle "for one's own needs" but also as the arena of daily conflicts with the police and the marshal body of the PCI. Savasta presents it as a dramatic experience:

Three days of conflict with the police; I went out in the morning, went to fight, came back home to eat, went back in the afternoons, until the evenings. It was a sort of Londonderry, a battle made of Molotov cocktails and stones to conquer five metres of land, ten metres at the crossing ... all 'till a boy from the Collettivo dei Castelli was killed, and they killed him in front of me, while we were attacking a police post. The policeman was shooting, and this boy died, and I took it very badly, very badly. I came back from these fights in the evening and then, at night, there was this incredible shoot-out because ... we all came back, armed, and fought with the wrath of God, that is armed fights with the police, in fact there were policemen hurt by bullets. (Life History no. 27: 434)

The events gave new strength to the ongoing debate on the organization of violence and mass mobilization, a debate that, according to Savasta, involved a large number of activists: "When we took to the streets we had three or four hundred people, only with the Comitato comunista Centocelle; it was a big reality, that involved especially school kids, and some neighborhood kids, and discussed violence in extremely normal terms. So, until '76 I was involved in this type of discussion" (Life History no. 27: 435). In fact, criticism of the Red Brigades was especially linked to their clandestinity and therefore their distance from social struggles, more than their use of violent forms of action.

With the concrete failure of the attempt to combine armed struggle and mass mobilization, however, Savasta's fascination with the Red Brigades increased "because the Red Brigades, nobody knows what they are, one thinks it is an extremely compact organization" (Life History no. 27: 444). A small network of former Centocelle militants (among them Savasta's girlfriend, Emilia Libera) entered into contact with the BR through a fellow activist: "It stays in the family, it's all in the family, we talked with someone we had known since 1972" (ibid.: 446). After their recruitment, they formed a Centocelle brigade that continued to intervene in the neighborhood, although no longer to stimulate "mass struggles" but rather to "recruit a series of vanguard people in that situation" (ibid.: 449).

The choice of armed struggle thus emerges as a natural consequence of involvement in a radicalized community:

It is useless to joke, that it was possible to do other things, given the way in which things were, given the roles, the function of the parties and the function of the society. In those years, in that situation it was unavoidable for some people, a few or many as they were – it may be they were not so few after all – to take that route. (Life History no. 27: 447).

When he eventually entered the BR in 1976, Savasta thought that "the things we were doing were going to blossom in a true insurrection, or at least open guerrilla warfare" (ibid.: 448).

Savasta was recruited to the Red Brigades by Valerio Morucci, who – although older – shared a similar story. Born in Rome in 1949 into a nonpolitical family of artisans, Morucci encountered politics – lost his innocence, in his words – in the so-called battle of Valle Giulia in 1968, when the police charged students occupying the Roman universities and the students reacted. As Morucci recalls, "after 15 minutes of panic, one after the other, the kids move ahead, taking up stones and throwing them at the police. I did not think much, the gesture was known and they were hitting with their batons everywhere. And I threw ..." (Morucci 2004: 66). Repression and reactions to it accompanied Morucci's life as an activist in the Potere Operaio, and its marshal body:

They were hitting us badly, all the time. The government had chosen the hard line. A line which passed through the batons of the Celere [special public order police], tear gas shot at the people and through charges with trucks. Many died because of it. Tired of being hit, I was charged with doing something. In a short time, given the success of the Molotov cocktails and of the squads I had organized, I was charged with founding the illegal structure of Potere Operaio. (ibid.: 80–2 passim)

However, it was only in 1976 that Morucci joined the BR, after the failure of a series of attempts to bridge political and military action.

The community to be defended was the counterculture of the radical Left, in which political and friendship ties overlapped. Peer pressure stemmed from a milieu in which violence was accepted as a given. Militants there "have consumed the final phase of the groups and are more determined than those who were 18 years old in '68, who had a slower and more classical process of acquisition of a political culture, much more inherited from the traditional left, even if in a critical way, these are instead strange types, very peculiar ... an incredible difference" (Life History no. 29: 28–9).

The context in which this path spread was the product of the escalation of political fights, in which individuals were involved at a very young age. In the words of a militant,

the choice is there but it is not the choice as the people imagine the terrorist at the end of the 1970s, with the clandestine organization that challenges the state. The organization was inside the struggle, the aim was therefore not armed struggle per se, but to solicit a further step of determination or toughness in the social struggle ... until the Moro kidnapping I had no impression of political isolation. (Life History no. 29: 341)

Radicalization was, if not triggered, at least strengthened by the preexistence of an armed conflict. At the meso level, these types of activists often introduced some organizational and ideological innovations, as they tended to be not only younger but also less disciplined and less loyal to the ideological orthodoxy. Whereas their political socialization was not rooted in the family and therefore happened later, their mobilization toward armed struggle was quicker than that of the militants who followed the other path.

Socialization to violent politics in fact acquired a particular relevance for a second generation of activists who either joined the BR later or founded other underground organizations. One of the Italian left-wing militants of this second generation recalled the speed of his radicalization: "My first march was on October 1, 1977; in February 1978, I joined an autonomous collective; in April-May of that very year, I was already supporting [the clandestine group] Front Line" (quoted in Novelli and Tranfaglia 1988: 300).

Acceptance of violence tended to increase among later generations of social movement activists. A first-generation left-winger described this difference as follows: "All of us who had been politically active before, had a lot of difficulty with respect to the military action, to the very fact of carrying arms.... Those who had no prejudice at all were the younger ones, those who were 18 or 19 years old" (Life History no. 5: 65). A militant of the first generation described his uneasiness with the growing propensity of young activists toward violence. He recalled in fact that he had participated in several radical groups but often quit, as he thought they were too extreme. He exited a first group after they started to organize robberies. Of a second group, he said that he wanted "to do a work, also military yes, but linked to the masses ... but they started to make discourses more and more militaristic, and I again quit" (Life History no. 16: 201). In a third one, he was suspended after he opposed a plan for a kidnapping. Then,

1977 explodes and I call the boys and say, well, when there are the mass, we go and with the mass movements ... and we went, but I tried to calm them down, because there were these very young proletarians, they came with us. But after the first march, as they wanted to break everything, I said no, we break nothing here, we break only what needs to be broken, they have broken already even too much. (ibid.: 204)

Similar paths emerged in left-wing clandestine organizations in Germany. Those who joined the RAF were "bound to each other to form a network, by means of personal acquaintances, of shared participation in communes, also of love stories, and in some cases even of a shared social work" (Neidhardt 1982: 341). Later on as well, activists "ultimately became members of terrorist organizations through personal connections with people or relatives associated with appropriate political initiatives, communes, self-supporting organizations, or committees – the number of couples, and brothers and sisters was astonishingly high" (Wasmund 1986: 204). The first generation of RAF members also had a stronger link with the Old Left than did the following one. The founders of the RAF and of the Bewegung 2 Juni (June 2nd Movement [B2J]) had also been members of the student movement. One of them, Horst Mahler, had become a member of the SPD in 1956, later joining the circle of people around Harry Ristock, leader of the Jusos (young Socialists) chapter of Berlin Charlottenburg. An activist within the SDS (Social Democratic Students) since 1959, he was expelled (purged, in his own words) from the SPD, which had declared membership in the SDS as incompatible (Mahler 1977: 77). As he recalled, "my attempt to keep a politically positive relation to the state so failed" (quoted in Baum and Mahler 1979: 39). His political career then developed in the New Left, and he faced direct experiences of repression when, at the time of the Cuban Missile Crisis (1962), he was arrested and charged with insulting the American occupation force and violating the law on public meetings (Mahler 1977: 77).[3] In contrast, several of the members of the second generation came from groups that had been built for the support of "political" prisoners (such as Rote Hilfe [Red Help] and Schwarze Hilfe [Black Help]).

ACTIVATION OF MILITANT NETWORKS IN RIGHT-WING ORGANIZATIONS

Two generations have also been singled out in the radical Right; these generations exhibit differences in family background and paths of socialization through which militant networks were activated.

To begin with, the sociographic characteristics of the activists are different from one generation to the next. In general, according to a quantitative study,

---

[3] Several RAF founders – including Manfred Grashof (a conscientious objector to military service whom Mahler had defended in court), Grashof's girlfriend Petra Schelm, Mahler, and Mahler's girlfriend Renate – came in 1969 from a small group that had come into contact with Andreas Baader and Gudrun Ensslin. Their first action was an attack with four Molotov cocktails against a public building in the Märkische Viertel (Aust 1985: 90). Examples of social engagement include the actions of the radical therapeutic group known as Sozialistisches Patientenkollektiv in Heidelberg. "At the outset of these careers stood a serious social engagement that did not confine itself to verbal propagation of revolutionary goals but was realized in practical social work" (Rasch 1979: 81). Some members of the first RAF generation also lived in the same communes as one another (Speitel 1980a: 36–7). Future RAF members were involved in work with juvenile prisons and poor neighborhoods (e.g., Märkische Viertel in Berlin).

neofascists were mainly men (males comprised 93 percent of members, in contrast to left-wing organizations, which were 77 percent male), and neofascist groups attracted people both below twenty and above forty years old. They were more likely than their left-wing counterparts to come from medium-sized cities but were also overwhelmingly from Rome (41 percent) (Weinberg and Eubank 1987: 84–6). Family ties were frequent: 60 percent of right-wing activists had siblings within the movement, and some had marital (18 percent) and parental (12 percent) relations with members of the radical Right (ibid.: 84). They were young (about two-thirds were below thirty when arrested), had not experienced much geographic mobility, and came from well-to-do families.

There were, however, some differences between early and late neofascists:

Members of the Nuclei of Armed Revolutionaries, Third Position and the other late organizations tended to be much younger at the time of their arrest/identification than their counterparts in New Order, National Vanguard and the other early neo-Fascist groups (gamma = 0.57). Furthermore, the second wave groups were somewhat more likely to include women (gamma = 0.53) and they were far more concentrated geographically than the earlier ones. As measured by both their places of birth and residence, the later neo-Fascists were substantially more urbanized and Rome-centred than their predecessors. There were no statistically meaningful differences between members of the two groups as regards prior political experience or occupational background. (Weinberg and Eubank 1988: 539–40)

Besides these sociographic differences, the first generation was still linked to the old fascist regime, often through strong family ties. In his work on life histories, Veugelers (2011: 242) has empirically proved the role of "dissenting" radical Right families in transmitting "a neo-fascist potential," by "teaching their children oppositional framings of history, society and politics," which seems particularly relevant for the first generation. In a hostile environment dominated by the narrative of resistance against the Nazis (and their fascist allies), these families functioned in fact as protected spaces in which old fascist narratives survived, and young people were socialized to them. According to Veugelers's data, 53 percent of the twenty-one militants of right-wing clandestine organizations he analyzed had right-wing fathers, and 36 percent had right-wing mothers – even though right-wingers made up only 8 percent of the total population. Most of the remaining ones came from nonpartisan families (only one had a left-wing father, and three had a father who voted for a party of the center). In fact,

half had at least one parent who voted for the MSI or the Monarchist Party. One father was a former MSI organizer who later edited a neo-fascist periodical and wrote a book that justified his Fascist past. Another was an official in the MSI labour union (CISNAL). Also later on, they socialized mainly with right-wingers: "my parents don't have many social relations and, as I told you, the ones they do have are all from the same political environment." (ibid.: 250–1)

As many as seven fathers out of twenty-one had been members of the Salò militia (ibid.: 252).

The interviewed activists stressed the importance of these family traditions. One of them observed that "my father admired Mussolini, you know that image of Mussolini, everything in order ... 'in those days, right, you could leave the doors unlocked and you wouldn't get robbed'" (cited in Veugelers 2011: 250). Similarly, another recalled:

My father had more or less the same ideas as me, even though he did not approve extremism, conflict with what I would define simply as the system. Let's say that even my older brother has the same ideas, more or less ... my younger brother is not too different ... so I come from a family that, let's say it never criticized the Fascist period, that's for sure. (ibid.)

In fact, an activist defined the influence of his father, a former RSI fighter, as "enormous, enormous, even at the unconscious level" (ibid.). Still another remembered his parents' "nostalgic attachment to a certain number of values such as God, father, and family" (ibid.: 253).

In the family, right-wing militants were socialized through books and discussions with family members. As one activist said,

as for my father's books, I read them because they were around the house, so I nourished myself on this kind of culture. They were all books that talked about the war we had lost, about the betrayal of Mussolini, about the massacres by the Partisans. Not that my father read only these; these are only the ones that really captured my imagination. Let's say that when I was a boy I was highly impressed by that lost war. (Veugelers 2011: 251)

Another concurred, "Undoubtedly the climate I absorbed at home as a child was a bit unusual. When I was ten years old, eleven years old and I was reading my first books, in the library at home I found books about the lost war, the war betrayed – what you would call the climate of postwar neo-fascism" (ibid.). Specific narratives of the past were kept alive in these families:

Children of right-wingers learned the alliance between Italy and Germany gave Europe its best chance of defeating Bolshevism and limiting the spread of Anglo-American power. The Allies who defeated Italy were invaders, not liberators. The Italian Social Republic of 1943–45 was a noble experiment, not an abomination. Soldiers who fought for Fascism were heroes, not villains. Partisans were opportunists and butchers, not patriots and defenders of freedom. Italians punished in the anti-Fascist purges were victims, not criminals. (ibid.: 252)

Often in continuity with these family traditions, most of the neofascists had had experiences in the MSI and related youth and student organizations; thus one could talk of "the radicalization of people who were already on the Right" (Weinberg and Eubank 1988: 539–40). In fact, the logic of action of the first generation was oriented toward an authoritarian shift, to be reached through the support of some parts of the state (see also Chapter 6). Of a first-generation leader, another right-wing activist said that he had a political perspective of a *golpista* type. He thought we could bring the country to such a level of terror to make exceptional measures and the intervention of the army necessary. This aim had to be reached through a series of attacks of growing gravity. His discourses were terrifying, as he defined himself as supporter of a theory of "pure terrorism"; he talked of indiscriminate massacres, and attacks to carry out, one after the other, in different cities, or in more places at the same time. (cited in Ferraresi 1995: 245)

The story of Pierluigi Concutelli is typical for the first generation of right-wing radicals. Concutelli, who was the grandchild of a high-ranking member of the fascist regime and had two neofascist uncles, declared, "I have chosen to be on the side of the losers, those who have been defeated" (quoted in Ardica 2008: 24). In the family environment,

I listened with my mouth open to the narrations of the former-fighters of the Salò Republic: of the African and Russian Fronts, of the young people who had left, searching for the "beautiful death," of the fights in the mountains between the black brigades and the partisans. Terrible rumors circulated on the red triangle in Emilia Romagna, of mass executions, mass graves full of corpses in black shirts, of women that had been raped because they were "guilty" of having a fascist husband or boyfriend....
They had cancelled our deaths. (ibid.: 33, 34)

In 1956, at only twelve years old, he participated in a demonstration organized by the MSI against the Soviet invasion of Hungary; at fourteen, he was beaten during his first action of leafleting (ibid.: 31).

It was during the 1960s and early 1970s, however, that he radicalized. The legacy of the fascist regime was still heavily influential in the radical Right: the sections of the MSI were full of "statues of the Duce.... Demonstrations were organized to remember Benito Mussolini and celebrate the March on Rome. And Ezra Pound, rigorously dressed in black shirt and high stifles, always had a *posto d'onore* [prestigious location]" (Ardica 2008: 27). Within the MSI, however, radical activists, among them the university students of the FUAN, started to criticize the party as too moderate: "I considered the party ... as a greenhouse where even the most promising plants were destined to remain small, to dry and die" (ibid.: 38).

With one foot in and one foot out (he had been in the ON since 1971, but also in the MSI's FUAN at the same time [Ardica 2008: 60]), Concutelli was increasingly socialized to violence. As he himself recalled,

in Palermo, we started to go around armed not only with leaflets, but also with the monkey wrenches ... for months, our main hobby was ... to go in front of the schools, armed with motorbike helmets, and sing a revised, corrected and palermitan-ized version of "All'armi siam fascisti." And we charged them....
The comrades marched against the war in Vietnam? And there we were, twenty of us, to cut the march in two. Running, punching, using our helmets to hit them. Every day the same story. An infernal life. We were extremely few, while the "reds" were hundreds, thousands....
We were the elite of a minority. A minority in the minority. (ibid.: 46–7, 61, 77)

In fights with political opponents, there was an escalation from monkey wrenches to guns, as, historical defeats notwithstanding, in the environment of the "Salò veterans, to get arms was easy" (Ardica 2008: 12): "In the tombs, in those years, there were few bones, and a lot of iron" (ibid.: 26). Violence was justified initially as defensive: "We were men and women ... with no right to citizenship in the Italian Republic. Everything was licit against those who professed post-fascist or fascist ideas ... always a climate of civil war ... and we, stupid or maybe too young, have fallen in the trap. Responding to violence with violence" (ibid.: 68). In time, however, violence came to be seen by Concutelli and his friends as the only political strategy: "We realized that the leaflets were useless, that our posters were ignored. That none of our beliefs was taken seriously ... I was ready: the armed struggle became the only alternative in front of me" (ibid.: 69–70). Especially after the ON was declared illegal, "those who stayed over, were ready for the armed struggle" (ibid.: 78).

Wanted by the police, Concutelli entered clandestinity, organizing the radical Right into what he planned to be "a pyramid formed by small pyramids: the cells spread over the territory. Nuclei independent from each other ... and always ready to obey the orders and act" (Ardica 2008: 79). After massive arrests in 1976, he launched the Gruppi di Azione Ordinovista, which "had to be a way to reorganize the movement, by now totally fragmented ... [in] a compartmentalized, rigid structure, spread all over Italy" (ibid.: 136). The killing of the public persecutor Vittorio Occorsio, who had been in charge of the investigations of the ON, was meant to show that "the time of the chat was over. It had to be the first act of response, the first true act of war of the fascist after 1945" (ibid.: 110). The use of a machine gun in the killing was to "give an even more military taste to the action" (ibid.: 113). He and his comrades in fact claimed responsibility for the killing, declaring: "The special tribunal of the MPON has ... judged Occorsio guilty of having, because of his opportunism, served the democratic dictatorship persecuting the militants of Ordine Nuovo and their ideals" (ibid.: 113).

Although they kept in contact with Concutelli and his generation, the type of activists on the right changed in the second half of the 1970s. In fact, the second-generation right-wingers stressed their search for innovation. A militant of Terza Posizione, Gabriele Adinolfi, remembered his fascination with the student revolt in 1968. When he joined the radical Right, he wanted "a generational change ... something innovative, youthful ... a chance to be free from hypocrisy and to be able to decide one's own destiny" (Cento Bull 2007: 140). In justifying their turn against the state, they presented the shooting of a police officer as an attack on "people who of their own will have become pillars for the defence of the Italian state" (Veugelers 2011: 254). NAR founder Fioravanti remembered that "in that period some kids agreed to try to have children in the same period, so that they could grow together, with the same ideals, assign them the task to make a revolution, but in twenty years.... They were known as the 'bucolic fascists'" (quoted in Bianconi 1992: 34). For this second generation, in fact,

political activism no longer aimed to overthrow the democratic regime. It now consisted of terrorist attacks devoid of any political aim, whose sole purpose was to strike at some of the hated symbols of the "system" – a procedure known as "armed spontaneity." This strategy was based on two facts. First, it was realised both that there was no hope of convincing the "renegade" MSI to adopt a revolutionary stance and that the coup d'etat scenario had led to the strengthening rather than the destabilisation of the system. Second, there was the arrival on the scene of a new generation of activists with no historical memories of Fascism. Their commitment tended to be personal and existential, rather than ideological or political. It grew, first and foremost, out of a need to assert themselves. They had an instinctive solidarity, on the ground, with anyone who was anti-system: from Italian left-wing terrorists operating as loners, with the Palestinian Fedayeen, and from the Argentinean Monteneros to the IRA. Their "armed propaganda" which preached the slogan "Let's build action" left the task of putting together a new consensus to the language of violence. (Chiarini 1995: 33–4)

As written in the *Quex*, "It is not towards power that we aim, nor, necessarily, towards the creation of a new order.... It is the struggle which interests us, action in se, everyday fighting in order to state our nature" (*Quex*, 1980, no. 3, cited in Ferraresi 1995: 279). The very logic of action changed from the first to the second generation. As Weinberg and Eubank noted,

these second generation formations differed from their predecessors in a number of ways. While members of the earlier generation had some reason to believe their violent actions might bring about the collapse of the democratic regime, the later ones could hold out no such expectations. Their public expressions of purpose seem correspondingly less focused on the achievement of concrete political objectives and more on the use of violence as a means of personal expression. The statements of these second generation neo-Fascists abound with references to the Japanese Code of Bushido, the Islamic concept of Jihad and the fantasy writings of J.R. Tolkien. Moreover, the initial wave of neo-Fascist terrorists were admirers of the Italian state, especially its "separate corps" of military and police officers. They had sought to overthrow the democratic regime as a means of strengthening the state. In contrast the later neo-Fascists saw the Italian state as a hopelessly corrupt institution, not to be strengthened but to be destroyed. Accordingly, unlike their predecessors, the second generation groups carried out attacks on the state and its personnel, including judges, prosecutors and policemen, in a way the first generation did not. (1988: 537)

Especially in the second generation, the increasing brutality of the daily fights with adversaries contributed to a growing acceptance of violence. One activist stated,

Eventually, the fascists are forced ... to carry guns and to use them, because they are attacked ... because when those of the Student Movement arrived, but they arrived in 150, 200 of them. Carrying their monkey-wrenches, you could not really discuss.... It is in those situations that we, the fascists, start to use guns. (interview with A.D'I.: 60, in Fiasco 1990: 201)

Recruitment thus happened in an increasingly radicalized milieu – what Fioravanti defined as "fights among gangs, in our generation's fashion" (quoted in Bianconi 1992: 51). The life history of Valerio Fioravanti – as an example of an activist of the second generation – is very different from those of the first generation. Raised in a nonfascist family, as a teenager he went to the United States, where he lived first with a Jewish family and then with a single white father who had adopted two black children. His commitment to clandestine violence developed later on in a subcultural radicalized milieu. Attracted to commitment in the radical Right by his younger brother Cristiano, in 1975 he bought a gun to bring to the Milan funeral of a seventeen-year-old activist of the MSI's Fronte della Gioventù, Sergio Ramelli, who had been killed with iron bars by left-wing militants. Fioravanti declared during the trial:

There was violence against my brother, and here I felt a sense of injustice that pushed me to engage in politics, as he did. My first attitude was retribution: they had burned my mother's car, and I burned theirs; the hit they had given to my brother I've given back to others. The things went this way, for several years, growing with time. Violence called violence. (ibid.: 51)

In the same year, a militant of the MSI's FUAN, Mikis Mantakas, was shot dead during fights with political adversaries. Near him when he was killed was a classmate of Fioravanti's, Franco Anselmi, who would keep Mikis's bloody balaclava hat as a reliquary. Anselmi was also the victim of an aggression that left him almost blind. Fioravanti recalled before the Padua judges:

I started in this period to go to the MSI section of Monteverde. It was the period in which engaging in politics on the right meant leafleting, injuring political adversaries, taking control of the neighborhood, a period that will culminate in 1978. The right-wing youth looked especially to aggregate with each other, they felt the need of *cameratismo*, they needed to feel strong and respected as a group. (quoted in Bianconi 1992: 59)

Adversaries were "those with long hair and long beards: ugly, dirty and evil, we called them" (ibid.).

In this milieu, he met his future girlfriend, Francesca Mambro, who recalled having engaged with the radical Right "not after a lucid choice but simply because the right in that period was put in a ghetto from a left-wing milieu that used its numerical strength to impose its presence on the street" (quoted in Bianconi 1992: 64). She also personally knew another right-wing militant, Mario Zicchieri, who was shot dead in 1975 in front of an MSI section of Prenestino (in revenge for the killed right-winger Antonio Corrado; he was mistaken for a Lotta Continua activist). She was then attracted to the radical right-wing group Lotta Popolare and its interest in the marginal people, as well as other traditional left-wing topics. In 1976, she was arrested at the road blockade to protest the death of MSI city councilor Enrico Pedenovi, killed in Milan as revenge for the assassination of the left-wing activist Gaetano Amoroso (ibid.: 66).

In this second generation, moreover, the rupture with the traditional neofascist milieu was stronger. The second generation's lack of taboos against violence even led to tensions with older members. An Italian second-generation right-wing radical recalls that, after some assassinations, "the senior members of the group seemed to be preoccupied with the legal consequences.... They started to look at us in a strange way" (quoted in Fiasco 1990: 172). In 1976, with the development of a campaign against state repression, "the old leadership loses control over young activists 'formed in the action and for the action'" (Ferraresi 1995: 278). Although the group that would found the NAR grew in the MSI section in Roman Monteverdi, its members were expelled by the leaders of the MSI. Later on, they started to meet in the headquarters of the FUAN and eventually were disclaimed by the MSI, which had lost control over "these kids who talk of authoritarianism and free love, alienation of labour and ecology, even of women's liberation" (quoted in Bianconi 1992: 105). Even Concutelli declared the activists of the NAR and Terza Posizione, with their spontaneity, to be "stupid and dangerous" (Ardica 2008: 178).

During this evolution, justification for violence became even more existentialist. When his friend Franco Anselmi was killed during a robbery organized by the group, Fioravanti wrote in a sort of memorial,

I've lost the prejudices of right and wrong.... If I had to die in the struggle, that will be my biggest party. No cry and no priest. Songs and dancing. And do not speak of me as an innocent victim. Do not say that I was crazy, but the son of a new moral.... The only thing I would like to leave as an heritage is a suggestion: get free of all inhibitions, find the taste to obey to instinct and passions. (Bianconi 1992: 97)

He also declared that they imitated the left-wing clandestine groups, "their seriousness, their total commitment, their organizational perfection" (ibid.: 33). Another extreme Right militant defined his "rebellion" as

an existential question as well as a cultural one, being able to live within ourselves and, if possible, in free, or rather "freed" areas, alternative life styles to mercantilism or utilitarianism. Then to affirm what we called "counterpower" ... and finally the ability to influence the cultural sphere and so being able to overturn the ready-made patterns of thought imposed by Marxism and Christian Democracy. (ibid.: 140)

ACTIVATION OF MILITANT NETWORKS IN ETHNIC ORGANIZATIONS

The ETA has also experienced two generations; family networks were more important for the first generation, and identification with a broader community was more important for the second.

Members of ethnonationalist underground organizations are usually presented as less isolated than those of other clandestine groups, enjoying a solid support base from friends and, especially, family. This was particularly true for the first generation of ETA members. As noted, under Franco's dictatorship, nationalist codes were reproduced especially in the family and the church, as well as in gastronomic and sports associations and informal networks of friends. As is typical in many cases, the three ETA founders had been part of the same school and Catholic group. During the Franco years the Basque hiking and mountain-climbing clubs functioned as cover-ups for clandestine meetings (Pérez-Agote

1984), during which the ETA "chose to make many of the contacts that led to recruiting in earnest" (Clark 1984: 154).

During these years, ETA militants mainly entered the armed group through personal networks of relatives and extended groups of friends (*la cuadrilla*), or via socialization through dense social networks of interrelations in the larger radical Basque nationalist movement (Dominguez Iribarren 1998: 22–6; Reinares 2001).

In contrast with other underground organizations, ETA militants tended to enjoy "normal" relationships with family and friends. In fact, interpersonal links strengthened by kinship and friendship through which social and group cohesion have been fostered are central to the structured radical nationalist subculture that supports the ETA.[4]

In research on a large number of ETA militants, Fernando Reinares observed many differences between the generation that joined in the first half of the 1970s and the one that did so in the 1980s–1990s. Based on an analysis of 600 ETA militants recruited between the beginning of the 1970s and the mid-1990s, his description is resonant with what we observed in the Italian case:

> The *etarra* of yesterday was, normally recruited with an age somewhat above 20 years, descended from autochthonous families, which lived in small and medium localities with a widespread use of Euskera. Adolescent when he is captured and coming from urban areas with less Basque-speaking, often grown up in areas with high presence of immigrants, the *etarras* [freedom fighters] of today are very similar to the young European radicals of his generation that participate in violent groups of neonazi ideology and other totalitarian anti systemic movements. (2001: 19)

Language and religion played an important role in the beginning, in what was also a generational revolt against the passivity of the previous generation. Of the first years, when no violent action happened, a founder declared:

> Those were the best years ... and it was extremely positive work, that is conscious-raising work carried out by groups.... During this time, no armed action was carried out, the only thing that the armed front did was to beat up some teacher that crossed the line a bit.... There were also people ready to paint slogans on walls and things like that. (Pérez-Agote 2006: 87)

As a militant of the first generation observed,

> those who created ETA were radicalized people who understood what losing the war meant and began to see their parents totally exploited by the defeat, left without a cent, therefore I had to respond to this, although my father couldn't; he was impotent, before with a war that he lost and then the struggle to raise his children, he had enough to face. So I found myself obliged to sentimentally react to this situation in Euskadi. (ibid.: 89)

---

[4] This is particularly true in specific regions within the Basque territory. Almost half of all members of the ETA came from the province of Guipuzcoa (Reinares 2001). The spatial concentration of a strong radical nationalist subculture is indeed important for mobilization.

The family nurtured the nationalist identity: "A pattern developed within the family whereby, through osmosis, what was silenced was transmitted and even magnified by virtue of such silence. It lent a magical, sacred, mysterious and mythical character to the secret intimacy of the family universe" (ibid.: 97–8).

In the Basque countries, militant networks were activated in the dense milieu of nationalism. There, repression had produced a "closed and secretive subculture, given its obvious need to remain hidden" (Pérez-Agote 2006: 75). In fact, "the reproduction of truth that contradicted the official version was confined to the private realm and the microsocial dimension of certain public institutions. Contexts beyond official control included the family and some forms of intersubjective relations within cuadrillas, relations among cuadrillas during poteo, and voluntary associations functioning secretly as forums of political socialization" (ibid.: 77). Especially in the beginning, "one joined ETA though neighborhood contacts. One joined through other groups like those of the parish, or the scouts; in the neighborhood, whenever there was a dance group, *ochotes*, choirs, etc.... because their families would have been nationalist, their general surroundings too, and of course they themselves" (ibid.: 91).

Goio, a leader of the ETA-PM, is a typical representative of the first generation. Born in 1950 in a village where Euskera was spoken, he was socialized to nationalist myths by his mother. Taught to speak Basque at home, he remembered his feelings of not only frustration but also increased ethnic identification when he had to defend his language before Francoist repression. As he described, "already when you're ten or eleven years old, you learned what Franco's repression was" (quoted in Reinares and Herzog 1993: 22). He already felt a nationalist as a teenager, and his commitment increased when his sister's friend and two others in his village were arrested as ETA members. In the same period, a couple of ETA members joined his *cuadrilla*, that is, his group of close friends. Undecided as to whether to become a priest, at fifteen he moved to San Sebastian. There, in 1967, he agreed to leaflet for the ETA, which he joined in the beginning of the 1970s. In danger of arrest, he went to the French Basque territory, where he remembered a comfortable life of "fun, bars, drinks.... And there was also something that was even more important: each of us had the feeling of being a small king, we were all small kings in front of our family, our friends. This was solidarity" (ibid.: 28). At twenty-three, he entered the ETA Executive Committee, choosing the ETA-PM in 1974. As Francoism failed in its attempt to destroy the nationalist milieu, this became a recruitment area for the ETA. In fact, since the 1960s,

there was a tremendous upsurge in the group activity of youth, cultural, hiking and dance associations. The close-knit realms of the neighborhood and town made up this associative and interpersonal network. In the associative world, under openly declared and functionally specific objectives, a strong degree of youth socialization took place. Through such activity interest was stimulated in social and political questions. As a result, those involved joined a generically nationalist symbolic universe that was reproduced daily through the activity of the cuadrilla and poteo. (Pérez-Agote 2006: 101)

Thus "in the Franco era, the mountain became ... a form of struggle. One of the strongest ways of protesting at that time was a mountain celebration, the Bizkargi [mountain] picnic etc. They were completely banned by the Civil Guard because it was the place where the Basque spirit was really preserved" (ibid.: 93). Hiking associations were, according to an ETA member, "consciously organized" for their political function (ibid.: 179).

As in the other cases, recruitment into the ETA took a long time – especially in the first phases – as did a career inside the organization. The use of violence did raise moral problems (Clark 1984), as Goio expressed: "You think about that, ask yourself questions, but, well, you think, you have to do it, because someone has to do it" (Reinares and Herzog 1993: 29). He remembered, however, that the first order to participate in an assassination would come "after you have already spent many years in the organization" (ibid.). In the first ETA handbook the reference to "our responsibility in front of God and the fatherland" testifies to attention paid to the ethical justification for violence – and, in fact, in 1965 the ETA consulted a collective of priests on the legitimacy of using violence (Itcaina 2007: 126). A much less problematic relationship with violence in the second generation is in fact stigmatized by older ETA members. According to one of them, "at that time it was not as nowadays. Before, when you entered in an armed commando, you had already passed through broader types of activities. You reach that a bit like a culmination.... Not today. People enter directly in the armed commando, with arms" (Reinares 2001: 36). In fact, although in the beginning certain actions were questioned from the point of view of religious beliefs, a gradual disinterest toward religion emerged in the following generations (Pérez-Agote 2006: 88).

With the passing of time, ETA activists tended to be younger and to have direct experiences with armed action even before officially entering the group. In addition, their ethnic background changed. In the 1970s, 43 percent of the members studied had two parents with Basque names; an additional 28 percent had only fathers and 12 percent had only mothers with Basque names. Only 17 percent came from families with no Basque name from either side; in contrast, this demographic made up 41 percent of the entire population of the Basque countries. In addition, 4 percent, in contrast to 19 percent of the entire population, were born in towns where more than 40 percent of the population spoke Basque. Only a quarter of them, in contrast to more than 40 percent of the entire population, were born in large cities (Reinares 2001: 41–3). According to Reinares's data, they came mostly from Guipuzcoa. The second generation came instead from big cities, where less than 10 percent of the population speaks Euskera; some even came from migrant families.

Motifs changed accordingly. In the beginning, motivations were mainly nationalist and separatist: the militants fought for "Euskadi independent, reunified and *eskaldun*, because the term socialist was barely used" (Reinares 2001: 52). In the first generation, "it is normal that among those who militated in ETA the internalization of the attitudes and beliefs proper to the Basque nationalism started during his childhood and in his original family" (ibid.: 54). In fact, there are frequent references to family examples of resistance during the civil war. A member of the ETA in its first years of existence remembers, "In my family, they always spoke about my uncle … he died in the battle of Matxitzako, in the fight between the marine of the government of Euskadi and the national marine" (ibid.: 55). Memories from the activists' family lives included the possession of a reproduction of Picasso's *Guernica*, the playing of the (banned) hymn of the Basque soldiers and other Basque songs, a hidden *ikurrina* (the Basque flag), attendance at *ikastolas* (unofficial schools where Basque was spoken), and the (prohibited) use of Euskera as a family language. Family support was therefore a recurrent memory, an important motivation that gave the impression that joining the ETA was a family tradition – in the words of an *etarra*: "I enter ETA, I believe, because of the family tradition" (ibid.: 60). Another recalled, "My family always helped … as economic support for those who had to leave the country … for the prisoners in Segovia before the amnesty, and for the Burgos trial earlier on" (ibid.: 61). One militant even stated, "I always say that I entered ETA thanks to my mother" (ibid.: 61).

First-generation Basque fighters often reported frustrating experiences related with ethnic background. For monolingual Basque-speaking children, entering schools was traumatic. As an ETA member remembers, "When I got to the school I realized that no one talked like me: I felt, then, a feeling of loneliness" (Clark 1984: 153). Children from Basque-speaking families were stigmatized and sometimes even punished. First-generation *etarras* remember, for example, that "the professors did not understand that those who did not speak their language could not understand a topic or another. So, clear, we were the last of the class, the most stupid, those who were punished more often…. When we spoke *Euskera* with each other, we were punished" (Reinares 2001: 66). In fact, especially for the first generation, the linguistic difference was politicized from a very young age; the strengthening of a Basque identity then transformed a stigmatized handicap into a militant commitment (Itcaina 2007: 288, 298).

As for the second generation, according to a first-generation ETA member, in the 1980s members became instead "less nationalists and more preoccupied with social issues, much more preoccupied with issues such as marginality, unemployment" (Itcaina 2007: 43). At the same time, the proportion of workers dropped (from 50 to 16 percent), and instead the proportion of students increased (from 5 to 33 percent) (ibid.: 43). In fact, the militants who started to join the organization after 1975 were said to be mainly

not interested in labor organizing, participating in the neighborhood associations or joining the new Basque social democratic parties. Instead, many advocated a terrorist strategy, using death threats and indiscriminate killings as a bargaining chip in negotiations with the Spanish government over the new legal order. According to the younger militants, guns and bombs could be effectively used in a ruthless game of dare. If Madrid truly wanted peace and civility, it would make the necessary constitutional changes that ETA's militants wanted. Otherwise, unarmed bystanders would suffer. (Zirakzadeh 2002: 75)

Generational tensions often took dramatic forms. According to an older member, in the new generation, "they just want to break things, to break for the pleasure of that" (Reinares 2001: 46). Wishing to preserve the ETA tradition of violent action, the new recruits "began to threaten the former ETArras who now advocated peaceful forms of politics. The youths harassed, sometimes maimed and occasionally even killed the ETA veterans who had laid down their arms. Horrified, the older generation of ETArras – including some of the earlier gunmen – began to accuse the youths of behaving irrationally, celebrating violence for its own sake and no longer recognizing ETA's ultimate social and political goals" (Zirakzadeh 2002: 76).

ACTIVATION OF MILITANT NETWORKS IN RELIGIOUS ORGANIZATIONS

Militant networks have been confirmed to be important for Islamist fundamentalists as well. Sociological research on jihad has stressed the role of informal networks, with intense affective focusing, in the recruitment of suicide bombers. Among members of al-Qaeda (and of the PLO), friendship and kinship are frequent (Sageman 2004). In a study of jihadist organizations, "about two thirds of the people in the sample were friends with other people who joined together or already had some connection to terrorism" (Sageman 2008: 66), and about one-fifth had relatives in the group. Sageman (2004) singled out some clusters that played different roles in different moments: for example, a central staff that had met in Afghanistan, a network of Southeast Asians made up of disciples of two members of the central staff, and Maghreb Arabs who had migrated to France.

Within Islamic fundamentalism, as in the previously discussed cases, differences have been noted between the first generation, which was more rooted in specific nationalist culture, and the second, which is made up of many Western-born Muslims who identified with a distant suffering community and joined an already-radicalized conflict. In al-Qaeda, among other groups, (at least) two generations have been singled out.

In the first generation, leaders mainly came from the Middle East and were bonded together in Afghanistan. According to Olivier Roy, "Al Qaeda's first-generation members shared common traits: all came from a Muslim country and had previous records of political activism; almost all went directly from the Middle East to Afghanistan. They had little experience of the West, and had a traditional way of life (traditional marriages, and their women kept at home)" (2004: 301).

In repressive Arabic countries, social movements developed within mosques as well as Islamic NGOs, including hospitals, schools, and cultural centers. Professional organizations or student associations represented important networks for both reformist and radical Islamist groups. In general, the importance of religious places in facilitating mobilization in repressive regimes is related to their capacity to provide mobilized networks. As the authoritarian nature of several regimes jeopardized political mobilization, "the Mosque was the one institution the state had the most difficulty dominating or controlling. Religion, mosques and mullahs became a rallying point when there was no space allowed for any other" (Esposito 2006: 147).

Moreover, these movements do not use only terror; several Islamist organizations in the Middle East have developed charity activities. In his economic approach to violence, Berman suggests that religious prohibitions are productive for the community because they "increase the availability of members for collective activities such as mutual aid, an essential part of what makes radical religious communities cohesive" (2009: 81). In this sense, radical religious groups "operate as economic clubs. They collectively provide both spiritual services and an entire array of concrete social services through mutual aid systems" (ibid.: 118). He recalls, in fact, that "charity is a pillar of mainstream Islam and that radical Islamist groups like the Muslim Brotherhood are famous for running religious schools, orphanages, soup kitchens, clinics, hospitals, and even youth centers and soccer clubs, all operated as charities" (ibid.: 77).[5] The importance of these social services increased with the declining capacity of Arabic states to provide welfare (Ahmed 2005). Similarly, Islamic student associations are said to have provided space for the formation of informal nets.

These informal networks facilitated the spread of Islamic organizations. Recruitment in Islamic groups occurred through activities such as "attending religious lessons at a nearby mosque, joining an informal study group, or accompanying a friend or neighbor to special prayer services in observance of an Islamic holy day" (Rosefsky Wickham 2004: 232). The legitimacy of those institutions reduced the perception of risk, as "Islamic lessons, seminars, and prayer meetings offered some of the few socially sanctioned venues for graduates of both sexes to congregate outside the home" (ibid.: 233). Socially embedded Islamic groups also allowed for different degrees and forms of involvement, and therefore for a gradual integration into the organization. Additionally, "most residents had a brother, cousin, friend or neighbor involved in Islamic prayer circles or study groups, and Islamist participants frequently maintain close relations with non-activist peers" (ibid.).

Within a religious environment, especially for the first generation, family continuities are often stressed. One example is Ayman al-Zawahir, who grew up in Egypt, in an oppositional academic family. His grandfather was a famous

---

[5] Hamas and Hezbollah developed social institutions and helped the local population with day-to-day survival: "In this sense, Hamas is not a terrorist organization using social service provision as a front to disguise its other activities.... The social services come first" (Berman 2009: 132). In fact, among the social services provided to the community are 130,000 scholarships and 135,000 microcredit loans to needy families managed by Hezbollah and the forty Hamas social welfare organizations. These groups provide not only food, clothing, and shelter but also education, training, libraries, sports clubs, and medical relief, amounting to 40 percent of social welfare institutions in the West Bank and Gaza (Pape 2005: 188, 191–2).

religious scholar and former rector of Al-Azhar University; his great-uncle had been a leader of the Libyan resistance against the Italian occupation; and his uncle was arrested for his devotion to Sayyid Qutb (he was executed in 1966 for his commitment to building an Islamic state). Criticizing the Egyptian government as corrupt, Ayman founded a group that, in the 1970s, joined with other groups to form Jamaat al-Jihad. As a medical doctor, he went to Pakistan with the Red Crescent society to treat people injured by the Soviet troops in Afghanistan and saw the Islamic revolution in Iran as a successful example to follow. After the repression of the Islamist movement by Sadat, and Sadat's subsequent murder, Ayman was arrested as a conspirator. Said to have betrayed his comrades under torture, he was convicted and given a three-year sentence; he left prison as a hardened radical (McCauley and Moskalenko 2011).

Family links were particularly important to the Middle Eastern Muslims who chose to go fight in Afghanistan. One of them remembers his mother saying, "My son, get up and go! Look what they are doing, they are raping our sisters and killing our brothers" (cited in Hegghammer 2010: 62). Another declared that he went to fight "all for the love of his brothers" (ibid.). And still another confessed: "I wasn't actually a dedicated Muslim … [my brother] saw me and said 'look at you, you're not a man, you're wasting your time'" (ibid.: 137). Osama bin Laden's father is also described as very pious, and as passionately committed to the Palestinian cause (Esposito 2002: 4). Some teachers were also supportive, to the point of accompanying their pupils to Afghanistan.

For Saudi Arabian militants as well, the decisions and acts that led them to join the jihad were collective ones, often influenced by family links. As Hegghammer recalls in his reconstruction of the Saudi Arabian jihad,

> the process of joining the jihad was fundamentally a social experience, and the main vehicles of mobilization were networks of kinships and friendships. The idea of going to Afghanistan or Bosnia often came from a friend or relative who had already visited…. Group adherence emboldened individuals and reduced the psychological barrier to departure. There are several examples of groups or pairs of old friends who traveled together to Afghanistan. Others went to Afghanistan with an older brother. (ibid.: 67)

Militants' life histories were in fact often rooted in the evolution of conflicts in their homeland. For many of them, politicization started in their Arabic country of origin, as in Algeria after the coup d'état in 1991, or in Egypt during the authoritarian turn of the 1990s, or in Palestine, given increasing Israeli repression. For activists living in the Middle East, the impact of political repression on their lives helps to explain their radicalization. Repression in their home country often accompanied a slippery slope. In Egypt, suppression by the Nasser regime radicalized elements of the Brotherhood and led individuals to transform the ideology of modernist Islamists into a "rejectionist call to arms," followed by growing stigmatization of the West as responsible for the victimization of Muslims all around the world.

Friendship ties were also strategically developed during the recruitment processes. In particular, differently from al-Jihad, which worked underground, al-Jamaa – in the words of one of its members – "believed in the public work. In the universities, in the towns, in the streets. [...] The public revolution. How can we move the public!" (cited in Malthaner 2011: 80). Al-Jamaa in fact recruited its militants after building personal relations in aboveground protest, especially at the student level. This trend emerges, for instance, in the life history of Khaled al-Berry, as reconstructed by Stefan Malthaner (based on Al-Berry 2002):

A particularly close bond existed between al-Jamaa and its immediate (youthful) following at secondary schools and the university, which was based on a distinct collective identity and subculture, as illustrated by the account of Khaled al-Berry, a middle-ranking member of al-Jamaa al-Islamiyya in Assiut between 1987 and 1989. He had joined a local group of al-Jamaa members while still a student at secondary school and later became a leading activist at the university of Assiut. In his school and later at the university, al-Berry's efforts involved raising awareness among pupils and students by distributing leaflets and giving speeches. His attention then focused on those students whom he judged to be particularly "receptive." With that group he made efforts to establish trust and a close personal relationship by demonstrating concern for their problems, supporting them in various ways, or by giving them small gifts.... Building a personal relation, al-Berry stresses, was the most effective way to reach young people and channel them to become followers and possibly members. Al-Jamaa methodically trained its recruiters in methods to establish close personal rapport and gave them a small budget for presents and other forms of support.... Close personal relationships insofar extended beyond the group of "full-members" to an immediate following of associates, disciples, and possible candidates for joining the group, who became socialized into sharing a common perspective and lifestyle. (2011: 146)

The social characteristics of the membership also changed with the evolution of the conflict. Whereas initially al-Jamaa al-Islamiyya members were male university students who had often recently immigrated from Upper Egypt, in the early 1990s there was a larger number of members who were younger and less educated and who came from rural areas. According to Malthaner, "these numbers indicate not only that the group moved its activities from universities to villages and neighborhoods, but also that it seems to have recruited heavily among local residents and, consequently, developed a membership originating within and linked to the local communities" (2011: 152).

Even though – as Khosrokhavar (2006) concluded from research on Muslims in French prisons – they are very different from one another and show "les visages les plus variés,"[6] second-generation militants share some characteristics. From the early 1990s, as Olivier Roy observed, "a new breed of militants slowly emerged" (2004: 301). The second generation of AQ is mainly made up of

---

[6] Roy (2004) distinguished different types of these militants, such as politicized rebels, who are fascinated by anti-imperialism; religious nomads, who come from other religions; former drug addicts; and antiracists. In general, re-Islamization is presented as a result not of community pressure but of an individual search, often after meeting with an Afghan veteran in a mosque.

migrants; these individuals are sometimes from working-class backgrounds, are often born-again Muslims, and have a deterritorialized supranational network. They often have had experiences in the West: "This new breed was above all more largely uprooted than its predecessors, had few links (if any) to any particular Muslim country, and moved around the world, travelling from jihad to jihad" (ibid.: 302). Most had left their country of origin to study or work abroad (often in the West). All were Westernized in some way, none had attended an Islamic *madrassa*, many were trained in technical or scientific disciplines, and all spoke Western languages. Moreover, before their conversion, they often followed Western customs, drinking alcohol and smoking (ibid.: 311). They tended to have had a promiscuous sexual life and did not have a traditional Muslim marriage within the kinship group. Many of the second generation are said to have had past experiences with petty crime (but not with organized crime). In this sense, they are examples of a deterritorialized form of clandestine violence, in which specific conflicts in the Middle East and elsewhere play a role as a narrative but not as a direct experience (Roy 2008). Members of the second generation of activists tend not to go back to their country of origin to fight for Islam. However, some of them have gone to fight in other countries where they perceived Muslims to be in danger. Whereas several second-generation Western Muslims fought in Bosnia (Roy 2004: 314), others joined the guerrillas in Chechnya or Kashmir. Regarding this second generation, Roy (2008: 15ff.) referred to a violent youth movement, made up of young people who had broken with their families and acted outside of their traditional community bonds. Recruitment is more often driven by fascination with violence than by ideological indoctrination.

Within the second generation of Islamists, networks are rooted in groups sharing a certain geographic origin (e.g., Kashmir), in Muslim student associations, or in radical mosques. According to research findings based on 200 people involved in terrorist acts and plots in Western Europe (Bakker 2006), most of the subjects came from families with foreign origins – in general, those living in France had origins in Algeria; in Spain and the Netherlands, Morocco; and in the UK, Pakistan. Most had a lower- or middle-class background (respectively 39 and 30 individuals out of 72 subjects for whom class information was known). Of the 103 people for whom information on jobs was found, only 12 had a skilled occupation, whereas the percentage of unskilled workers and especially unemployed people was higher than in the Muslim population of Europe as a whole. One-quarter had previous criminal records, mainly for nonpolitical crimes. As in the other cases, people tended to join in groups: out of the 242 people analyzed, 50 had kinship relations and 43 friendship ties with other members. The average age was 27.3 (Bakker 2006).

For these activists, some mosques had functioned as places of propaganda and recruitment. Networks were formed around the Al-Quds Mosque in Hamburg, from which several 9/11 attackers came; the Finsbury Park Mosque in London; and the Abu Bark Mosque in Madrid. Repression and also self-control have significantly reduced this potential use. Prisons – in which Muslims are over-represented – have been said to provide another milieu for recruitment, as Islam became a religion of the repressed, and belonging to it was a positive mark of difference.

Among this second generation, groups of friends frequently joined together, sometimes after re-encountering old friends from their native country after they had migrated (e.g., five of the seven Madrid bombers played together in the same village in Morocco). An encounter with a radical preacher is a step that has been said to have brought entire groups of friends to join militant Salafism, as "the majority of those involved in militant Salafism become so in the context of a group" (Egerton 2011: 151). Recruitment in the second generation is described thus:

There is a general pattern of radicalization in Europe. A politicized middleman from the Middle East (usually with an "Afghan" background) contacts a group of local friends, often involved in petty delinquency or drug abuse, whose ethnic origin is less relevant than their sense of isolation and uprootedness, and who find in radical Islam a positive protest identity, even when they have no previous record of religious practice. (Roy 2004: 315)

In the second generation of European radicals, experiences of discrimination are often mentioned as a cause of identification. In research on the Islamic al-Muhagirun in Great Britain, Quintan Wiktorowicz (2005) described a process of cognitive change of future members linked to an identity crisis and experiences of discrimination. One of the militants who planted bombs in Paris in the mid-1990s – a French Algerian who had gone to Pakistan for training – stated,

I'm neither Arab nor French. I'm Muslim…. When I walk into a mosque, I'm at ease. They shake your hand, they treat you like an old friend. No suspicion, no prejudices…. When I see another Muslim in the street, he smiles, and we stop and talk. We recognize each other as brothers, even if we never met before. (Kohlmann 2004: 142)

This does not indicate, however, a lack of integration. Even for non-Europeans, there is intense contact with the West: "It is not a deficit of modernity, but a super-exposition to it" (Khosrokhavar 2006: 21). In fact, "the problem is in a reinter-pretation of Islam, built upon their individual experience, as a function of a sentiment of rejection, humiliation and of lost honor face to a West that they feel as the more foreigner the more it is near" (ibid.: 22). For instance, the story of Mohammad Siddique Khan, one of the four suicide bombers responsible for the 7 July 2005 attack in London reveals a life embedded in a modernized environment. Born in Leeds in 1974, after the attack he was presented in the media as a "quiet, studious boy" who "considered himself Western, and insisted his mainly non-Muslim friends on calling him 'Sid.' Moreover, while he was a teenager, Khan never showed interest in religion and rarely went to a mosque" (Transnational Terrorism, Security and the Rule of Law 2008d: 36). While in college, he had volunteered to help disadvantaged youngsters, a commitment he kept after college, when he became an engaged Muslim: "He told associates he had turned to religion after a far from blameless youth that had seen him involved in fights, drinking and drug-taking" (ibid.). Social networks also played an important role in his life history. At his workplace, the Hamara Youth Access Point (HYAP), he met the other three London bombers, all of whom attended the Omar "Stratford Street" Mosque in Leeds (ibid.: 37).

For the second generation of migrants, however, religious conversion often develops in situations of tension between traditional values and assimilation into Western society. According to Sageman, in Western countries, Muslims' radicalization occurs when young migrants are disconnected from family and peers through a sort of double isolation. They have learned the ambitions of the West but feel discriminated against. So they join groups that interpret this as a result of a war against Islam. An example of this progression is Muhammad Bouyeri, the killer of Theo van Gogh (Bakker 2006; Transnational Terrorism, Security and the Rule of Law 2008d). Of Moroccan origins and born and raised in a suburb of Amsterdam with strong presence of Moroccan and Turkish migrants, he was described as a good, gentle, and cooperative boy, although not excellent in school. Growing up, however, he became increasingly angry over the Palestinian situation, coming to support Hamas. After being arrested for a violence-related crime, he radicalized in prison. When released, he started to study as a social worker and volunteered for a community center, organizing soccer games and neighborhood cleanups. Wanting to establish a youth center, he lobbied the parliament and the city council, without success. The articles he wrote for a local journal became more radical over time, from calls for cross-religious tolerance to radical statements about the Dutch police (whom he called Nazis) and the war on Iraq (in which the Netherlands participated). After losing his job, he was recruited by a group of militant Islamists in Amsterdam and probably approached by jihadists.

In the diaspora, the suffering of distant coreligionists is intertwined with experiences of discrimination, giving them a specific meaning. One of the Islamists interviewed in jail in France declared that, through religion, he had "learned to respect myself, and not to respect the West" (Ouaman, quoted in Khosrokhavar 2006: 140). This sentiment was also expressed by Moussa, a militant who came from a nonpracticing family, spoke three languages ("Je suis pas un déshérités" [ibid.: 49]), and framed his claims in nationalist terms: "What we want is a Muslim government, not a Frenchisized, not an Americanized one, a Muslim one, and that's it" (ibid.: 48). He declared that he felt humiliated as a Muslim by Americans and Israel. Similar are the claims of Ahsen, a grandfather who holds a degree in science and fought against the French in Algeria; he declared that "our problem is not that the West does what it wants *chez lui*, but that it does what it wants *chez nous*" (ibid.: 73). Ahsen also believed that "Ben Laden acted in order to push away the Jewish from Palestine, or the Americans from Arabia" (ibid.: 74).

This identification as Muslim then strengthens sensitivity toward "distant issues." One militant stated that he felt such an interest "when I hear of the Israeli missiles over Palestine..." (Khosrokhavar 2006: 142); he also criticized

France because it claimed to promote democracy but supported the coup d'état in Algeria. A similar, gradual identification with distant issues is visible in the life history of one of the 9/11 bombers, Mohamed Atta. Born in 1968, he is an Egyptian from a nonreligious family. His two sisters are university professors who do not wear a veil. The son of a lawyer, Atta graduated with a degree in architecture from Cairo University. He studied city planning in Hamburg in the early 1990s and then worked part time for a German planning firm for five years; he lost his job in 1997. In 1999, he wrote a dissertation on the souk of Aleppo, in Syria, that is, on a pre-Islamic city. As he started to perceive the West as humiliating the Islamic world, he became more devout, especially during a pilgrimage to Mecca in 1995 and then to Afghanistan in 1999. He moved to the United States in 2000. In nationalist tones, he expressed regret that Egypt opened up to the West without concern for the well-being of Egyptians. Similarly, two other members of Atta's Hamburg cell, Marwan al-Shehhi (from the United Arab Emirates) and Ziad Jarrah (from Lebanon), arrived in Germany in 1996 and radicalized while in Germany. Both from middle-class backgrounds, they are said to have initially taken on Western tastes, including smoking and listening to music. Descriptions of the Hamburg cell stress a team spirit, accompanied by development of fraternal bonds out of isolation. Similarly, Omar, one of the British al-Qaeda radicals, is said to have developed awareness of Muslim suffering while helping victims in Afghanistan and then in Pakistan; he described his actions as "helping the Mujahidin who were fighting the Goliath" (Holmes 2005: 69).

In conclusion, given the heterogeneity of the Muslim population in terms of language, nationality, and ethnic group, for those living in the immigration countries, identification with Islam implies a reinvention of Islam (Roy 2004).

ACTIVATION OF MILITANT NETWORKS: CONCLUSIONS

Networks assume a fundamental value in recruitment into clandestine organizations. In all four types of clandestine violence, participation in groups of relatives, friends, and political comrades favored the recruitment of individuals into underground groups. Involvement in the milieus that served as relays – or connections – for the radical component of broader movements was one condition that increased the likelihood that a particular individual would participate in a radical movement organization. According to this trend, one's chance of being recruited into a movement increases with participation in specific personal networks actually connected with more militant areas. The peer groups to which individuals belonged played a very important role in determining their successive political choices (for instance, joining a more structured movement's organization), particularly in passages from low-risk to high-risk activism.

Participation in radical milieus was facilitated by family and friendship ties and then escalated in everyday experiences of violent confrontations with police and militia groups. Throughout the networks of friends-comrades, friendship reinforced the relevance of political commitment, while political commitment strengthened some friendship ties, and groups of political friends became closed units. Within the movement environment, personal networks are connected with one another, and new networks emerge from old.

Networks exercised peer-group pressures, influencing the construction of external reality. Group memberships then became relevant at two levels: physical proximity within a networks of peers and identification with an imagined community. Homophyly, in terms of sociodemographic characteristics and the beliefs that derive from such characteristics, was then reinforced by the social influence of others in the group; friendship and common values strengthened each other, thus producing emerging social norms that were then enforced through the group's capacity to distribute prices and punishments (e.g., Sageman 2004).

Some characteristics of these networks changed in the evolution of the history of the underground organizations, and with these changes came a shift in the balance between types of networks. Via long-lasting, relational processes, clandestine groups developed from politicized networks and also contributed to the creation of new groups. In all four types of clandestine groups, we could in fact distinguish (at least) two generations, which differed in terms of sociographic characteristics and also political milieus and attitudes toward violence. The first generation was more closely linked to old political traditions (of the Left, the Right, nationalism, or pan-Islamism). Family ties were more often important in the recruitment process, producing a precocious politicization into free spaces, in which the ideals of resistance for the Left, fascism for the Right, Basque identity for the ETA, or religious devotion for the Islamist groups were nurtured. In particular, founders of clandestine groups often came from politically committed families, in which they were socialized to specific values and were provided with specific narratives about the world. Further, as a result of more cautious strategies of recruitment by the clandestine organizations, entrance into clandestine groups was slower, involving a gradual break with those traditions. Violence was learned gradually.

The second generation of militants grew instead within an environment that had already been radicalized by clandestine organizations. Whereas family traditions were more varied, militants were socialized to violence at a very young age and also joined the underground when they were still very young. Experiences with violence long predated entrance into the underground. Harsh struggles between the extreme Left and the extreme Right as well as between activists and the police in Italy; the unsolved center-periphery conflicts in Spain; and the severe conflicts that involved Muslim groups in Afghanistan, Bosnia, and Chechnya all contributed to producing new generations of militants with lower taboos against violence. Recruitment of peer groups thus proceeded at a fast pace, involving groups of often extremely young activists.

As mentioned in the introductory chapter, my explanation stresses emerging qualities rather than causal determination, as "the 'whys' or 'reasons' for joining arise out of the recruitment itself" (Snow, Zurcher, and Ekland-Olson 1980: 799). In this sense, it goes beyond the traditional social movement agenda that has looked at networks and motivations as preconditions for action, instead stressing the emerging nature of such networks. As Wood (2003: 15) observed in the case of insurgents in El Salvador, the most important networks are not the preexisting networks but those formed in action, as "these networks were not based on strong antecedent communities" but rather emerged with collective action. Motivations emerged in action as well – as she recalls, "insurgent *campesinos* did not act because they were confident they would receive land as a result of their participation. Rather, reasons for which participants acted referred irreducibly to the wellbeing of others as well as oneself, and to processes, not just outcomes" (ibid.: 19). Costs were therefore transformed into rewards, such as the pleasure in agency, a "positive affect associated with self-determination, autonomy, self-esteem, efficacy and pride that comes from the successful assertion of intention" (ibid.: 235). Commitment was process driven: it was not what they got that motivated them; rather, motivations emerged as they were getting there. Opportunity structures were therefore produced along the way.

5

Organizational Compartmentalization

ORGANIZATIONAL COMPARTMENTALIZATION: AN INTRODUCTION

Parallel to, and partially overlapping with, the organization of Ordine Nuovo were the Nuclei Territoriali di Difesa dello Stato or NDS, which operated under the direction of the army, and had as one of their goals the implementation of a so-called Piano di Sopravvivenza, consisting ostensibly of resistance or guerrilla action in the event of a Soviet invasion…. The Nuclei were divided into Legions (up to thirty-six in all) and each Legion consisted of civilian and ex-military personnel who could be relied upon as staunch anti-communists and be trained and eventually utilised by the army. The fifth Legion, active in Verona, was led by Major (later Colonel and then General) Amos Spiazzi, who, by his own admission, started to recruit neo-fascist and neo Nazi elements, so much so that he practically incorporated the Verona group of Ordine Nuovo into the Nuclei. (Minna 1984: 35–6)

There are the conditions for a spontaneous struggle, SPONTANEISM! Be then the slogan that the vanguard sends to comrades. To make a Cuib, three or four comrades are sufficient. (*Quex*, no. 2, 1979: 8, cited in Ferraresi 1995: 282)

Although the organizational characteristics of groups in clandestinity have been considered as relevant in understanding their choices, as these two quotes, which refer to Italian radical Right clandestine groups, show, they do indeed vary. In particular, they indicate that the organizational structure in the Italian radical Right changed dramatically in the course of a decade, moving from a hierarchical to a horizontal structure.

In the evolution of social movements in all of the types of clandestine violence examined in this text, we have witnessed both the radicalization of some social movement organizations (SMOs) and the moderation of others. As mentioned (see Chapter 3), we therefore have to look for specific explanations for both contrasting paths by considering the effect of the protest cycle on different SMOs and trying to explain their institutionalization, disappearance, or radicalization. This means addressing long historical processes in which specific phases of radicalization are located, as already-existing SMOs provide organizational resources for those that follow, thus influencing their strategic choices. In addition, SMOs exist within a particularly volatile environment, in which the mobilization of protest may move rapidly from a peak to a decline. In trying to adapt to environmental transformations, they transform themselves, but not all in the same direction. Although some contextual conditions exist at the onset of clandestine organizations, they are filtered through organizational processes.

Moreover, in turn, radical organizations favor the diffusion of violence. Even if they cannot be considered as the primary cause, the presence of other organizations that advocate violence plays an important role in the development of clandestine organizations. Underground organizations evolve within and then break away from larger, nonviolent social movement organizations. Exploiting environmental conditions conducive to militancy, splinter groups undergo further radicalization and eventually create new resources and occasions for violence. These radical groups, in other words, themselves become agents, or entrepreneurs, for the propagation of violence.

How does this happen? I suggest in this chapter that, in the four cases examined here, adaptation to both increasing repression and decreasing support brought about an *organizational compartmentalization*: that is, groups became increasingly isolated in their structures – hierarchical but also fragmented. Whether they were centralized or networked, the increasingly bounded potential for strategic choices brought the underground organizations to detach themselves from their external environment. Previous studies on radical political organizations offer quite opposite approaches to organizational decision making. The ideological perspective defines radical organizations as ideological sects that are based on emotional commitments and governed by internal dynamics. The instrumental perspective considers them instead as instrumental actors who logically relate means to ends to bring about changes in their environment. Studies of political violence have often shifted between the two.

Sociological analyses have focused on the ideological characteristics of the radical organizations. So, for instance, German commentators traced the ideological roots of the RAF to traditional left-wing ideology (for instance, Rohrmoser 1981), and Italian scholars have ascribed the ideology of the Red Brigades to the workerist tradition – that is, to a splinter branch of Marxism that stressed the autonomy of workers' action from parties (Galante 1981; Ventura 1980). The evolution of exclusive conceptions of Basque nationalism into (more) inclusive conceptions has been analyzed in depth (Jauregui Bereciartu 1981). As for religious groups, their very reliance on revealed truth and absolute beliefs has been considered as facilitating (if not promoting) fanaticism (Juergensmeyer 2000). In this perspective, the ideologies of radical organizations tend to be considered as the main causes of political violence.

Other scholars have considered that interests, rather than ideas, influence choices in violent organizations. Martha Crenshaw (2011) presented terrorism as a political strategy adopted by groups that are endowed with some preferences and that select courses of action from a range of perceived alternatives.

Radical forms of violence are often strategically chosen when, in conditions of scarce resources, other methods have failed to attain the radical changes that are demanded. In fact, terrorism is considered as an arm of the poor; for example, it is used when groups have few members and little mobilization capacity, when the state uses heavy repression, and when there are time constraints (impatience for action) or expectation of regime vulnerability (see also Smelser 2007: 52). Successful examples from other armed groups help in spreading violence.

Ideas and interests are, however, not necessarily opposed: interests are not inherent in some material conditions but are cognitively constructed, and strategic choices not only are normatively constrained but also depend on the perceived external opportunities and organizational resources. The choice of repertoires is, therefore, influenced by aims and strategies but also limited by norms and perceptions of opportunities.

Parallel to the ideas-versus-interest debate is the question of how decisions are made in clandestine organizations. One image, which is developed especially within terrorist studies and re-emerges with each new wave of violent attacks, is that radicals are incapable of strategically oriented action, seeing as their behavior is erratic. In another approach, they are instead assumed to have (more or less) hidden goals, which are in some cases connected with dirty games in the system of international relations. As we will see in what follows, decision making in these four radical organizations emerged neither as spontaneous reaction nor as totally calculated strategies but rather showed the environmental limitations on (bounded) strategic choice (Crenshaw 2011).

Relying especially on social movement studies, I address these debates, keeping in mind the complexity of processes in which both instrumental reasoning and perverse effects are intertwined. Because it concentrates on the meso level, social movement research seems particularly valuable in allowing us to look at the organizational fields in which violent organizations move and at not only their internal competition but also their relations with their enemies. Drawing on organizational approaches to social movements, I bear in mind both instrumental behavior and vicious circles.

Attention to SMOs has been at the core of the resource mobilization approach, whose proponents stress "both the rational-economic assumptions and formal organizational thrusts" (Zald and McCarthy 1987: 45). Social movement organizations must mobilize resources from the surrounding environment, whether directly in the form of money or through voluntary work by their adherents; they must neutralize opponents and increase support from both the general public and the elites (e.g., McCarthy and Zald 1977: 19). Stressing its instrumental logic, a social movement organization can be defined as a "complex, or formal, organization which identifies its goals with the preferences of a social movement or countermovement and attempts to implement those goals" (ibid.: 20).

However, SMOs are also sources of identity for the movements' constituencies as well as their opponents and the public (della Porta and Diani 2006). In fact, SMOs play an identification function and can be defined as "associations of persons making idealistic and moralistic claims about how human personal or group life ought to be organized that, *at the time of their claims making*, are marginal to or excluded from mainstream society" (Lofland 1996: 2–3, italics in the original). In social movement literature, the first approach has been dominant. As Clemens and Minkoff have recently noted, with the development of the resource mobilization perspective, "attention to organization appeared antithetical to analysis of culture and interaction. As organizations were understood instrumentally, the cultural content of organizing and the meanings signaled by organizational forms were marginalized as a topic for inquiry" (2004: 156). In recent approaches, however, SMOs are increasingly considered as "contexts for political conversation," characterized by specific etiquettes (Eliasoph 1998: 21). Different visions and norms explain why not all SMOs react in the same way to similar external challenges.

Attention to norms increased with the evolution in the sociology of organizations from a closed- to an open-system approach, and then to neoinstitutionalism. In organizational studies, a closed-system approach has traditionally focused on organizations as self-sufficient systems, whereas an open-system approach has suggested that they are influenced by the resources they can mobilize in their environments.[1] Later on, according to the neoinstitutional approach in organizational theory, the focus has shifted from the technical to the sociocultural environment (Scott 1983: 161). According to two proponents of this approach: "The new institutionalism in organizational theory and sociology comprises a rejection of the rational-actor models, an interest in institutions as independent variables, a turn towards cognitive and cultural explanations, and an interest in properties of supra-individual units of analysis that cannot be reduced to aggregations or direct consequences of individuals' attributes or motives" (DiMaggio and Powell 1991: 8–9).

In my research, I share some of the concerns expressed by the neoinstitutional approach in an attempt to combine the analysis of environmental impacts with that of organizational choices, as constrained by organizational norms. In particular, I consider organizations as socializing agents and as producers of norms, which "do not just constrain options: they establish the very criteria by which people discover their preferences" (DiMaggio and Powell 1991: 11). Organizations are therefore not just means for mobilization but also (or even mainly) arenas for experimentation.

I also share with the neoinstitutional approach a focus on cognitive mechanisms: organizations do not automatically adapt to their environments; environmental

---

[1] These approaches can be distinguished mainly by the (relative) roles assigned to environmental influence and organizational agency, respectively. With the development of organizational sociology, the so-called closed-system approach presented internal organizational factors as "the prime causal agents in accounting for the structure and behaviour of organizations" (Scott 1983: 156). In the 1960s, the open-system approach stressed instead the technical interdependence of organizations and their environments, whereas later the metaphor of the garbage can was used to describe decision making in conditions of highly ambiguous preferences and little information on environmental constraints and opportunities (see March 1988).

pressures are filtered by organizational actors' perceptions.[2] Although I consider environmental constraints as potentially important in shaping organizational behavior, I believe that organizations play an important and active role in shaping their environments. For social movements, as for other social actors, the organization is therefore not just a means but also an end in itself. The same applies to clandestine organizations.

I suggest that organizational evolution happens during long-lasting processes in which several actors interact; thus organizations are relational in character. Looking at social movement studies for inspiration, my analysis of clandestine organizations develops from a few observations. Organizations are open systems; that is, they are influenced by the environment with which they interact. This environment can be defined as an organizational field, made up of all the actors with whom the organizations enter into contact. Clandestine political organizations develop therefore in relation to one another and to the external environment, which includes not only opponents (mainly repressive state apparatuses) but also concentric circles made up of other violent organizations, other organizations belonging to the same social movement family, and potential sympathizers. Drawing on these assumptions, I suggest that, at the meso level, the process of radicalization of social movement organizations as well as underground organizations includes a progressive *encapsulation* of some social movement organizations.

As seen in Chapter 3, radicalization develops in dense organizational fields, from competition between various organizations that conflict with one another on the use of violence (among other issues). Clandestine organizations evolve within and then break away from larger, nonviolent social movement organizations. Exploiting environmental conditions conducive to militancy, these splinter groups undergo further radicalization and eventually create new resources and opportunities for violence.

Organizational dynamics develop in the underground, through a progressive encapsulation. Underground, the organizations become increasingly compartmentalized and closed to the outside. Groups that go underground to perform low-level actions of violence then tend, under the pressure of state repression as well as internal competition for leadership, to escalate their forms of violence, moving toward the use of lethal and sometimes indiscriminate violence. Isolated from potential supporters and forced to self-finance through holdups and

[2] Organizations are, that is, constructed. Neoinstitutionalists marked a shift from Parsons's conception of norms internalization (with a concept of utilitarianism derived from Freud) to an emphasis on cognitive processes, derived from ethnomethodology and phenomenology and their focus on everyday action and practical knowledge (DiMaggio and Powell 1991: 15ff.) based on the assumption that "organization members discover their motives by acting" (ibid.: 19). Important for this analysis is Bourdieu's notion of *habitus* as "a system of 'regulated improvisation' or generative rules that represent the (cognitive, affective, and evaluative) internalization by actors of past experiences on the basis of shared typifications of social categories, experienced phenomenally as 'people like us'" (ibid.: 26).

kidnappings, the clandestine organizations sometimes enter into relations with criminal groups (see Chapter 6). In addition, their ideology tends to become increasingly obscure to outsiders, developing into an instrument for internal consumption (see Chapter 7).

Organizations are important actors: they select their own structures, action strategies, and ideological frames. As we will see, these developments derive in part from the tensions between different organizational aims. Radical organizations, like other political organizations, aim at attracting sympathizers through structure, actions, and frames that are apt for propaganda. In doing this, clandestine organizations compete in a crowded organizational field, in which they need to outbid their competitors. We have seen that organizational competition is a potential cause for violence as, especially in situations of declining mobilization, violence is an instrument for attracting consent (see Chapter 3).[3] Once in the underground, tensions with (sometimes legal) kindling organizations can bring about an investment in more violent forms of action.

The most important aim of organizations is to mobilize resources in their environment and allocate them to perform different external and internal tasks. As with other political organizations, underground ones need to address sometimes conflicting goals, those that are externally oriented – aiming at legitimizing goals and methods of the organization – and those that are internally oriented – aiming at maintaining the organization itself (della Porta 1995: chap. 4). The balance among them varies in different historical moments, as strategic choices are not only made but also limited by environmental and normative constraints. In particular, clandestinity develops a logic of its own, broadly limiting the range of available options as well as the organizational capacity to construct them. As clandestine organizations fight their adversary, the state, in this struggle their very choice of clandestinity brings them toward a military conception, which tends to isolate them from a broader social movement environment focusing on resisting state repression.

The specific constellation of environmental conditions and normative constraints will influence which organizational model is chosen by clandestine groups. Renate Mayntz observed that these groups, like most other types of organizations, tend to combine aspects of hierarchy with aspects of networks. As for hierarchy, they share the following features:

1. They have a clearly defined leadership – e.g. the *cupola* (SL), *army executive* (IRA), *majlis shura* (Islamic Jihad), *council* or again *majlis shura* (Al Qaida). 2. They are differentiated both vertically and functionally. All terrorist organizations covered (again

---

[3] Social psychology has linked radicalization not only to cognitive mechanisms such as social comparison (as extreme opinions are more admired) but also to intergroup competition that is said to produce hostility toward a threatening group. External threat produces cohesion, whereas continuing threat produces escalation. Outbidding is a version of this phenomenon that develops when there is competition among groups struggling for the same cause (McCauley and Moskalenko 2011).

including Al Qaida) have specialized units directly below the top leadership level. In some cases the main distinction is between a military and a support branch, in other cases various units distinguished by functions such as finances, procurement, propaganda etc. are related to the operative units in a matrix-like fashion. All terrorist organizations have furthermore a clearly circumscribed third level of operative units, the famous cells. 3. Vertical communication dominates. (2004: 12, emphasis in the original)

However, clandestine organizations also share characteristics that are typical of a network structure, such as the following:

1. There is no detailed central steering of operations; the operative units, or cells, enjoy a considerable degree of autonomy in planning their day-to-day actions and in the execution of acts of terrorism, sabotage etc. 2. The organization reacts quickly and flexibly to situational exigencies (threats as well as opportunities) by changing plans and the function of individual members. 3. The organization has a relatively open and fluid boundary. New cells are continuously created, and dissolve. At all levels except the top leadership, there are members with different grades of identification with the organization. (ibid.)

Although it is true that these different elements might enter into reciprocal tensions – and this applies also to all forms of organizations – the balance of the two types of elements can have positive effects.[4] Conceiving of all organizations as balancing the different principles rather than definitively opting for one or the other ideal type helps in identifying some specific features, such as (1) the presence of a particular mode of control, with a large scope for autonomous action but also a central leadership, steering activities around centrally formulated strategies; (2) the presence of a latent relationship, with little face-to-face communication either between levels or within the rank-and-file units; and (3) strong identification, based on ideological indoctrination and practical learning (ibid.: 13).

As we will see in what follows, clandestine political organizations have different organizational formats: some look more like an army, and some more like a party; some are more compartmentalized, and others less; some ask their members to go underground, and others do not. The comparative analysis shows that the chosen structure is justified by more general visions. Thus, for instance, left-wing organizations tend to develop structures that imitate democratic centralism; right-wing groups are more prone toward hierarchical structured leadership; ethnonationalist groups develop to a greater extent along the lines of a military model; and religious groups include responsibility for religious purity. However, all groups tend to experiment with similar tensions between military and political action and between centralism and compartmentalization and, in general, to develop from political organizations toward a sect model.

---

[4] In fact, "the different features of a hybrid organization can counteract each other, and in this way contain the negative effects following from each pure type, such as the rigidity of hierarchy and the centrifugal force of network structure. In the case of terrorist organizations, the addition of network elements to a basically hierarchical structure is held to be necessary to maintain operational effectiveness in the face of constant threats of discovery and repression" (Mayntz 2004).

In what follows, I will analyze the organizational models and their evolution in these four types of clandestine organizations. Common to all of them is a mechanism of organizational compartmentalization, which features progressive encapsulation from the external environment and fragmentation.

ORGANIZATIONAL COMPARTMENTALIZATION AND LEFT-WING ORGANIZATIONS

The Brigate Rosse (BR) was founded in 1970 in Milan by militants of one of the many radical leftist groups, the Collettivo Politico Metropolitano (CPM). Some of these militants came from a small group from the traditionally red city of Reggio Emilia, the Collettivo Politico Operaio (CPO); others came from a student group active at the University of Trent, the Università Alternativa, and the Centro Informazione di Verona. In 1968, members of the three groupings founded the group Lavoro Politico, whereas other members of the CPO of Reggio Emilia joined the left-wing organization Lotta Continua (LC). After some experiences in a Marxist-Leninist group (the Partito Comunista Italiano Marxista Leninista [PCIml]), some activists from Lavoro Politico joined with activists of the Collettivo Politico Operaio Studenti of Borgo Manero (a town on the outskirts of Milan) to found the Collettivo Politico Metropolitano, which later gave birth to the BR.

The group tried in the beginning to keep a "double level of militancy": the organization itself would be clandestine, but its members had to engage in political activity, in particular, in the industrial conflict. However, house searches and arrests of members following a series of BR bombings and a few "demonstrative" kidnappings pushed the group underground.

The organizational structure was inspired by the traditional democratic centralism of left-wing organizations. According to the BR statute, decisions had to be conveyed from the top down, from the National Executive Committee to the territorial columns and, then, to the local (neighbor- or factory-based) brigades. Beyond the territorially based columns, fronts were responsible for various areas of activity (groups of workers, military actions, and so on). Although initially decisions were mainly made by the historical founders of the group, around 1972 an executive committee was set up, with the task of directing the actions of the columns and fronts. In a step toward centralization, a strategic direction was created to establish the political line, regulate the internal life of the organization, and allocate the budget. The structure was hierarchical: in it, representatives of the city-level columns (of which there were initially only two, for Turin and Milan) were co-opted (Caselli and della Porta 1984: 160–1).

Moreover, increasing repression pushed the organization to implement separation between the different organs, so that each member tended to know only a few others or at least was allowed to interact only within his or her own small group. After a wave of arrests in 1972, the BR focused on the construction of a clandestine structure, including the acquisition of hideouts, around each of which an operative group was formed. Rules of clandestinity also started to be more rigidly implemented, with fewer opportunities to interact with movement activists or even to participate in protest activities.

Recruitment was a long-lasting process that ended in clandestinity. Attention focused especially around the small, extreme Left groups that seemed more promising in terms of proselytism. The idea of the fronts, which were intended to allow workers of one factory meet and talk with those of another, was never effective, given security concerns. Their activity thus became increasingly focused on preparation for action.

The very names of the fronts and the roles they played testify to the declining role of political propaganda and the increasing attention to the military war against the state (see also Chapter 6). Not only did the Front of the Factories tend to lose power to the Logistic Front – a common criticism made by BR militants – but in the mid-1970s the Front for the Fight against the Counter-Revolution was created and was substituted for the Mass Front (which had represented an evolution of the Factories' Front). The militants in prison created the Brigate di Campo.

Although initially the individual choice to go underground was made when necessary to escape arrests, being "regular" (that is, in hiding) was later considered a sign of higher commitment. The group's hierarchical turn is testified by the increasing power of the full-time, regular militants over the "irregular" ones, especially during the second half of the 1970s. In fact, the role of these full-time militants – who had renounced their legal life – was increasingly emphasized. Whereas no structure open to sympathizers existed, only the regular militants – defined as the "more conscious and generous cadres produced by the armed struggle" (BR, *Alcune questioni per la discussione sull'organizzazione*, 1972) – could aspire to become part of the "vertical structure of command" (ibid.).

Given its smaller dimension, the RAF was in theory more decentralized, aiming at forming "simply structured groups of eight to ten persons (in which to build the command level) if possible in all the cities of the federal states" (cited in della Porta 1995: 116). In its first years, it operated in six German cities (Steiner and Debray 1987: 117–30). As in the previous example, however, the imprisoned leaders played an important symbolic role; Andreas Baader in particular was described by his comrades as "the leader of the RAF because from the very beginning he had what the guerrilla needs the most: willingness, awareness of the goals, firmness, collectedness.… In these five years we learned from Andreas – because he is what we can define as an example – … to fight, fight, and fight again" (ibid.: 155). "Andreas," added Ulrike Meinhof in 1975, "is for us what Fidel is for Cuba, Che for Latin America, Lumumba for the Belgian Congo, Ho for Vietnam, Marighella for Brazil, Malcolm X for the blacks in the USA, George [Jackson] for the prisoners in the USA … the personification of a collective leadership" (ibid.: 158).

As was the case for the BR, compartmentalization followed waves of arrests. According to a RAF document from 1971, although the organization initially tried to keep connections with a broader movement, experiences of repression forced it deeper underground:

Our initial concept of the urban guerrilla implied a link between urban guerrilla and mass work. We all wanted to work in the factories, in the neighbourhoods, in the existing socialist groups, we wanted to influence the discussion, to experiment, to learn. It became clear that this was impossible. The control of the political police over these groups, their meetings, their discussions is so widespread that it is impossible to take part in them without being singled out and put into their dossiers. (quoted in Steiner and Debray 1987: 125)

Compartmentalization and centralization were not irreversible trends but were affected by environmental conditions: they tended to diminish in more supportive environments, and vice versa. For instance, in some periods both groups decentralized their organizational models and created structures open to sympathizers (such as the RAF's antifascist committees and the BR's Nuclei of the Proletarian Movement of Offensive Resistance).

Also, in both countries, the latecomer clandestine organizations, in open criticism of the BR and RAF, tried to keep their structures more open and decentralized. So did the Prima Linea (Front Line [PL]) and the Formazioni Comuniste Combattenti (Communist Fighting Formations [FCC]) in Italy and the Bewegung 2 Juni (June 2nd Movement [B2J]) and the Rote Zellen (Red Cells [RZ]) in Germany. The FCC aimed at "clandestinity in military action but not in proselytism" (FCC, *Statuto*, 1978). The PL's fighting worker squads or fighting proletarian patrols and the FCC's proletarian armed squads were open to sympathizers who did not share all the aims of the organizations but were nevertheless willing to participate in actions on a small scale and on a local level; these participants were autonomous in their choices (even though their commanders participated in coordinating efforts).

Both groups originally planned to use horizontal decision making. In the PL, each territorial *nucleo* (nucleus) had to elect a delegate (or commander) who had to meet with the others in an organizational conference, during which they had to elect local commandos, who in turn had to elect the national commando and the national executive (della Porta 1990: 230). Fronts or commissions were set up to address specific tasks, such as support for their comrades in prison, propaganda, information on repression, and logistics.

Similarly, in Germany, the B2J wanted to combine legal and illegal work; the RZ asked its members not to go underground and, instead, to participate in legal protest campaigns. The B2J defined its "battle as part of the entire resistance. The urban guerrilla embodies imagination and energy, qualities that the people have" (B2J, *Die Entführung aus unserer Sicht*, 1975: 2). They in fact openly criticized what they stigmatized as the hyper-underground and hierarchical organizational model of the RAF. As a member of the B2J stated,

"We did not have directive cadres like the RAF. We considered ourselves part of the left-wing movement. Our aim was to support the mass campaigns with militant actions" (cited in della Porta 1995: 132). The B2J was in fact structured into something akin to affinity groups, made up of three to nine people who had often known one another before joining the clandestine organization. The small groups were autonomous from one another, but they had plans to hold assemblies of delegates of the various nuclei, which however never materialized (della Porta 1995: 118).

The RZ was also formed by several semiautonomous groupings that were supposed to grow in number as their revolutionary ideas spread. The RZ aimed in fact at "organizing counter-power in small nuclei that work and fight autonomously in the different social fields.... And at a certain point, when we will have many, many nuclei, then the definition of the urban guerrilla as mass perspective is fulfilled" (Revolutionäre Zelle, *Revolutionärer Zorn*, 1975: 8). According to the German judges,

the different groups of the organization exist and operate according to a principle of the most strict separation.... Nevertheless, there are various types of contacts between the various groups. Those members who have been in the organization for a longer time, and therefore have the deepest knowledge of the organization of the Revolutionary Cells and a dominant position in their group, maintain these contacts. (quoted in della Porta 1995: 118)

This decentralized structure resonated with an egalitarian ethos: "In our group, we were all equals," said a militant (ibid.). Decision-making processes had to be "the product of common discussions and editorial meetings of members of different groups that were held before a final decision was made on the content of the publication" (Revolutionäre Zelle, *Revolutionärer Zorn*, 1975: 23).

This decentralized model, however, worked only for short periods, as it was ill fit to face repression. As a result, like in the other examples, there was a move to centralization. For instance, the general assembly of PL members (according to the statute, the supreme organ of the organization) was discontinued because of security concerns. For similar reasons, the structures open to sympathizers (the squads) disappeared, and power was centralized in the national executive.

So, after a couple of years, all the mentioned organizations either disappeared or changed their structures toward a more compartmentalized model, which ended up fueling the very isolation it was supposed to address. In both cases, internal dynamics pushed the groups deeper underground. Internal conflicts developed, especially among different generations and militants inside and outside prisons, on the relative balance of political and military action, and on the degree and forms of legitimized violence.

Centralization in the underground also favored factionalism, by reducing the possibility to express dissent; at the same time, compartmentalization reduced the opportunities for debate. Personal conflicts over leadership interacted with widespread divergences about the "right" strategy to contrast state repression and societal isolation. Organizational fractionalization, as characterized by the evolutionary dynamic, is evident for example in the organization that survived the longest: the BR. Until the end of the 1970s, the organization had not suffered any divisions – beyond the departure of three of its leaders at the start of the decade. The end of the decade, however, witnessed a series of successive splits. Internal conflicts were the expression of different strategies to deal with organizational difficulties. The common element of the various separatist groups was the accusation made to the national leaders that the group was suffering from "militarism," defined as "detachment from the political attitude to intervention." Such a criticism was expressed by activists involved in the first division, which took place in 1979. In a document sent to the daily paper *Lotta Continua* (*The Struggle Continues*), a group of dissidents (among which the most well known were Adriana Faranda and Valerio Morucci) accused the organization's founders of disconnecting from their base and not understanding current social transformations. The organization's reply to these criticisms was verbally violent; a few months later, the main spokesmen for members of the first generation of the BR, who were serving sentences at Asinara Prison, courted controversy with the new leaders, accusing them of "bureaucratic and militaristic detours," being "incapable of participating with the people," "bad management of the Moro kidnapping," and, furthermore, excluding activists in prison from the internal debate over the organization. This break was diplomatically resolved for tactical reasons, but the brigadiers of the historical nucleus would subsequently support the creation of other separatist groups such as the Colonna Walter Alasia in Milan or, in 1981, the Prisons' Front, which would lead to the Party of the Proletarian Guerrilla of the Metropolitan Proletariat. In these cases, too, the main criticism of the leaders of the organization was that they had lost touch with collective movements. The same was true in the PL, from which came the groups that formed the Per il Comunismo and the Nuclei Left. Several of these splits developed around the tensions between military and political logic.

Fractionalization became particularly acute in the 1980s, as various groups proposed different solutions to perceived defeats. For the Brigate Rosse, this was a phase of virulent division between the Brigate Rosse–Partito della Guerriglia and the Brigate Rosse per la Formazione del Partito Combattente, which divided BR members not only outside but also inside prison. As recalled by Prospero Gallinari – who, from prison, supported the actions of the latter, while other founders of the BR (including the founder Renato Curcio) were supporting the former: "This is Novara and these are us. The break of a generation. We are so increasingly small that, at best, we hate each other cordially. But this prison framework also represents a break from the outside world, from the state where you find not only what's left of the armed struggle but all social movements" (2006: 319). Although it was smaller, the RAF was also torn by internal conflicts. In 1972, the bombing of the headquarters of the publishing house Springer, in which several workers were wounded, was strongly criticized by one of the RAF's founders, Gudrun Ennslin. In 1977, Karl-Heinz Dellwo, who was one of the group's imprisoned leaders, attacked his organization's support for the Palestinians who had hijacked a Lufthansa plane. Dellwo was also critical of the kidnapping of the president of German entrepreneurs, Hanns Martin Schleyer, and the killing of the hostage (cited in Seufert 1978).

In conclusion, as repression pushed militants into hiding and sympathizers abandoned the group, the organizational model became increasingly hierarchical and militarized but also compartmentalized and fractionalized.

ORGANIZATIONAL COMPARTMENTALIZATION AND RIGHT-WING ORGANIZATIONS

The right-wing clandestine organizations that emerged at the end of the 1960s also tried to combine political and military activities.

Founded in the 1950s with the stated aim of strengthening the state through the elimination of parties and trade unions, the National Front (Fronte Nazionale [FN]) was organized into city-level delegations, with a visible level and an underground level. The second (level B) was, in fact, formed by armed groups that had the task of organizing multiple "minor criminal actions, aggressions, clashes," thus creating alarm in the public opinion and consequently pushing "the Armed Forces, so long humiliated ... to intervene so as to re-establish the law" (cited in Ferraresi 1984: 61). The National Front's underground units were "prepared to strike when the appropriate time came" (Weinberg and Eubank 1987: 40).

The organizational model of the Ordine Nuovo (New Order [ON]) was similar. With its about 600 members (Franzinelli 2008: 426–7), the ON had a very centralized political directorate. The group was structured into "sectors," which included sections dedicated to organization, propaganda, financial initiatives, high school scholars, university students, workers, parallel organizations, press relations, external affairs, activism, and ideology. In addition to the Direzione Nazionale, there was the Consiglio Nazionale, composed of regional leaders, regional and provincial directorates, and three Ispettorati di Zona for the northern, central, and southern regions (Minna 1984: 34). Its "seminars of political formation" included instruction on the theory of revolutionary war, organization of a revolutionary group, techniques of financing, and organization of self-defense (ibid.: 35). Clandestine structures also existed, however. In addition to the hidden organizational structure of the Nuclei Territoriali di Difesa dello Stato (see the incipit to this chapter), there were cells. Each "comprised a small number of activists and, to ensure a high degree of secrecy, the cells were in contact with each other only through their leaders," who reported directly to the national leaders (Cento Bull 2007: 31).

The Avanguardia Nazionale (National Vanguard [AN]), which comprised about 500 members, had a federalist structure, with somewhat autonomous regional units (Franzinelli 2008: 424). It had action squads in several Italian cities. Since its foundation, the AN "engaged in a variety of acts of 'neo-squadrism.' Rome, and especially its university was the locale for many of these punitive expeditions. Illustratively, a student, Paolo Rossi, was killed during a scuffle between a National Vanguard contingent and a leftist student group in 1966" (Weinberg and Eubank 1987: 37).

As in the other cases, environmental changes were reflected in organizational ones. After the ON was outlawed in 1973, its members converged with those of the AN and formed a new group, the Ordine Nero (Minna 1984: 61). The organizational structure of the group was "formed on vertical lines and articulated horizontally in isolated compartments, that did not communicate with each other, but only with the top" (ibid.: 61). A court described two levels in Ordine Nero: an official one devoted to nonviolent action and oriented to obtaining support from the militants of the neofascist movement and an unofficial one responsible for massacres, which had to remain anonymous (Ferraresi 1995: 247). Members of the groups had been responsible for the assassination of a police officer, Antonio Marino, during a postdemonstration street fight in Milan in April 1973. In the same year, another activist, Nico Azzi, died while placing a bomb on a train.

As mentioned in Chapter 3, since the mid-1970s, the old right-wing radical organizations had been in crisis. In the second half of the 1970s, however, a new generation of young activists emerged, taking the radical Left as an example, in particular imitating its emphasis on spontaneity. More specifically, regarding organizational structure, "after 1977, the model of internal organization and the modality of action of the extreme right imitated more and more those of the subversive left" (Minna 1984: 68). Loosely coupled networks of groupings developed inside schools and neighborhoods at both a visible and an invisible level, in some cases from inside sections of the MSI.

When political violence picked up in the second half of the 1970s, the dominant organizational ideal became a sort of right-wing anarchism. The proposal was "to leave, immediately, any organized groups; abandon strategy and hierarchy.... Attest with groups of very small size, do not look to enlarge the spontaneous groups beyond the size that allows for action." This structure had to be "agile, immediate, no need for hierarchies" (Minna 1984: 84). Armed spontaneity was based on "the formation of small groups, that acted and disappeared with great rapidity, connected to one another in a fluid way ('political,' not hierarchical or structural) and therefore reciprocally autonomous, even though they moved in an heterogeneous environment, where tendentially everybody knew everybody.... There was frequent overlapping militancy and actions could be claimed by more than one organization" (Ferraresi 1995: 299).

Of the journal *Quex*, which aimed at loosely coordinating these various groupings, one of its militants stated, "as an organization, we are a bluff" (*Quex*, no. 2, 1979: 12, cited in Guerrieri 2010). Similarly, Costruiamo l'Azione (Let's Construct the Action) was an umbrella organization, coordinated around the homonymous journal that was published between 1977 and 1979, in

which people's committees, coordination efforts, and initiatives were advertised
(Ferraresi 1995: 303).[5] The group had an interest in typically left-wing topics
such as internal colonialism against the south, attacks on workers' rights,
repression, and prisons. Costruiamo l'Azione launched the so-called strategy
of the archipelagos, a loose network oriented toward the creation of committees
for a revolutionary struggle. As Guerrieri summarized,

on the basis of this strategy the single neo-fascist formations would, without losing their
individual identities nor their freedom of action, have had to act according to a unique
revolutionary objective. To achieve this aim, all monolithic organisational *solutions* were
rejected in favour of collaboration among the various groups, in order to form an indistinct
circuit of men and means. In reality "Costruiamo l'Azione," precisely as the fruit of
mediation – referred to previously – was one of the first groups of the period to which
vertical structure did not apply. On the basis of the latter organisational model, political
debate was reserved to leaders, and any contribution from the base was overlooked. This
was not the case within "Costruiamo l'Azione." Here, a subversive project began to emerge
from the bottom up through penetration and the linking of work carried out not on
structural or ideological bases, but exclusively political ones. In this view, each single
individual or group was called on to operate in the name of a common political aim.
(2008: 104)

Terza Posizione, founded in 1978 by activists of Lotta Studentesca, presented
itself as an attempt to bridge spontaneity and organization. Inspired by the
Romanian Iron Legion, the group had a legal branch, made up of small local
cells spread on the national territory; these were known as "the *cuib* – nursery in
Roman – which through a very strict hierarchical structure were to respond to
the leaders of the territorial nuclei, who in turn depended on central organs,
made up of territorial heads and national leaders." There were also, however,
two clandestine levels: "While the operational nucleus was the armed wing of
'Terza posizione' and fulfilled the role of sourcing funds for the organization
through robberies and kidnappings, the legion was made up of the 'elect,' those
whose role would be to form the leading class after the revolution planned by the
group had taken place" (Guerrieri 2010: 71).

Finally, the most deadly organization of the period, the Nuclei Armati
Rivoluzionari (Revolutionary Armed Nuclei [NAR]), presented themselves as
a "spontaneous movement." Fioravanti explained that "NAR is an acronym
behind which there is no single organization, with directive bodies, with chiefs,
periodic meetings, or programs.... Any armed fascist groups, formed even on an
occasional base, for just one action, can use the acronym NAR" (quoted in
Bianconi 1992: 36). In the leaflet in which it claimed responsibility for the
assassination of the judge Mario Amato, the organization declared:

All too often we hide ... behind phrases like "we have no arms" or "we have no money."
Money and arms can be found on the street and a knife is enough to begin with. [...] There

---

[5] The journal was also linked to the Movimento Rivoluzionario Popolare.

is no need for either "hideouts" or great "organisations." Three trusty comrades and a lot of good will are enough. And if there aren't three, two will do, and don't tell us there aren't two trustworthy comrades! But even if that were true it is our job to continue searching for them, or, if necessary, to create them. To create spontaneous armed action. We end this document by telling those who accuse us of not being "political enough" that their politics does not interest us, only the struggle, and struggling does not leave much room for idle chatter. [...] And to those who accuse us of being desperate criminals we say that our "desperation" is better than cowardliness. To those who need help, help will be given, but lead awaits those who continue to pollute our youth preaching that we wait or similar. (cited in Guerrieri 2010: 76)

In the Italian radical Right, however, the plan to combine legal and illegal activities by keeping a decentralized structure failed. Whereas the underground organizations of the second generation disappeared, crushed between state repression and internal violent fights, bitter struggles continued to characterize the history of the extreme Right, with the most politicized groups despising the antipolitical stand of skinheads and (right-wing) football hooligans, with political parties that strategically used more populist claims entering into tensions with social movement organizations that were more oriented toward action, with traditionalist Catholics stigmatizing the followers of esoteric rituals, and so on.[6]

The growing reliance of the extreme Right on network structures, with autonomous cells connected through new media, is in part a by-product of repressive policies. The tendency toward a decentralized and compartmentalized structure is long-standing. A recent comparative analysis of radical Right groups in Italy, Germany, and the United States (Caiani, della Porta, and Wagemann 2011) also noted a fragmented capacity for networking, although with variable degrees of intensity in different contexts and times.

Similar trends have been noted in other radical Right organizations. The white supremacist networks in the United States are described as relatively decentralized, with multiple centers of influence but no strong divisions (Burris, Smith, and Strahm 2000). In general, the radical Right is said to evolve toward a cellular structure, becoming a sort of leaderless resistance (de la Corte Ibanez 2006: 294ff.). Also in some other countries, internal differences appear so great that scholars find it difficult to identify one concept that links the radical Right (Bjørgo 2005: 2).

ORGANIZATIONAL COMPARTMENTALIZATION AND ETHNIC ORGANIZATIONS

The organizational structures of the ETA also changed, developing a tendency toward compartmentalization that was linked, in this case, with – increasingly tense – relations with structures open to sympathizers. As in the previously

---

[6] Tensions between the political and countercultural wings were clearly expressed by Italian radical Right leader Franco Freda, who defined the skinheads as folkloristic and plebeian, writing, "They have to study.... They do not reflect. And we need instead disciplined soldiers" (cited in Marchi 1994: 175).

discussed cases, the ETA's organizational model adapted to the complex inter-actions of repression and fluctuating support for the organization.

Organizational changes accompanied the ETA's evolution. To begin with, an increase in the complexity of the organizational structure followed an increase in the number of members, which grew from about 50 in 1959, to about 300 between 1960 and 1965, to 450 in 1966, and to about 600 in 1969.[7] In the 1970s, police data reported 70 commands of 4 to 5 militants each (Muñoz Alonso 1982: 147), with peaks of about 1,000 members. In fact, the Fifth Assembly approved a complex and specialized structure, with several layers of authority.

While the growing number of militants moved the ETA toward more complex structures, repression pushed the organization increasingly underground. Already in 1950, a wave of arrests had brought an awareness of "what it meant to act clandestinely" (Clark 1984: 25). In 1965, the ETA Executive Committee (EC) declared the group to be "a clandestine organization whose only objective is to obtain as rapidly as possible and using all means possible – including violence – the independence of Euskadi" (ibid.: 37).

Centralization also followed the failed attempt to keep a horizontal structure. In 1962, an executive committee was created to lead the organization between one assembly (the coordinating organism) and the next. The national assembly, which was the supreme decisional structure, was made up of about fifty leaders (members of the EC, heads of various branches, chiefs of the territorially struc-tured *herrialdes*, and leaders of subunits in them) (Clark 1984: 207). At that time there was also a "tactical executive committee" and a small assembly, made up of four fronts and *herrialdes* with three geographical levels (down to the village level). However, the meetings of the national assembly had to be discontinued for security reasons. It is significant that the assembly, which until 1965 had met once per year, met only irregularly between 1966 and 1974 and disappeared after 1975. In the early 1980s, the EC was made up of a *maximo dirigente* and seven members responsible for propaganda, intelligence, political office, *commandos illegales*, *commandos legales*, and international operations (ibid.: 213).

As in the case of the BR, compartmentalization implied the increasing impor-tance of clandestine members. In 1964, after a wave of arrests, the Third Assembly created the role of the *liberados*. These were militants who were already known to the police; they were granted full-time status as *etarras* and received a salary from the organization. Each *liberado* controlled a *herrialde*. They also constituted parallel structures open to sympathizers who were devoted to offering logistic support, finding shelter, collecting funds, and so on. A political office was created in 1965, at the Fourth Assembly, yet the organization also contained *kommandos*, who specialized in assaulting banks and factories.

The structure of the ETA included a functional dimension (either fronts or branches) and a territorial one (with six *herrialdes*). In 1962, at the First

---

[7] In 1972, a fusion with EGI Batasuna brought in about 500 activists, but their number then went down again to about 200 in 1974.

Assembly, the ETA defined a structure of five fronts, which dealt with internal publications and communication, cells and study groups, mass propaganda, legal actions, and military actions. In 1965, at the Fourth Assembly, fronts were replaced by branches (*ramas*). In particular, the activism branch replaced the military front (Clark 1984: 37). At the Fifth Assembly (in 1966–7), the organization was restructured into four fronts: cultural, political, workers', and military. This division followed a broader organizational strategy:

> The Basque country had to adopt anti-colonialist guerrilla tactics, something which Krutvig clearly explains when he distinguishes between social revolutions and national revolutions. In the former only three fronts are necessary: political, economic and military. However, in revolutions of national liberation as is the case in the Basque country, a cultural front is necessary as given the specific linguistic-cultural and national nature of the Basque country with respect to its oppressors, it acts as supreme director of the other fronts. (Jauregui Bereciartu 1986: 602)

In practice, however, the military front became increasingly dominant:

> The cultural and economic fronts have been of little relevance, at least from the point of view of strict organization. The cultural movement and the movement to resuscitate the Basque language and literature coincide with the time when ETA became extremely important, but, strictly speaking, one cannot talk in terms of a cultural front in ETA but of numerous groups of intellectuals who strongly sympathise with ETA's actions and whose interests coincide to a certain extent as far as objectives and ends are concerned. Thus, the structure of ETA was, in fact, reduced to two fronts: the political and military. In theory, after the Vth Assembly, the political front was to find itself in a situation where it had absolute priority over the military to the extent that the latter would become a kind of armed band subject to the strategy established by the political front. In practice, however, it is quite clear that the military front has always exerted greater influence than the political. This is one of the key questions that must be taken into account when considering the evolution and later development of ETA activity, that is the absolute priority of praxis and activism over theory and doctrine. (ibid.: 602)

In 1968, as a reflection of the growing interest in labor struggles, the economic front was substituted by the workers' front, which however remained subordinated to the military front until it split from the ETA in 1974.

This complex structure proved difficult to implement, especially as internal tensions developed on a number of issues. In 1966, the plurality of opinions within the ETA brought about conflicts between a workerist side, which wanted to reconcile national liberation and social revolution; a more traditional intransigent nationalist side; and a "third current, constituted by an extraordinarily heterogeneous ideological conglomerate, which was a firm advocate of activism and armed conflict. Its members were united against occupation and advocated third world-style revolutionary means of attaining the liberation of the Basque country" (Jauregui Bereciartu 1986: 597). This third current prevailed, and those who argued for the other two positions were expelled. At the Fourth Assembly, however, a similar constellation developed that still contained a communist component, those who wanted to create a Basque working-class party, as well as the anticolonialists, who wanted to update nationalism, and the military front, which defended the primary role of armed action.

Compartmentalization also facilitated fragmentation. Between 1968 and 1975 there had already been an evolution toward decentralized cells, coordinated by an operating directorate in France, whereas the *herrialdes* were discontinued (Clark 1984). Cells or commandos – which were responsible for a small area of operation (a neighborhood or a village) and formed mainly by natives – were composed of about five men (occasionally a woman) who continued to live at home. The structuration of the small cells reflected a base rooted in other cellular structures, such as climbing clubs (*mendigoitzales*). Whereas the *liberados*, also called *illegales*, were often responsible for armed attacks (half of those arrested in 1979 and 1980 were *liberados*), the *legales* were unknown to the police. Some of them worked as links, some functioned as "mailboxes," and some gathered information on targets.

At the same time, compartmentalization fueled factionalism. As with most clandestine groups, the history of the ETA is rife with splits – especially involving groups that privileged the class cleavage over the nationalist one, as was the case with the ETA Berri in 1966 (which then went on to found the Movimiento Comunista de Espana in 1970), the Celulas Rojas in 1970 (which then founded Soiak), and the ETA VI Asemblea in 1972 (which founded the Revolutionary Communist Ligue/Liga Komunista Iraultzaielea [LKI]). In 1973, there was a split in the cultural front (which later formed the Basque Popular Socialist Party and later Herri Alderdi Sozialista Iraultzailea, the People's Socialist Revolutionary Party [HASI]). In 1974, the workers' front was expelled and formed the Patriotic Revolutionary Workers Party. All of these groups would later join the radical nationalist party Herri Batasuna (HB). In the same year, the main split between the ETA-PM and ETA-M took place. In the years to come, competition would also increase: the Berezi group developed from the ETA-PM, and the Commandos Autonomous were formed by members of the Berezi group and by the ETA-M's former militants. Emerging in 1978–9, the Commandos Autonomous remained decentralized, refusing to take orders from any of the ETA factions.

Most of these splits reflected differences regarding strategic choices. Organizational issues were key to the main split, in 1974, between the ETA-M, whose militants wanted the organization to focus on revolutionary military action, and the ETA-PM, which was joined by those who instead gave priority to political considerations. The ETA-M declared independence from the mass organization of the armed nucleus, which was responsible for military activity, claiming that it was impossible for a single organization to combine military action and grassroots forms of activism. The ETA-PM, representing the majority of the organization, stressed instead the need to coordinate military and political action under the same leadership to exploit the favorable climate for mass action, without giving up armed struggle.

Both options had, however, inherent weaknesses. The repression of the mid-1970s (with the executions of anarchist Puig Antich in 1974 and of three members of the left-wing clandestine group Revolutionary Antifascist Patriotic Front [FRAP] and two ETA members in 1975) facilitated the military option (Muro 2008). The ETA was in fact almost dismantled in a few months, as more than 500 activists were put in jail and more than that were sent into exile (Wieviorka 1993: 160), and only one commando remained operational. The choice to keep a balance between a political and a military option was particularly damaging for the ETA-PM: "It first did it by rendering it vulnerable to police repression, and later by quickening opposition between the political faction, which was becoming increasingly intent on being the vanguard of all Basque resistance movements, and the military faction, which was becoming increasingly adamant in refusing all attempts to supervise its activities" (Wieviorka 1993: 160).

In the mid-1970s, the ETA-PM also divided into a military and a predominantly political wing, resulting in conflicts over leadership. The leader of the political wing, Pertur (whose real name was Eduardo Moreno Bergareche), denounced was he saw as a situation in which the use of weapons was getting out of control, internal fights risked becoming violent, and activists had become more cynical. On 23 July 1976, he disappeared after meeting with Apala (Miguel Ángel Apalategui Ayerbe), the leader of the military wing, to talk over their disagreements. Pertur's disappearance led to suspicion that he had been killed by the other faction within his organization (Wieviorka 1993: 161). The ETA-PM quickly disappeared after its military wing joined the ETA-M, while other members founded the Basque Revolutionary Party (Euskal Iraultzarako Alderia [EIA]). After 1977, a section within the ETA-PM obtained a pardon, declared a unilateral truce in 1981, and, in 1982, abandoned armed struggle to form the left-patriotic party Euskadiko Ezkerra (Patriotic Left [EE]), which was later joined by the EIA.

The ETA-M evolved instead into an increasingly compartmentalized format. When it split in the summer of 1974, the ETA-M aggregated the majority of the militants of the military front. In a document it explained: "We decided not to enter in the democratic legality and to keep our clandestine structure," as participating in democratic legality would mean either renouncing armed struggle or attracting repression of the movement. The document also recognized that the strategy of the four fronts (political, labor, cultural, and military) had failed in its aims of organizing the various "sectors with interest similar to ours," and at the same time had exposed the activists to repression (*Agiria*, quoted in Ibarra 1989: 106). It finally expressed the fear that compromises and pacts would dilute the aims of social and national liberation.

Compartmentalization, militarization, and factionalism were also observed in the evolution of the left-wing and right-wing clandestine organizations in Italy. What is different in the organizational structures of the ETA, as compared with the left-wing and right-wing groups we have just looked at, is the relevance of structures open to sympathizers. The complex structure of the so-called Basque Movement of National Liberation (MNLV), which existed mostly within the KAS (Koordinadora Abertzale Socializta, or Socialist Patriotic Coordinator Committee), functioned as a resource for and a constraint to the ETA. The Basque Movement of National Liberation is made up of a complex network of legal, semilegal, and illegal social and political organizations – newspapers; a party (the HB); a trade union (the Patriotic Workers' Committee [LAB]); ETA prisoner groups; sports, cultural, free-time, and neighborhood associations; and bars and squatter houses – which acts as an infrastructure to ensure the persistence of the ETA (Waldmann 1992: 241).

The KAS was established in 1975 to coordinate activities in support of Txiki and Otaegi, two ETA militants sentenced to the death penalty. Even after their deaths, the KAS continued to coordinate various groups close to the ETA. For example, the group Herri Batasuna established itself as an electoral force, as well as a movement of popular unity of the *abertzale* (patriotic) Left. In 1979, HB obtained 15 percent of the vote, becoming the third party in the Basque Country; at the European elections in 1989 it became the largest political force, holding 20 percent of the vote. After 1979, HB-elected members refused to occupy their seats in the Spanish and Basque parliaments, instead using their positions to voice protest.[8]

The HB electorate reflects some characteristics of ETA membership: it is overwhelmingly male (59 percent), young (55 percent of members are less than thirty-four years old), and mainly working class (73 percent). It is not by chance that the Basque trade union LAB is another member of the KAS. Strong mainly in Guipuzkoa, it accused other unions of supporting repression. Bolstered by growth particularly during the crisis of heavy industry in late 1970s, in 2000 it became the third-largest union, organizing 15 percent of the Basque labor force.

The youth organization Jarrai is also part of the MNLV. Particularly active in the campaigns against NATO, military service, and unemployment, Jarrai addresses issues ranging from drugs to squatters, the environment, Basque rock, and same-sex couples; it is also said to play an important role in the coordination of street violence during the so-called *kale borroka*, which have been held since 1994 and are based on the example of the Palestinian intifada (see Chapter 3).

The organizational structure of the ETA, which emerged from continuous but constrained adaptation to environmental changes as well as defeats, challenged its very survival. The very illegality of the organization has imposed a strong turnover in the leadership following the rhythm of arrests and, later on, assassination. Repression also radicalized the ETA by bringing about new and more radical generations, which were increasingly committed to armed struggle (see also Chapter 8). Specialization also fueled competition for scarce resources

---

[8] For example, in 1991, nineteen members of HB contested a speech by King Juan Carlos, interrupting his discourse by singing the Basque anthem, "Eusko Gudariak."

among the various fronts. In general, "the most serious problem lay in ETA's attempts to combine armed struggle and nonviolent activity in the same organizations" (Clark 1984: 70).

ORGANIZATIONAL COMPARTMENTALIZATION
AND RELIGIOUS ORGANIZATIONS

Jihadist groups have been seen as moving from a hierarchical organizational model towards a more horizontal one. However, as in the previous examples, their organizational structures have changed in response to some external challenges.

In particular, in AQ's case, the organization developed from a hierarchical structure into an increasingly decentralized structure. As Mishal and Rosenthal synthesized,

> Al Qaeda started out as a hierarchical organization, transformed into a network system, and later – after the 2001 attack in Afghanistan – dispersed into a Dune [moving] organization…. Al Qaeda gradually transformed its structure from being a strictly hierarchical model to a variety of network structures – leading up to its current highly dispersed and multistructured organizational design. Each of these structures co-exists alongside others. Yet, the emphasis on a specific structure varies along Al Qaeda's existence with accordance to exogenous constraints and endogenous beliefs. (2005: 273)

Successful repression pushed the organization toward a simpler and more clandestine structure, but the organizational evolution was also influenced by the involvement, since the second half of the 1990s, of various groups such as the Egyptian al-Jamaa al-Islamiyya and al-Jihad. In fact, three different periods have been distinguished in al-Qaeda's organizational development.

The forerunner of AQ was a group called the Office of Service, founded in Pashawar by Abdullah Azzam, a former Palestinian Muslim Brother who had abandoned the PLO because of its nationalist and secular character (Roy 2004: 295). A cleric, Azzam theorized about an Islamic holy struggle against Muslim suffering in Bosnia, Sudan, Somalia, Afghanistan, Albania, Egypt, Syria, and Kashmir. In 1985 he founded a training camp for Arab fighters in al-Sadda, focusing on the reading of holy texts as well as military practices. He was joined there by Osama bin Laden, who founded AQ, whose name can be translated as "the solid foundation."

During this first period of its life, scholars stress the hierarchical characteristics of AQ. Initially, there was a pyramidal structure at the center of al-Qaeda, led by bin Laden and supported by a consultative council (*shura*), which enjoyed the trust of the leader. At the top of this hierarchical structure Osama bin Laden served "as the Emir General, a role that some have likened to that of a corporate chief executive officer. Coordinating directly with Osama were the members of the Shura Majlis, his cabinet or council of leaders. His closest friend and partner, Ayman al-Zawahiri, functionally guided the group on matters related to Islamic ideology and law, and continues to do so" (Borum and Gelles 2005: 747).

As in other clandestine groups, AQ was functionally divided into departments, which included military (responsible for a guerrilla group in Afghanistan, as well as various cells around the world), financial, and propaganda departments. One distinctive feature was the presence of a department for religious matters, devoted to overseeing the religious orthodoxy (de la Corte Ibanez 2006: 297).

The advantages of a hierarchical structure have often been emphasized in research on al-Qaeda. At the moment of its foundation, al-Qaeda was located in a specific territory and possessed a centralized – charismatic, one could say – leadership. AQ is described as being characterized at that time by "a well-defined, top-down system of communication; well-defined and rigid positions and responsibilities; a rigid command chain; and clear time horizons for operations. This organizational structure is conducive to stability because it hinders communication between members operating at the same level who may share grievances or seek to challenge the organization's leadership" (Chhabra 2010: 2). This model has been said to resonate with some general values of political Islam. In contrast to society-oriented groups, which focus on individual change and aim at expanding free spaces (Yavuz 2004: 278), state-oriented Islamic movements tend to be vertical and elitist in their organization.

In the first years of its existence, according to Hegghammer, al-Qaeda seems to have been "more of an alumni society than an active military organization" (2010: 100). In addition to being organizationally weak, al-Qaeda was also fragmented, because, after Soviet withdrawal from Afghanistan, its leaders had made different choices. However, when they moved to Sudan in 1992, Osama bin Laden proceeded to restructure the group. Still small in membership (composed of no more than a few hundred people), the organization gained consistent resources, thanks to its rich leader, among others.

The leaders linked to the resistance in Afghanistan were then replaced by younger leaders who were militarily less skilled, some of whom came from the Egyptian Islamic Jihad. The groups that converged in al-Qaeda developed from networks of the fighters who went to Afghanistan, Bosnia, and Chechnya and then "returned to Europe or the Middle East with greater ideological commitments, deeper loyalties to a particular community and military experience" (Singerman 2004: 157). These resources were then invested into the formation of military structures. Because those who frequented the al-Qaeda camp in Afghanistan belonged to other groups as well, their experiences in Afghanistan also affected their organizations at home. Some of them, in fact, "came from existing organizations and gave them a more radical twist when they returned to their home countries" (Roy 2004: 298). In particular, in Egypt, it was the decision to form a military wing that marked the turning point in the evolution of al-Jamaa, which had previously emphasized open proselytism (*da'wa*).

In the second half of the 1990s, however, AQ developed into a more networked organizational format. Its experience in Afghanistan also established a rich potential for transnational networking. Given his previous direct commitment, bin Laden was able to network with the many jihadist groups who had fought in

Afghanistan, as well as with irredentist groups in Kashmir, Philippines, or Chechnya. Al-Qaeda then grew when Osama bin Laden formed an alliance with the leader of the Egyptian Islamic Jihad, Ayman al-Zawahri, forming, together with other Islamist groups from Pakistan and Bangladesh, an international umbrella organization, which was then responsible for the attacks against US installations in Kenya, Yemen, Saudi Arabia, and Tanzania. To these allies bin Laden offered training camps and other resources, with increasing success.

Between 1998 and 2001, the creation of the International Islamic Front for Jihad against Jews and Crusaders, which included various national organizations from Pakistan, Egypt, Bangladesh, and other countries, hinted at a future network structure. Although the most important actions of this organization (such as the bombings in the United States, Kenya, and Tanzania) were supervised by the central organization, cells tended to be autonomous – so much so that they have been defined as franchised groups, and al-Qaeda has been defined as a network of networks.

The decision to organize a global jihad required a transformation into a network structure in which AQ presented itself as a hub, located at the center. In this period, there was still a territorial base in Sudan and Afghanistan from which the network was steered; this base led to the 9/11 attacks. AQ thus increasingly became a cross-national military alliance of national liberation movements – or at least it aimed to be such. However, after 9/11, the organizations decentralized into an increasingly loose network that has been said to resonate with the tribal structure of power in the contexts in which the organization was rooted (McAuly 2006: 279). From a visible organization that runs training camps in a specific territory, Afghanistan, "al-Qaida has transformed itself into a global jihad movement increasingly consisting of associate groups and ad hoc cells all over the world" (Eilstrup-Sangiovanni and Jones 2008).

Especially after 9/11, AQ is in fact said to have evolved into a deterritorialized networked organization (Borum and Gelles 2005), with very limited communication between semiautonomous cells. Owing to its transnational nature, "Al-Qa'ida has always been an organization that depended as much on local initiatives as on top-down direction, and in the aftermath of 9/11 it has dispersed even more. Its complex organizational structure is something between a centralized hierarchy and a decentralized flat network" (Crenshaw 2009: 1). In particular, the loss of Afghanistan as a territorial base generally transformed AQ into an umbrella organization with relatively poor control of the activities of its various cells – which remained indeed broadly autonomous, often with a high chance of being subject to police control and low military skills. In fact, AQ has been defined as more of an ideology than an organization.

In this loose network we find, on the one hand, national-level affiliated organizations, such as AQ in the Arabic Peninsula (in Yemen), AQ in the Islamic Mahgreb, the Moroccan Islamic Combatant group, and the Somali al-Shabab (Crenshaw 2009: 3). Scholars also place within this category the Egyptian Islamic Jihad and the Islamic Movement of Uzbekistan and Jemaat Islamiyyah in

Indonesia (Byman 2003). These interactions are mainly limited to occasional exchanges of resources and temporary coalitions, rather than construction of a structured alliance. Tensions are high, as many of these groups have mainly territorially bounded aims. On the other hand, there are small groupings, such as the Bali, Casablanca, London, or Madrid cells, that are often vaguely inspired by AQ in terms of principles and beliefs but tend to lack any logistical links – so much so that AQ has been said to have remained more a label or a brand than an organizational structure (Eilstrup-Sangiovanni and Jones 2008: 40).

This type of decentralization has been seen as an adaptation to external pressures, in particular to the military reactions to the 9/11 attacks. After 2001, as aforementioned, the US occupation of Afghanistan challenged AQ's capacity to control the network. Even though it still offered logistic support to various local jihadists, AQ refrained from long-term coordination efforts (Eilstrup-Sangiovanni and Jones 2008: 7). According to this "dune" model, the organizational activities emerge at intervals, there is no specialization or division of tasks, and command and control are minimal (ibid.: 7). The Internet therefore became more important, not only for operational communication but also as an instrument for mobilization through indoctrination, as leaders use Web forums as well as Web sites to distribute various types of documents worldwide (ibid.: 11). New technologies helped the development of virtual Internet communities that find and exchange information about Muslim suffering in the world.

The capacity of the center to control the periphery thus radically declined:

Al-Qaida's most successful operations took place when the organization possessed a hierarchical structure. In the 1990s al-Qaida had a significant degree of hierarchy and formal organization in the top tier, though lower levels remained more loosely structured…. This leadership oversaw a tidy organization of committees with well-defined positions and responsibilities. When defined to include its regional affiliates, al-Qaida assumed a more networked form with regional hubs acting as subcontractors, who maintained substantial autonomy. But although some operations were carried out with local autonomy and limited hierarchical management, successful ones typically received close supervision from above. Indeed, the top tier closely managed the 1998 bombings of U.S. embassies in East Africa and the September 11 attacks. Moreover, al-Qaida until 2001 was not stateless; it used Afghanistan under the Taliban as a base to centrally plan and coordinate terrorist operations around the world. (Eilstrup-Sangiovanni and Jones 2008: 34)

Out of necessity and opportunity, as in the other analyzed types of clandestine political violence, the trend has been toward increased autonomy of the various groups. In particular, jihadist terrorism in Europe has been described as thoroughly decentralized (Coolsaet 2005), with mainly horizontal forms of recruitment (Nesser 2006a, 2006b). The jihad in the West is clearly organized around semiautonomous cells, whose connection with AQ varies from top-down control (as with the Hamburg cell), to loose contact, and to mere inspiration (as in the case of the bombers in Madrid and London) (Neumann and Rogers 2007: 12–15).

Even these groupings are loosely connected internally. The Hofstad group, responsible for the assassination of Theo Van Gogh, is described as "loose, haphazard and contingent" (Egerton 2011: 74), neither demanding nor receiving exclusive loyalty from its participants (ibid.: 77).[9] In fact, "the best way to conceive of the militant milieu in the Netherlands in the early twenty-first century is of several fluid and overlapping groups, all of whom shared some information and memberships, with the Hofstad group exerting particular influence on establishing the terms of debate and with a perceived willingness to act upon their words" (Egerton 2011: 77). The London attackers coalesced in an informal group that met at an Iqra Islamic bookshop in Beeston, where videos and other online materials could be consulted. The Hamburg cell responsible for the 9/11 attacks also came from a fluid net: "People came to the group for a variety of reasons. Many left, often disturbed by the radicalization and fervor of the others within" (Egerton 2011: 152). Those who did not leave consolidated their relations, focusing on jihad and the duty of martyrdom. So, "local groups, based on local solidarity (neighborhood, family, university) and with few or no ties to Al Qaeda take the label and act according to what they see as Al Qaeda's ideology and strategy" (Roy 2004: 323).

Therefore, the network structure of the organization changed from a star structure, with bin Laden at its center and control of information and operation located in the center, toward the less centralized network structure of a multi-channel net (Arquilla and Rondfelt 2001). Al-Qaeda thus became "a network that pooled the funds and talents of diverse jihadi Muslims, shopping around for opportunities to work together against common enemies" (Sadowski 2006: 215). In fact, "although officials often give them names (al-Qaeda in the Middle East or Jama a Islamiyya in Southeast Asia) that suggest the existence of formal organizations, these terrorists really work through informal networks. They raise funds and acquire weapons from diverse sources, acting independently and without central leadership" (ibid.: 233). So, al-Qaeda has been said to have become, at the same time, an organization and a trademark: "It can operate directly, in a joint venture, or by franchising. It embodies, but does not have the monopoly of, a new kind of violence. Many groups are acting along the same lines without necessarily having a direct connection with Al Qaeda" (Roy 2004: 294).

Opinions are split on the balance of the pros and cons of loosely networked structures. Among the advantages is the fact that a loosely coupled structure allows the adhesion of different groups, with different aims – in particular, connecting those with specific territorially bounded concerns with the "global jihad." However, it also reduces internal coherence, favoring splits as well as reducing control over the members and their activities, up to a final defeat.

---

[9] Adherence to the Salafi method of religious interpretation is said to allow for the building of loose networks (Wiktorowicz 2001, quoted in Singerman 2004).

ORGANIZATIONAL COMPARTMENTALIZATION: CONCLUSIONS

This chapter has addressed the question of organizational evolution in the underground. As violent entrepreneurs, clandestine groups contribute to shaping their
environment, as well as being shaped by it. In line with neoinstitutionalist explanations, I found that organizations are constrained by the very norms they contribute
to spreading. After splitting from larger social movement organizations, the militant
groups studied here initially aimed at propagating their ideas to a broader base of
reference. However, they tended to develop into sects. Changes in structure were
neither erratic nor merely the result of instrumental reasoning. Organizational
structures were adapted in action, from complex relations among a number of
different actors who reacted to their own construction of external reality.

These four types of clandestine violence displayed different organizational
structures, which resonated in part with the organizational repertoires dominant
in the social movement families within which the groups developed. Past forms
of underground violence have been said to differ from contemporary ones in
terms of organizational structure. If in the past underground organizations
developed mainly into hierarchical, although compartmentalized, structures,
contemporary extreme forms of political violence seem to follow a different
model, with a strongly networked structure made possible by new technology
and legitimized by widespread norms. Research on the Islamist groups, however,
indicated a complex development that was also influenced by their interactions
with repression, on the one hand, and their potential basis of support, on the
other. As Mayntz (2004) had predicted, we observed different balances of
hierarchical and networked structures in the groups. They tended to have a
defined (even if ever-changing as an effect of arrests and killings) leadership and
had a functional division of labor that reflected some main organizational
purposes (and multiple tasks). They also showed network characteristics in the
autonomy of (compartmentalized) structures and their fluid borders. In their
evolution, some groups (mainly left-wing and ethnonationalist) tried to keep a
centralized structure; others (such as right-wingers and religious groups) opted
for a network style.

Some differences could be explained by the available organizational resources.
In general, the clandestine groups we observed were rather small, even (especially
in the case of the extreme Right and the extreme Left) tiny. The larger the group
and the richer it was in material and military resources, however, the more
complex its structure tended to be. In particular, when clandestine groups have
some control territory, be it small or large (like the ETA in the Basque Country or
Islamist radical groups in Egypt), they need to develop organizational structures to
deal with the external environment. At the same time, large illegal groups – like
organized crime networks – can never fulfill their aspiration to centralization,
given not only repression outside but also continuous conflicts inside.

Beyond material resources, norms were also important. As is the case for
forms of protest (see Chapter 6), forms of organization are limited in space and

time (Clemens 1996), and – we might add – by social movement families. Any specific organizational model is more likely to be adopted "to the extent that the proposed model of organization is believed to work, involves practices and organizational relations that are already familiar, and is consonant with the organization of the rest of those individuals' social worlds" (Clemens 1996: 211). So on the left, some horizontal structures had to resonate with participatory traditions: the democratic centralism of the communist organizational tradition entered into tension with the more anarchist forms. On the right, hierarchical structures were largely consonant with an elitist organizational culture, even if some late-riser groups proposed a more spontaneous organizational model. Ethnonationalism stressed a military model to fight against the invader but also kept channels open to sympathizers. The global AQ adopted an umbrella structure to coordinate multiple and diverse national and transnational jihadists. In addition, organizational structures were built on specific tasks that were normatively defined: the left-wing groups had fronts to intervene in the factory, or do "mass work"; the ethnonationalists built structures for "national liberation"; religiously inspired clandestine groups have organs to deal with religious purity.

Context mattered, not only in the forms of reference base but also in terms of strength and strategies of opponents. Repression was especially relevant for the clandestine organizations whose very choice of clandestinity was an adaptation to police and judicial investigations. Also, for groups that initially wanted to keep a political logic, the engagement with repression brought about an increasing focus on military structure, whereas, given security concerns, horizontal structures failed victims of compartmentalization, which also reduced their capacity to impose a centralized structure, fomenting factionalism. The context was, however, constructed and deconstructed by the militant groups, which acted therefore on the image they built of their reality.

Writing about social movements, Hanspeter Kriesi (1996) has described their internal structuration as deriving from the following: (1) formalization, with the introduction of formal membership criteria, written rules, fixed procedures, formal leadership, and a fixed structure of offices; (2) professionalization, understood as the presence of paid staff who pursue a career inside the organization; (3) internal differentiation, involving a functional division of labor and the creation of territorial units; and (4) integration, through mechanisms of horizontal and/or vertical coordination. In all of the clandestine groups discussed in this text, I noted a common evolution toward compartmentalization, featuring (1) development of vertical forms of power, with decreasing power of horizontal structures and sympathizers; (2) militarization, with increasing power of the military functional bodies and of the "regular," full-time, and underground militants; (3) encapsulation, as a decreasing capacity to implement communication among units; and, finally, (4) factionalism, with internal struggles and continuous splits.

6

Action Militarization

The ETA used kidnappings to demand policy decisions, and sometimes also money. Their use increased from one per year in 1970 and 1973, two in 1976, and one in 1977, to four, eight, and seven respectively in 1978, 1979, and 1980. The lethality of the kidnappings also grew as the motive behind them changed, moving from a logic of negotiation to one of punishment.

In the beginning, kidnappings were staged as Tupamaros-style actions, which ended with the liberation of the hostage. So, for instance, in 1970, the ETA kidnapped the honorary West German consul in San Sebastian, Eugen Beihl, asking for the release of fifteen ETA members on trial, but then freed him before the special tribunal decided on the case. In 1971, the owner of a factory on strike, Lorenzo Zabala Suinaga (who was of Basque origin and spoke Euskera), was held prisoner by the Basque separatists; he was asked to rehire without sanctions all workers, as well as to grant wage increases. The kidnapping of Zabala was a turning point toward a workers' movement, justified by the ETA's journal *Zutil* with the words, "All bosses are the same for us ... whether they have Basque surnames or not changes nothing.... All of them exploit us" (Pérez-Agote 2006: 65). He was also released after all conditions had been met. The kidnapping of Felipe Huarte in January 1973, also during a labor conflict, was similar; in exchange for his freedom an $800,000 ransom was requested.

Also partially oriented to negotiation was the ETA-PM's 1979 kidnapping of Javier Ruperes, leader of the Unión de Centro Democrático (UCD) and chairman of its international relations committee. However, this time the requests were more focused on the organization itself: an amnesty for most prisoners and the return of the rest to the Soria prisons in Euskadi, as well as the withdrawal of Spanish law enforcement authorities from the Basque provinces. Ruperes was to be freed after the government made good on its promises to release prisoners and to create a special parliament committee to investigate charges of torture.

Kidnapping continued in the years to come, but more often ended up with the assassination of the victim. The kidnapping of Jose Antonio Ortega Lara, a minor civil servant seized in 1996 and held for 532 days, lasted much longer than previous kidnappings. The year after, the ETA kidnapped the city councilor of a small town, Miguel Angel Blanco Garrido, asking for the end of the dispersion policy of 460 convicted ETA members. As the request was not met, and notwithstanding mass demonstrations against violence in major cities (half a million marched in Bilbao), he was shot dead by the organization.

We see a similar – telling – evolution in the BR's kidnappings. The first four, between 1972 and 1973, were propaganda actions that lasted from a few minutes to a few hours, whereas the later ones more often ended with the assassination of the victims. The first victim, Idalgo Macchiarini, a corporate executive at Sit Siemens, was accused of "particular rigidity against the workers" in contract negotiations. The second was a right-wing unionist from CISNAL, Bruno Labate, who was accused of having hired neofascist squads at Fiat. An entire document was devoted to the "anti-worker responsibilities" of the executive director of Alfa Romeo, Michele Mincuzzi. The fourth kidnapping victim was Ettore Amerio, director of personnel at Fiat, who was accused of having cooperated with Labate in hiring neofascists. All of the kidnappings were justified as actions oriented to getting information on repression and dismissals in the factories; after the (usually short) "interrogations," the victims were released (after pictures were taken), and the information they delivered was printed and circulated. However, this was certainly not the case for the kidnapping and killing of the president of the Italian Christian Democratic Party, Aldo Moro, and the assassination of his five bodyguards in 1978. Even though the BR asked for the release of prisoners, only to meet a firm refusal by the large majority of the political parties, in its choice of victim as well as the development of the event, the Moro kidnapping appeared more as an act of war than a Tupamaros-style demonstrative action.

Although kidnappings were used by both the ETA and the BR throughout their histories, their modalities changed. Similar alterations were seen in other forms of violent action. This chapter deals with these transformations in the action strategies of the clandestine organizations, in their forms and their targets, and, especially, in the logic behind these actions. Not only did clandestine organizations produce a mix of violent and nonviolent actions, but the violent forms varied a great deal. As we will see, the action choices in the underground are in part oriented by a consequential assessment of potential supporters as well as of the repressive strategies and repressive capacity of the state. This also means that the lethality as well as the targets of different underground groups diverge, adapting to the context in which they operate. Nevertheless, the choice to use violence in its extreme forms brings about some emergent developments, as it tends to isolate the organizations from potential supporters as well as increasing repressive state pressure. In this chapter, I look in particular at *action militarization*, which implies a shift toward increasingly cruel actions as well as a focus of the target selection toward organizational survival.

Clandestine political violence is only one part of a more complex repertoire used by different collective actors, under some circumstances. Armed groups aim at inspiring people by their example, using violence as a dramatic form of action that is capable of capturing the attention of various targets. Violence is often justified as a symbolic refusal to participate in an oppressive system, but it is also used to obtain media attention. Given its reduced costs (versus, for example, hiring guerrillas), political violence has been called a weapon of the weak.

However, using violence, especially in its most extreme forms, also has many limitations and constraints, which acquire different weights in different contextual circumstances. In fact, violence polarizes conflicts, transforming "relations between challengers and authorities from a confused, many-sided game into a bipolar one in which people are forced to choose sides, allies defect, bystanders retreat and the state's repressive apparatus swings into action" (Tarrow 1994: 104). First, violent action may cause an escalation in repression. The state holds a monopoly on the legitimate use of force, and most challenges to that monopoly are doomed to fail, transforming political conflict into a military confrontation in which the state has by far the greater firepower (della Porta 1995). Second, political violence has high costs because it implies a potential loss of popular sympathies. Although it is true that a lack of resources may encourage the use of more extreme tactics, "this impulse is constrained … by the erosion of support occasioned by repression and moral backlash. The crucial question, therefore, is whether the government's additional responsiveness to violent protest will provide sufficient compensation for the movement's smaller size" (DeNardo 1985: 219).

If clandestine groups tend to define violence as a means to an end, there is also a mystical view of rebellion as a means of individual expression, a sort of redemptive act, or an assertion of the will (McCormick 2003: 477). Beyond its low material costs, violence has the advantage of binding the individuals to the cause (e.g., see Fanon 1961).

A parallel distinction exists among scholars of violence, between those who assume rationality in decision making and those who stress nonrational logics (ibid.: 481). For the first group, the choice to use violence follows some preferences and is consequential, that is, based on the assessment of its anticipated consequences. So, the different degrees of brutality in civil wars have been explained as "part of a rational strategy aiming to punish and deter civil defection under specific constraints" (Kalyvas 2006: 245). Selectivity is considered as a basis for efficacy in deterring defection and insuring compliance: massacres reach their aims if the killing is – to a certain extent – selective. They are strategically useful especially when control of the population is declining or contested, and defectors are addressed as a way to set an example. Similarly, Pape's (2005) study on suicide bombers stressed efficacy as a motif.

In contrast to those who assume rationality, other scholars have suggested the importance of looking inside the clandestine organizations to understand how their specific features influence their choices of repertoire of action. Clandestinity, secrecy, and group-dependency exert important constraints on decision making. The type of ideology to which a group subscribes might increase or limit its propensity to kill. For instance, according to Engene's data on Western Europe (2004: 107), at least in recent periods, ethnonationalist conflicts tended to be more deadly than either right-wing or left-wing ones. Between 1950 and 1995, as many as 1,489 deaths caused by acts of terrorism took place in the UK (54 percent of the total number of terrorist-related deaths in Europe), most of which were related to the troubles between Catholics and Protestants in Northern Ireland; another 650 (24 percent) occurred in Spain, most of which were linked to the ethnonationalist conflict in the Basque Country. Italy, with its widespread right-wing and left-wing violence, comes third among European countries, with 298 victims (11 percent). Acts of terrorism leading to injury or loss of life amount to 41 percent of the total number of acts of terrorism in the UK and 50.5 percent in Spain, as compared to 28 percent in Italy; in parallel, the number of acts of terrorism that lead to loss of life make up 29 percent, 41 percent, and 20 percent of the totals, respectively (ibid.: 111). More recently, in a large-N study of 395 underground organizations active between 1998 and 2005 (only 68 of which had killed ten or more people), Asal and Rethemeyer (2008) found that a religious and ethnic-religious ideology (as well as large size in terms of members and territorial control plus connectedness) is causally linked to the lethality of these events.

No doubt, the groups we analyze use very radical forms of action. Engene (2004: 60) analyzed 8,916 terrorist attacks in Europe between 1950 and 1995, 39 percent of which involved bombs, 18.5 percent armed attacks, and 14 percent firebombs. A total of 1,470 people lost their lives in these actions (1,035 actions killed only one targeted victim) (ibid.: 65). In 1970 terrorist attacks increased drastically, and the number of victims per year remained around 100 until 1980. Most (78 percent) of these actions were performed by ethnonationalist groups, as compared to 10 percent by the radical Left and 8 percent by the radical Right (ibid.: 68).

It would be misleading, however, to say that clandestine groups aim just to produce as much material damage as possible, or that their choices are not normatively constrained by a (changing) definition of what is morally justified, as well as by the context in which they act (with repression playing a particularly important role). It has been observed that urban riots staged by excluded ethnic minorities as well as exclusionary riots against ethnic minorities have typically aimed at specific concessions, and rioters tend to practice much more self-restraint than usually admitted (Hobsbawm 1959). Similarly, and contrary to a widespread stereotype, underground organizations do not aim at destroying as much as possible or at leaving as many victims as they can.

Some research has also identified various logics, whose balance shifts over time. In my previous research, I have singled out propaganda-oriented actions, aimed at raising support in a specific group of the population, and internally oriented ones, focused on the clandestine group itself (della Porta 1995). Distinguishing between a logic of influence and a logic of security, McCormick (2003: 496–7) notes the tensions between the two, as well as the different points of equilibrium different groups can achieve in different times. In a similar vein, Luis de la Calle and Ignacio Sánchez-Cuenca distinguished a strategy of attrition against the state, which aimed at forcing the state to make concessions (e.g., killings of members of security forces to push the state out of the territory), and a strategy of control, which is related to maintaining the security and popularity of the organization in its territory, by punishing those who do not comply with the rules set by the clandestine organization (2006: 5). Whereas the attrition logic includes indiscriminate attacks and attacks against security forces (army and police) and state officials (politicians, judges, and other officials), control logic includes support-seeking campaigns as well as actions against informers and traitors (ibid.: 7). According to all these classifications, forms of action and targets are important indicators of the group's organizational logic.

As we will see in what follows, the clandestine groups I have studied in this volume have chosen different forms of action and different targets. Left-wing groups tended, at least in the beginning, to target factories. Ethnic clandestine groups often attacked the army. Right-wingers and religious fundamentalists were more often responsible for "untargeted" bombings. Especially when and where more environmental resources were available, the choice of targets and forms tended to be influenced by the characteristics of the radicalized social movement militants that the clandestine groups addressed, seeing as they were oriented to propaganda and recruitment. However, similarly, these groups developed toward the use of increasingly lethal actions that were more often oriented toward internal aims. In fact, in all of the four types of clandestine violence addressed in the following parts, the more isolated the groups and the stronger the repression, the more they gave up propaganda aims and focused on organizational survival.

ACTION MILITARIZATION IN LEFT-WING ORGANIZATIONS

The left-wing clandestine groups tended to focus many of their actions on propaganda activity, addressing targets that were stigmatized in the left-wing social movements and avoiding forms of action – such as bombs – that were rejected in that environment. However, the logic of their action changed over time, as they became increasingly involved in a sort of war with the state, giving up hopes of recruiting in broader social movements.

In Italy and Germany, between 1970 and 1983, about half of the actions of the clandestine left-wing groups (61.6 percent in Italy and 44.1 percent in Germany) were externally oriented propaganda actions, targeting the social and political adversaries of the social movements they addressed. Reflecting those movements' characteristics, in Italy, the main targets were linked to the factories (45 percent of the propaganda actions targeted factories and factory

TABLE 6.1. *Targets of Armed Italian Clandestine Left-Wing Groups*

Targets	BR		Others		Total	
	%	#	%	#	%	#
Propaganda in factories	40.4	262	11.2	67	26.8	329
Social propaganda	5.7	37	30.7	184	17.6	221
Political propaganda	23.9	155	9.7	58	17.1	213
War against the state	17.1	111	17.4	104	17.1	215
Military defense	5.2	34	4.8	29	5.1	63
Self-financing	7.1	46	25.4	152	15.1	198
Other	0.5	3	0.8	5	0.5	8
TOTAL	52.0	648	48.0	599	100.0	1,247

Note: As more than one option is possible for each event, the total is larger than the number of cases. The percentages have been calculated on the number of options.
Source: Elaboration of data obtained from judicial acts; reported in della Porta 1990: 216.

workers versus 16 percent against political targets), and in Germany the targets were related to anti-imperialist struggles.

Even inside each country, different groups preferred different targets, reflecting, once again, the specific social movement bases they wanted to address. In Italy (see Table 6.1), the more traditional left-wing BR focused its actions on the factories, especially those in which more radical struggles had erupted and, especially in the beginning, against stigmatized right-wing trade unionists and "small bosses" as well as political targets. The latter targets made up 40 percent of all of the BR's actions (as compared to 11 percent of those of other groups), and the former targets made up 24 percent (as compared to 10 percent of those of the other groups).

The groups that emerged in the second half of the 1970s concentrated instead on "social" propaganda, targeting real estate agencies, small businesses, drug dealers, neuropsychiatrists, night watchmen, computer services, and advertising agencies (della Porta 1990: 216). Thirty-one percent of their actions fell into this category, as compared to a very low 6 percent of the BR's actions. The targets of the second generation of clandestine organizations thus reflected the themes of the radical movements active in the second half of that decade, as the groups focused on housing, cost of living, unemployment, and drugs, as well as agencies involved in the penetration of social control in the private sphere of individual lives (such as psychiatrists and computer shops).

In parallel, in Germany, the RAF's propagandistic action was mainly oriented to anti-imperialism; the B2J chose "solidarity" action with the Irish independents; and the actions of the RZ reflected the campaigns of new social movements of the 1970s on the cost of transport, nuclear power, or technology. As an RZ militant explained, "we wanted to address marginal groups, where dissatisfaction and even misery were dominant. So we arrived at such actions as printing fake transport tickets or welfare tickets" (quoted in della Porta 1995: 122). Later on, in the 1980s, RZ's actions targeted the institutions considered responsible for the restrictive policy toward immigrants and refugees seeking political asylum.

In both countries, however, the groups also carried out internally oriented defensive actions, aiming at the survival of the underground organizations (such as bank robberies, accidental shutouts during arrests, and punishment of so-called traitors, which made up 37.3 percent of all actions in Germany as compared to 21.1 percent in Italy), or targeting the police, the judiciary, or the prison system.

In parallel to compartmentalization processes at the level of the organization, defensive actions increased over time (see Table 6.2). In Italy, the proportion of terrorist actions against the repressive state apparatuses grew from 20 percent in 1970 to 50 percent in 1982. Between 1978 and 1983, three-fourths of terrorist attacks were directed against the military state apparatuses (della Porta 1990: 246). The number of actions of revenge against traitors increased from only one before 1979, to four between 1979 and 1980, and to thirteen in 1981 and 1982 (della Porta 1990: 247).

This trend is even clearer if we look at the evolution of the two largest Italian clandestine organizations, the BR and PL (Table 6.3). In both cases, we can

TABLE 6.2. *Evolution of the Targets of Italian Left-Wing Groups (1970–1983)*

	Political Organizations	Trade Unions	Gov. Bodies	Repressive Establishments	Factories	Other	Total
1970	25.0	–	–	–	75.0	–	4
1971	58.8	5.9	5.9	5.9	23.5	–	17
1972	23.1	28.2	2.6	10.3	35.9	–	39
1973	–	23.1	–	–	76.9-	–	17
1974	10.9	8.7	–	19.6	54.3	6.5	46
1975	15.3	12.5	1.4	15.3	54.2	1.4	72
1976	4.9	12.6	2.9	27.2	51.5	1.0	103
1977	27.7	4.1	5.1	15.4	45.1	2.6	238
1978	15.1	2.5	7.1	41.6	31.1	2.5	179
1979	9.5	2.2	7.3	34.1	43.0	3.9	125
1980	7.2	2.4	12.0	20.8	54.4	3.2	195
1981	13.3	3.3	8.3	30.0	43.3	1.7	60
1982	8.2	–	–	49.0	36.7	–	49
1983	33.3	–	–	33.3	33.3	–	3
TOTAL %	14.9	5.6	5.8	27.3	43.7	2.7	–
TOTAL #	170.0	64.0	66.0	312.0	500.0	31.0	1,143

Note: As more than one option is possible for each event, the total is larger than the number of cases. The percentages have been calculated on the number of options.

Source: Elaboration of data obtained from judicial acts; reported in della Porta 1990: 245.

TABLE 6.3. *Evolution of the Targets of the BR and PL (1970–1983)*

	Brigate Rosse				Prima Linea			
	Propaganda	War against the State	Armed Defense	Self-Financing	Propaganda	War against the State	Armed Defense	Self-Financing
1970–6	72.2	11.0	4.1	8.2	80.0	10.0	–	10.0
1977	91.3	5.4	2.2	1.1	63.5	20.6	1.6	14.3
1978	59.2	35.7	1.0	4.1	66.3	14.1	4.3	15.2
1979	73.8	18.5	3.1	4.6	52.1	23.9	7.0	15.4
1980	70.1	23.9	1.5	2.9	15.8	10.5	5.3	18.3
1981	59.5	19.0	14.3	7.1	–	–	–	100.0
1982–3	5.4	21.6	32.4	35.1	–	–	–	–
TOTAL %	70.0	17.2	5.3	7.1	58.0	17.9	4.3	19.5
TOTAL #	453.0	111.0	34.0	46.0	149.0	46.0	11.0	50.0

Note: As more than one option is possible for each event, the total is larger than the numbers of cases. The percentages have been calculated on the number of options.

Source: Elaboration of data obtained from judicial acts; reported in della Porta 1990: 248.

observe a decline in the number of propaganda actions. Actions in the factories were dominant in the beginning. Among the very first actions of the BR were, in the fall of 1970, attacks against the cars of high-ranking members of Sit Siemens and Pirelli Bicocca as well as, later on, against those of exponents of the right-wing unions. Leaflets were distributed that explained, at length, the individual responsibility of the targets. The same is true of the kidnappings mentioned in the incipit of this chapter, and of some break-ins at the headquarters of radical Right unions as well as the MSI – including one incident in which two right-wing militants were (apparently accidentally) killed. Actions against factory targets would continue in the following years, including the director of personnel at Ansaldo, the factory medical doctor at Fiat, and a corporate director of Singer, who was accused of having decided on many workers' dismissals. Between 1977 and 1978 eighteen of the people who were wounded and one of those who was assassinated were employees at Fiat, Lancia, Sit Siemens, Alfa Romeo, Breda, Pirelli, Ansaldo, and Italsider, all of whom were considered symbols of the "command system" in the factories.

At the same time, however, beginning in the mid-1970s, actions began to be aimed at more political targets, especially in the Christian Democratic Party – which was believed to be acting at the heart of the capitalist system. In the second half of the 1970s, in an attempt to gain support among emerging social movements, left-wing organizations carried out actions targeted at not only university professors but also the press (including the assassination of Carlo Casalegno, vice-director of the Fiat-controlled daily *La Stampa*). In the 1980s, splinter factions (e.g., the Walter Alasia Column) would attack factory targets or "anti-imperialist" targets (in Veneto).

While this type of propaganda action began in general to decline, in parallel, there was an increase in actions oriented against repressive state apparatuses (especially the police), as well as in unplanned shoot-outs during chance encounters with police and actions geared toward the financing of the organization. One of the first actions of revenge against repression was the kidnapping of Judge Mario Sossi in 1974, followed by break-ins at the offices of the institution responsible for prison management and culminating in the planned assassination, in 1976, of the Genoa public prosecutor Francesco Coco. Especially in the second half of the 1970s, the long list of assassinations of police officers is linked to the attempt to block the trial against the founders of the BR as well as to the campaign against the creation of high-security prisons. In 1979, the revenge activities escalated with the (apparently unplanned) killing of a communist factory worker, Guido Rossa, accused of having denounced a colleague to the police and, in 1981, with the assassination of the kidnapped Roberto Peci, the brother of a former BR militant who had collaborated with the judges. Two private policemen were killed in 1982, the sole purpose of which was to denounce the supposed betrayal of another militant. In addition, an army truck was attacked in Salerno, and three policemen were killed during the action. Action against the police hit not only rank-and-file but also high-ranking officers, sometimes those with specific investigative tasks. Explaining the shift from the initial low-level forms of action to more brutal ones, a leader of the organization recalled, "We could not continue to burn cars ... there was already the image of the BR as those who burn cars.... Instead, we wanted to be *guerrilleros*" (Franceschini, Buffa, and Giustolisi 1988: 57). Similarly, after a few attacks with an emphasis on propaganda, the RAF also became increasingly involved in internal aims, such as support to imprisoned comrades.

Although all of these actions were a reaction to isolation, as well as attempts to recruit among already-radicalized militant milieus, they contributed to isolating the organizations even further: bank robberies tended to be stigmatized as common crimes, shoot-outs with police had limited appeal for potential sympathizers, and attempts on the lives of former militants considered as traitors were strongly criticized.

As for the forms of action, both Italian and German left-wing clandestine organizations privileged actions against property over actions against individuals, even though the total number of victims was high, especially in Italy (there were a total of 179 deaths – including those of militants in the underground organizations – in Italy, as compared to 41 in Germany). There were, however, internal differences among the various groups in each country. In Italy, the BR, looking for recruits among those who had already joined the underground, carried out a greater number of bloody acts than any other group. The other groups were addressing a broader constituency of militants who favored radical action but were opposed to killing: 28.9 percent of the BR attacks were thus aimed at people, as compared to 7.7 percent of those carried out by other leftist underground groups (della Porta and Rossi 1984: 19).

Similar distinctions existed among the German terrorist groups. There, the RAF was responsible for most of the terrorist attacks against people, whereas the other clandestine groups exercised more restraint. Aiming at increasing sympathies in a broader environment, the RZ organization also used nonviolent forms of protest: for instance, "since in many cities of the FRG the police brutally attacked the demonstrations against the increase in the transport price, the RZ have distributed 120,000 fake tickets in West Berlin" (RZ document, cited in Fetscher, Munkler, and Ludwig 1981: 176).

However, the propensity toward bloodier forms of action tended to increase over time (see Table 6.4). In Italy, if we distinguish different forms of violent action, between 1970 and 1983 we observe a decrease in the proportion of attacks against property, which declined from 100 percent in 1970, to 80 percent in the two following years, to 8 percent in 1982, and to none the following year. In reverse, we have an increase in the proportion of assaults against people, which started at a low 4.3 percent in 1973, remained below 10 percent the following two years, increased to 15 percent in 1977, and then rose above 25 percent in the following years, with a peak at 66.6 percent in 1983. In parallel, we can also note an increase in the percentage of occasional shoot-outs with the police, which started in 1974, then grew in the first period of organizational

TABLE 6.4. *Evolution of the Tactics of Italian Left-Wing Clandestine Violence (1970–1983)*

Year	Bombings	Robbery	Incursion	Armed Conflict	Seizure	Ambush	Total
1970	100.0	–	–	–	–	–	4
1971	82.4	17.6	–	–	–	–	17
1972	79.5	12.8	5.1	–	2.6	–	39
1973	50.0	14.1	14.1	–	21.4	–	14
1974	63.0	4.3	17.4	4.3	6.5	4.3	46
1975	67.6	9.5	6.8	4.5	4.1	8.1	74
1976	70.0	5.8	7.8	5.8	1.0	9.7	103
1977	57.9	8.6	16.2	1.5	1.0	14.7	197
1978	56.3	10.0	9.2	0.8	0.4	23.3	240
1979	43.0	17.3	9.5	3.9	1.7	24.6	179
1980	44.3	26.0	3.1	3.8	2.3	20.6	131
1981	22.2	28.6	4.8	7.9	12.7	23.8	63
1982	8.2	42.9	2.0	22.4	–	24.5	49
1983	–	33.3	–	–	–	66.6	3
TOTAL %	52.5	14.8	9.0	3.8	0.6	17.5	–
TOTAL #	609.0	171.0	104.0	44.0	28.0	203.0	1,159

Note: As more than one option is possible for each event, the total is larger than the number of cases. The percentages have been calculated on the number of options.
Source: Elaboration of data obtained from judicial acts; reported in della Porta 1990: 248.

crisis (the following three years), and continued after 1979, peaking at 22.4 percent in 1983. About 80 percent of the assassinations committed by left-wing underground organizations between 1970 and 1982 were carried out after 1977 (della Porta 1990: 241).

A similar type of evolution can be observed if we focus on the BR, whose first, unplanned assassination happened in 1974, followed by a planned wounding the year after; the first planned assassination occurred in 1976, followed by as many as sixteen killings in 1978. To give one more example, the proportion of the PL's actions against people (as opposed to actions against property) grew from 8 percent in 1977, the year the organization came into being, to 31 percent in 1979.

We find a similar evolution in Germany. The RAF's illegal activities initially consisted mainly of robberies or attempts to free imprisoned comrades. However, this changed later on, when the organization began to carry out kidnappings and assassinations, some of which occurred during shoot-outs with the police. Similarly, the B2J specialized in bombings against state apparatuses and bank robberies but then became involved in actions against people.

In general, it seems that the more isolated the group, the quicker its evolution toward more lethal forms of action. For instance, in Germany, the RAF quickly progressed toward the most lethal forms of action, whereas in Italy the BR's forms of action escalated more slowly. In Germany, the number of victims increased in 1975 and 1977, with ten assassinations in each of the two years. In Italy, terrorist attacks peaked for the first time around 1974–5 and a second time in 1979 and then sharply declined, although the most brutal forms continued to be used for several years. Attacks against people rose to between 20 and 25 percent in 1977–82 and then to 67 percent in 1983.

On the other hand, the spiral of increasing – and increasingly destructive – violence was interrupted when violent social conflicts erupted within the social movement family. At such times, even the BR or the RAF tended to invest in less lethal forms of action that could bring them more sympathy in the radicalized social movement environment. These phases, however, did not last long; in fact, in dense clandestine environments the intraorganizational competition itself brought about increasingly militarized actions aimed at impressing radical militants already in the underground.

ACTION MILITARIZATION IN RIGHT-WING ORGANIZATIONS

The use of violence in the radical Right in Italy only partially followed the trends toward higher lethality of action, even though there was indeed, especially in the second half of the 1970s, a move from primarily propaganda-oriented actions to actions relating to a greater extent to a private war with the state.

In the political violence of the Italian extreme Right, we observe an initial period of the most lethal and untargeted attacks between the end of the 1960s and the first half of the 1970s (see Figure 6.1). Also on the right, attacks against people grew, together with other forms of violence that were, particularly in the first years, more widespread within the extreme Right than within the extreme Left. The registered episodes of right-wing violence (which totaled 2,925 between 1969 and 1982, against 1,173 episodes of left-wing violence) numbered 148 in 1969, doubled to 286 the next year, remained around 400 in the following years, dropped to 154 in 1975 and 110 in 1976, and then grew again to 279 in 1978. As many as 73 percent of violent episodes involving the radical Right happened between 1969 and 1975, versus only 17 percent of those involving the radical Left (della Porta and Rossi 1984).

One characteristic of radical Right violence was the higher proportion of unclaimed attacks as compared with the radical Left. In fact, the radical Right claimed 17 percent of the total number of attacks (524 claimed attacks versus 2,545 unclaimed attacks); in comparison, the Left claimed 55 percent (2,188 claimed attacks versus 1,792 unclaimed attacks), with an increase over time. In addition, anonymous bombings increased since 1968, while new neofascist groups proliferated, engaging in street battles and assaults against left-wing opponents (della Porta and Rossi 1984).

Radical Right attacks were also bloodier than those by the extreme Left. The radical Right was responsible for 51 clandestine attacks against people, versus 272

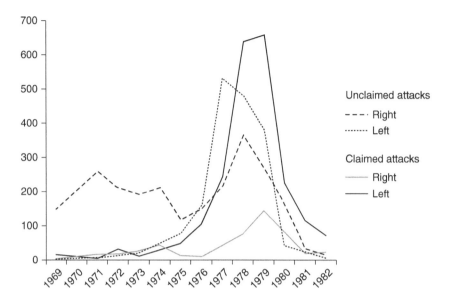

FIGURE 6.1. Claimed and unclaimed attacks on the right and on the left, 1969–1982.
Source: adapted from della Porta and Rossi 1984: 18–19.

for the Left. However, these attacks represented 758 persons wounded or killed, including 186 deaths; this compares to 360 wounded and 164 deaths for the Left. As many as 689 were the victims of massacres; 138 of these victims lost their lives (ibid.). Most of the massacres happened between 1969 and 1974. During these years, 53 people died and 351 were wounded in the massacres of Piazza Fontana in Milan in 1969 (17 deaths), on a train in Calabria in 1970 (6 deaths), in Piazza della Loggia in Brescia in 1974 (8 deaths), and on a train in San Benedetto in Val di Sambro, also in 1974 (12 deaths) (Ferraresi 1984: 57–72; Galleni 1981: 52). In 1974, a series of bombings accompanied the two massacres in Brescia and on the Italicus, and rumors spread of a new attempted coup d'état, involving members of the police and the army (Ferraresi 1995: 254). Even though a final judicial conclusion has not yet been reached (and probably never will be), the AN and ON are considered to have been involved in these massacres as well as in attempted coups d'état during this period (Ferraresi 1984).

Bombing was indeed a widespread form of violence for the radical Right. In 1969 alone, there were 312 attacks with bombs for which the extreme Right was seen as responsible. Moreover, a compilation that covers the years 1969–80 attributed to the extreme Right 83 percent of violent events between 1969 and 1975, as well as 63 out of 92 homicides (della Porta and Rossi 1984). The most deadly years were therefore those in which the protest cycle peaked, and when there were rumors of institutional support for the radical Right. As a militant recalled, in 1974, "there was the greater integration between the political and the military, as there were talks about the possibility to realize a sort of coup d'etat ... so aiming at a coup d'etat becomes our tactics ... because through it, we can free us from communism, which is the main enemy" (interview with S.C.: 53, in Fiasco 1990: 170).

The mid-seventies represented a turning point (see Chapter 3). Thirty-five percent of the 8,400 attacks attributed to the Right between 1969 and 1980 took place after 1975 (see Galleni 1981). The lethality of the attacks remained high in the ensuing years. Between 1975 and 1980, right-wing clandestine groups were responsible for 115 assassinations (85 of which were victims of the massacre in the Bologna railway station, for which right-wing radicals were sentenced, even though they denied responsibility). Between 1977 and 1979, as many as 3,000 attacks were attributed to the neofascists.

Also on the right, there was a change in targets, with a progressive focus on organizational survival. In the second half of the 1970s, together with the "fake opposition" of the MSI, the strategy oriented to a coup d'etat of the previous generation was stigmatized as de facto supporting the existing regime. Thus, some of the former members of the ON, in a sort of imitation of the left-wing radicals, started to theorize about an armed spontaneity, giving birth in 1977 to Terza Posizione (a third position between the Right and the Left).

Left-wing activists nevertheless remained a main target for violent actions. Using a faster dynamic than those on the left of the political spectrum, the radical Right groups focused on a sort of war of the bands with their political adversaries. In 1979, the Nuclei Armati Rivoluzionari assassinated left-wing adversaries and assaulted the headquarters of the Partito Comunista Italiano (Communist Italian Party [PCI]), injuring twenty-five people in 1979. They claimed twenty-nine bombings in 1978, forty-three in 1979, and thirty-two in the first half of 1980. When the state reacted with judicial investigations and repression became effective, however, right-wing clandestine organizations started to perform actions oriented toward the disarticulation of power by attacking the state's transmission belt of power. After losing institutional protections, the extreme Right turned against state institutions.

Disillusioned by the lack of resonance in the military, neofascist groups started to attack the state, which they considered to be increasingly penetrated by communists. The bombs against Carabinieri in Peteano in May 1972 had already indicated a shift toward a fight against the state. According to the testimony of one of the bombers, the action was meant to signal a definitive break with the institutional instrumentalization and the start of an independent political battle against the regime and its supporters (quoted in Panvini 2009: 214). In fact, "the reference to the need of a struggle against the State represented a relevant semantic shift that indicated a change in the strategy of the extreme right" (ibid.: 212). One of the militants who claimed responsibility for the Peteano massacre defined it as part of "a logic of breaking with the strategy which was followed by forces which I had thought were revolutionary, on the Right, and which instead followed a strategy which was dictated by the national and international power centers located at the top of the state" (Ferraresi 1995: 235).

Additionally, violence soon turned inward and was used – in a particularly brutal way – to punish presumed traitors. The list of former activists killed by their comrades because they were suspected of having collaborated with the police or even having stolen money from their own organizations grew over time. Already in 1979, the NAR had mistakenly killed someone they took for a traitor. In 1981 two other radical Right militants were accused of betrayal and were killed by their fellow activists (ibid.: 65). The NAR even organized a campaign against the leaders of the Terza Posizione (TP), who were accused of having instrumentalized and then abandoned young people for their own ego-tistic purposes. In a leaflet claiming responsibility for the assassination of a policeman, the NAR also took responsibility for the killing of "the infamous traitor Luca Pericci.... The dement exploiters Francesco Mangiameli ... the infamous traitor Marco Pizzarri" (cited in Ferraresi 1995: 339). According to NAR militant Francesca Mambro, the assassination of Pino De Luca "has to be framed within a military campaign against those elements that we considered as 'exploiters' and that, 'till then, had had a lot of room to live exploiting the others" (quoted in Bianconi 1992: 2111). In the early 1980s, two radical Right activists, Ermanno Buzzi and Carmine Palladino, were killed in the high-security prison in Novara, by a "revolutionary tribunal" formed of fellow right-wing prisoners who suspected them of betrayal. In fact, in the militants' memory, punishing traitors became a sort of perverse moral obligation. As a former militant wrote, "we have no power to follow or masses to educate. For us, what is important is to respect our ethic, that says that you have to kill your enemy and destroy the traitors" (ibid.: 66). A sense of honor was invoked in the choice of targets for revenge action: "Until any single comrade is revenged, nobody has the right to desist" (ibid.: 76).

In this period, robberies and holdups were also carried out more often, to finance the clandestine organizations (although proceeds were sometimes split equally between the organization and the robbers); they often ended in shoot-outs with the police. Logistical links with organized crime thus became increas-ingly influential (Fiasco 1990: 167). Recalling that period, an activist stated,

The only contacts we had were with those who could sell us arms. Joking, we said: "once upon the time there were Indians of various tribes; we are those who were expelled by all of them: the Broncos. The only people with whom the Broncos can talk are the Comancheros, who sell arms and whisky." This is how we felt. (interview with S.C.: 141, in Fiasco 1990: 183)

One of them, Giliberto Cavallini, also admitted to "contacts with the Milanese criminal milieu ... developed for logistic and contingent needs" (quoted in Bianconi 1992: 175).

In conclusion, right-wing clandestine organizations also tended to lose their capacity to act against political, outwardly oriented objectives, transforming themselves into bands and/or sects that invested most of their time and resources into the organization of their own survival. In the words of a right-wing radical, their very isolation moved them inward: "Given our size, what is left for us is just revenge. The most we can do it to take revenge for the killed comrades. And the revenge is sacred" (ibid.: 86).

ACTION MILITARIZATION IN ETHNIC ORGANIZATIONS

The history of the ETA also shows an evolution in action strategies – not a linear one, but one influenced by contextual conditions such as state repression as well as the presence and characteristics of a potential base that the organization wanted to address and influence.

Scholars have singled out different periods in the lethality of the ETA's activities, which totaled 836 victims in 597 attacks between 1968 and 2007 (Sánchez-Cuenca 2009), more than 90 percent of which were attributed to the ETA-M (24 were attributed to the ETA-PM and 32 to the Commandos Autonomous Anti-Capitalistas; de la Calle and Sánchez-Cuenca 2006: 17). Although it was founded in 1959, the ETA started killing only in 1968. Between 1968 and 1977, the ETA maintained a low level of lethality; most of its assassinations occurred between 1977 and 1981. The decade between 1982 and 1992 saw some stability at a relatively low level of lethality, although this was interrupted by some peaks in 1987 and 1991. After that, ETA violence drastically dropped.

In its first years of existence, in fact, the ETA limited itself to timid symbolic actions, such as the writing of graffiti (which included the ETA symbol and the slogan "Gora Euskadu askatuta," that is, "Long live the Basque Country") or public display of the Basque flag. On 18 July 1961, the first action involving use of force happened during the anniversary of the beginning of the civil war, when the ETA derailed a train of Francoist ex-combatants traveling to San Sebastian. However, so much care was put into avoiding casualties that even material damages were extremely limited (Clark 1984: 110). Nevertheless, 110 activists (including many leaders) were arrested, tortured, and sentenced to up to twenty years in prison, while intense and indiscriminate repression hit the whole Basque population.

Only in 1968 did the first, unplanned killing occur. On 7 June, two ETA members were stopped at a police control. One of them, Txabi Etxebarrieta, opened fire, killing a policeman. A few hours later, he was found and shot dead in retaliation by the police, leading to widespread protests in major Basque cities. On 2 August, the ETA retaliated in turn, with its first planned assassination in the more than eight years of its history: it killed the police chief of Guipuzkoa, Melito Manzanas Gonzales, who had been accused of torturing Basque prisoners. Many activists were arrested during the state of exception, with suspension of constitutional guarantees following the assassination. Although the number of assassinations remained low for a few years (a total of four between 1968 and 1973), on 30 December 1973, the ETA carried out the most effective of its actions: the killing of the prime minister, Franco's chosen successor, Admiral Luis Carrero Blanco.

In 1975, the competition between the ETA-PM and ETA-M underlay an escalation of action, as both organizations attacked the Guardia Civil and the police as a way to push the Spanish government toward negotiation (Tejerina 2001: 44). In that same year, on the day of a demonstration in support of Franco, the ETA killed three other policemen in Madrid.

Paradoxically, ETA violence increased exponentially during the transition and consolidation, allowing the Basque organization, whose capital of reputation had increased enormously after the Carrero Blanco assassination and the Burgos trial, to remain a relevant force even as conditions changed. ETA victims were distributed by year as follows (see Figure 6.2): two in 1968, one in 1969, none in 1970 and 1971, one in 1972, six in 1973, nineteen in 1974, fifteen in 1975, eighteen in 1976, ten in 1977, sixty-five in 1978, eighty in 1979, and ninety-six in 1980 (Calleja and Sánchez-Cuenca 2006: 151; Laurenzano 2000: 122, cited in Muro 2008: 122). The peak of ETA activities between 1977 and 1981 coincided with the period of the first democratic elections, the constitutional referendum, and the referendum on the Statute of Autonomy for the Basque Country, as well as during intense radical Right violence between 1978 and 1982 (Sánchez-Cuenca 2009: 10ff.). In fact, "violence by the extreme right with regards ETA does not reduce the lethality of ETA, quite the opposite: it would seem that it sparks off a spiral of acts of vengeance" (ibid.: 14).

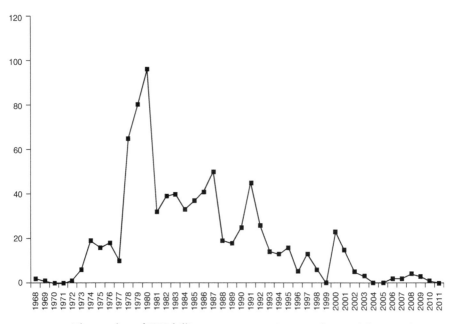

FIGURE 6.2. The number of ETA killings per year, 1968–2006. *Source*: Muro 2008: 187. Permission to reproduce gratefully acknowledged.

Unlike the actions of the radical Left in Italy and Germany, bombings against bystanders were also occasionally practiced (14 percent of ETA victims died in bombings). There was an indiscriminate attack in September 1974, although the ETA denied responsibility.[1] In 1979, instead, the ETA-PM did claim responsibility for bombings in public places against the rising tourist industry. Even when the ETA issued warnings, they were not always effective, as was the case on 29 July 1979 in Madrid, when three bombs in the Atocha railway station and in the Barajas airport caused five deaths in total. In July 1987, a bomb at a Hipercor supermarket in Barcelona caused twenty-one deaths, two of whom were children, and in December of the same year a car bomb at the civil guards' living quarters in Saragoza killed eleven, among which were five children. Bombings (usually with warnings) were never discontinued. On 30 December 2006, a bomb in Madrid's international airport caused 35 million Euros of damage and killed two people sleeping in one of the parking lots.

A high level of lethality characterized ETA actions during two local conflicts over the construction of some large infrastructures in the Basque Country. During the protests against the construction of a nuclear power station at Lemoniz (which was later cancelled), the ETA was responsible for 246 acts of sabotage and the killing of five people, among them the chief engineer of the Lemoniz plant, José Maria Ryan, and its project manager, Angel Pascal. In 1978, bombings at the Lemoniz site killed two and wounded fourteen. In 1981 and 1982, two engineers working on the construction of the plant were killed. A second violent campaign developed against the construction of the Leizaran highway, against which the ETA organized 158 acts of sabotage.

In general, the initial concern to minimize risks for bystanders diminished, as is evidenced by a number of casualties during bombings of building or attacks against military targets. The use of bombs (especially car bombs) was in fact linked to the largest number of accidental and indiscriminate victims: 64 out of a total of 126 – that is, 50.8 percent, as compared to only 3.4 percent of the 527 victims killed by firearms – were accidental or indiscriminate (de la Calle and Sánchez-Cuenca 2004: 65). As the 1980s proceeded, indiscriminate explosions became more common and selective assassinations with pistols less so. In 1987, for instance, an ETA cell bombed a shopping center in Barcelona, killing 21 people and wounding more than 100 (Zirakzadeh 2002: 76).

In the 1990s, violence changed its form to include low-level types previously stigmatized by the organization:

Younger recruits in particular, ignoring advice from earlier generations of ETArras, increasingly adopted vandalism as their preferred methods of pressing the Spanish government. According to government officials, youths claiming allegiance to ETA carried out approximately 5,000 acts of politically motivated vandalism, such as arson, breaking windows and trashing offices of political parties, between the years 1996 and

---

[1] A bomb in the cafeteria Rolando, in front of the Spanish government's Bureau of Security in Madrid, killed nine and wounded fifty-six.

2000. In 1996, politically motivated destruction of property – for example, burning buses and town halls – resulted in property damages in excess of $24 million. In addition, some young ETA affiliates began to surround political opponents in the streets and beat them. More than 650 street attacks on political opponents occurred in the year 2000 alone. (Zirakzadeh 2002: 84)

The targets of ETA actions also changed over time. Among the victims of ETA assassinations between 1968 and 1980, 68 percent were law enforcers, 8 percent politicians, 9.1 percent bystanders, 1.4 percent accidental victims, 2.4 percent entrepreneurs, and 4.2 percent people killed in retaliation (Clark 1984: 135). In general, victims of the ETA were mainly military: between 1978 and 1983, the ETA killed thirty-seven army officers as well as policemen. In the course of the 1970s, the main targets became not only the Guardia Civil and the police but also increasingly right-wingers, suspected traitors, and businessmen who refused to pay the revolutionary tax or were kidnapped for ransom.[2] To the attacks against representatives of the state (police, military, senior politicians, etc.), we have to add those against journalists, judges, prosecutors, civil servants, academics, businessmen, and especially low-profile politicians (Muro 2008: 156; Sánchez-Cuenca 2001: 73).[3] With this move, the ETA started to attack Basque people, in what was called a "socialization of pain," which was oriented to involve a broader range of the population as potential targets, thus increasing its resonance in the public opinion and its institutional impact. This logic became dominant in the 1990s. According to Sánchez-Cuenca,

until 1992, violence was used to put pressure on the State: the preferred targets were the police, the Guardia Civil and the army. After the fall at Bidart, the terrorists decided to change tactic and carry out attacks on state representatives and officials. While politicians and state officials form only 2.6 percent of fatalities during the war of attrition (1977–1992), this figure reaches 21.7 percent during the following phase (1992–2007). (2009: 6)

In general, the ETA strategy of involvement in environmental, labor, and antinuclear conflicts and the radicalization of Basque youngsters through street fighting (*kale borroka*) aimed at capitalizing on social movement mobilization, recruiting new militants, and reinforcing local bonds of participation (Kasmir 2002; Tejerina 2001).

---

[2] This was the case of Ybarra's kidnapping in 1977, during which the ETA asked for the liberation of twenty-three prisoners. As the French police arrested Apala, leader of the Berezi Comandos, Ybarra was killed.

[3] In 1976, the ETA-M killed the president of the provincial assembly of Guipuzkoa. In October 1977, Augusto Unceta, president of the provincial assembly of Biscaya, was assassinated with his two bodyguards. Later, the Comandos Autonomos killed a member of the PSOE who had a working-class background. Later, there was the killing of Gregorio Ordonez, a member of the Partido Popular (PP) and deputy mayor in San Sebastian, in 1995. Until May 2003, twenty-three PP and PSOE politicians were killed (de la Calle and Sánchez-Cuenca 2004: 64).

The organizational logic in the selection of the victims changed as well. According to de la Calle and Sánchez-Cuenca's data, 26.8 percent of the ETA's killings were selective (based on the behavior of the victims), 54.9 percent generic (based on their occupations), only 4.8 percent indiscriminate, and 13.5 percent collateral or accidental (2004: 14). The lower propensity of ETA supporters (and HB voters) to accept indiscriminate killings explains their lower rate when compared with the Provisional Irish Republican Army (PIRA) in Northern Ireland (15.6 percent [ibid.: 14]).

Also, in the case of the ETA there was a growing focus on organizational survival. Especially with the passing of time, robbery was increasingly used as a source of organizational resources (there were fifty robberies in 1978 alone [Clark 1984: 227]), in addition to ransoms and revolutionary taxes imposed on local entrepreneurs. Revolutionary taxes also became more significant over time.[4]

In contrast to the trends of the BR and right-wing terrorism, in the case of the ETA (see Figure 6.3) the proportion of victims from military forces (policemen

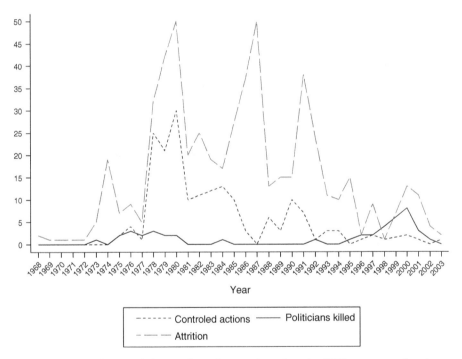

FIGURE 6.3. Evolution of the number of strategic actions by ETA per type of action. *Source*: De la Calle and Sánchez-Cuenca 2006.

---

[4] Resources were mainly kept in France, although there are rumors of training occurring in Algeria, Lebanon, Libya, and South Yemen.

and soldiers) dropped with time, from 59 percent of people assassinated between 1978 and 1998 to 29.7 percent between 1995 and 2003 (de la Calle and Sánchez-Cuenca 2004: 63). Conversely, the proportion of politicians and state functionaries killed increased from 1.6 percent to 29.1 percent in the same period (ibid.).

The number of revenge assaults against supposed traitors tended to rise. In 1978, there was the assassination of the journalist Portell, who was accused of trying to arrange a ceasefire. In the 1980s, seven ETA members were killed after being accused of having betrayed the organization, the most infamous case being Maria Dolores Gonzales Katarain (nicknamed Yoyes), one of the few women in ETA leadership, who was assassinated in 1986 by an ETA commando in her village. However, this type of assassination was discontinued in 1988 following strong negative reactions. As many as ninety-seven of the victims were accused of being police informants (de la Calle and Sánchez-Cuenca 2004: 68). In Guipuzkoa and Biscay in particular, types of action aimed at control became dominant in the last period. As de la Calle and Sánchez-Cuenca noted, after 1992, "there is an important and statistically significant fall in attrition (from 72 per cent to 60 per cent), and a spectacular increase in the percentage of state officials and politicians killed (from 3 per cent in the attrition period to 29 per cent in the last period)" (2004: 25).

In conclusion, in ethnic organizations actions also tended to become more inward oriented and bloodier.

ACTION MILITARIZATION IN RELIGIOUS ORGANIZATIONS

For underground religious groups as well, the choice to use violence and its development is influenced by instrumental as well as normative reasoning. Given the multisited nature of the Islamist groups, we can single out spirals of nested escalation in the forms of action.

One escalation can be seen in the various conflicts in the Middle East, where clandestine Islamist organizations emerged. In Egypt as well as in Algeria, mass and indiscriminate attacks were not present since the very beginning of such groups; rather, the degree of brutality and the legitimation of action against the civil Muslim population developed gradually, from an interaction of local as well as national and supranational dynamics.

In Egypt in the 1970s and 1980s, violent Islamist groups initially targeted their political opponents – especially left-wing students – as well as their religious ones, the Christian Copts. In the 1990s, we observe a move toward hitting not only state institutions (police, security forces, and government officials) but also the tourist industry and foreign banks. As local conflicts escalated and Islamist groups tried to win territorial control in some areas, violent actions even began to be targeted at Muslims, those who were accused of either betraying or simply not supporting radical Islamism. Of the 137 people killed by al-Jamaa in just one year, ninety were policemen; the rest were mainly Christians and foreign tourists, including, since 1992, attacks on tourist ships on the Nile, tourist buses, and tourist sites (Malthaner 2011).

In the same period, violence against Christians also escalated, bringing about increasing criticism of the radical Islamists. Through the politicization of intra-religious conflicts, traditional fights also took new and more dramatic turns. This is the case, for instance, in the violent spiral that developed in the village of Sanabo (near Assiut) from the assassination of eleven Christian peasants, together with a teacher (shot in front of his class) and a health inspector on 4 May 1992. According to Malthaner's reconstruction, based on official accounts, the escalation started over the sale of a house and involved a Christian family and a Muslim one, the latter of which counted some radical Islamists among its members. Previously, however, a member of al-Jamaa had been killed by the Christian family. In retaliation, "militant Islamists had been preventing public Christian ceremonies and wedding celebrations in the village, had forced the local Christian community to pay a special 'tax,' and on several occasions had carried out 'punishments' against people in the village" (Malthaner 2011: 163). Later, radical Islamists attacked a bus carrying Christian tourists, assassinated a Christian doctor, and set fire to a church and dozens of Christian homes. In 1992, al-Jamaa al-Islamiyya killed thirty members of local Christian communities, most of whom lived in the area of Assiut. As many as 110 Christian victims were counted between 1992 and 1997 (ibid.: 164).

Action repertoires also escalated. In 1992, bomb attacks, ambushes, and assassinations increased after the killing of al-Jamaa's spokesman, Ala Mohieddin. The number of people killed during attacks further grew from 80 in 1992 to more than 200 in 1993. Malthaner vividly describes escalations in repertoires of action, especially in some localities where Islamist groups tried to develop a sort of territorial control, in conflict with state institutions. This was the case in Imbaba, where al-Jamaa had imposed, through violent intimidation, territorial control "which allowed the group not only to assert themselves as new 'patrons' providing order, controlling crime, offering social services, and mediating in conflicts. In addition, they also used their power in the neighborhood to impose an Islamic order and rules of moral conduct" (2011: 147). However, attempts to control everyday life – including the prohibition of activities that were fully legitimated by local customs (such as playing cards or smoking water pipes) and the imposition of something akin to revolutionary taxes – produced resentment, to which the organization responded with increasingly violent efforts to "prohibit the evil." Since 1991, this focus on imposing through violence what they saw as Islamic rules for everyday life brought about attacks against video stores as well as Christian shops.

Violence also escalated in interactions with the police. The Islamist groups brutally reacted to repression, which had increased with the growth of intra-religious conflicts – involving arrests and the killing of presumed Islamists.

Violence eventually started to hit Muslims accused of being collaborators. In 1993, three such cases were reported by newspapers and human rights organizations. In September 1994, al-Jamaa killed a farmer accused of denouncing to the police the Islamist militants who were hiding in his fields. Five more murders of suspected collaborators followed in the next few months, reaching a total of eight in 1994 and spiraling to thirty-eight in 1995. As Malthaner recalled, not only did actions against collaborators increase but the range of behaviors included in the category also broadened:

In December 1994, police in Mallawi found a list of alleged "traitors" that included more than 150 names, suggesting that killing "collaborators" had become a strategic component of al-Jamaa's violent insurgency. Thereby, the category of "collaborators" broadened over time. In addition to people allegedly informing the police about the groups' activities, any person cooperating with the authorities now became a target. In December 1995, a farmer was killed because he drove a tractor in an operation to clear sugar-cane fields, a hideout for the militants. Several months before, the imam of a local mosque was murdered, allegedly because he resisted al-Jamaa taking over his mosque, and mayors and traditional village guards in particular became the target of attacks. (2011: 174–5)

Eventually, especially since 1996, the struggle against the community ended in the isolation of al-Jamaa. Attacks against Muslims brought about decreasing support, especially among merchants. The related declining trend in voluntary donations pushed the organization to resort to extortion, of not only Christian but also Muslim shopkeepers. In a vicious circle, these actions produced a further decline in the support for the violent group.

This isolation in turn reduced constraints on violence; there was a decrease in the number of attacks in 1996 and 1997 but at the same time an increase in their brutality, including massacres in which victims were mutilated. In February 1996, eight unarmed Christians were killed near Assiut; a few weeks later, eighteen Greek tourists were killed in an assault at their hotel in Giza because their Greek flag had been mistaken for an Israeli one. The attack was claimed as revenge against the Israeli Grapes of Wrath operation in Lebanon.

Attacks on tourists also escalated in the second half of 1997, until the vicious circle of isolation-brutality-isolation ended in the massacre in Luxor in November 1997, during which fifty-eight tourists and four Egyptian guards died at the Hatshepsuth temple in the Valley of Kings. As Malthaner observed, "the Luxor massacre in particular proved a turning point in the development of the conflict. It shocked and appalled all sectors of the public, including Islamist sympathizers and parts of al-Jamaa itself, and thus contributed to clearing the way for the historic leadership's ceasefire initiative, which was announced in December 1997" (2011: 166).

A similar evolution, though with different timing and higher lethality, was observed in Algeria. Under increasing repression by the Algerian authorities, the GIA's actions escalated in terms of forms and targets. Initially focused on military and police personnel, in 1993 the targets were expanded to include government officials and then foreigners, oppositional groups, journalists, artists, intellectuals, and even ordinary citizens, all considered as apostates and infidels (Malthaner 2011: 50ff.). As the organization stated, the jihadist operations were "targeting all the symbols of the infidel regime, from the head of state through the military and ending with the last hypocrite working for the regime"; also "the nationals of the resentful crusading countries are a target for the mujahidin because they represent part of the wicked colonialist plan" (quoted in Hafez 2004: 51). In 1994, customs and tax employees as well as teachers were called to immediately stop working for the apostate ruler, and the next year the wives of public employees were asked to leave their husbands if they did not leave their jobs. In 1996, the organization prohibited any contracts with the state and the use of tribunals, threatening to kill those who did not pay a tribute to the GIA or who prayed in the wrong mosques, as well as women who did not wear the *hijab* or who voted in elections (ibid.: 51).

While these local and national conflicts faded away, al-Qaeda's appeal to a global jihad grew in reaction to the defeats of nationally bounded Islamic rebellions in Egypt and Algeria; this growth was accompanied by a move from territorially bounded guerrilla tactics to deterritorialized clandestine political violence. At the same time, however, its repertoire was built on those high levels of violence, developing from the escalation of clandestine organizations as well as the brutality of civil wars in Afghanistan and Bosnia. This might explain why al-Qaeda's activities rapidly reached high levels of lethality. In fact, according to the dataset of the MIPT Terrorism Knowledge Base, the attacks associated with al-Qaeda and its recognized affiliates in the Arabian Peninsula, Iraq, and the Maghreb have caused more than 12,000 injuries to victims and more than 5,000 fatalities (Bakker and Boer 2007). The thirty-two incidents attributed to al-Qaeda up to 2007 had injured 8,864 and killed 3,464. A very high degree of lethality is also to be found in the affiliated group in Iraq, the Al-Qaeda Organization in the Land of the Two Rivers, with 3,764 injuries and 1,888 fatalities in 216 attacks, as compared to 126 fatalities in 47 attacks by Al-Qaeda Organization in the Islamic Maghreb and 14 fatalities in 5 attacks in Saudi Arabia (Al-Qaeda in the Arabian Peninsula) (MIPT Terrorism Knowledge Base, cited in Bakker and Boer 2007: 14–15).

Indeed, AQ focused on bombings, which constitute 81 of the 131 actions coded in the START database, which covers the core AQ organization (see Figure 6.4). Main targets were US and Western objects outside the West (see Figure 6.5). This was the case for the bombing of the Khobar Towers in Riyadh in 1996 and of the US embassies in Kenya and Tanzania in 1998, as well as the attacks in Tunisia (April 2002); Pakistan (May 2002); Kuwait, Yemen, and Indonesia (October 2002); Kenya (November 2002); Turkey (November 2003); Jordan (November 2005); and Algeria (December 2007). Exceptions to this trend include the bombing of the World Trade Center (WTC) in New York in 1993 and the 9/11 attack in New York and Washington, DC, in 2001, as well as the bombs in Madrid (March 2004) and London (July 2005). Several attacks on Western targets happened in Saudi Arabia between 1996 and 2005. Groups affiliated with AQ are considered responsible for the attacks on a nightclub in

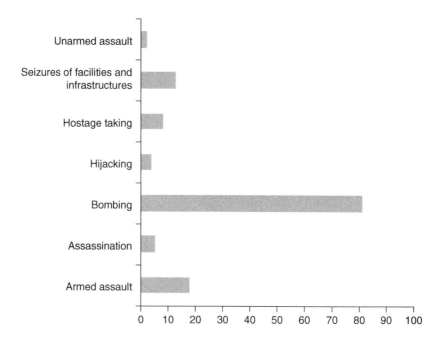

FIGURE 6.4. Al-Qaeda attacks (1995–2010) per form of action. *Source*: START. Permission to reproduce gratefully acknowledged.

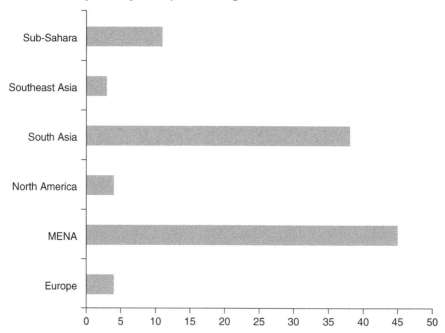

FIGURE 6.5. Al-Qaeda attacks (1995–2010) per geographical region. *Source*: START. Permission to reproduce gratefully acknowledged.

Bali (2002), a hotel near Mombasa (2002), and Jewish sites in Casablanca (2003), as well as a bomb in Amman (2005) and many car bombs and assassinations in Iraq (2003–7).

Different phases have also been identified in the development of AQ activities. Initially, AQ concentrated on the training and funding of Muslim resistance jihads in Chechnya, Kashmir, Indonesia, Georgia, Azerbaijan, Yemen, Algeria, and Egypt (Gunaratna 2003). In 1993, however, the aforementioned bomb at the World Trade Center killed 6 and injured more than 1,000 passersby. Two years later, a car bomb at the offices of the Saudi National Guard in Riyadh killed 7 people, and in June 1996, a bomb outside a military complex in Dharan, Saudi Arabia, that housed US Air Force personnel killed 19 US citizens and injured 372.

The second phase, characterized by the construction of a jihadist front, led, in August 1998, to attacks by suicide bombers on US embassies in Nairobi, Kenya, and Dar es Salaam, Tanzania, which killed 224 people. The Kenyan government was accused of having let the US army attack Muslims in Somalia, as well as of supporting Israel. In October 2000, a Zodiac boat filled with explosives detonated near the United States Ship (USS) Cole in the port of Aden, in Yemen, killing seventeen US servicemen and injuring thirty-nine. As recalled at the beginning of this volume, on September 11, 2001, in the most lethal of the attacks attributed to the group, nineteen al-Qaeda activists hijacked four commercial aircrafts, two of which were exploded into the Twin Towers in New York and one into the Pentagon in Washington, DC, resulting in a total death toll of 3,000 (Koschade 2006).

Notwithstanding the strong US military reaction, most attacks happened after 9/11. According to the START database, in fact, AQ attacks peaked in 2002–3, declining later on (see Figure 6.6).

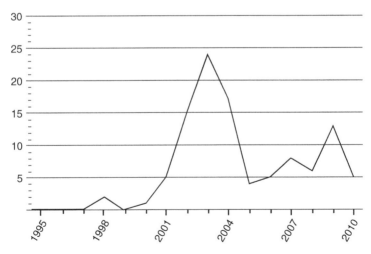

FIGURE 6.6. The number of al-Qaeda incidents (1995–2010) per year. *Source*: START. Permission to reproduce gratefully acknowledged.

A list of AQ's most serious attacks after 2001 includes the following:

In April of 2002, in Tunisia, an al-Qaeda bomber detonated a truck carrying natural gas outside a historic Jewish synagogue, which killed 21 people. On May 12, 2003, in Riyadh, Saudi Arabia, four expatriate housing complexes were attacked by suicide bombers in explosive filled vehicles. 25 bystanders were killed in the attacks, later attributed to al-Qaeda. Later that month, twelve al-Qaeda linked suicide bombers attacked Spanish and Jewish sites in Casablanca, Morocco, killing 33 people.... In November, two Jewish synagogues in Istanbul, Turkey were bombed killing 23 people. Just days later, the British Consulate, and the British owned HSBC bank were attacked by suicide bombers, killing a further 27 people. Joint responsibility was claimed between al-Qaeda and the fictional "Great Eastern Islamic Raiders Front." The al-Qaeda financed and backed Indonesian Islamic extremist group *Jemaah Islamiyah* (Islamic community) was responsible for the bombing of night clubs in Bali on October 12, 2002, which left over 200 people dead, including 88 Australians. The group is also responsible for the Marriott bombing in Jakarta on August 5, 2003, which killed 17 and injured 100, and the bombing of the Australian Embassy in Jakarta, on September 9, 2004, which killed ten and injured over a hundred. (in Koschade 2006: 8)

In all these actions, lethality remained high, whereas the focus moved increasingly to the civil population, which was in fact the main target in forty-eight attacks (see Figure 6.7). The attacks on a nightclub in Bali in 2002 and a housing complex inhabited by Westerners in Riyadh in 2003 have been cited as examples of adaptation to increasing repression, through the targeting of Western "soft" objects (Borum and Gelles 2005: 278). In general, after 9/11, "the group's increasingly fluid and disaggregated nature has necessitated a move toward assaults that are cheap and easy to manage, and that can be executed through locally based affiliates (who may be more or less an integral part of the wider international jihadist network) as and when circumstances require" (ibid.).

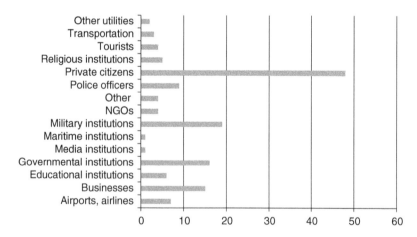

FIGURE 6.7. The number of al-Qaeda attacks (1995–2010) by target. *Source*: START. Permission to reproduce gratefully acknowledged.

The lethality of attacks was also extremely high in Iraq and Afghanistan, where suicide bombs killed not only military invaders, government officials, and Western contractors but also Muslim people. For example, in August 2003, a car bomb at the UN headquarters in Iraq resulted in 22 deaths (and more than 150 injured). Hundreds of attacks have occurred in recent years, for which a wide variety of groups – such as the 1920 Revolution Brigades, the Islamic Army in Iraq, the Mujahidin Army, al-Qaeda in Iraq, Ansar al-Sunna Army, and the Salah al-Din al-Ayubi Brigades – have claimed responsibility (Hafez 2006). Related to the war on Iraq were the bombings on 11 March 2004 of four trains in Madrid, which killed 190 people and injured more than 1,400. Responsibility for the attack was claimed by a cell professing to belong to al-Qaeda, even though it was only connected to it. Similarly, on 7 July 2005, suicide bombers detonated explosive devices on three London Underground trains and a bus, killing 56 people and injuring more than 700. The Secret Organisation Group of al-Qaeda in Europe claimed responsibility.

Other highly lethal attacks, also in reaction to the war, took place in Saudi Arabia. In May 2003, twenty-six people were killed during an armed terrorist raid of a building that housed employees of American companies in Riyadh. In November of the same year, again in Riyadh, a truck bomb killed eighteen. In May 2004, another armed raid on an American-owned petrochemical plant in Yanbu'al Bahr killed seven, and another on an oil installation ended with the killing of twenty-two of the fifty hostages. In December of the same year, four people died during an assault on the US consulate in Jeddah (Hafez 2006). Additionally, in October 2005 a bombing by Jemaah Islamiyyah killed twenty-three people in Bali, and in July 2006 a train bombing by the Pakistan-based Lashkar-e-Taiba (Army of the Righteous) killed 207 in Mumbai.

In conclusion, shifts in forms of action as well as targets can also be noted in the religious type of clandestine political violence, and they follow a trend toward increasing isolation.

ACTION MILITARIZATION: CONCLUSIONS

Clandestine organizations use a mix of violent and nonviolent forms of action, with violent actions displaying different degrees of lethality and brutality as well as varying degrees of discrimination in the choice of target. Forms of action and targets of action might also follow different logics, variously defined as the logic of propaganda versus the logic of survival (della Porta 1995); the logic of influence versus the logic of security (McCormick 2003); or the logic of control versus the logic of attrition (de la Calle and Sánchez-Cuenca 2006).

Research on civil wars has explained lethality based on the preferences of the recruits (Weinstein 2007) or the balance of forces in a certain territory (Kalyvas 2006). Research on social movements has stressed the various costs or risks and benefits of political violence. In this chapter, I have tried to look inside the clandestine groups, to understand the characteristics and evolution of their forms of action. To summarize the results reported in this chapter, the evolution of the action repertoires of the organizations studied emerged under the influence of the environmental opportunities, in terms of both the opening up and the closing down of windows of societal support as well as repressive institutional strategies. Competition among underground organizations also increased the degree of lethality of their forms of action.

To begin with, we observed some specificity in the repertoires of action of the various groups, which exhibited variation in the level of brutality but also the degree of selectivity in the choice of targets. Some forms of action were normatively excluded by some groups but not by others. Thus, the Italian left-wing radicals did not use the untargeted massacres employed by the Italian right-wing radicals. The Italian radical Right used massacres but never resorted to suicide bombing, which was used by some Islamist groups. The ETA did organize bombings but usually gave warnings to police to avoid casualties.

In addition, the targets varied greatly from one type of clandestine violence to the next. Not only did the Left target the Right and vice versa, but left-wing groups also focused attention on factory workers and other potential constituencies in mobilized social groups, whereas the extreme Right more often struck randomly. The symbols of Spanish colonization were targets hit by the ETA, whereas AQ focused on the far enemy. Additionally, the radical Left and the Basque ETA stressed a consequentialist logic to a greater degree than did the radical Right and Islamist groups.

Beyond these diversities, however, the cases showed some similarities in an evolution that I have defined as action militarization, in which the groups' actions become increasingly radical in their forms and inner-oriented in their aims. Although the analysis did not allow for a systematic cross-sector check for the impact of organizational age on forms of action, we could nevertheless observe that the organizations tended to follow a trend over time. Action often grew in brutality (especially in left-wing and ethnonationalist groups), as well as in the level of lethality. Action also became less discriminate, delving increasingly into the very groups the clandestine organizations wanted to mobilize: the Left for the BR, the Right for Italian neofascists, Basque people (in the so-called socialization of pain) for the ETA, and the Muslim population for AQ. Eventually, violence was also used more often to regulate not only ideological but also personal internal conflicts.

Moreover, although action tended initially to propagate the aims of the clandestine organizations in the broader population, with the passing of time – and rising and more focused repression – all the groups concentrated their attention on the internal war with the state. The police, the military, and the judiciary were targeted with increasing frequency by Italian left-wing and right-wing radicals alike. Repression also increased betrayals and fear thereof, as the clandestine groups started to kill within their own ranks, in actions oriented toward taking revenge for presumed collaboration with authorities or discouraging those who wanted to leave the organization.

Territorial control had mixed effects on their organizational repertoires. In Egypt, Algeria, or Iraq (and to a much lesser extent in the Basque Country), territorial control initially facilitated interaction with the population. However, it also pushed toward extracting resources from the very people the clandestine groups wanted to attract, resulting in increasing negative public reactions and growing isolation of the clandestine groups.

In all cases, the processes of action militarization were gradual, feeding on broader conflicts. In the case of the Islamist clandestine groups, we can observe the nesting of several conflicts, with complex spirals of radicalization. In general, past experiences, whether with sympathetic authoritarian regimes (e.g., in the case of the Italian radical Right) or with repressive authoritarian regimes (in the case of Basque nationalism), also influenced the degree of acceptance of violence among the reference groups and therefore the organizational use of more lethal and brutal forms of violence.

In fact, the militarization of repertoires of action interacted with the support for violence in different communities. As the case of the radical Right indicates, the forms of action (e.g., the use of massacres) as well as their targets (the general population or state institutions) changed radically, adapting to the transformation in the preferences of the bases of reference. Therefore, as aforementioned, the Italian left-wing groups showed more constraints on their militarization paths than did the other groups: the radical Right, which built on an already more elitist culture; the ETA; and, especially, AQ, which originated within some of the most polarized conflicts of the era. Although many of these limits tended to be forgotten in the face of increasing institutional repression and societal isolation, clandestine organizations did in some cases discontinue the use of forms of action that had produced strong criticism among potential sympathizers (as in the case of punishment of those who quit the ETA). Alternatively, organizations tried – as in the case of the Italian left-wing groups in the mid-1970s or the ETA in the past two decades – to sponsor less brutal forms of violence (such as proletarian expropriations in Italy or street riots in the Basque countries) that would be more palatable for radicalized social movement actors. In neither of the two cases, however, were these attempts successful.

7

Ideological Encapsulation

Allah ordered us in this religion to purify Muslim land of all non-believers, and especially the Arabian peninsula where the Ke'ba is. After WWII, the Americans became more aggressive and oppressive, especially in the Muslim world ... we believe that the biggest thieves and terrorists in the world are the Americans. The only way for us to fend off these assaults is to use similar means.... We look at ourselves and our brethren as worshippers of Allah who created us to worship him and follow his books and prophets. (John Miller's 1998 interview with Osama Bin Laden, "Why We Fight Reminder," cited in O'Boyle 2002: 40–1)

It is a fundamental principle of any democracy that the people choose their leaders, and as such, approve and are party to the actions of their elected leaders.... By electing these leaders, the American people have given their consent to the incarceration of the Palestinian people, the demolition of Palestinian homes and the slaughter of the children of Iraq. This is why the American people are not innocent. The American people are active members in all these crimes. (bin Laden's "Statement from Shaykh Usama Bin Ladin, May God Protect Him, and Al Qaeda Organization," al-Qal'ah [Internet], 14 October 2002, cited in Blanchard 2007: 4)

The near-term plan consists of targeting Crusader-Jewish interests, as everyone who attacks the Muslim Ummah must pay the price, in our country and theirs, in Iraq, Afghanistan, Palestine and Somalia, and everywhere we are able to strike their interests.... And the long-term plan is divided into two halves: The first half consists of earnest, diligent work, to change these corrupt and corruptive regimes.... As for the second half of the long-term plan, it consists of hurrying to the fields of jihad like Afghanistan, Iraq and Somalia, for jihad preparation and training. Thus, it is a must to hurry to the fields of jihad for two reasons: The first is to defeat the enemies of the Ummah and repel the Zionist Crusade, and the second is for jihadi preparation and training to prepare for the next stage of the jihad. (statement by al-Zawahiri, July 2007, cited in Blanchard 2007: 13)

As shown by these quotes referring to different periods in the evolution of AQ, the definition of the self and the enemy changed over time, because it was intertwined with transformation in the group's organizational and action repertoires. Similar transformations in narrative constructions can also be seen in other clandestine groups.

As we will see in this chapter, political violence is normatively justified by the organizations and the activists that make use of it; these justifications adapt to the shifting organizational targets and forms. In explaining the behavior of clandestine violent groups, researchers have often addressed their ideology. It has been said that radical beliefs represent the world causally, with a high level of abstraction, and develop dichotomous, black-and-white visions that present the members of the group as morally superior elites (Crenshaw 2011). An essentializing thinking is indicated by overly simplified generalizations, fear of contamination, and use of a style of language that refers to the enemy as all the same, as evil. Clandestine organizations in fact develop narratives that tend to provide a Manichean vision of the world, with good on one side and evil on the other. Hatred often grows from the belief that the enemy has a bad essence. Scholars frequently note a reciprocal essentialization in terrorism and counterterrorism (McCauley and Moskalenko 2011).The search for a "dream time" as a way to escape feelings of futility has been linked to the development of myths of self-sacrifice and purification, as well as to romantic dreams of virility, glory, and crusade (Griffin 2003). The concept of a crusade resonates with this Manichean and fighting view:

The fusion of hero with the idea of self-sacrifice perhaps finds its most telling expression in the idea of the "holy war" which occurs in several religious traditions (e.g. the crusade, the jihad) and invokes a collective ethos in which an entire army or people is involved in a communal battle with Evil. This calls upon a small elite within the community to be prepared to sacrifice itself for a cause that transcends the realm of the human in its significance and thus guarantees immortality of some sort for all those who lay down their lives in the struggle. (ibid.: 65)

Death is therefore seen as a prelude to rebirth (ibid.: 67). Especially for religious forms of violence, it has been observed that narratives of martyrdom fuel spirals of revenge, when martyrs are constructed as characterized by a purity of motifs and when ritualization spreads these images. In this sense, the power of suicide bombing is linked to mobilization by sacrifice – that is, the establishment of a new scale on which others must situate themselves (McCauley and Moskalenko 2011).

Adhesion to specific ideological systems has also been addressed in recent policy-oriented definitions of radicalization processes. Typically, the EU has defined violent radicalization as "the phenomenon of people *embracing opinions, views and ideas* which could lead to acts of terrorism" (European Commission 2005, emphasis added). Ideological radicalization (such as the adoption of certain ideas) has thus been defined as "the mental prerequisite to recruitment" (Jenkins 2007: 2). In recent times (as well as long ago), various religious narratives have been used to justify violence (Juergensmeyer 2000). Although differences in religions are hardly a genuine source of political conflict per se, some scholars suggest that their content can shape conflict behavior in the direction of either escalation or de-escalation of violence (Hasenclever and Rittberger 2000).

The very concept of an ideological explanation for violence has been, however, challenged. Many scholars have in fact been skeptical about the existence of a tendentially direct link between ideology and ensuing practices. As observed by the report to the European Commission by a group of independent experts,

> Clearly, the espousal of a particular ideology does not guarantee that a radicalisation process will ensue. Many other elements and their interplay must be present for the individual to progress through the personal and social transit that radicalisation into violence entails. In fact, previous studies of several European terrorist groups have made clear that ideology had a varying degree of relevance in that process. Moreover, individuals in need of an ideological framework very often develop an instrumentalised cut-and-paste interpretation of a given ideology in order to justify their recourse to violence. (Expert Group on Violent Radicalisation 2008: 15)

Militant organizations rarely rely on well-formulated ideology; they more often borrow fragments from various sources (Crenshaw 2011). Moreover, not all of those who use clandestine political violence have radical beliefs, and not all radicals use violence (ibid.).

With reference to religious fundamentalism and its radicalization, a debate developed on the proper role to assign to general ideological systems. It has been remarked, in fact, that religious cultures provide a toolkit of concepts, myths, and symbols from which militant organizations can selectively draw to construct strategies of action (Hafez 2004). However, the determining factor that makes a situation more or less conducive to violence is not the type of religious belief or specific stream within it but instead the concrete institutional balances that develop to impose tolerance on both the state and the religious institutions.[1] As Esposito reminded us, "Islam like every other world religion neither supports nor requires illegitimate violence" (Esposito 2011: 137). For example, even though the group Hizb al-Tahir shares some general visions with jihadist groups, it has refused violence, and only in some countries do its members refer to jihad in their call to armed struggle (Kepel 2005). Indeed, social movement studies consider ideology to be an inappropriate concept for what is actually a flexible (and often superficial) narrative that links a number of frames that define an individual's identity, opponents, and motivation to action (see Chapter 1).

Even within clandestine groups, different narratives have been said to influence the forms and degree of violence, as well as the logic used for its justification: "The ideal typical content of ideologies associated with extremist movements – some of which turn to terrorism – has displayed the greatest variation" (Smelser 2007: 87). Left-wing ideologies are said to justify violence on the basis of a consequentialist discourse – that is, violence is justified because it is effective toward the cause, as it can either directly overthrow the state or provoke the state into brutal repression,

---

[1] As, for example, Stephan's critique of Huntington's clash of civilization theory clearly indicated.

thus spreading awareness of the need for a violent uprising. This also seems to be the case for ethnic groups, which "often admit that killing and bombing are not good things per se and even that they are wrong in certain specific contexts and thus that they should be avoided in those contexts." In contrast, "fascist or hate groups may not see their acts as necessarily wrong in themselves, in the sense that they see their targets as morally irrelevant, whether they be black, Jewish, communist or an abortion doctor" (O'Boyle 2002: 27–8). Religious fundamentalists also tend to justify violence deontologically, as an instrument of the will of God (O'Boyle 2002: 27).

In my analysis, I point to the evolution of macronarratives, beliefs, values, and the like as linked (relationally) to the symbolic resources available in the environment. I suggest that organizational compartmentalization and action militarization is linked to ideological encapsulation, with an evolution toward increasing elitism and Manicheism, as well as an essentialization of violence as valuable per se.

Clandestine groups select their macronarratives from within existing narratives and tend to combine – often eclectically – several narratives or parts of narratives:

In the search for ideological formulas that would explain their situations and give meanings to and motivate their activities, interest groups have at their disposal whole cultural traditions of their own and other societies, a range of legitimizing values (e.g., freedom, equality and justice), past ideologies of all stripes, a population of historical heroes or villains; recorded or living memories of past social movements, and perceptions of the economic, political and cultural scene. (Smelser 2007: 58)

They in fact build on continuities with a dominant discourse, linking the organization to broader traditions (e.g., see Tololyan 1987, on Armenia).

Social movement studies have suggested that, when feeling excluded from the political system, social movements tend to escalate their demands, both elaborating radical frames of meaning and taking on a revolutionary rhetoric. In the 1960s and 1970s, Italian left-wing movements adopted the frame of the betrayed resistance, and German activists adopted that of the missed resistance. In the Basque countries, ethnonationalists resorted to the long-standing narrative of oppression of the ethnic minority. Nationalist frames were used to justify forms of violence and were certified by powerful actors. In the Basque Country, the pacted transition was not sufficient to legitimize the Spanish state, which was accused of following the fascist tradition established during the long-lasting Francoist regime of resorting to torture against Basque patriots. Violent organizations of the extreme Right motivate individuals to action through discourses that often refer to previous narratives on the superiority of one race (religion, gender, sexual orientation, and so on) over others (O'Boyle 2002: 28); blood and honor are some main justifications of violence (Bjørgo 2004; della Porta and Wagemann 2005). In the case of Islamic fundamentalism, religious and nonreligious authorities certified violence as belonging to a deep-rooted tradition.

This does not mean that political violence derives directly from the presence of narratives that justify violence. In fact, the choice of violent forms of action is often debated within the radical milieus, in not only instrumental but also ethical terms, and it is often linked to contingent moments. Radical narratives engender radical violent repertoires only when political opportunities trigger escalation (della Porta 1995). Moreover, as we will see in this chapter, the narratives developed by different types of clandestine groups vary in time and space, evolving through attempts to not only propagate their ideas among potential recruits but also adapt to defeats. Following turning points in their organizational structures and repertoires of action, to justify a progressively more compartmentalized structure and military action, clandestine groups tend to lose their capacity to convince outsiders and increasingly become instruments of internal consumption (Moyano 1995). This research shows that, especially in the period of their emergence, the discourse of clandestine groups tends to echo the ideological preferences of the national social movement family, tying their frames to previous traditions and helping the group adapt to changes in the environment. This explains why the narratives vary among the different groups, adapting to the potential base of recruitment as well as to state repression (and its effect on the clandestine milieu itself). In all cases, however, they seem to develop in action, accompanying shifts in strategies.

IDEOLOGICAL ENCAPSULATION IN LEFT-WING ORGANIZATIONS

In the left-wing underground, justifications for violence are sought in the traditional, revolutionary discourse of the Left, even though different groups have bridged their discourses with different left-wing ideologies.

The BR developed a Marxist-Leninist narrative, singling out the working class as the revolutionary subject and violence, initially, as a necessary defense against a forthcoming fascist coup d'état, which the BR believed would be promoted by the bourgeoisie in the attempt to regain control in the factories by means of "the growing despotism against the working class, the militarization of the State and of the class struggle, the intensification of repression as a strategic measure" (BR, *Brigate rosse*, 1971). Particularly strong was the myth of the (betrayed) resistance against the Italian fascist regime and the Nazi occupation. For the BR, the armed organization is a vanguard, and, as early as 1973, they wrote of the need for building the fighting party, as "a party of fighting cadres ... the advanced part of the working class, and therefore departed but also organically part of it" (cited in della Porta 1990: 221).

Following the narrative evolution in the social movements to which they referred, the other Italian terrorist groups defined social oppression as a question more of individual alienation than of economic exploitation: state power was seen as controlling the private lives of individuals, with the urban youth as leading revolutionary actors. Their role was conceived as "bridging the gap between the fighting organization and the proletarian fighting" (PL, "Court of Turin," 1980), or the creation of a "clandestine network" (FCC, *Statuto*, 1978).

In Germany, too, the discourse of the first organization to develop, the RAF, was more traditionally leftist than those adopted by the later groups, although it was more anti-imperialistic than most Leninist references. Given the assumed betrayal of the German working class, the RAF looked for a revolutionary subject among the young people in asylums, the inhabitants of the parts of the city centers that were about to be renovated, apprentices, and married working women. The RAF's emphasis on the Third World in the anti-imperialist fight allowed for a "pretence of success" (Neidhardt 1982: 355). According to the RAF, the Left in the metropolis had the role of building the "international brigades for the victory of the people's war in Quan Tri and Hue, Palestine, Lebanon, Angola, Mozambique, Turkey" (cited in ibid.: 357). The RAF "perceived itself less as a real instrument of liberation than as an example of self-liberation. It presented itself as a beacon of light" (ibid.).

The narratives of the B2J and the RZ were instead more influenced by the anarchist and anti-authoritarian wings of the left-libertarian movements. In particular, the RZ openly criticized the pessimism of the RAF, observing that "the history of the last years shows how little the masses here are corrupted and how fertile the ground can be" (quoted in della Porta 1995: 132). Referring to the activists of the antinuclear movement, a writer for *Revolutionärer Zorn* (Revolutionäre Zelle, *Revolutionärer Zorn*, 1978), the RZ outlet, stated, "We do not have to organize the militants ... but we have to support them and to act in combination, like the yeast in the dough." After listing the movement campaigns that involved some guerrilla action, the RZ authors rhetorically asked, "Comrades, are these movements still in your head today? Or do you think that they have no meaning? Are they not important enough for internationalism? Or do you find them insignificant because they do not pursue exactly the same politics as the RAF?" (ibid.).

In all clandestine groups, increasing repression and societal isolation brought about a clear evolution in their dominant narratives, which can be seen in the details of the story of the longest-lasting organization, the BR. The self-image of the Italian left-wing groups changed: the "armed branch of the movement" or the "armed movement" became the "army"; the "brigade" or "squad" became the "party." In an internal document from 1972, after the first wave of arrests, the BR stated the importance of organizing in a clandestine way, while still stressing the need to remain linked to mass struggles:

Clandestinity is an indispensable condition for the survival of a politico-military, offensive organization that operates within the imperialist metropolis. The condition of clandestinity does not impede the organization from developing within the forces of the autonomous area. Beyond the conditions of clandestinity, it is therefore fundamental, in our experience, a second condition in which the militant, although he belongs to the organization, still operates in the movement and must therefore appear and move in the political forms that the movement assumes in the legality. Operating in clandestinity gives an advantage over the class enemy that lives exposed in its men and installation. (Soccorso Rosso 1976: 125)

References to mass movements were frequent in this first period. A 1971 document states that

the BR action has as necessary reference the objectives proper to the mass movement. It is therefore indispensable to pay the highest attention to the fact that the BR would not work as a "military arm of the masses," do not, that is, substitute themselves to the masses in the course of their struggle. Their task is indeed to stimulate the action of the movement, trying to channel it into the strategic perspective of the people's war, develop its strength, give them security and a new trust in their own possibilities. (BR, *Organizziamo un grande processo popolare*, 1971)

Nevertheless, armed struggle already began to be considered as the most important task, "as it is around the armed struggle that the class autonomy is aggregated, not vice-versa" (ibid.). It was therefore fundamental to reach the "phase of the armed struggle."

The main reference point for the BR in their first years of existence was the workers who struggled in the big factories, as well as the "camp of the resistance." In an *autointervista* (self-interview) in 1973, the BR appealed to "the forces that since 1945, at the margin of the official guidelines of the labour movement have always expressed the continuity of the revolutionary pressure of the working class and the more recent forces that enrich with the content of '68 and '69 the patrimony of the autonomy" (*Potere operaio del lunedì*, no. 61, 16 July 1973, quoted in Manconi 1990: 70). The organization of the masses thus required "the construction, in the factory and the popular neighborhoods of the articulation of the proletarian state: an armed state that prepares itself for the war" (ibid.).

The first turning point came as early as the mid-1970s, when the BR stated the need to move toward the creation of the "fighting party," "as the real interpreter of the political and military needs of a class stratus, 'objectively' revolutionary and the articulation of the armed fight at class level, on the various fronts of the revolutionary war" (Soccorso Rosso 1976: 277). This also implied organizational changes, such as a shift from the conceptualization of itself as a self-appointed "historical nucleus" to a strategic direction. As a BR document stated in 1974,

today with the growth of the organization and of its influence, of its complexity and political and military responsibility, this historical nucleus is de facto insufficient. A redefinition and an extension of the *quadro dirigente* [the leadership] is needed. We therefore propose to our comrades the constitution of a revolutionary council that collects and represents the tensions and revolutionary energies that have matured in the fronts, the columns and the irregular forces. This council must be the highest authority of the BR.

At the same time, the enemy became increasingly identified with the state. As the BR wrote in its Strategic Resolution of 1975, "the state assumes in the economic field the function of a large bank at the service of the big international corporations.... It becomes a direct expression of the big multinational corporations; it becomes the imperialist state of the multinationals" (Soccorso Rosso 1976: 270). The BR had started their action by working against what they saw as the risk of a fascist coup d'état. In 1971, in their sixth communiqué, they recalled "Piazza Fontana, Pinelli [an anarchist arrested with the accusation of having carried out the massacre, who died in prison under dubious circumstances], comrades in prison, Della Torre [a trade unionist killed by the Mafia] and many others fires, fascist squads which are protected by the police, judges which make politics for the government, serfs of the patronat" (cited in Manconi 1990: 59). As early as 1971, the BR denounced the growth of a "revolutionary law-and-order block," based on "the growing despotism of capital over labour, the progressive militarization of the state and the class struggle, the intensification of repression as a strategic element" (reported in Soccorso Rosso 1976). In the factory, the turn to the right was expressed, according to the BR, "in the intertwining of two lines, which have always existed: the technical productive restructuring and the political persecution" (BR, *La crisi è lo strumento usato dalla reazione* ... , 1973). The BR criticized the "neo-Gaullist twist" as a repressive design that "expands and aims not so much at the liquidation of the 'democratic' state, as fascism had done, but at the most ferocious repression of the revolutionary movement" (della Porta 1990: 104), through a "new dictatorship" and a "neofascist turn" in the factories (ibid.).

With the closing down of spaces of intervention in the factories, the BR shifted its focus to the state, which it described as an expression of the imperialism of the big corporations: the "Imperialist State of Corporations" or the SIM (Stato Imperialista delle Multinazionali) (BR, *Risoluzione della direzione strategica*, 1975). The "strategic isolation of the workers' struggles" required its members "to expand the revolutionary initiative to the vital centers of the state" (BR, *Contro il neogollismo* ... , cited in della Porta 1990: 223) through a "convergent attack to the 'heart of the state'" ("Risoluzione della direzione strategica of 1975," in *Controinformazione*, 7–8 June 1976, quoted in Manconi 1990: 69).

In fact, it became the task of the armed vanguard to fight the political struggle against the state. This was explained as a consequence of the weakness of the "workers' autonomy" outside the factory:

If in the factories the workers' autonomy is strong and organized enough to keep a status of permanent insubordination and conquer a growing space for itself, outside the factories it is still weak, to the point that it is not able to oppose resistance to the forces of the counterrevolution. This is why the counterrevolutionary forces tend to move the main contradiction outside of the factory. (BR, "*Contro il neogollismo* ... ," 1974)

The response to the "strategic encircling of the revolutionary forces" was therefore the extension of the "revolutionary initiative to the vital centers of the state:

this is not a facultative choice, but a necessary one in order to keep the offensive also in the factories" (ibid.). Within this political project, the BR began to consider the Christian Democratic Party as "the organized center of the reaction." At the same time, it emphasized that the struggle must address the repression of the revolutionary forces: "Free the comrades in prisons, take revenge on the regime judges" (ibid.).

In addition to continuing to aim at adapting to the changing discourses of social movements, in the late 1970s, the BR also moved its attention to the marginal urban youth, which came to be seen as cadres for the growing "Proletarian Movement of Offensive Resistance" (BR, *Risoluzione della direzione strategica*, 1978). They therefore promoted an "open civil war." As we can read in the *Risoluzione della direzione strategica* from 1978, "the disarticulation of the enemy's forces is, therefore, the last period of the phase of armed propaganda, and it progressively introduces that of revolutionary civil war." Gradually, the BR, along with the other left-wing groups in the underground, eventually abandoned its interpretation of the armed struggle as a stimulus for a revolutionary process; the role of the organization became to witness a revolt that survived the end of class struggle.

The BR's definition of the enemy gradually grew to include social democracy. According to the BR (*Risoluzione della direzione strategica*, 1978 and 1979), the bourgeois state alternated between fascism and social democracy. Although in the past there had been attempts at authoritarianism, the neocorporatist project assigned to the Communist Party the task of controlling the working class.

At the same time, the adversary became less concrete and, instead, more immanent. Outside the organization there was only evil, and everything but the organization was evil. Although in the beginning the specific and personal responsibilities of targets were discussed at length, the enemy eventually became increasingly abstract. So, for instance, after accidentally wounding the twin brother of a chosen target, the BR proclaimed that "a twin is worth the other" (cited in della Porta 1990: 252).

The tasks of the armed organization then changed from armed peace to fully developed civil war. Thus, in 1978, the BR wrote that

> to disarticulate the forces of the enemy means to develop an attack whose main aim is still to propagate the armed struggle and its necessity, but at the same time it already starts to operate also upon the tactical principle proper of the next phase: the destruction of the enemy's forces. The disarticulation of the enemy's forces is therefore the last period of the phase of the armed propaganda and progressively introduces that of the revolutionary civil war. (BR, *Portare l'attacco* ... , 1978: 41–2)

The growing "strength and deep-rooting" of the revolutionary forces was the claimed reason for the increasing complexity of the military action, which also had to respond to the "militarization and concentration of military forces in the defence of the vital organs" of the Stato Imperialista delle Multinazionali.

Destruction of the imperialist forces thus became the only possibility to "politically and militarily disarticulate" it (ibid.: 42–3).

In a parallel evolution, the RAF declared that the German working class had become an aristocracy and was corrupted by capital to such a degree that it was no longer possible to address any political activity to the German workers. Its leaders located the "real front of the fight" between imperialism and the people in the Third World, defining the RAF as the revolutionary subject: "We are the revolutionary subject. Everyone who begins to fight and resist is part of us" (RAF, *Die Aktion des Schwarzen September in München: Zur Strategie des antiimperialistischen Kampfes*, 1972). They stated they were fighting a *verknastet* (imprisoned) and *psychiatrisiert* (one that is subjected to psychiatric controls) society, dominated by a new fascism. The B2J, which had started out with a critique of the militarism of the RAF, ended up justifying kidnapping and killing.

In general, the discourses of the clandestine organizations became less comprehensible from the outside. As former militants of clandestine groups declared:

> we did not limit ourselves, as in the first documents, to analyze, in a more or less mystifying way, the reality, looking for trends in which to locate our action. The new theorizations do not propose an analysis, but rather a new vision and a way to live the reality starting from the existential condition of the metropolitan guerrilla. They no longer talk of a civil war to promote through guerrilla action, but of the war as ... the only complete expression of the proletarian consciousness and struggles at the actual level of capital development.... The guerrilla would be the only means to break a social control, which is first of all a control upon consciousness.... It is not necessary to reach a civil war stage; you just have to see it, in action, in your everyday experience. (Detenuti del Carcere di Brescia, *Documento*, 1981: 8)

Thus their language became ever more cryptic. A BR leader talked of the *brigatese* as "that cryptic language that we had invented year after year, as another prison in which we had jailed our own brains" (Fasanella and Franceschini 2004: 202). In a previous work, I concluded my analysis of the ideological changes in the Italian and German underground organizations as follows:

> As the ideologies of the various underground groups evolved, they became less functional as propaganda and increasingly oriented towards the integration of the militants.... The terrorists' language also changed. The terminology and categories of Marxism-Leninism or other doctrines that pervaded the social movement family and which the militants had originally found useful for explaining their activities in terms accessible to the external world, gradually disappeared from terrorist documents. Instead, terrorist groups developed special, cryptic languages, consisting of terms coined within the organization. Obscure or incomprehensible to anyone outside the group, these languages possessed a highly symbolic value for the members. (della Porta 1995: 132–3)

Although the clandestine organizations began with different narratives to appeal to the specific milieus in which they tried to recruit, following repression and isolation those narratives evolved toward increasingly dichotomous and militarized visions of the external reality, and their language became progressively more cryptic.

IDEOLOGICAL ENCAPSULATION IN RIGHT-WING ORGANIZATIONS

Right-wing groups also attempted to connect their organizational frames to broader narratives, adapting them to a changing environment through an evolution from primarily instrumental to primarily existential justification for armed struggle.

Nostalgia for the fascist regime was common to various groups that cooperated and competed in the right-wing milieu in the 1960s. As the Italian judge Rosario Minna observed, "in the sixties, the extraparliamentary right looks to be characterized by unconstrained *ducismo*, with various groupings that fight with each other" (Minna 1984: 47). From fascism – and Duce-ism – the first generation of the extreme Right inherited some narrative characteristics, such as the rejection of modernity and democracy.

The extreme Right criticism of modernity was rooted in its historical development as a reaction against the illuminist principle of equality, along with widespread anti-intellectualism that saw in the French revolution the origins of a crisis of civilization (e.g., see Tarchi 1995). As an interviewee from a right-wing clandestine group observed, "teen-agers were taken by those absurd ideas, and believed that those impossible ideas could be implemented in practice.... Eventually, you think you abhor the French revolution, the bourgeoisie that produced trade, the industry" (interview with Stefano: 22, in Fiasco 1990: 169).

According to the Italian radical Right, indeed, fascism was seen as having brought about an ethical revolution that was much more radical than the traditional conservative policies, by imposing values such as authority, hierarchy, honor, loyalty, and especially the supremacy of the national community as a "secular religion" (Ignazi 1994: 46). In fact, antimodern decadence, aristocratic elitism, and the refusal to accept philosophies of reason and logic have been considered as typical topoi of the extreme Right: "The enemy is the modernization of the society, the institutionalization of rational models, a universalist egalitarianism among peoples and groups" (Ferraresi 1994: 151). Right-wing extremism often

> points to a kind of resurgence or "rebirth" in order to create a new revolutionary order, a new society, and even a new man. This goal cannot be achieved except through a general, collective, unitary effort by the whole nation. [...] The idea of resurgence from a dark period; the emphasis of the nation as a collective, organic body; the projection into a glorious and beaming future. (Ignazi 2002: 24)

The activists were said to "envision the 'good old days' in wildly unrealistic ways" (Merkl 1997: 20). In the AN, the external situation was defined as characterized by four ages of decadence, which had to be fought against through the development of the spirit of the legionary.

As in traditional fascism, the main enemy was singled out as parliamentary democracy, which the ON defined as "a most unfair and illiberal system, as it gives power to the less capable and the most sectarian, as emanation of the parties" (Ferraresi 1984: 244). As a radical Right interviewee recalled,

Avanguardia Nationale said it in all its documents, that it saw in the democratic state, in parliamentarism, a tumor, a very damaging infection to the principal values of the man: honor, tradition, loyalty. It saw a danger in this society, because it is a society of the economy, the merchants, so it saw a very great danger for the man's spirituality. (interview with D.M.: 28, in Fiasco 1990: 205)

The struggle was therefore, "against democracy and the liberal state, because I thought they were ... an historic evil" (interview with V.V.: 41, Fiasco 1990: 208). For the radical Right, the state had to be totalitarian. The immediate enemy, however, was communism; right-wing groups experienced an evolution toward an increasingly conspiratorial vision in which the red subversion looked like an immediate threat that attacked the very fundaments of the society (Ferraresi 1984: 70).

References to exclusive forms of nationalism were also frequent. In general, the "renaissance of a largely imagined purity of the nation" (Prowe 2004: 131) created a kind of nationalistic myth in the form of a populist and romanticist ultranationalism (Minkenberg 1998: 33), which also had quasi-religious aspects (Forndran 1991: 15; Minkenberg 1998: 41). An exclusive definition of the nation was combined with an aggressive attack on – or even denial of – the other, which was defined in ethnic, religious, or (in the Italian case) political terms. This Manichean us-versus-them distinction allows for the definition of the in-group in opposition to the out-groups (Taggart 2002). In fact, a main aspect of right-wing violence has been seen in the delegitimation of an "inferior community" (Sprinzak 1995). In the eyes of the Italian extreme Right, whereas the nation was considered as the basic unit, Europe was criticized by right-wing militant Franco Freda for its lack of an homogeneous European civilization: "Latin American guerrillas are nearer to our vision of the world than the Spaniards, loyal to the priests and the USA; the Vietnamese guerrillero, with his sober spirit, is more similar to us than the stupid Italian or French or western terrorist; the Palestinian terrorist is nearer to us than the English Jews or Jewish like" (cited in Ferraresi 1984: 275).

In addition, however, the clandestine organizations active in the late 1960s and early 1970s believed that their society was ready for a revolution, one that was resonant with the fascist one. Extreme Right groups clearly coupled authoritarian, antidemocratic political conceptions with the cult of a heroic elite. Common to the groups discussed in this text was an emphasis on action per se, even up to fascination with heroic death, and an identification with a minority that was refused by the mainstream society – "proscribed, rejected" (Ferraresi

1994). For example, the ON declared itself "a revolutionary movement; our action will be therefore revolutionary; the times ... are ripe for a revolutionary action" (ibid.: 64). There was also, as in the fascist ideology, an emphasis on the power of ideas and the heroism of the political soldiers who "fight for the ideas" (ibid.: 65). According to the theorization of its leader, Graziani, a revolutionary movement had to use violence because it was bound to be repressed: the "will of the revolution to survive" would provoke an awareness of one's own right to counterviolence. The ON was defined as an order of people loyal to principles and ideas. The patria was considered as the place where you fight for ideas (Ferraresi 1984).

Similarly, the Avanguardia Nazionale, which was put under trial for reconstitution of the fascist parties, stressed antiegalitarian, elitist discourses. It defined itself as "an elite of heroes. Heroic is our lifestyle, rich of those values that allow ascending to the divine, heroic is our battle against a system that violates us and humiliates us" (quoted in Ferraresi 1984: 71). Violence was exalted as a way to build this battle spirit. According to an AN leaflet: "We are for the fight, man against man. Before they leave, our people are morally prepared to break the bones even to someone who cries on his knees" (ibid.: 258). However, like the aforementioned examples, their image of the future society was, at best, vague. As another militant observed, "if I had to say, by which means Ordine Nuovo aimed to conquer power, I do not know. And not even the chiefs had thought about that. Clemente Graziani, when we sometimes had dinner together he said: 'let's hope they do not give us the power, as we would not know what to do with it'" (interview with S.C.: 62, in Fiasco 1990: 173).

The narratives spread among militants of the extreme Right organizations in the second half of the 1970s had clear linkages with the fascist past. However, they also addressed issues that were central for their left-wing opponents. As one of them recalled, "at the juvenile level this will develop in the Campo Hobbit, where they started to talk about struggle, the women's problem, ecology, alternative energy, social communication, trade union problems" (interview with P.L.C.: 27–8, in Fiasco 1990: 164). Indeed, Terza Posizione focused on the environment and unemployment, and the Movimento Rivoluzionario Popolare declared the desire to unify the radical Left and radical Right. In general, marginal groups became a potential basis of reference. As an activist declared,

I consider as potential reference for all our action all that area that the sociological Frankfurt school has aptly defined as "area of refusal." ... This brought us to consider as homogeneous areas that were very diversified at their origins. Among them, the so called Workers' Autonomy, but also all those deviant areas, from those of criminality to those of mental hospitals, from social marginalization on the territory, the so called *banlieus*. (*Corte d'Assise di Roma*, 1992, quoted in Fiasco 1990: 168)

Some activities attempted to "claim an identity of the province versus the metropolis" (interview with P.L.C.: 48–9, in Fiasco 1990: 177).

Thus right-wing organizations visited some of the main narratives of their political adversary, the Left; to that end, a former militant spoke of "the para-doxical attempt to transform the right in the left" (interview with P.A.: 53, in Fiasco 1990: 173). The use of left-wing arguments was in part instrumental: "There was a mixture of themes that we thought we could use in a tactical fashion, a different language, that could allow us to approach peoples in differ-ent areas, those who were not rooted in left-wing movements" (interview with S.C.: 46–7; in Fiasco 1990: 166). At the same time, however, it also reflected competition in the radical right-wing milieu: "The social vision that you have in the fascist environment is extremely simplified.... You do not imagine the com-plexity" (interview with S.C.: 62, in Catanzaro 1990: 205).

Moreover, the more isolated the right-wing clandestine groups became, the more often they discarded the very idea of conquering political power – that goal of control of the state that was so central for the previous generation. As a radical Right journal stated,

it is not power we aim at, not even necessarily towards the creation of a new order. These are remote possibilities. We have to give priority to a political praxis that is essentialist practice. It is in the struggle that we are interested, in the action per se, in the everyday struggle to affirm one's own nature against a society that constantly aims at suffocating us. (*Quex*, no. 3: 6–8, cited in Guerrieri 2010: 283)

As aforementioned, as right-wing militants began to target their attacks at state representatives, especially judges and policemen, as well as drug dealers, journalists, and opponents from the radical Left, their massacres were criticized and so was the "golpisme of the regime." Repression was expected to make sympathizers of the Right aware of the need for counterviolence (Ferraresi 1984: 251). In fact, the right-wing organizations saw radical forms of violence as an instrument to trigger repression against small groups of militants, which would, as a result, broaden the struggle by involving the population "that will fear us and admire us, despising at the same time the state for is incapacity to protect itself and protect the population" (*Quex*: 287, cited in ibid.: 287). In particular, the militants exhibited a growing glorification and aesthetic exaltation of death (Fiasco 1990: 160).

As in the previous examples, the definition of the enemy expanded: from the political adversary to the "near one," including the "traitors" in the radical Right. In 1980, the journal *Quex* justified the massacres of civilians by drawing a parallel with the bombings of World War II: even though the targets were not military, the aim was nevertheless to weaken the enemy (quoted in Fiasco 1990: 163).

IDEOLOGICAL ENCAPSULATION IN ETHNIC ORGANIZATIONS

ETA narratives also changed over time, adapting to the environmental context, in terms of both potential social support and repression. Consequential reasoning tended to prevail, at least at the beginning. However, the macronarrative was sensitive to changing environmental conditions. In particular, confrontation with state repression fueled an increasingly militaristic approach to politics, and various groups split on issues of tactics and strategy.

During the ETA's organizational evolution, tensions emerged on four main issues, as summarized by Robert Clark:

(a) ethnicity versus class as an organized principle for the revolution; (b) nationalism versus socialism as a guiding ideology; (c) the conduct of the struggle based solely on ethnic Basques versus integrating non-Basque immigrants in the conflict; and (d) the use of "direct action" or "activisms" (euphemisms for insurgent violence) versus non violent organizing among the masses of industrial workers. (1984: 32)

Because it was working within a complex milieu of potential supporters located in the "patriotic left," the ETA tried to keep a precarious balance between the ethnic and class identities that were both mobilized in the Basque countries. The organization developed from a small group that defined itself, in the First Assembly in 1962, as a "Basque revolutionary movement of national liberation" that was asking for a federated Europe based on ethnonationalities and that was aconfessional and antiracist into a Marxist organization (Fourth Assembly, 1965). It attempted first of all to regenerate an old nationalism, inheriting the romantic vision of the founders of the PNV – in particular the ideas of a remote past, in which all Basque people were equal, and of the Basque Country's eternal right to independence (*fueros*) (Jauregui Bereciartu 1981; Muro 2008). It thus presented itself as "the continuation of a long line of Basque patriots who gave their lives for the independence of the Basque country" (quoted in Muro 2008: 133). It has been noted that

if we look at its ideological evolution we can see that the adoption by ETA of the doctrine of classic nationalism covered several important aspects: firstly, what may be called regeneration in the sense of what is essentially Basque (that is the recovery of the Basque spirit) and in an inward-looking sense (that is the rejection of all that is Spanish); secondly, the assumption of the Basque historical myths (the Basque people as a noble, just, democratic, freedom loving people that has reached this state of degradation as a consequence of the submission to and occupation by a reactionary, feudal country – Spain); thirdly, the consideration of the immigrants as foreigners; fourthly, a visceral anti-communism in opposition to a doctrine that is radically incompatible with what is peculiarly Basque; and finally, various socio-economic concepts based on the social doctrine of the Catholic Church, through the encyclicals of Leo XIII and Pius XI. (Jauregui Bereciartu 1986: 593)

The ETA constructed important organizational myths based on the nationalist narrative, which constructed a golden age (located in the Middle Ages, or even in the sixth century), that is, a time when the Basques were proud citizens of an independent state, followed by a dark period of decadence. In addition, it referred to tradition to promote the myth of the fighting Basques. To forge a fighting character, the Basques, with their proper social and cultural characteristics, were portrayed as a people who had struggled for their independence throughout more than 150 years of war. The emphasis put on this fighting spirit emerged in particular in the commemoration of events such as the abolition of the *fueros* (in 1876) or even the Battle of Roncesvalles (which occurred more than 1,200 years ago), in which the Basque forces were said to have defeated Charlemagne. The Kingdom of Navarra was celebrated as an independent Basque state and the Carlist Wars (a nineteenth-century confrontation during which contenders fought to establish their claim to the throne in the name of the Spanish tradition) were portrayed as wars of liberation; the civil war was defined as yet another Carlist war, to defend the nine months of Basque sovereign statehood during the republic (Muro 2008).[2]

Beyond the aforementioned continuities, however, ETA ideology made innovations to previous Basque nationalism in various ways. Not only did the ETA proclaim its aconfessionalism, but the bases of the nation were also differently defined than in the first wave of Basque nationalism. Whereas the traditional nationalism was exclusive, based on the distinctive characteristics of the Basque race, the ETA stressed the use of the Basque language as the basis for being considered as Basque: "Ethnos substituted for race, the language was established as an essential factor of the Basque ethnos, and the division of the nation into a political nation and an ethnic nation was established: in short, the nation becomes an ethnos with a conscience" (Jauregui Bereciartu 1986: 594).

Traditional Basque nationalism was also updated through the adoption of a Third Worldist national liberation approach. According to the vision of the founder of Basque nationalism, Sabino Arana, the Basque Country was occupied by a foreign state. One innovation versus previous nationalism included the introduction of anticolonial frames imported from the Third World (Jauregui Bereciartu 1986; Tejerina 2001). This theory was advanced in particular by Federico Krutvig, who, in his book *Vasconia*, published in 1963, defined the Basque Country as a Spanish colony fighting for independence. From the awareness of anticolonial liberation struggles and of the European New Left came an inclusive conception based on the will to be Basque (Muro 2008).

Also new vis-à-vis the traditional Basque nationalist discourse was the bridging of nationalist and socialist discourses. In the first period of its existence, the participation of several of the ETA's activists in a wave of strikes had important consequences for its organizational ideology, introducing a hitherto absent language of class struggle. In fact, labor protest

caused some changes in ETA thinking, including the appearance of a new terminology with such concepts as bourgeoisie, working class, class war, objective conditions for

---

[2] It is not by chance that the myth of the struggling nation survived in the discourse of Herri Batasuna: "Euskal Herria was deprived of all its political right by force, and being confronted by such dispossession, our nation has defended its rights and organized its self-defence, combining different forms of struggle, for the last 150 years. This constant clash with the Spanish state has generated a movement of resistance which has had a progressive evolution in terms of political consciousness and other internal and external factors" (HB, *Urrats Berri*, 1992: 25, in Muro 2008: 128).

revolution, a stress upon the need to create a direct link between the Basque national fight for liberation and the demands of the working class, and the establishment of a distinction between middle-class nationalism and nationalism of the people. (Jauregui Bereciartu 1986: 595)

The debates on the combination of class and ethnic struggles interacted with those on intransigency versus cooperation with Madrid. Violence was initially justified as an essential part of a traditional myth of regeneration (Muro 2008). Although the justification of violence was not present in ETA documents until 1961, at the Second Assembly in 1963 a revolutionary war (supported by the population) was presented as a core strategy and was linked to the defense against repression by a consequentialist justification for violence: "In a system that did not allow ETA members to express their grievances through institutional channels, violence synthesized their regenerative programme of secession and revolutionary warfare. ETA gradually adopted a discourse which justified the use of physical force" (ibid.: 103). In the words of an ETA ideologist, beyond Franco's repression, in general "achieving political independence by a people is internationally considered something illegal (according to the concept of legality of already existing states). This is why an oppressed people has no other means of achieving national independence and sovereignty except by illegal means" (Krutwig 1973: 328, in ibid.: 104).

The role of insurrection as a spiral of repression-action-repression was thematized at the Third Assembly, in 1964. Algerian liberation, and in particular Franz Fanon, inspired a conception of action as oriented at producing indiscriminate repression, and therefore popular resentment. The planned spiral of action-repression-action was explained by the ETA in this way:

Let's suppose that an organized minority produces material and psychological damages to the organization of the state thus forcing it to answer, and violently repress the aggression. Let's suppose that the organized minority succeeds in avoiding repression and makes it so that repression hits the popular masses. Let's finally suppose that said minority succeeds in having, rather than panic, a rebellion of the population so that it helps and supports the minority against the state so that the cycle of action-repression can repeat itself, each time with greater intensity. (*Bases teoricas de la guerra revolucionaria, ponencia de la IV asemblea de Eta*: 1, cited in Ibarra 1989: 69)

The main idea is that "before every revolutionary violence there is always the repressive violence of the state.... It is not just a question of responding; we have to force them to respond to us" (*Zutik*, no. 50: 294, cited in Ibarra 1989: 70).[3] In this context, an increase in armed struggle was justified as helping the masses,

---

[3] Examples of actions intended to elicit a response include not only violent actions but also the opening of an *ikastola* or a strike (with solidarity and repression) – in fact, "any simple claim, cultural or of any other type" (Ibarra 1989: 72). The ETA also developed the myth of the *guerrigliero etarra* (*José Luis Zabilde's Insurreccion en Euskadi*, 1964).

who "need an army that can face the repressive force of the system.... In sum, a military apparatus that, facing the other oppressive military apparatus that is the fascist state, damages its action and offers the only possibility to fight with its own arms" (ibid.: 89).

The function assigned to armed struggle is thus to provoke one's opponents: "The aims are to favour, protect and support the organization of the working class and of the people, so that it can pursue and direct the revolutionary struggle of national and social liberation of our people. At the same time, the revolutionary action should be directed to divide the oppressors, aiming at radicalizing the contradictions inside the exploiting class" (Ibarra 1989: 95). Violence was thus evaluated (consequentially) for its results: "The armed struggle did effectively contribute to make the contradictions of the system and its repressive character more evident and acute, complementing the revolutionary work oriented to claims-making and raising awareness at the mass level" (*Zutik*, no. 164, May 1974: 379, cited in Ibarra 1989: 86).

The ETA has certainly been sensitive to changing political opportunities, defining its role in different ways in the different steps of democratization. Since 1974, the ETA's aim became to attack the state; that is, it chose the option of the military front, "weakening the regime, by making the internal contradictions between liberals and ultra-fascists more acute" (Ibarra 1989: 97). The ETA reacted to the political evolution in 1975 and 1976 by theorizing a double strategy, featuring a distinction between an offensive tactical option and a defensive strategic one. The assumption was that when the five conditions set out in the so-called KAS platform were accepted, there would be a shift to a struggle oriented to defending the conquered people's power.

Thus the following double strategy was presented. The first (tactical) objective was offensive: to conquer democratic freedom. Democracy was considered as a positive evolution, granting more freedom of action than did the repressive authoritarian regime. However, the ETA did not trust the democratic path to political and social change, and it remained prepared for a revolution, as conquering power was seen as the only way to grant social justice and the rights of the nation. In its self-image,

1) ETA defines itself as a independentist organization following a Basque strategy, that is, that propagates the instauration of a re-unified Basque state as the unique definitive solution to national oppression; 2) ETA defines itself as a revolutionary organization at the service of the working class, that is, that promotes the conquering of the power by the popular classes, under the direction of the working class, and the instauration of the socialist society, which implies the socialization of the means of production; 3) ETA promotes, inside the bourgeois democracy, a strategy of popular power, based upon the empowering of the autonomous organisms of the popular Basque classes, as a priority over participation in the electoral mechanism. (*Zutik*, no. 67, 1976: 5, cited in Ibarra 1989: 110)

Second, once democratic freedom was achieved, the ETA planned to enact a strategic but defensive use of armed struggle. As "the bourgeoisie does not leave with good manners its conditions of privileged class," there would be need for an "armed popular power, that defends all the patriotic popular sectors from any antidemocratic aggression" (ibid.). Armed struggle was then to be used to defend democratic achievements, as "in this new stage, we cannot foresee the type of armed struggle that will be convenient, but we can anticipate that it would need to have defensive characters, face with the attempts of an oligarchy to impose itself upon the people with the use of force, so violating the constitutional legality" (ibid.: 111). In fact, the organization announced that "with the peace, ETA will not practice the armed struggle, but will not either be inactive. To the contrary, it will expand itself, to form cadres and acquire the material means the most important possible, both in quality and quantity; in the moment in which there will be the minimal aggression against our people, ETA will be active" (*Punto y ora*, no. 29, March–April 1977, cited in Ibarra 1989: 114.)

The justification for violence, and therefore for the ETA's very existence, needed updating during and after the transition. Born in a dictatorship, the ETA found it difficult to adapt to democracy: "When the Franco years came to a close and Spain began its transition back to constitutional democracy however, ETA was ill prepared to adjust to the changed political environment" (Clark 1984: 57). In the years of Suarez, given the slow pace and contradictions of the democratic transition, the ETA motivated its continuation of armed struggle by denying that Spain had become a democracy. Moreover, later on, the changing circumstances – the rise to power of the PSOE government, signaling democratic consolidation; the presence of a monarchy; the pacted transition, which had jeopardized a true rupture; nonapproval of the Constitution by the majority of Basques; and torture and killings of patriots – were presented as proof of a continuous decline that required a strenuous struggle (Muro 2008). So, in 1978, the ETA explained, "Many people are wondering, why is ETA still active after Franco's death and with the process of democratization of the Spanish state under way? ... These people thought that we were simply anti-Francoist patriots.... ETA will try to exist and to struggle in the most appropriate way for the creation of a Basque socialist state, independent, reunified and Basque-speaking" (*Deia*, 21 March 1978, cited in Clark 1984: 106–7).

After democratization, increasing violence and the shift of targets toward nonmilitary people were still justified as functional to a negotiation that (especially since 1977) was deemed to be a substitute for the strategy of action-repression-action:

When a guy from the PSOE, PP or PNV goes to the funeral of a *txakurra* ["dog," a term used for a police officer], he has a lot of words of condemnation and crocodile tears. That's because he does not see himself in danger.... But if they go to the funeral of a party member, by the time they go back home they might start thinking that it is time to find solution or they might be the next ones. (quoted in Muro 2008: 156)

Parallel to this evolution was an evolution in the justification of violence. The ETA's conception of itself and definition of the enemy changed toward an increasingly Manichean view. Determining the right balance between violence and mass action and between military and political logic was always a contentious issue. In fact, sources within the ETA acknowledged that "if the struggle between the armed ETA groups and the Spanish state takes to the front, there is the risk that it appears as a private war of ETA, alien to the interest of the popular masses." So, at the very beginning, for example, the choice to kill Manzanas, who was considered an enemy of the Basque people, was meant to communicate that the "ETA identifies itself with the masses, that have been victims of the fierce repression personified by this criminal." The organization was also aware that "the unity between ETA and the masses, which the revolutionary praxis requires, dictates that the merely military necessity of the revolutionary struggle is subordinated to the political needs" (leaflet, Iraultza, cited in Ibarra 1989: 73).

The attempt to combine a legal social movement with armed struggle – the main object of internal divisions – remained central in the decade to come. The presence of a strong ethnonationalist movement in the Basque Country pushed the ETA to continually adapt its narrative of social and political liberation to external potential opportunities and threats. As the group declared in the 1980s,

the Basque Movement of National and Social Liberation developed in the last years as the consequence of an objective reality of national and class oppression, and of subjective conditions of revolutionary awareness and will.... KAS has a concrete political project that passes through the tactical alternative of a democratic rupture and the strategic objectives of a reunified Euskadi, *eskaldun* [Basque-speaking], independent and socialist. (cited in Ibarra 1989: 142)

However, the ETA was also aware of the difficulty of articulating workers' or social struggles and armed struggle – the belief was that "the military activity will never substitute for the mass struggle, but would need to complement and strengthen it" (quoted in Ibarra 1989: 92). In fact, rather than participating in a unitary front, the ETA developed its own organization, with divisions open to the masses (e.g., since 1974, with the founding of the LAB).

These tensions brought about an evolution toward an increasingly dominant militaristic vision. As in the previous examples, we can note in the ETA a clear progression in the importance attributed to the use of violence. Under Franco, armed struggles gradually became the main form of action for the organization. As we read in one of the ETA's documents,

we conceive of the armed struggle as a supreme form of the struggle of the working class. Our liberation as a class and as a people will be possible through the armed insurrection of the proletariat and of the rest of the people in Euskadi in a technical revolutionary articulation with the rest of the people that compose the Spanish state. (*Resoluciones de la primera parte de la VI asemblea de Eta-V, agosto de 1973*, cited in Ibarra 1989: 86)

Or, "thanks to the military activity – in reality, political – of ETA, the Basque masses, recently and violently repressed, wake up from their lethargy" (*Resolucion sobre la lucha armada*, internal document written in 1972, cited in ibid.: 86–7).

The ETA evolved consistently toward the recognition of the primacy of armed struggle:

As has always happened throughout the history of ETA, the more extreme tendencies and those more directly linked with armed activity became more dominant, with the other tendencies being expelled. ETA had arrived at the definitive consolidation of a tendency which exalted the strategy of armed conflict to the point of converting it into an end in itself rather than a means of attaining political objectives. The anti-colonialist tendency has since served as nothing more than an instrument for providing minimum ideological support to the armed conflict and the actions of the activists of the organization. (Jauregui Bereciartu 1986: 598)

In fact, after 1970, discussions within the ETA "have centred only around problems of strategy and political tactics; even so they have been of greater intensity than previous debates before this date" (ibid.: 598).

In a very pluralistic organization, violence worked as a sort of glue. ETA declared itself nonsectarian and accepted recruits with strikingly different political beliefs and even with diverse knowledge and interest in Basque cultural practices, such as speaking its difficult indigenous language. By the mid-1960s, ETA included self-described social democrats, communists, Catholic advocates of producer cooperatives, Maoists and anarchists. The pages of the movement's clandestine publications (especially the underground newsletter called "Zutik") contained debates over the types of political institutions, social arrangements and cultural reforms that should be established in a newly independent Euzkadi. Some activists yearned for a society with a large number of self-directing worker cooperatives; some wanted strong unions and a large public sector; some desired an exclusively Basque-speaking country; some advocated cultural pluralism for the region. ETArras also disagreed over the sort of territorial independence (or "separation") that they hoped their movement would secure. Some desired immediate and complete secession from Spain and gradual integration with the small Basque territory within France. Some, however, supported the continuation of a Spanish state but its transformation into a federation of self-governing regions. Some desired significant increase in provincial self-rule; some championed municipal self-rule. Some hoped that in the foreseeable future, smaller, self-governing regions would replace all existing European states. (Zirakzadeh 2002: 72–3)

A militaristic vision increasingly became the minimal common denominator; it was stressed to overcome internal divisions between different narratives present within the organization. Throughout its historical evolution, the ETA gave priority "to the political praxis and especially to armed conflict over doctrine or theory." In fact,

if we leave to one side ETA's first three years during which time the organization theoretically covered such heterogeneous fields as Basque history, legal and political institutions, the Basque language and culture, the different political currents such as "fuerismo," Carlism, Francoism, Falangism, Marxism, etc., democracy, human rights, the relationship between the church and the state, the nation or the state, it can be clearly seen that from 1962 onwards ideological questions were exclusively subject to the search for a valid revolutionary model for the fulfillment of the ultimate objectives. (Jauregui Bereciartu 1986: 599)

Therefore, the ETA also evolved from a consequentialist discourse toward an essentialist one. Eventually, the ETA narrative became characterized by

a genuine mysticism surrounding the guerrilla, a revolutionary messianism which virtually borders on delirium and a blind faith that armed violence is the only way of attaining the objectives sought after. This revolutionary illusion, very much in keeping with the feeling of anguish produced by the disappearance of the Basque people, acquired romantic, irrational and tragic connotations closely related to the idea of sacrifice and death as an indispensable condition for the achievement of the future happiness and resurgence of the Basque mother country. (ibid.: 601)

In the words of the ETA, "the work of this organization is to create in the mass the subjective conditions, in the sense of making a war and organize it in view of conquering its irreversible objectives: it plays, that is, a role of vanguard" (*Zutabe*, no. 22, December 1980, cited in Ibarra 1989: 143).

The emphasis on armed struggle was therefore a way to address organizational dilemmas and internal divisions. In conclusion, "in radical Basque nationalism, ideological contrasts, cultural differences and political pluralism could be superseded through both the boundary-building effect of violence and the powerful street presence of nationalist symbols. Thus the roster of Basque nationalists includes not only peasants, small businesspeople, cultural traditionalists and Marxists, but newer subcultures like environmentalists, punks and gays" (Conversi 1997, quoted in Kaufmann and Conversi 2007).

IDEOLOGICAL ENCAPSULATION IN RELIGIOUS ORGANIZATIONS

Research on the ideology of Islamist underground organizations shows some specificities as well as general trends, which tend to conform to those observed in other types of political violence.

The radical Egyptian groups shared with other clandestine groups the narrative of a glorious past followed by a period of decadence. In this, they were inspired by Sayyid Qutb who, after being arrested in 1954, wrote a book in prison called *Milestones*, in which he presented a pessimistic view of Muslim societies, which had allegedly abandoned religion, and he "designated a vanguard of committed Muslims for the role of eliminating this ignorance.... Before the vanguard could set out to confront and change society, they first had to separate from it and free their minds from its corrupting culture" (Malthaner 2011: 64).

As in the previous examples, violence was justified as the only way out of decadence. Claiming that Islamization of the society and the state from below, through social and political work on the grassroots level, was not possible under the authoritarian regime, the jihadist groups pursued a strategy of secretly preparing to overthrow the regime through a coup d'état. An early attempt to do so was the attack on the Military Academy in Heliopolis in 1974 by a group led by Salih Sirriya, which ended with the arrests of most of its members (Kepel 1985: 93). In 1980, several jihadist groups, among which was one group led by Ayman al-Zawahiri, forged an alliance (ibid.: 71). But, especially from the mid-1990s on, al-Zawahiri, noting the failure of attempts to bring about Islamic regimes in single countries such as his native Egypt, started to insist on the need to mobilize the global *ummah* against the common enemy (Mandaville 2007: 253).

The jihad was initially addressed not to the foreign invader but to the "corrupt regimes" in the Arab world. Later, however, the focus shifted toward Western powers. Osama bin Laden is said to have learned Sayyid Qutb's totalitarian vision of Islam from one of his teachers. A devout Palestinian disciple of Qutb's ideas, who studied in Egypt and was a member of the MB, Abdullah Azzam stressed the religious obligation to conduct a jihad against Western invaders of Muslim countries. According to Azzam, the jihad not only had to be defensive (against the invaders), but it also had to target the military forces, not the citizens. For Azzam, al-Qaeda was a vanguard, as

> every principle needs a vanguard to carry it forward and, while focusing its way into society, puts up with heavy tasks and enormous sacrifices. There is no ideology, neither earthly nor heavenly, that does not require such a vanguard that gives everything it possesses in order to achieve victory for this ideology. It carries the flag all along the sheer, endless and difficult path until it reaches its destination in the reality of life, since Allah has destined that it should make it and manifests itself. (cited in Gunaratna 2005: 3)

In the early 1990s, especially after the US intervention in Somalia, the existing Islamic networks that were supported by Saudi Arabia and Pakistan became more openly anti-Western (Roy 2004: 292). In this period, "al-Qaida's violence was rationalized primarily as the struggle to defend the entire *ummah* from non-Muslim aggression" (Hegghammer 2010: 102).

After the perceived success of the Mujahidins' guerrilla insurgency against the Soviet Union in Afghanistan, the objective became to free other Muslim lands – mainly in the Middle East, and starting from Saudi Arabia. Although at its foundation al-Qaeda concentrated on the near enemy, it was especially the invasion of Iraq, with the increased American military presence in Saudi Arabia – the "land of the two holy places," that is, Mecca and Medina – that united the groups behind the idea of a global jihad focused on the far enemy. In particular, bin Laden strongly opposed Saudi support for US intervention, especially after the Iraqi invasion of Kuwait.

The entrance of US military troops into South Arabia was an important step in the definition of a global jihad, as Saudi Arabia was considered to enjoy special status, having maintained its independence throughout the century. At the same time, Saudi Arabian authorities were considered as "scum," because they had betrayed the global Islamic community, but not as direct targets (Hegghammer 2010: 107). The fight was considered as a path to "reinstituting confidence in the hearts of Muslim masses" (quoted in ibid.: 107).

Especially after 1996, Israel and America became the main enemies: faced with an international coalition of "Jews and Crusaders," AQ started to consider the struggle for the establishment of a Muslim state as no longer a regional one. The narrative of al-Qaeda focused, then, on two sequential goals: first, the ejection of foreign forces and influences on secular and corrupt regimes from Islamic societies and, second, the creation of a society governed by sharia law, based on the Qur'an, as a way to restore the caliphate for the entire global Muslim *ummah* (Kepel and Milelli 2008). In his "Declaration of War against the Americans," published in August 1996, bin Laden stated that "the people of Islam had suffered from aggression, iniquity and injustice imposed on them by the Zionist-Crusaders alliance and their collaborators; to the extent that the Muslims became the cheapest and their wealth as loot in the hands of the enemies" (cited in Bakker and Boer 2007: 28). Their suffering testified to the fake claims of the "crusaders" to protect human rights and democracy, as "all false claims and propaganda about 'Human Rights' are hammered down and exposed by the massacres that took place against the Muslims in every part of the world" (bin Laden, *Ladenese Epistle*, 1996, cited in Greenberg 2005: 160). Similarly, he denounced the cruelty of the authoritarian and corrupt governors in the Arab countries. Given "deterioration of the economy, inflation, ever increasing debts and jails full of prisoners," the use of peaceful means toward reform was seen as having failed and being bound to fail (ibid.: 162).

This change in the definition of the enemy coincided with a change in leadership, as the Egyptian militants, led by al-Zawahiri, gained increasing power. Also influenced by Qutb and a former member of the MB, al-Zawahiri had been jailed after Sadat's assassination in 1981. Having been affected by the radicalization in Egypt, in contrast to Azzam, he supported a more offensive attitude and the enlargement of the target to include the civil population.

This evolution culminated in 1996, with the declaration of the individual duty of Muslims to resist the new crusade led by Americans, Jews, and other allies against Islam. For bin Laden, such attacks were to be seen by Western citizens as retribution for US policy, because Muslim "blood was spilled in Palestine and Iraq. The horrifying pictures of the massacre in Qana, in Lebanon, are still fresh in our memory" as well as "massacres in Tajikistan, Burma, Kashmir, Assam, the Philippines, Fatani, Ogaden, Somalia, Eritrea, Chechnya, and Bosnia-Herzegovina" and in Palestine ("Declaration of Jihad," *Al Islah* (London), 2 September 1996). Therefore, not only did the enemy become global, but that enemy was also to be hit everywhere: as bin Laden declared in his *Tactical Recommendations*, "the first duty and the best works you can undertake for God is to aim at the Americans and the Jews everywhere on earth" (cited in McPhillips 2010: 34). Although the immediate aim is still defined as liberating the Muslim land from the invaders, one must also pursue the aim of installing Islamic regimes there "to free the land unbelief and to apply the law of God there" (ibid.: 37).

The evolution of the conception of AQ from that of a vanguard to that of the base for an Islamist network was marked, in 1998, by the document "Jihad against Jews and Crusaders: World Islamic Front Statement." Signed by Osama bin Laden and Ayman al-Zawahiri, among others, the document ruled that

to kill the Americans and their allies – civilians and military – is an individual duty for every Muslim who can do it in any country in which it is possible to do it, in order to liberate the al-Aqsa Mosque and the Holy Mosque from their grip, and in order for their armies to move out of all the lands of Islam, defeated and unable to threaten any Muslim. (cited in Bakker and Boer 2007: 30)

The narrative of the global jihad for the global *ummah* culminated in 2001, with the attacks of 9/11. In October of that year, Osama bin Laden appealed to Islamists around the world: "Our concern is that our *ummah* unites ... and that this nation should establish the righteous caliphate.... The *ummah* is asked to unite itself in the face of this Crusaders' campaign, the strongest, most powerful, and most ferocious Crusaders' campaign to fall on the Islamic *ummah* since the dawn of Islamic history" (quoted in McPhillips 2010: 17). The need to resist the new crusaders is emphasized with reference to the position of the United States and its allies in Palestine, Iraq, Kashmir, Somalia, Chechnya, Sudan, the Philippines, and Lebanon, thus bridging the near and distant enemies.

Similarly to the anti-imperialist armed groups in the 1970s (such as the RAF and the Weather Underground), which aimed to bring about war at home (Varon 2004), al-Qaeda justified its violent actions as a way of making Western citizens suffer what Muslims have suffered in the past and are still suffering today. This suffering belongs to a narrative of oppression, which is part of a broadly supported discourse that resonates with an anti-imperialist rhetoric (Roy 2004).

As mentioned in the incipit of this chapter, the killing of civilians in American and other Western countries is considered as justified, as they are deemed responsible for the deeds of the governments that they elected and financed (by paying taxes). Along the same lines as bin Laden's statement cited in the incipit of this chapter, Mohammad Sidique Khan – one of the bombers in the 2005 attacks in London – proclaimed in a video: "Your democratically elected governments continuously perpetrate atrocities against my people all over the world. And your support of them makes you directly responsible, just as I am directly responsible for protecting and avenging my Muslim brothers and sisters" (quoted in Egerton 2011: 9–10). Another of the bombers confirmed: "To the non-Muslims of Britain: you might wonder what you have done to deserve this. You are those who have voted in your governments, who in turn have, and still to this day, continue to oppress our mothers, children, brothers and sisters, from the East to the West, in Palestine, Afghanistan, Iraq and Chechnya" (ibid.: 10).

The Madrid bombers also declared their action to be justified as "a response to your collaboration with Bush and his allies. This is a response to the crimes you have caused in the world" (ibid.: 86).

In parallel to the described transformation, the fundamentalist groups developed an increasingly dichotomous view of good against evil. The struggle was increasingly framed as one between the Americans and their allies, on the one hand, and the Islamic nation, on the other:

The whole world is watching this war and the two adversaries; the Islamic nation, on the one hand, and the United States and its allies on the other. It is either victory and glory or misery and humiliation. The nation today has a very rare opportunity to come out of the subservience and enslavement to the West and to smash the chains with which the Crusaders have fettered it. (OSC Report – FEA20041227000762, 27 December 2004, cited in Blanchard 2007: 7)

Democracy was considered as a Western trick. So, in a December 2004 statement, bin Laden "urged Muslims to oppose the creation of democratic governments in Iraq, Afghanistan, and the Palestinian territories; to resist non-Islamic reform movements in other Islamic societies; and to overturn existing regimes deemed insufficiently-Islamic by Al Qaeda such as the Saudi monarchy" (Blanchard 2007: 12). At the same time, Western democracies were criticized for failing to live up to the expectations they themselves spread, as stressed in the criticism of US detention centers at Guantanamo Bay, Cuba, and Abu Ghraib, Iraq. In Iraq, where al-Qaeda Iraq (AQI) was responsible, between 2003 and 2006, for 30 percent of the 514 suicide attacks (Hafez 2007: 89), the organization explained its use of suicide bombers by describing the need to fight "the strongest and most advanced army in modern times ... arrogance, tyranny and all its big numbers and advanced weapons" (ibid.: 121). The killing of civilians was further justified because the occupied forces "are hiding behind ordinary Muslims in markets and other public places so that it is nearly impossible for the jihadists to fight the enemy without inflicting unintentional harm on other Muslims" (ibid.: 133). In fact, it was during this period, and through the influence of al-Zawahiri and the resistance in Iraq, that the radical Takfiri doctrine justifying the elimination of Muslim leaders who do not implement sharia is said to have penetrated AQ (Borum and Gelles 2005: 477).

The evolution of the situation in Iraq also weakened the appeal to a global Islamic *ummah*, as a result of increasing tensions between Shia and Sunni Muslims. Whereas bin Laden encouraged the creation of a broad front, Abu Musab al-Zarqawi targeted the Shiites in the name of the Sunni-led insurgency. In fact, "the Islamic Army of Iraq, the Mujahidin Army and the Ansar al Sunna Sharia Council announced the formation of a Jihad and Reform Front in May 2007 as a means of disassociating themselves from what they reportedly considered to be Al Qaeda's indiscriminate targeting of Iraqi civilians" (Blanchard 2007: 10). The narrative justifications for killing Muslims in Iraq are linked to accusations against Muslims who collaborate with the enemy: this includes not only Shiites in general but also those Sunnis who voted and thus accepted Western domination.

The change in targets coevolved with another rhetorical turn. Whereas debates on religious fundamentalism have stressed the search for martyrdom, especially in the beginning of the movements, Islamists justified violence instrumentally. The call to jihad was initially framed in a consequentialist form. For example, in Egypt, the assassination of Sadat was considered as politically correct, given his repression of the Islamist movement. As Malthaner observed, after Sadat's assassination,

While they appreciated martyrdom, the attackers also rationalized the assassination in political terms, as an act to punish Sadat for the harm he had done to Muslims and for the preceding crackdown against the Islamist movement. And they hoped to "give a lesson" to his successor and that their deed would be a step towards an Islamic order: *"... they thought that now the sharia would come."* Leaders of al-Jihad discussed the strategy and political implications of the attack in terms of a political rationale, weighing the risks against possible benefits and both, leaders and perpetrators, considered the attack part of the struggle for an Islamic order in Egypt: *"They did not start from the wish that they want to go to heaven, and therefore they killed him. No! They wanted to change the system, of course!"* (2011: 74, emphasis in the original)

Al-Qaeda defined jihad as an individual imperative, as "without shedding blood ... no degradation can be removed" ("Declaration of War against the Americans Occupying the Land of the Two Holy Places," 1996). Guerrilla war was thus justified as the weapon of the poor, as well as by its own instrumental value as the only language understood by the West (Kepel and Milelli 2008: 64). Similarly, in the "Declaration of War," we read: "It must be obvious to you that, due to the imbalance of power between our armed forces and the enemy forces, a suitable means of fighting must be adopted i.e. using fast moving light forces that work under complete secrecy" (quoted in ibid.: 432). In the "Letter to the American People," AQ declared,

You attacked us in Palestine.... You attacked us in Somalia.... You have starved the Muslims in Iraq.... These tragedies and calamities are only a few examples of your oppression and aggression against us.... The American people are the ones who pay the taxes which fund the planes that bomb us in Afghanistan, the tanks that strike and destroy our homes in Palestine, the armies that occupy our lands in the Arabian Gulf, and the fleets which ensure the blockade of Iraq.... It is saddening to tell you that you are the worst civilization witnessed in the history of mankind." (quoted in Greenberg 2005: 218–23 passim)

The past success of violence was also mentioned as a way to justify one's own choices. According to a declaration in "In the Shadow of the Lances," published in 2003, "with guerrilla warfare the Americans were defeated in Vietnam and the Soviets were defeated in Afghanistan. This is the method that expelled the direct Crusader colonialism from most of the Muslim lands, with Algeria as the most well known. We still see how this method stopped Jewish immigration to

Palestine, and caused reverse immigration of Jews from Palestine" (quoted in Greenberg 2005: 432). The economic crisis in the United States, the fall of the stock market, and the weakening of the dollar, all linked to the ensuing break-down of trust, are considered by the organization as positive effects of the massacres of 9/11.

Violence was therefore justified as the only way out, when other channels fail to affect the situation. As in the previous examples, violence was increasingly justified as essentially (and not just instrumentally) good. The videos of suicide bombers in Iraq often cite a narration of humiliation – with recurrent reference to the "wounds of Palestine" and the "wounds of Chechnya, Afghanistan, Kashmir, Indonesia, Philippines, and Iraq" (Hafez 2007: 101). The killing of US civilians is then justified with reference to the inequality of resources, as well as the arrogance of the enemy. According to a video,

[the holy warriors] faced the strongest and most advanced army in modern times. They faced its arrogance, tyranny and all its big numbers and advanced weapons.... When the holy warriors noticed this huge disparity in numbers and armaments between them and the enemy, they looked for alternatives to amend this deficiency and fill this gap so that the light and the fire of jihad will not be extinguished. Brigades of martyrs, whose sole goals are to please God and rush to the heavens, have set out and attacked the sanctuaries of infidelity and broke its armies. They inflicted severe punishment and injuries on the enemy and hurt its reputation! (quoted in ibid.)

With the increasing repression and isolation of fundamentalist organizations, however, there was a growing focus on the inherent and absolute value of martyrdom. In addition to its usefulness, violence was therefore justified by the (greater) evil of the other: the justificatory form employed within bin Laden's speeches, articles, and interviews became overwhelmingly deontological. The heroic martyrs of the Afghan war became a main example of fighters; for instance, they were praised by Azzam as

a small group: they are the ones who carry convictions for this religion. An even smaller group from this group are the ones who flee from this worldly life in order to act upon these convictions. And an even smaller group from this elite group, are the ones who sacrifice their souls and their blood in order to bring victory to these convictions and ambitions. So they are the cream of the cream of the cream. (Sheykh Abdullah Azzam, *Martyrs: The Building Blocks of Nations*: 3)

The cult of martyrs increased after 9/11. Altruism, piety, and commitment were stressed as the most honorable motivations of the perpetrators of the attacks. According to an al-Qaeda statement,

The heroes who offered themselves for the destruction of the strongholds of the enemy did not offer themselves in order to gain earthly possessions, or temporary fame, or a transitory desire. Rather, they offered their souls as a sacrifice for the religion of Allah almighty, defending Muslims whom American hands had mistreated by various types of torture and forms of domination and subjugation in every place [...] the only motive these young men had was to defend the religion of Allah, their dignity, and their honor. It was not done as a service to humanity or as an attempt to side with Eastern ideologies opposed to the West. Rather, it was a service to Islam in defense of its people, a pure act of their will, done submissively, not grudgingly. (cited in Wiktorowicz 2004: 173)

So bin Laden proudly declared, "Your problem will be how to convince your troops to fight, while our problem will be how to restrain our youth to wait for their turn in fighting and in operation" (bin Laden, *Ladenese Epistle*, 1996, cited in Greenberg 2005: 184).

Similarly, in Algeria, the GIA grew increasingly exclusive. In 1994, it issued a communiqué declaring itself the only legitimate jihadist organization; the next year, it gave FIS leaders one month to repent and join the GIA, threatening bloodshed if they did not obey (Hafez 2004: 48). In parallel, the image of the outside world became increasingly polarized: the jihad was to aim at apostasy, infidels, and tyranny. Anyone who sustained the regime (even tacitly) was considered as an apostate and an infidel, and the struggle had to target apostate and infidel rules all around the world (ibid.: 48–50).

IDEOLOGICAL ENCAPSULATION: CONCLUSIONS

Specific ideologies have often been given responsibility for radicalization processes. Marxist-Leninist, fascist, ethnonationalist, and religious constructions have indeed been twisted and fitted within specific narratives used by clandestine organizations to justify violence. In the case of the Italian Left, the Marxist-Leninist discourse of the beginning of the movement evolved toward the singling out of a "social proletariat" that had to take over the revolutionary role of the working class of the big factories. Anti-imperialism and anarchist frames were present in the German Left. The Italian right-wingers built on some main fascist topoi, such as the preference for totalitarianism over democracy, an exclusive nationalism, and an emphasis on the heroism of the few. The ETA made innovations to traditional Basque nationalism, through a more inclusive definition of ethnic identity as well as a fusion of socialist and Third Worldist frames. As for Islamic fundamentalism, its narrative has especially developed within some Salafist conceptions.

We have stressed, however, that, rather than focusing on preexisting ideologies, explanations for radicalization should look at the manipulation of such ideologies by violent groups, which connect old frames to new ones, legitimizing radical means. As Egerton rightly notes, "the problem is, to cite Islam, or any religion, suggests that it is an entity that can be definitively identified and understood" (2011: 20). Not only do the texts (religious or otherwise) have to be interpreted, but they have also existed for a long time without being used to justify violent action. Even though al-Qaeda uses religious language, "the very fact that the code involved is ancient while the behavior we want to explain is recent suggests the inadequacy of causal theories that overemphasize the religious element" (Holmes 2005: 135). What is more, the very same ideologies have been used to justify more moderate positions; thus their reinterpretation as justification for killing and/or self-immolation implies radical breaks with the ideological tradition.

Transformation of the definition of the self (more and more as an heroic elite), of the other (more and more as "evil"), and of violence (more and more as intrinsically good) is brought about not by the original big narrative but rather by a mechanism of adaptation of frames to changing contextual challenges through what I have defined as ideological encapsulation.

Even though it is not the direct consequence of one ideology or another, violence is discursively justified: "Clandestine high-risk activities, especially violence, require a great deal of justification and motivation" (Hafez 2004: 42). A common mechanism of radicalization is, we noted, the narrative construction of a violent past by the entrepreneurs of violence.

The development of narratives that justify violence should be seen as an evolution during which symbols and discourses are adapted to other organizational changes. They develop, that is, in action, from various sets of relations with other actors. As in the previous chapters, we noted differences among the various groups, which could be explained in part by the resonance of some narratives – and justifications for some forms of violence – in their base of reference, as well as by the roots of such narratives in the history of the broader movements to which the clandestine organizations refer. Most radical forms of violence were difficult to justify in the radical Left, which in fact experienced a very gradual evolution, with a strong emphasis on the need to defend the labor movement from the repressive reaction of capital and the state. Right-wing groups exhibited a revisitation of the fascist myths, including strong representation of a heroic elite of soldiers. The ETA, although it made radical innovations to the previous ethnonationalist definition of self and enemy, stressed an image of a long-suffering nation that had to fight with guns against the occupying forces. The Islamic jihad was justified as a defense against new crusaders who wanted to impose their own religion.

However, we also noticed some similarities in the chosen narratives and rhetoric of clandestine groups. In trying to root their claims within broader cultural traditions, they presented visions of a glorious past (the resistance for the Left, fascism for the Right, the *fueros* for the ETA, and the caliphate for the Islamists) followed by decadence, against which a heroic vanguard had to react. Members of these groups justified violence as a response to the tyranny of those in government and declared that the time was ripe for rebellion. According to a Manichean view, the evil of the enemy justified violence as the only way out in a situation in which democracy and freedom were denied first of all by the state. Primacy of action went together with fascination with military action.

The narratives of the clandestine groups discussed in this text also shared a similar evolutionary trend: an ideological encapsulation. After using defensive and consequentialist fames in the beginning, the underground organizations tended to promote progressively more moralist and mystic discourses, which were sometimes mixed with religious messianism. Moreover, in all cases the groups' discourses tended to increasingly become instruments for internal consumption, rejecting more factual arguments and becoming more abstract and obscure. Increasing ambiguity also helped them avoid confronting external reality (Edelman 1971: 65–83). In time, faced with repression and isolation, they tended to use less consequentialist frames, and to stress (especially in the case of the extreme Right, but also on the left) a more essentialist view of violence as satisfying per se. At the same time, the image of the enemy tended to become more immanent, and to include a growing number of noncombatant categories: ultimately, all those who did not fight with the organization. Their vision of themselves also tended more toward the exaltation of a vanguard, an elite of heroes or even martyrs who were suffering and dying for the survival of an acquiescent community. In addition, the narratives converged in stressing action over ideology, and especially the role of the military over politics. Finally, although it initially addressed the masses, the language of these organizations tended to become increasingly cryptic and self-referential. In sum, the ideology adapted to organizational choices in terms of action strategies, rather than vice versa.

8

Militant Enclosure

KEEPING COMMITMENT IN THE UNDERGROUND:
AN INTRODUCTION

The former militants of the (US-supported) Mujahidin resistance in Afghanistan, as well as the numerous armed conflicts in the Middle East, Chechnya, or former Yugoslavia, which contributed to the spreading of a military vision, are particularly relevant to the development of the global network of Islamic fundamentalism. The Gulf War in 1990–1 was a turning point because it "brought U.S. troops to the Arabian peninsula. The movement that became the global Salafi jihad might have faded away but for the continuous presence of these troops" (Sageman 2004: 40). After September 11, the war in Afghanistan pushed Salafi jihadists to look for protection in other countries such as Pakistan and Iran, where they disseminated military skills and ideological motivations (Hafez 2007: 166ff.). Similarly, resistance to the American invasion of Iraq involved a heterogeneous coalition, made up not only of Salafi jihadists but also of members of Hussein's Ba'ath Party; again former soldiers and secret service officers played an important role (ibid.: 37).

During the resistance against the Soviet occupation, thousands of Arab Afghans – many from upper- and middle-class families of the Arabic Gulf region – joined the various groups of Mujahidin with headquarters in Peshawar, Pakistan. This helped in developing the notion of universal Muslim brotherhood. Notwithstanding some tensions with the Afghanis, participation on the battlefield fostered feelings of solidarity. One explained: "For me, this battle was really a big boost that motivated me to carry on. It gave us the assurance that no one is hit except if that was destined for him by Allah" (Kohlmann 2004: 13). As Abu Abdel Aziz declared: "The Jihad in Afghanistan was a great experience. Whoever was involved in this experience had the great desire that Allah would keep them engaged in the Jihad" (ibid.: 17). Osama bin Laden himself stated: "What

I lived in two years there, I could have not lived in a hundred years elsewhere" (cited in Esposito 2002: 9).

After the withdrawal of Soviet troops in 1989 and the internal divisions in the resistance, many fighters "largely returned to domestic economies with limited opportunities and to highly charged political environments where the 'Afghans,' as they were called, were immediately deemed politically suspect and suspicious, due to their travel" (Singerman 2004: 158). The perceived sense of injustice enhanced their solidarity. "The 'criminalization of politics' produced activists and sympathizers who create their own political world, with different rules and norms, where the transcendental ends justifies the means" (ibid.: 164). The war in Afghanistan was a formative moment for several of those who joined AQ, as "the strength of Al Qaeda is that it is made up of veterans of the Afghan wars, who know each other and have developed an esprit de corps in the Afghan 'trenches' (sangar) or training camps" (Roy 2004: 294).

Some of those who had fought in Afghanistan then moved to Bosnia, where, in 1992, Bosnian Muslims had rebelled against a self-proclaimed independent state for fear of Serbian violence. The Arab-Afghanis arrived, after having been expelled from Afghanistan, as displaced men who

faced a serious problem, because return to their countries of origin meant certain arrest, torture, and likely death. At the time, a Saudi spokesman for the Arab-Afghans in Jeddah explained in the media, "the Algerians cannot go to Algeria, the Syrians cannot go Syria, or the Iraqis to Iraq. Some will opt to go to Bosnia, the others will have to go into Afghanistan permanently." (Kohlmann 2004: 16)

So "hundreds of Arab mujahideen veterans caught in the civil turmoil in Afghanistan and with nowhere to go found asylum in Bosnia" (ibid.: 11). There, they met European Muslims; as a result of this encounter books were shared and translated into several languages, and European Muslims passed on their knowledge of computers. Of the about 700 foreign fighters in Bosnia, many came from Egypt, with experiences in the student movement and/ or in al-Jamaa; others came from Saudi Arabia, and still others from Europe, where they or their families had migrated and where they had sometimes been active in Muslim charities. For many of them, the war in Bosnia was to be read not as one of Serbians against Muslims but as one of Christianity against Islam (ibid.: 25).

Whereas for many Islamists commitment was kept alive in war situations, as I discuss in this chapter, in the other types of clandestine violence individual participation in violent activities also created affective and cognitive resources that linked individuals to their organizations. It is these processes, rather than individual characteristics, that explain why militants keep their loyalty to organizations, even when the organizations tend – as shown in the previous three chapters – to transform their structures, strategies, and discourses. In this, I hope to show the utility of moving from a search for the psychological or sociobiographic characteristics of "terrorists" to an analysis of relational, constructed, and emergent processes.

Research on political violence has looked at various characteristics of the individuals who participate in underground organizations. Early studies pointed at psychopathologies such as dependent or identity-seeking personalities. According to some, "madness, especially paranoia, plays a role in contemporary terrorism" (Laqueur 2001: 80). However, there is no indication that militants of clandestine organizations suffer from psychological disorders or are brainwashed pawns (Silke 2003: 94). As Horgan synthesized, "there remains little to support the argument that terrorists can or should be necessarily regarded as psychopaths owing to the nature of offences committed" (2003: 6). In fact, although research based on secondary sources tended to perpetuate this myth, studies based on interviews with militants stated their normality (Silke 2003). Narcissism (impulses mainly oriented to the ego) has never been proved to be more widespread than average among members of clandestine political organizations, and no distinct personality traits have been found among members of the Front de Libération du Quebec (Morf 1970), the RAF (Rasch 1979), or the Red Brigades (Jamieson 1989). In the Basque Country, it was noted that "the overwhelming majority of *etarras* are well within the range of functioning and sane human beings ... [and] have relations with loved ones that are normal to the point of being mundane" (Clark 1984: 141).

These psychopathological explanations, which had faded in the analyses of ethnonationalist and ideological forms of violence, re-emerged after 9/11. Recent contributions on radicalization again suggested – but did not prove – the presence, among people prone to radicalization, of personality traits such as hypersensitivity to humiliation, depression, or anxiety (for a review, see Victoroff 2005; for a critique, see Sageman 2004). However, research on jihadist activists concluded, once again, that they are neither mad, nor immature, nor ignorant (Sageman 2008). Psychopathologies are not absent, of course, but they are no more widespread than in the overall population, and, when they appear, they are more frequent among militants at the fringe than among the most active (Silke 2003). This is due in part to a selective recruitment, as usually candidates who show signs of psychopathology are not admitted into the clandestine groups, because they are suspected to pose a potential risk for the security and reputation of those groups (Ricolfi 2005: 107).

Dismissing psychopathologies, another approach has focused on grievances. "'Terrorists' are said to come from the most deprived groups of the population, to be frustrated by their positions, and to look for revenge. Sentiments of injustice, exclusion, and humiliation have always been powerful forces in politics and prime movers for change" (Expert Group on Violent Radicalisation 2008: 9). If poverty per se is not a direct cause of violence (Gurr 2006: 88), it is said to bring about frustration and, then, despair, which is then reflected in various forms of violence. In contrast to absolute deprivation, which refers to poverty in general, relative deprivation implies a comparison of one's own position with that of significant reference groups (Gurr 1970).[1]

Explanations of several forms of political violence have in fact mentioned economic and social inequalities as causes of grievances, and therefore as predictors of commitment to clandestine violence. For instance, civil wars are said to be started by individuals who want to redress past injustice (e.g., Gurr 2000). The potential basis for radical Islam, in particular, has been linked to feelings of humiliation, guilt, and shame that derive from perceptions of discrimination (see, among others, Juergensmeyer 2000; Richardson 2006a, 2006b). According to the report of the EU Independent Experts, "from the late 19th century to the present day, all such diverse significant political radicalisation waves that resulted in terrorist action share a number of structural features. First, they all thrive in an enabling environment which is essentially characterized by a widely shared sense of injustice, whether real or perceived, among concerned segments of the population or whole societies." Profiling population groups that possess some specific characteristics as "at risk of radicalization" thus became a widespread counterterrorist tactic.

Research on civil war, which has bloomed in the past few decades, has debated the links between structural causes and individual behavior. As for many other phenomena, an indicator of economic precondition – the GNP per capita – has emerged as the only robust and consistent correlation with violence across various studies, using different techniques (Sambanis 2005). As the report of the Task Force of the APSA noted, "this finding is significant for it ties the emergence of political violence to the economic characteristics of the state. The finding is perplexing however because it is not exactly clear what is measured" (APSA 2007).

As for the psychopathology approaches, empirical evidence was at best inconsistent. In fact, the grievance theory seems to work only partially. The assumption of an automatic frustration-aggression chain does not take into account that individuals react differently to frustration (Horgan 2003). In addition, empirical findings are inconsistent, as different indicators are used and results vary for different underground organizations or subtypes of civil wars (see, respectively, Gurr 2000; Sambanis 2000).

Moving from grievances to greed, recent approaches to political violence instead stressed instrumentality. According to this vision violence is an instrument of greedy individuals used to obtain material benefits. Large-N studies have located "greed" at the onset of civil wars, suggesting that civil wars are explained

[1] Relative deprivation is produced by the "actors' perception of discrepancy between their value expectations and the goods and their value capabilities" (Gurr 1970: 24). One's condition is evaluated in comparison with reference groups, with one's own position in the past (or, even, one's expectations for the future), or with an "abstract ideal, or the standards articulated by a leader as well as a 'reference group'" (ibid.: 25).

by the combination of incentives and opportunities in specific political and economic situations (e.g., Collier and Hoeffler 2004; Collier and Sambanis 2002; Elbadawi and Sambanis 2002). This approach assumes that motivations for rebellion develop when challengers believe that they "can profit from seizing or seceding from the state (i.e., after dividing expected loot or tax revenue among organizational members) and/or when they believe that they are able to sustain themselves through the period of confrontation with political authorities by effectively paying for dissident activity (i.e., hiring rebels away from supporting the state and/or remaining neutral)" (APSA 2007). The opportunities for rebellion, especially as concerns the expected cost of the rebellion (arms and labor) and the perceived incapacity of the government to mount a counter-insurgency, have thus been addressed. In this view, "terrorists are simply the members of their societies who are the most optimistic about the usefulness of violence for achieving goals that many, and often most, support" (Pape 2005: 8). Suicide missions in Israel, Lebanon, and occupied territories related to the Arab-Israeli conflict are seen as having the potential to boost the morale of members and populations, enhancing the prestige of the organization versus competitors (Ricolfi 2005: 99). Selective incentives for members, such as prestige for their family and community or compensation in cash, have also been mentioned.

Empirical research has challenged the view that militants of clandestine groups are members of the most aggrieved social strata. In an early study, Russel and Miller (1983) pointed out that terrorists tend to be single males between twenty-one and twenty-four, with university experiences (especially in the humanities), and they tend to come from the middle or upper classes. Further research found, however, that not only does the expected social background change by group and by country but radical groups are often joined by activists with different socioeconomic and cultural backgrounds (e.g., Sageman 2004). In particular, for some periods, left-wing terrorists had been assumed to be frustrated members of the middle classes, whereas right-wing ones were said to come from alienated lower strata. But this was not true in all countries: for example, in Germany, left-wing radicals tended to come from the middle class and right-wing ones from the lower class, but the opposite was true in Italy (Merkl 1986; Wasmund 1986; Weinberg and Eubank 1988). In fact, Italian right-wing radicals are not recruited from the poor and less educated:

If anything, the distribution appears skewed towards the upper end of the occupational spectrum. A little over a quarter of the neo-Fascists were drawn from the free professions (law, medicine, journalism, architecture) or came from high status backgrounds in business. In view of the group's age distribution, the fact that 21 per cent of the neo-Fascists were students does not come as a surprise. More interesting is the substantial proportion from small business backgrounds (shopkeepers, salesmen, etc.), which combined with industrialists or business managers produces a figure of nearly a quarter drawn from the Italian business community. Finally, a substantial number of police and military personnel, that is individuals trained in the use of violence, were attracted to the neo-Fascist formations. (Weinberg and Eubank 1988: 539–40)[2]

Furthermore, some groups tend to represent a broader range of social classes than others. Looking at 48 cases analyzed in depth, supplemented by data on 171 Basque political prisoners as of October 1974 plus 228 arrested for ETA crimes in 1979 and 1980, Clark (1984) observed that 31 percent had a working-class background, 30 percent were from the lower middle class, 12 percent were from the middle class, 2.5 percent were from the upper class, 18.5 percent were students and priests, and 6 percent were unemployed (none of these percentages were very different from those of the general population).[3]

As for the Islamists' class backgrounds, it was initially suggested that they tended to be uneducated, unemployed, socially isolated single men (see Pape 2005). Later on, however, research consistently contested those statements, noting higher-than-average social background as well as education, with no sign of a particularly strong religious commitment. Among suicide bombers, 76 percent of those with Arabic origins were from middle- or working-class backgrounds, and only 17 percent were from lower classes (ibid.). Of a total of 134 Islamists imprisoned for violent crime, 18 were upper class, 56 middle class, and 28 lower class. As for their occupations, 57 were professionals, 44 semi-skilled workers, and 33 unskilled workers at the moment of joining. Their education was mainly secular (114 out of 137), and they were fairly well educated (88 percent had finished college). The sociographic characteristics of Pakistani terrorists were similar: aged between eighteen and thirty, 30 percent were upper class, 50 percent were middle or lower middle class, and 20 percent came from poor strata (Hassan 2006). Looking at suicide bombers related to the Israeli-Palestinian conflict, Ricolfi (2005) observed that most of the bombers were single young men about twenty-five years old (the average age was 22.7, and 55 percent were between 19 and 23) whose social background, income, and education was higher than those in the general reference population. In addition, their level of education tended to be high: a very low 10 percent of Arabic suicide attackers had only a primary education; 54 percent (much more than in the total population in their societies) had a secondary education. There is also evidence that Hezbollah did not mainly recruit among the impoverished groups, and the same is true for Hamas (Maleckova 2005). Similarly, Fatah's members often come from well-off families, even if the status of refugee is dominant in their identity (Post 2005).

---

[2] Professionally, neofascists were overrepresented among small business owners (who made up 12 percent of neofascists versus 3 percent of left-wingers), career military officers and police officers (16 percent versus 1 percent), free professionals (15 percent versus 5 percent), and businesspeople and aristocrats (11 percent versus 1 percent) (Weinberg and Eubank 1987: 17–18).

[3] The few women were mainly recruited through men and were assigned principally to logistical tasks.

Family conditions vary as well. Among the ETA members analyzed by Clark (1984), 90 percent were male, most were young, and only 10 percent were married, whereas as many as three-quarters of the jihad activists are married (Pape 2005; Sageman 2008). Data on suicide bombers in Israel and Lebanon indicate that they were mostly single males aged about twenty-one who did not come from poor origins and who had a mixed secular-religious background (Merari 2005: 76–7). Of the 381 suicide bombers studied, 15 percent were women, but there were many internal differences: whereas there are no women in al-Qaeda, women represent 60 percent of Chechens and 71 percent of the Partîya Karkerén Kurdîstan (PKK), the Kurdish Workers' Party (see Pape 2005).

Regional backgrounds also vary. Of 172 Mujahidins studied, 31 came from Saudi Arabia and 24 from Egypt (Sageman 2004). As many as 70 percent joined the group in a country different from that of their birth, and 14 percent were second-generation migrants. The stories of radical Islamists in Europe tell of mainly integrated people who are often radicalized on distant events (in Palestine, Afghanistan, Iraq, and Chechnya). Clearly, a background of migration is dominant. Of 250 militant Salafis in the West, only 23 percent were not migrants themselves, and some of them came from migrant families (Egerton 2011: 101, 117).

In addition, family socialization and values vary. Of the Mujahidins studied by Sageman (2004), about 33 percent were raised in jihad-affiliated families and one-third in very religious ones, but the majority did not pray regularly in a mosque, and less than half attended *madrassas* or mosque schools (Hassan 2006). Thus "members of the global Salafi jihad were generally middle-class, educated young men from caring and religious families, who grew up with strong positive values of religion, spirituality and concern for their communities" (Sageman 2004: 96). However, about half (55 out of 117) of the suicide bombers studied by Pape (2005) were not religiously devoted in their youth.

The ideas that militants belong to specific sociographic types have been used in counterterrorist strategies to profile categories of people as potential terrorists. According to the application of old frustration-aggression theories, (first or second generation) migrants in particular are considered to be more rebellious the more that the group to which they belong is economically, politically, or culturally marginalized, and/or the less they are integrated into the host society. The assumption is therefore that "as the number of causal factors and intensity of exposure increases, so does the potential for radicalization. Somebody who belongs to a marginalized social group, who experiences discrimination, who feels humiliated as well as depressed, and who has recently lost a family member, is more likely to turn to radicalism than somebody who is only relatively deprived" (Transnational Terrorism, Security and the Rule of Law 2008a; see also 2008b, 2008c).

This risk is considered higher for the individuals who are more deeply engaged in identity seeking – for instance, for second-generation migrant youth that do not feel integrated either into their parents' society or with their native peers.[4] This is assumed to imply that "the need to belong might drive young, identity seeking individuals into the arms of potential recruits and radical groups" (Transnational Terrorism, Security and the Rule of Law 2008a). Islamism, particularly militant Salafism, is said to offer a community to people who are isolated and uprooted. In fact, several accounts "see militant salafism as attractive because it offers profoundly dissatisfied individuals the possibility to enjoy redemption from a life of social transgressions, petty crime, educational underachievement, aimless drifting and/or a traumatic experience" (Egerton 2011: 35).

Nevertheless, the lives of the European jihadists do not often conform to this stereotype. In reality, only some are "social misfits, criminally insane or professional losers. Most fit a nearly opposite profile: typically they are psychologically normal, have better than average economic prospects for their communities, and are deeply integrated into social networks" (Pape 2005: 23). Moreover, "many militants have also travelled widely, meeting, training and fighting together with other likeminded individuals" (ibid.: 119). And they do not go back to fight in their countries of origin, instead joining an imaginary *ummah*: "Theirs is a process of projectively imagining, built on the types of experiences mediated by movement and media that negate the need for geographically present experiences" (ibid.: 125). The biographies of many radical Muslims tell of well-integrated people who are radicalized by distant events.

Profiling the type of individuals who, on the basis of some biographic characteristics, are considered as potential terrorists is therefore not only useless – as militants of underground organizations vary on a number of characteristics – but also risky, as broad groups tend to be stigmatized as at risk of radicalization. This could lead to what criminologists define as secondary deviation: to be singled out as a potential danger to security or public order and treated as such might result in actual risks, as the individuals in question feel unjustly treated or are actually discriminated against. In a vicious circle, social groups that are considered as vulnerable to radical propaganda, because they are excluded and/or discriminated against, tend to be treated as potential terrorists, thus strengthening those feelings of exclusion and discrimination. As John Horgan has concluded,

the notion of a terrorist profile might be administratively attractive (even seductive, since it enables us to simplify an enormously complicated process into misleading and simplistic answers), but is unhelpful. Many of the personal traits or characteristics we attempt to identify as belonging to a terrorist are neither specific to the terrorist nor serve to distinguish one type of terrorism from another. (2005b: 48)

---

[4] Scholars have also found that an individual's propensity to identify with an aggrieved group may be one explanation for adhesion to underground organizations. The more individuals identify with a certain (alienated and marginalized) community, the more sensitive they are to the perceived unjust treatment of that community, and the more they are considered to be in danger of joining radical organizations when they perceive their reference group to be threatened.

In general, the focus on individual motivation has been criticized as a fundamental attribution error in social psychology (McCauley and Moskalenko 2011). Explanations that point to anger due to perceived injustice and aggression as motivations for radicalization do not consider that they refer to relatively short-term emotions that often last no more than a few minutes. Rather than psychopathology, McCauley and Moskalenko (2011) talked of a psychology of altruism and of identification, based on strong reciprocity and involving the attribution of a grievance as affecting a group.[5] This often happens along a slippery slope that "can move individuals to opinions and actions that are not anticipated at the first step" (ibid.: 57).

In what follows, I look at commitment to the underground as a continuation of the slippery slope that had brought activists to join the organization (Moskalenko 2011). Whereas in Chapter 4 I looked at recruitment by locating those who joined in broad activist networks, in this chapter I look at how commitment is maintained through the *militant enclosure* brought about by *affective focusing* – the progressive reduction of affective ties to small groups of comrades in the underground – as well as *cognitive closure*, which is linked to the parallel closing of channels of communication. Following suggestions in social movement studies, affective and cognitive processes are considered not as opposite mechanisms but rather as elements that interact with each other, as affective links are the bases of a certain construction of external reality that, in turn, fuels the focusing of positive emotion on an increasingly smaller community. In contrast to previous chapters, I consider these mechanisms in parallel for all four types of clandestine political violence.[6]

AFFECTIVE FOCUSING

Affective focusing is particularly intense in high-risk political activism. Throughout the networks of friends-comrades, friendship reinforces the relevance of political commitment, while political commitment strengthens some friendship ties, and the groups of political friends become closed units. Affective focusing on militant networks tended to increase as political activities grew more dangerous and as the group grew closer. The more radical the group, the more isolated from the movement culture it became, and the more the members' shared risks intensified an us-versus-them mentality.

Relations within the radicalized social movement milieu were intense. This is evidenced by the frequent use of the word "family," among others. As the Italian left-wing militants consistently recalled, "the comrades became my

---

[5] A positive identification, which tends to extend beyond those who are near, implies feeling good when the other feels good; vice versa, a negative emotion implies feeling good when the other feels bad. Identification is in fact steadier than emotions.

[6] The availability of sources on the different types of clandestine violence is particularly unequal for the mechanisms addressed in this chapter.

family" (Life History no. 5: 35); "Potere operaio was a small family" (Life History no. 16: 71); and "it is the sense of a family … we questioned the [biological] family, but looked for new certainty inside the group, which replaced what we criticized" (Life History no. 26: 16). One recalls that, with his girlfriend, "we started to associate with members of the factory collectives, to have common experiences, to go on holidays together" (Life History no. 12: 27).

In fact, participation in small legal political groups strengthened friendship ties. Political activists became best friends, while ties to nonpolitical friends weakened. Strong friendship ties with political friends tended to increase the importance of political involvement. In the words of Italian left-wing activists, "the most beloved friends" were those with whom he "handed out leaflets in front of the factories" (Life History no. 9: 32). "My friends were the comrades with whom I lived everything together" (Life History no. 28: 11), as when "friendship coincided with politics," it was "difficult to distinguish between friends and comrades, because politics occupied every moment of the daily life" (Life History no. 9: 30). German militants also stressed the "practice of solidarity, love, and reciprocal respect without competition and its anxieties" (Klein 1980: 144). Or, as an Italian activist put it, "the sense of the group was always very strong. It determined personal choice and actual behaviour towards society" (Life History no. 26: 5).

In addition, neofascists stressed "true friendship" using similar tones. An interviewee explained, for instance, that the sacrifices in terms of sociability were

compensated by a projection in a future dimension. In that moment, you do not feel a limitation, as you feel perfectly integrated in the group dimension. You consider relationship only possible with those who belong to it…. Relations with the others look banal. 'The others,' relatives, friends, are part of that category that do not really know who the person that is next to them is. They are totally de-valued. The small group, totally uprooted, develops relations only inside it. (interview with S.C.: 121, in Fiasco 1990: 179)

The small militant circle was made up of people "who really knew each other, deeply, who could live some values among themselves" (interview with V.P.: 68, in Fiasco 1990: 209).

As aforementioned, affective ties ultimately were vital to recruitment into clandestine organizations. Both the Italian and German left-wing militants testified that "loyalty" to friends compelled them to descend into the underground and that underground organizations were founded by cliques of friends-comrades. As an Italian left-wing militant declared, "as far as I am concerned it was up to emotional feelings, of passions for the people I shared my life with" (Life History no. 21: 28). Another confirmed, "A choice [made] in cold blood, such as 'now I will become a terrorist,' [did] not exist. It was *a step-by-step evolution, which passed through a kind of human relation*" (Life History no. 17: 31, emphasis added). Another remembered joining a clandestine organization as a way of "*devoting all of myself to this kind of involvement [that was] spiritually related … to my friend who had to go underground*, to this idea of our feverish lives … I had these images of the necessity, the rightness, the beauty of that kind of sacrifice" (Life History no. 18: 58–9, emphasis added).

In Germany as well, friendship ties were relevant to recruitment into underground organizations. Bommi Baumann explained: "I had joined the group because of Georg. I knew that he had decided to do certain things and I did not want to abandon him" (Baumann 1976: 185). Other German militants of the second generation became involved in the underground groups to express solidarity with friends – often comrades of the same commune – imprisoned during the first wave of arrests (Jäger 1981). Friendship keeps alive solidarity with the group, as it is inspired by "human solidarity" (Boock 1981: 113) and "loyalty towards people one knew from before and would not want to be defined by as a pig" (Speitel 1980c: 34; also Speitel 1980b).

For various reasons, affective ties became even more important in the underground than in legal organizations. Life in the underground is in fact often defined as characterized by "absolute human relations," "relations free from any material interest," "affective generosity," and "solidarity even in the small things." Friends in prison were, according to Italian left-wing activists, "an important element for continuing" (Life History no. 26: 68) as

> at the end of the game, either we are all outside or we are all inside [prison], because if some of us are out and some of us are in, I don't give up my friends…. This means that if my friends had drowned because of a belief that I shared with them, I would decide to drown; … *if they are there and I can't help them, I prefer to be with them.* (Life History no. 18: 58–9, emphasis added)

The PL was praised by its members as "the richest group in terms of human relations" (ibid.: 315). Similarly, a German left-wing militant declared, "You cannot cut the thick bonds the group has covered you with in the course of time. *One's whole existence was first of all in the group … the entire existence of all of us was first of all the group*" (Speitel 1980c: 34, emphasis added). The RAF was defined as a "family" that experimented with the "right forms of life for the future," pushed for "nonrepressive and open relations," and fought against "the imperialism that is inside ourselves" (cited in Böllinger 1981: 202), giving its members feelings of "warmth," "care," and "love" (Proll 1978).

Affective ties also provided important constraints against leaving the underground: the group relationship was in fact so intense, and individual identities were so embedded in the group, that the members believed it was impossible to live outside it. As an Italian left-wing militant noted, quitting the terrorist organization was considered as "betrayal of those who were in prison": "We continued to fight above all for our comrades who were in prison…. Choices [that could lead to] death, [to] individual death, were based on this very thing: solidarity with those who were in prison…. A solidarity that … had become reciprocal blackmail between those who were inside and those who were outside" (Life History no. 26: 69). Similarly, for those in prison: "It was a situation in which we were all for declaring the dissolution of the organization, the end of the experience of the armed struggle. But at that point the comrades outside wrote a very radical document in favour of 'continuing' the struggle, and rejecting their demands seemed to us immoral. So, all that happened many years later" (Life History no. 29: 48). A German imprisoned militant stated in a letter to his wife, "Now I understand things very clearly. We are inside for you, you are outside for us.... The struggle goes on. You fight outside, we fight inside" (cited in della Porta 1995: 179). In fact, exiting the underground was often a collective choice (della Porta 2008b). To the Italian radical Right militants as well, the clandestine community of the comrades provided them "with a human contact, that you do not find in the metropolis" (interview with M.M.: 151, in Fiasco 1990: 178).

Identification with a peer group of friends-comrades is extremely important for the mobilization of jihadist activists as well. As Olivier Roy writes in relation to European militants, "the group effect concerns 'the small group': the process of radicalisation takes place in the framework of a small group of friends (they knew each other before, used to have a common place of meeting: campus, local neighbourhood, networks of petty delinquency, etc.)" (2008: 16–17). Among these individuals, to justify the transition to violence, there was a feeling that everyone was joining.

Friendship and family ties strengthened Islamic networks. In Egypt,

> participation promoted feelings of belonging and an intimacy with peers based on shared commitment and routine. Graduates usually referred to others in their Islamic circles as *ikhawa*, brothers and sisters, and the close bonds were evident in warm embraces among members of the same sex, exchanges of personal secrets and confidences, and the readiness to assist one another in times of need. Beyond this, participation offered recruits a sense of psychic empowerment, transforming poorly skilled graduates with bleak economic perspectives into fellow-soldiers in the noble task of Islamic reform. (Rosefsky Wickham 2004: 234)

Militancy in the jihad thus appears to be a collective choice rather than an act of isolated individuals. In reference to the international jihadist activists' mobilization, Marc Sageman points out that "social bonds are the critical element in this process and precede ideological commitment" (2004: 135). In many cases it is a friend, relative, disciple, or acquaintance in the group who recruits the future militant (Bakker 2006: 56). The creation of cliques is "the social mechanism that puts pressure on prospective participants to join, defines a certain social reality for the ever more intimate friends, and facilitates the development of a shared collective social identity and strong emotional feelings for the in-group" (Sageman 2004: 154). The Hamburg cell responsible for the 9/11 terrorist attack (Taarnby 2005) as well as the network behind the Madrid bombings in March 2004 (Alonso 2007) are just two examples of how small circles of friends and relatives collectively join the jihad, keeping strong internal loyalties. In addition, the destiny of an Iraqi suicide bomber, Abud Ubeida, was linked to that of a friend who had participated in a suicide mission in 2005: "We made a pact that we would meet in heaven," he declared (quoted in Hafez 2007: 45).

The search for an alternative family inside a clandestine organization has been said to be particularly relevant for the second generation of European jihadists, who often break with their own families when joining, and for whom the peer group of affiliates becomes a second family. After experiences of prolonged periods of intense social integration that progressively distance members from previous relationships, being part of these groups strengthens individual beliefs, group identity, and the group's sense of brotherhood. This is well explained in the words of Shiv Malik:

People underestimate – or rather, people haven't come to appreciate – what it means to find a family again. Many of the jihadists broke with their parents, and they were cut off from everything. They don't want to leave the group because they don't want to be pariahs again. So the fatherly element is very important…. They hang out with each other, and they all become brothers. (interviewed July 2007; quoted in Neumann and Rogers 2007: 43–4)

For many activists, affective closure increased with the intensity of their activism, which culminated in a life in the underground in which everything was devoted to the organization. Activists talked of high-speed and intense experiences: "Crazy activism," "political activity … on a 24-hours-a-day basis," and "leafleting every day" (Life History no. 3: 45), that took "90% of my time" (Life History no. 12: 21) and left "no time to sleep anymore" (Life History no. 5). They participated "in nothing … but political activities" and went "to every single mass demonstration that took place" (Life History no. 18: 31); it was "a terrible activism, we never slept" (Life History no. 5: 85). Participation was characterized by a willingness "to give all ourselves…. The feeling of being influential, of being many, of having power" (Life History no. 13: 22–3), "living totally in function of the political group" (Life History no. 16: 190). The speed of the political experiences is also often recalled. Thus a militant recollects, "I started head foremost. In a sequence of progressive steps, in a few months I became a militant, in an atmosphere that I found absolutely fantastic" (Life History no. 12: 20). Another recalled "the very high speed at which I precipitated" (Life History no. 18: 16). A German activist similarly described how his "whole life changed in practically a period of only three or four months" (Speitel 1980a: 38). The political experience was totalizing and determined every aspect of their lives, as "everything was political in that period" (Jünschke 1988: 153).

For Italian right-wing radical groups, life was also described as composed of "Xeroxing, gluing posters, providing support for fellow activists in the university, engaging in physical fights, attending public speeches, working as an armed corps for the protection [of the MSI leaders]" (quoted in Pisetta 1990: 193). For a radical Right activist, "political violence is part of the political fight, is a means like [any] other" (ibid.: 205). According to another, "I did not feel any psychological shock, I thought it was normal" (in ibid.: 207).

Participants often cited a pleasure in action that sustained these high levels of militarism. The Italian left-wing activists spoke of "parties that followed some actions," a "large component of conviviality," and a "merry brotherhood." Life was described as pleasurable and exciting – "[We] had such a good time" (Life History no. 28: 11). Whereas "summer holidays were felt as ... very boring" (Life History no. 13: 33), activism developed in "a magic atmosphere. In the Statale you met girls, had your first love affairs. But, especially, you met the students of the other schools, and so widened your horizons" (Life History no. 12: 13). And "there were Saturday-night parties, when the parents were away; the first encounters with members of the other sex, the first joints; and the participants were all members of the movement, there was a public and a private life. Officially, one of the activities of the marshal body was to take information on drug dealers" (Life History no. 12: 14). Activism was defined as "very romantic ... very beautiful" (Life History no. 5: 103). Another militant recalls that "there was harmony inside, because we had always known each other" (Life History no. 21: 313). The German activists concurred in describing – at least during some periods – an atmosphere that was "always nice, and even fantastic when we planned some political actions, and when an action succeeded, then there was a real party at home" (Baumann 1976: 51).

High emotionality brought about a vicious circle of progressive affective isolation, as "to be politically active means to organize your everyday life in such a way, that makes it difficult to have relations with those who are not" (Life History no. 9: 250); there was "an escalation of feeling responsible and wanting to be committed" (Life History no. 27: 459). Socialization to violence happened in action. As a neofascist wrote, "why should I hide it? I took part in all punitive expeditions between 1949 and 1955 ... I learned to build bombs with war remnants ... ; I used iron fists, stakes, iron bars in the fights with the police and the social-communists" (quoted in Del Boca and Giovana 1965: 190).

This intense commitment often left a perception that they had no choice. As a left-wing militant stated, "to be frank, they [violent activities] did not produce any moral embarrassment. For instance, to set the deposit of the Magneti Marelli to fire, 40 billion of damages, but they were 40 billion of damages for the capitalists. We told the night-watchman not to worry; we gave him the time to save his car, because he was a worker" (Life History no. 12: 28). Another confirmed, "There was not a moment in which I chose, I said 'now.' It was an evolution towards a model of life, which became extremely exacting for the rest of my life. From that moment on, I did only [activism], full time" (Life History no. 29: 15). Direct experience with violence fed the "internalization of the idea that violence was legitimate for any communist militant" (Life History no. 13: 28).

Revenge for the fate of arrested or killed friends was a widespread legitimizing frame. On the left, the death of fellow comrades especially produced a strong emotional motivation to "resist": "The deaths of Matteo and Barbara [two young militants shot dead by the police] had such a strong emotional impact.... [We then entered] *a spiral of revenge and retaliation*, because when you are in that game, you have to play it" (Life History no. 17: 35, emphasis added). The violence perpetrated by opponents then justified the use of violence against others. Similarly, another radical left-wing activist recalled "the days when militants were killed during the marches, the years in which comrades were killed in fascist assaults" (Life History no. 13: 29). There was a militant antifascism, experienced as "the practice to get information on them, to go and get them … the polarization friend-foe, also linked to the contention on the very same space" (Life History no. 29: 20–1).

Moreover, on the right, a situation of everyday physical fights was meant to justify violence as the most effective form of revenge. A radical Right activist remembered "a situation in which to kill a fascist is not a crime, a situation in which the fascists cannot enter the schools, a situation in which the fascists cannot walk in the streets, a situation in which the fascists cannot live" (quoted in Pisetta 1990: 200). This brought about, in the words of a radical Right activist, "a logic of hatred, a logic of death" (ibid.: 196). Valerio Fioravanti recalled,

It was a very dangerous period for those who were active in politics, both on the left and on the right, there was a lot of violence. I remembered that when we went out at night my mother would wait for us until two or three in the morning and she used to tell us of the many explosions she had heard…. Where I lived we had five attacks, at Francesca's house there were two, they put a bomb on the windowsill in the mezzanine room where she slept, aged eighteen and with two younger brothers. (cited in Cento Bull 2007: 147)

Furthermore, he stated, "we invented a war to fight" (ibid.). In the words of another activist,

when during the trials they ask, "ah, but why did that guy have a gun?," I wanted to laugh. I wanted to laugh and tell them, But, shit, instead of saying why did he carry a gun?, why don't you ask yourselves how was it possible that a 15, 16, 17 year old kid had to get a gun in his hands, a knife in his hands, an hammer in his hand, an iron bar? (Ferraresi 1995: 343)

Stronger solidarity within radical groups coincided with intensified hatred for opponents, who, in the militants' eyes, became progressively dehumanized.

The push for revenge and the passivity of the MSI toward the victims of political adversaries and police were often quoted as reasons for leaving the party and taking up weapons. In the narrative of Stefano Delle Chiaie, the intense emotionality of those years comes to the fore: "There were deaths from both sides, each of us bore witness to the death on our side, to our own death. They were years of deep passion, deep faith … we thought only of achieving a beautiful death, this was our decadent romanticism" (Cento Bull 2007: 134). In these cases, the use of violence was then internalized as the only solution – as one of them said: "It is as if you asked a Red Indian or a Palestinian, or a Spanish fighter for the Republic or the national side whether it is right or wrong to fight – but he does not have a choice, either he deserts or he fights, no third solution … there were five attacks per day" (quoted in ibid.: 143).

As for radical Islamists, especially the younger, less-educated, and often unemployed later joiners of al-Qaeda in Saudi Arabia were motivated by revenge for the torture they had suffered themselves or seen inflicted on their friends by the Saudi Arabian regime. In addition, assisting friends who had been in jail was a way to get involved in the underground organization through a sort of secondary deviation (Hegghammer 2010: 197).

As the Islamist militants indicate, revenge is also felt to be a duty vis-à-vis distant causes with which militants identify. A common step in Islamic commitment is collective identification with a suffering community. As a militant stated, "our basic motive in Jihad was to defend Muslim lands. We were greatly affected by the tragedies we were witnessing and the events we were seeing: children crying, women widowed and the high number of incidents of rape" (cited in Hegghammer 2010: 61). Arab fighters in the distant war knew little about the lands to which they went to fight on the side of their coreligionists. As a Saudi who went to Bosnia said, "we were unable to understand where Bosnia was, was it in America, or in the southern hemisphere or in Asia? We had no idea where it was. When we found out that it is a part of the ex-Yugoslavia in Eastern Europe, we still had no idea of how many Muslims there were when Islam reached there" (ibid.: 48). Nevertheless, they went and saw "things that were more awful than anything we had expected," and then "we realized we were a nation, with a distinguished place among the nations" (ibid.: 61).

Despite some tensions with the Bosnians, who sometimes accused them of committing atrocities as well as instrumentalizing the situation for their own propaganda interests, the "Afghans" were respected for their military skills (Hegghammer 2010). For them, Bosnia was another step in the global jihad. In Bosnia, militants recalled their direct experiences with the atrocities of the war. One of them recalled, "I saw people who died"; "I saw a ten year old child who burned alive in Bosnia. It was a genocide" (Kohlmann 2004: 115). "I had Kalashnikov in my hands. I was blessed twice. I saw corpses" (ibid.: 119). In this international environment, claims quickly became global: "It is the global situation that pushed me towards theology" (ibid.: 101).

In these situations, as in Afghanistan, violence was perceived as the only way to achieve independence: "Writing, demonstrating, it is useless. It is demagogic. It is like doing nothing" (Kohlmann 2004: 104). In the words of another fighter, "Afghanistan was our school ... instead of fighting the Communist Russians outside Kabul, we are now fighting the Communist Chetniks Serbs outside Travnik. Even their tanks are the same. In Afghanistan, we hit the T-55s in the mountains. Here, we hit T-55s in the mountains" (ibid.: 92).

Development of an identity as a freedom fighter pushed militants to expand their armed struggle from one circumstance to the next:

We are coming here to die, not to leave. That is why we shall win.... The West says we are terrorists. But look what it did in Africa, in Algeria; nobody tells them that they are fascists and terrorists.... To become a member of the Mujahidin is something very serious, a sacrifice. You cannot return to your home once the government there knows that you are. Instead, we must follow the eternal path of jihad. (Kohlmann 2004: 118).

The armed diaspora continued after the Dayton agreements, which imposed the expulsion of foreign fighters: "We the Arab felt that our staying in Bosnia was not desirable anymore … we were compelled to flee to Kosovo" (ibid.: 200).

Direct experiences with war played an important role in the life history of one of the Arab Afghans and the founder of AQ, Osama bin Laden. Osama's father was born poor in Yemen and then moved to Saudi Arabia, where he became the Saudi royal family's preferred construction contractor and the richest man in the country. A passionate supporter of the Palestinian cause (Esposito 2002: 4), he died in 1967 in a plane crash, after divorcing Osama's mother. Osama attended an elite school, which was secular and Western-oriented. He was an average, quiet, and shy student. At fourteen, he joined an Islamic study group that discussed the ideas of the Muslim Brotherhood against Western domination, and he became concerned with the situation in the Arab countries. He then attended university and worked for his father's construction company. He liked horses and riding fast but was also described as quiet and courteous and seldom hungry. As Esposito recalled, "bin Laden was educated at a time when Islamic movements and religious extremist or jihad movements were on the rise in the broader Muslim world and within Saudi Arabia" (ibid.: 8).

After the 1979 Soviet invasion of Afghanistan, he took up Abdullah Azzam's call for jihad, channeling support to fight the Russians. When the Soviets withdrew from Afghanistan, he built an organization with Azzam to keep the Arabs (and Afghans) united but then returned to his company, frustrated by civil war in Afghanistan. He demanded a Saudi boycott of US products as a response to US support for settlement of Jewish Russians in Israel. He saw US forces in Saudi Arabia as infidels in the sacred land of Mecca and Medina, and this, as aforementioned, moved him toward the definition of a far enemy. Placed under house arrest, he was relieved of his passport, but his brother negotiated an extension for him to go to Afghanistan, where the Soviet troops had just withdrawn and civil war had begun.

In 1992, after the failure of his attempt to negotiate among the various fronts into which the resistance had split, bin Laden moved with about 200 AQ members to Sudan, where the National Islamic Front had taken power in 1989. There, he secured governmental contracts to build roads in exchange for land as well as the opportunity to provide jobs to his fellow comrades in exile. In 1994, the Saudi government revoked his citizenship and froze his property. Expelled from Sudan, he returned with tens of thousands of dollars to Afghanistan, where he was welcomed by the Taliban. It was there, in 1996, that he issued his "Declaration of War against the Americans Occupying the Land of the Two Holy Places" and launched a jihad against Americans in the Arabic Peninsula and the apostate Saudi government. He called at first for a boycott of American products but not for attacks against civilians, at least until 1998, when he built a world Islamic front with the Egyptian Islamic Jihad and

Islamic Group and the Bangladeshi Jihad Movement. He later organized bomb-ings of the US embassies in Kenya and Tanzania in 1998 (leading to 213 deaths in Nairobi) on the anniversary of the stationing of US troops in Saudi Arabia (7 August). In retaliation, on August 25, the US army dropped seventy-five missiles on AQ camps in Afghanistan, making Osama bin Laden a cult figure.

In conclusion, although he was not personally aggrieved in the beginning, bin Laden underwent a slippery slope, which included increasing direct experiences with violence as well as repression. Throughout this long trajectory, he came to be progressively identified with a community, and continued to increase his commitment to that community (McCauley and Moskalenko 2011).

COGNITIVE CLOSURE

Affective focusing has an effect in terms of a cognitive closure, insofar as all the information the militant activists receive is filtered through the group; this process defines their external reality by providing shared master frames of meaning. Unconventional beliefs are said to be more resilient, as high entrance costs also make exit more difficult, and the dependence on the group reduces availability to changing beliefs, thus enforcing uniformity (Crenshaw 2011). Political violence develops in contexts in which some cultural resources are available; it produces heated debates on violence itself; and it aims at producing emotional effects more than material damages. Because people need to "talk themselves into violence" (Apter 1997: 2), they need to find narratives with which their discourse can resonate. These are activated under historical circum-stances that make them relevant and salient (Crenshaw 2011). At the same time, "perceptions of the political and social environment are filtered through beliefs and attitudes that reflect experiences and memories" (ibid.: 1). Although radical beliefs are not themselves the cause of violence, the narrative frames through which the militants interpret their daily encounters with political violence tend to dramatize the significance of these events. This process happens slowly through a progressive closure of the channels of communication to the outside.

First of all, in the examples studied here, militants stressed action more than thinking. In Germany, "the Rote-Armee-Fraktion states the supremacy of the praxis" (Meinhof, cited in Neidhardt 1982: 355). So, as an Italian militant observed, an encounter with violence "has nothing to do with ideology" (Life History no. 9: 259). And an Italian left-wing activist added, "More than ideology as a culture of violence, the fundamental moments are some social situations you live, where I became familiar not only with the practice of violence, but also with the emotions that inspire them, the frontal opposition, hate" (Life History no. 29: 19). In fact, it was not so much the ideology that was relevant: "Most of the comrades of my group called themselves 'anarchic-trade unionists,'" wrote a German activist, "and so did I, although I did not really understand what it meant" (Klein 1980: 149). A notion of physical pleasure linked to the use of violence was all the more explicit in the extreme Right. In the words of a right-wing radical, "to be honest at the time I liked physical fights" (interview with M.B.: 194, in Pisetta 1990: 194).

For AQ members as well, commitment is not maintained because of ideology. As Olivier Roy observed, "they do not articulate before or after having been caught a political or an ideological stance ... we should certainly not discard entirely the fact that some quarters in Al Qaeda are writing or thinking in terms of ideology, but this does not seem to be the main motivation for joining" (2008: 13). The AQ narrative is in fact very simplistic, featuring an appeal to individual heroism in the name of a suffering *ummah*, which also redeems personal humiliation. As Egerton notes, "whilst militant Salafism has produced some profound thinkers articulating sophisticated arguments, the journey to become a militant Salafist in the West is rarely the result of prolonged self-reflection, theological investigation and political analysis. Many of those who have gone on to militancy demonstrate a very poor grasp of the Qur'an and hadiths" (2011: 97). Emotionality is emphasized over intellectualism.

The activists' image of external reality was in fact the product of small-group dynamics: in the social construction of reality, the frames of meaning provided by cliques of friends-comrades interacted with the reality of everyday experience. The militants' immersion in violence distorted their perceptions of external reality: direct experiences of violence produced, in fact, frames of meaning that justified violence. Internalizing the use of violence as ethically "right" increased an individual's propensity to take part in violent confrontations.

Activists increasingly portrayed the enemy as undifferentiated, abstract, and monolithic, and themselves as good, acting for people who could not defend themselves. They also found moral justification by comparing their actions with the (more inhuman) behavior of the enemy. "By declaring your enemies 'non-people,' and by denying their human qualities, you block moral scruples right from the beginning" (Wasmund 1986: 215). In Germany, victims were dehumanized as "pigs": "We say that policemen are pigs, that guy in uniform is a pig; he is not a human being. And we behave towards him accordingly" (Meinhof, cited in Jünschke 1988: 164). The RAF promoted a "fight of the human beings against the pigs in order to free humankind" (cited in Jäger 1981: 162). A Basque activist also declared, "I never saw a person, in blood and flesh. I was attacking a symbol ... I think I was not able to see the person. And if you do not see it, you do not suffer" (ibid.:99).

Another image that emerged was a more bureaucratic one: the targets were defined as "tools of the system." According to a German left-wing militant, "even today, I do not feel any general scruple concerning a murder, because I cannot see some creatures – such as, for instance, Richard Nixon – as human beings" (cited in Böllinger 1981: 203). The Italian militants also talked of the victims of their attacks as "wheels of the capitalist machine":

We lived the problem of death inside a grand ideology ... I am one of those who killed the policeman Lo Russo in Turin.... Well, I lived that murder inside this logic of the "role," because he was a warden, and he was well known as a "torturer," as we used to say, so I had all the justifications of the ideology.... For me it was a routine job. And this is the very aberration of the ideology: on the one side, there are your friends, and on the other, there are your enemies, and *the enemies are a category, they are functions, they are symbols. They are not human beings.* And so they have to be dealt with as absolute enemies so that you have a relation of absolute abstraction with death. (Life History no. 26: 62–3, emphasis added)

The process of selecting a victim also followed this "neutral" logic. An Italian left-wing militant reconstructed:

You make a political analysis, but then you need a victim. If you want to hit the Christian Democracy in a neighborhood, you need a target ... therefore, you start to look for this victim ... you read the newspapers, you infiltrate their meetings, and you try to find out. Then you have singled out your victim: he is physically there; he is the one to be blamed for everything. In that moment there is already the logic of a trial in which you have already decided that he is guilty; you have only to decide on his punishment. So you have *a very emphatic sense of justice*; you punish him not only for what he has done but also for all the rest. Then you don't care anymore which responsibilities that person has; you ascribe everything to him ... he is only a small part of the machine that is going to destroy all of us. (Life History no. 27: 45, emphasis added)

In parallel, militants increasingly defined themselves as belonging to a heroic elite, although the theories of different groups had different undertones. Some activists in fact stressed their role as neutral and cold. A German militant recalled that "most of the fear you feel disappears in the phase of the planning and repetition of the exercise until perfection.... *Then you become nothing more than a working gear*" (cited in Böllinger 1981: 189–90, emphasis added). An Italian similarly recalled: "You enter in a role, there are the rules, supra-ordered by the ideology, the organization, ... from the phase" (Life History no. 27: 455). This also helps militants identify with all those who are fighting, because, as a RAF member put it, "anybody who fights is one of us" (cited in Böllinger 1981: 202).

The militants of clandestine radical Right organizations reflected a narration, which was widespread in the Italian neofascist culture, of self-victimization but also heroism. The RSI was presented as a "desperate republic" that was working to recover the original revolutionary nucleus of fascism (Ferraresi 1995: 71). The ON wanted to form "men able to stand among the ruins" (Ferraresi 1995: 112). A neofascist of the first generation who was active in the MSI remembered:

None of us had a future. We had all taken a no-exit road; a road at the end of which there was only prison, or exile in a foreign country, or death. It looks like rhetoric. It is not. Of the leading groups of my section, no one is left. I have to be in prison for 30 years. Another for ten. Another one committed suicide. Two died in the Foreign Legion. One died doing *bravate* with an airplane. Another one killed himself running on his motorbike. One died as they cut his throat in Africa. (Salierno 1976: 132)

Later on, the radical right-wingers also perceived themselves as victims of the worst repression. A research study on the biographical materials of radical Right activists concluded that "the narrators present their 'in-group' systematically as a collective victim" (Cento Bull 2007: 124). As one of them declared in an interview, "the neo-fascist groups were the victims, precisely those who suffered the most from the state repression. I saw this with my eyes" (ibid.: 118). And another concurred, "We were the victims of the political situation, of the political unrepresentativeness of our community – a community exposed to fierce reprisal" (ibid.: 124). This victimization was presented as linked to the historical defeat of fascism: "We came from the side which had lost the war and hence we felt excluded so we were, even from the point of view of societal norms and daily life" (Stefano Delle Chiaie, cited in Cento Bull 2007: 134). Fioravanti remembered that "in the 1970s, the proportion was clear everywhere in Italy: one Italian over three was a communist and all stated that killing a fascist is no crime" (Bianconi 1992: 50). As a motivation to support the radical Right, militants stressed a sense of injustice. One of them recalled,

What really got me hooked politically was a series of what I would call historical injustices, you know, a reaction against what was imposed on me in what we read in school, let's say, that's the main reason for something that was born in me and brought me closer to a certain world. I remember reading books about history, about the war, the Resistance, and when I was a boy I asked myself, I said to myself: "Is it true? I mean, are all the good guys on one side and all the bad guys on the other side?" (quoted in Veugelers 2011: 251)

The heroism of a minority was emphasized. As fascism acquired a heroic aura, the neofascist milieu was presented, in comparison with the left-wing milieu, as "an entirely different environment, more heroic, more beautiful, more pure, at the same time more exalting, with stronger ideals of heroism, strength, courage, youth, life. Not that you could not find some of this with the extreme left too, but they were weaker, and I always had a love of everything heroic" (Veugelers 2011: 62). On the right, the militants found that the atmosphere reflected a commitment to the heroism of the few, even if such heroes were historically defeated. One of them declared, "I felt a community, a community of intention and sensibility" (Ferraresi 1995: 298).

Activists started to consider violence as a necessity. In the radical Right, militants believed that "usually regimes gain power after an armed struggle, using violence. This is how power was gained during the French Revolution, the Russian Revolution, the American Revolution – there was an armed struggle. This is what happened with Castro, with Hitler, with Mussolini. From what I can tell, history teaches this is one of the paths to power travelled most often" (quoted in Veugelers 2011: 254). As one of the AN's leaders, Stefano Delle Chiaie, declared, "we are an elite of heroes. Heroic in fact is our style of life, rich in values that alone permits us to approach the divine, heroic is our battle against a system that violates and oppresses us, heroic is our commitment to the forces of honor, loyalty and discipline" (Weinberg and Eubank 1987: 37). The ON's militants propagated order – the importance of which is evident in the very name of the organization – presenting themselves as not only a spiritual elite but also the best representatives of the Aryan race as soldiers and warriors: "The impression to spread was that of a closed and compact rank, capable of facing the challenges of an hostile environment, proud of his solitary wake" (Ferraresi 1995: 117). Furthermore, the events of Piazza Fontana were perceived as a turning point for the Right, as "things turned nasty after Piazza Fontana," when "the hatred and the fights went before the boundaries of physical [street] clashes" (Delle Chiaie, in Cento Bull 2007: 134).

It was thus common to consider oneself and one's group as the good ones in a world of evil. In the Basque countries, some ETA members went to confession before actions. "You never have the feeling that you are doing something bad … nothing bad, and nothing against God's doctrine, right? That is, you're struggling for the ideals of your people, to defend freedom" (Reinares 2001: 64). Similarly, radical Islamists progressively isolated themselves from outsiders, considering themselves as enlightened believers and everybody else as infidels. In this way, the perception of external danger magnified group cohesion (Cronin 2009b).

Violence was justified cognitively through different narratives. To begin with, it was presented by the militants of clandestine groups as historically legitimized: "We were supported … also by famous quotes from Marxist literature, in which violence appeared as absolutely legitimate, as part of the history of the working class. Once it [has been] decided that the historical conditions allow for that kind of organization, the rest is only a technical consequence" (Life History no. 12: 21). In the words of another Italian militant, "violence is not discussed, it is seen as absolutely normal" (Life History no. 5: 98).

Violence was in fact often presented as a very successful tool. Violence was justified as efficient – or, at least, as the only way out. The Italian militants boasted about being "deeply rooted at Fiat and Pirelli," being "in contact with the working class," and enjoying "a very widespread legitimation." Another activist similarly observed: "Legality does not allow you to solve these problems, political and also personal, of personal liberation. Guns start to be the solution" (Life History no. 27: 441).

ETA militants also read historical events as proof that "no country in the world became independent without death and violence" (Reinares 2001: 91). According to the account of an *etarra*, "therefore, let's say the only way … to oblige the state to recognize our rights as people is … a political and military strategy … the only possibility of a real change is the political and military pressures upon the poderes facticos" (ibid.: 91). The militants reconstructed Spanish history to highlight the success of armed struggle, especially in regard to the ETA's assassination of Franco's presumed successor, Carrero Blanco, in 1973. According to a militant, "people, once they have something, you do not change them with good manners. Only if you put pressure upon them and force them … I am convinced that without violence we would have not obtained the Estatuto, or the development of the Ertzaintza, we would have not got many

many things" (ibid.: 93). So they asked themselves, rhetorically, "Well, what is the strongest way to struggle today?" (ibid.: 104). For the extreme Right, action also naturally implied violence, as, in the words of militants of the time, "violence is part of the political struggle, it is a mean like another, I do not give a morally negative judgment" (interview with V.V.: 35, in Pisetta 1990: 205).

However, when defeats were difficult to hide, the militants nurtured images of themselves as a minority of heroes who want to offer a testimony. In Italy,

from 1980 on, the only aim [was] to resist…. There [was] no longer the idea of an advancing revolution: "Let's go on, we are many, we are beautiful." We [were] not beautiful, we [were] not many; we [were] only poor chaps who meet and say "O.K., let's try to do something while we wait, let's try to create again a revolutionary situation." … If we want to synthesize that in a slogan, it was to resist at any price, without allowing [the system] to reabsorb the movement and to impose social peace. (Life History no. 6: 50)

This elite heroism mystified isolation as a positive, self-chosen quality. According to a German interviewee, "it was wonderful to belong to [a group of people] who had a complete understanding of the world and who had really started to work hard, instead of sitting and complaining" (cited in Böllinger 1981: 189).

On the right, violence was also justified by a sense of superiority – "we felt superior" (interview with Roberto: 65–6, in Pisetta 1990: 206) – as well as by the feeling of living "in an incredible atmosphere, created by fake, true, presumed coups d'état to come" (interview with M.M.: 62, in Fiasco 1990: 171). Thus militants liked "to imagine oneself as a *guerrigliero*, that lives in the mountain and acts in the plains … with his arms, and his independent life" (interview with V.V.: 42, in Pisetta 1990: 209).

As for religious clandestine violence, participation in the global jihad became seen as glamorous, which attracted new recruits. As a Saudi militant recalls,

the youth used to envy those who went to Afghanistan and were greatly influenced by them…. When we used to look at the Afghan suits that the mujahidin who returned from Afghanistan wore as they talked in the street of Jidda, Mecca or Medina, we used to feel we were living with the generation of the triumphant companions of the Prophet, and hence we looked up to them as an example and an authority. (cited in Hegghammer 2010: 64)

How militants defined their situation was related to the identification of the other and the self. In this regard, references to a war analogy allowed the militants to legitimize violence. According to an Italian militant, "we had this tendency to find our gratification only at the military level; therefore we went and did what had to be done" (Life History no. 5: 57). Similarly, as Mahler recalls, "in clandestinity, one lives in a completely changed world…. *You see the world only inside a military model*, as a freed zone, or as a dangerous area. You do not see human beings so often any more…. When the world becomes so illusory, then you have to change yourself" (cited in Horn 1982: 149, emphasis added). He further explains: "We were from our point of view in something like a war. It was in order to be able to face the problem of death that *we defined ourselves as soldiers*" (cited in Jäger 1981: 164, emphasis added).

The use of military terms tended to spread this war analogy. As a German militant recalls, "they talked about cadres, units, and commandos *in a military terminology that suggested … that something like that really existed*" (Speitel 1980a: 41, emphasis added). And "the dominant feeling was instead that [what we did] was something for a military command, a military action" (cited in Jäger 1981: 164).

Militants developed "very special relationships with guns"; guns were said to "give you more strength" (Life History no. 27: 33) and to "have a charm … that makes you feel more macho" (Life History no. 16: 79). They occupied physical and mental space: "You are there to clean them or to charge them. You spend really a lot of time with this thing. You practice. Or you read books on guns. The deutsche *Waffenjournal* was the most beloved reading." Militants could feel "very secure of yourself because you keep a gun in your hands … [they give you] a crazy self-confidence" (Baumann 1976: 165).

On the radical right, the cult of guns was even more widespread. In the words of a militant, "arms, arms with that terrible fascination. You watch it, weigh it, carry it out, you feel different" (Ferraresi 1995: 81). Similarly, another stressed, "We could not even conceive that a fascist did not make all what he could to procure himself one, was not a maniac for it" (ibid.: 81). This implied also a very strong exaltation of death: "To die! To know how to die! All our mystics of courage evolved around the capacity to face death. A man's value was linked to him knowing how to die," declared a militant (ibid.: 79). And another confirmed, "All our tradition was based on the cult of the death, and of its symbols" (ibid.: 81). The celebration of dead heroes of the radical Right was particularly central in the NAR.

These images of the self and the other developed within increasingly isolated communities. As an Italian activist stated, "you built a network of friends, of personal relations always inside this circle. I think that already at that moment a kind of unconscious ghetto-like isolation took place" (Life History no. 13: 6). Similarly, one German activist acknowledged, "I became completely closed. Everything was political to such an extent that I did not meet human beings on a human basis anymore" (Jünschke 1988: 153).

Underground organizations in fact required total commitment, often including renunciation of external ties. As clandestinity drastically reduced external contacts, isolation from external channels of information strengthened commitment. In the memory of an Italian left-wing militant, "the majority of the group was closed towards some topics. They could not get information" (Boock 1981: 114). A German militant stated, "Today I would say that the politics of clandestinity and the prison have something in common: isolation. This politics brings an almost total insulation from the people that you would like to reach from the political point of view" (Proll 1978).

This isolation tended to produce and reproduce a distorted vision of society. In the words of an Italian activist,

it was a sum of small lies. In fact, each of us … tried to give credence to the image of an underground organization that was deeply rooted in society, which enjoyed more popularity, more support, more consensus [than it actually had]. This did not happen through big lies but through the small lies we told each other … [for example]: "but do you know that … the concierge understood that I am a member of the Red Brigades and not only does she not denounce me but, if she sees a policeman, she manages to warn me? Do you know that the people of that cafe understood who I am and, when I go there, the barman offers me a drink? Do you know that in that factory, when we wounded that foreman, they opened a bottle and drank a toast?" (Life History no. 11: 38)

According to the imagery enforced in the radical milieus, the "revolutionary forces" were growing stronger, and a civil war was ever nearer. For instance, a militant remembered that

when Moro was kidnapped, we were at a protest march of the workers of the Unidal, an alimentary factory … I remember that a copy of a special edition of the newspaper with the title "Moro kidnapped, his escort killed" was raised by the workers as a sign of victory. We were amused. Nobody realized how grave the situation was…. We went to the canteen and toasted, with the workers, to the near fall of the regime. (Life History no. 12: 34)

So, in time, the militants' relationship with external reality became increasingly detached. As a radical Right militant explained,

the world is like a physical space you have to go through, made of targets you have to hit…. The relationship between reality and the person that calls himself out of it is a parasitic one. The person is, that is, no longer autonomous, but needs an external reality which could reconfirm him in his own existence as a diverse one. It is a symbiotic relation. (interview with S.C., in Fiasco 1990: 184)

Adherence to group norms then made leaving the organization more difficult. As an Italian left-wing militant recalled, "the idea of quitting the organization produced feelings of guilt because after having already paid such a price, to quit meant to admit that all that we had done had been useless" (Life History no. 19: 63). Or – as another militant said – "*to go right to the end* … [was] the only chance for redemption I had, from a moral point of view, both for the violence I produced and the violence I suffered" (Life History no. 18: 73–4, emphasis added). Thus "*to pursue the way I had undertaken*" was perceived as the only option "to find – or, better, to try to find – a reason for my previous participation in a murder" (Life History no. 14: 19, emphasis added). In particular, in the high-security prisons,

hostile conditions become more bearable only if the prisoner can consider himself part of a larger community, of a somehow overdetermined truth, which allows one to see one's own existence as prisoner as only temporary. I am a member of the Rote Armee Fraktion, an anti-imperialist urban guerrilla who fights against the Federal Republic of Germany, because the FRG, side by side with the imperialist USA, represses its own people and exploits Third World peoples. Because I was and I am part of this struggle, the state has taken me prisoner, almost as a hostage, and is keeping me in these inhuman conditions in prison.... There cannot be an individual solution for me: my only support is the group, solidarity with the other comrades, and the continuation of the common struggle, even in these constrictive conditions.... *Only insofar as I keep my loyalty to the aims of the group, can I retain my identity and the hope that the situation will change....* The prisoner has only this choice between capitulation, which means destruction of the self and despair, and the spasmodic attachment ... to the group and its aims. (Boock 1981: 97–8, emphasis added)

Similar observations apply to radical Islamism. Islamism addressed some of the grievances of young people, giving them an explanation and a purpose. Many young militants mentioned experiencing cultural alienation, as well as the shock produced by the gap between extreme poverty and extreme affluence (Rosefsky Wickham 2004: 237). In turn, the internalization of the new value system strengthened within the net, producing a reordering of priorities. As an activist explained, "we read what we respected – religious only. It is a question of priorities" (ibid.: 240). Radical Islamism also provided confidence in the future, with the expectation that Islam would expand as the only source of moral guidance for a society in decay, as well as a space in which to develop one's own values, such as the taste for a spiritual and simple life. As for the London attackers, it was noted that they became a self-appointed vanguard and developed increasingly stronger emotional ties: "Separating from dissenting views and moderating voices, increasing isolation breeds an easier acceptance of radical messages" (Egerton 2011: 155). In the Islamist underground, "ties to each other replace those to people outside the group" (ibid.: 156).

MILITANT ENCLOSURE: CONCLUSIONS

Traditionally, explanations of commitment to clandestine organizations have looked at either psychopathologies, expecting militants to have dependent, identity-seeking personalities; grievances, expecting militants to belong to the (at least relatively) deprived groups of the population; or greed, expecting militants to be those who are the most ready to exploit environmental opportunities to improve their material resources.

In this chapter, an alternative set of explanations has been put forward, looking at the relational processes that enforce commitment to the underground. In all of the cases discussed, the militants who eventually chose, or were drawn into, the underground then developed a freedom-fighter identity, seeing themselves as members of an embattled community of idealistic and altruistic people fighting a heroic war against evil. In underground organizations, commitment, as a process through which individual interests became attached to socially organized patterns of behavior (Kanter 1968; 1972), was enforced through the development of a specific cognitive system.

Militants in all four types of clandestine violence stayed loyal to their underground organizations due to the convergent effects of affective and cognitive mechanisms. Strong friendship ties, intense involvement with comrades who share the same destiny, feelings of revenge toward enemies, and a battle spirit toward politics all contributed to an affective focusing around what was perceived as a heroic community, accompanied by, in parallel, a detachment from alternative focuses of identification. Affective ties acquired growing importance in all the steps that led from first involvement in the movement, to recruitment into the underground organization, and to persisting commitment. Beyond solidarity with intimate friends, myths also produced emotionally strong ties with a broader community of those who struggled along with the militants. The frequent use of terms such as "family" or "brother" testifies to the affective intensity of relations in the underground. A process of identification developed, therefore, through slippery slopes of intense commitment to a broader community that was seen as something to be defended and avenged. The group is said to offer "this type of identification-object in the form of comrades and leading personalities" (Böllinger 1981: 223). A sort of pleasure in action is often mentioned as producing positive, intense emotional feelings that further strengthened commitments.

In fact, clandestine political organizations have been defined as subcultures with a distinctive value system; in them,

we see not only the breakdown of normality but also the development of a counterculture, of an alternative system of norms and aims that establishes the frontiers, reduces the constraints, imposes compliance, and – in a situation of complete isolation from the external world – replaces the normal standard of right and wrong, good and evil with a different or alternative value orientation. (Jäger 1981: 157)

Affective focusing interacted with a cognitive closure. Because of their isolation, the underground organizations eventually became the sole point of reference for their members, progressively reducing their sense of external reality.

Participation in the underground nurtured a vision of the self as hero and martyr, of the opponents as absolute enemies, and of the situation as a war in which violence is necessary. Specific characteristics of the clandestine organizations that influenced this evolution of behavior include their illegality, small size, and secretiveness (Crenshaw 2011; della Porta 1995). The intimate relations among individuals strengthened by high-risk activism made individuals all the more dependent on the group. Clandestine political organizations also emerged as similar to sects in their intolerance of dissent. They became a sort of social infrastructure that provided essential emotional support, thus enforcing uniformity (Crenshaw 2011). In time, group solidarity tended to replace political aims.

The longer the life of the organization or the longer the individual's experience in it, the more demanding participation became – such that those militants living in clandestinity came to depend on the underground formations as their only means of survival, and indeed for their identity. As the underground group became the militants' only source of information, or at least the only source they were supposed to believe, their grasp of external reality became increasingly tenuous with the passage of time. The emphasis on cognitive coherence was all the more important because the process of individual socialization in radical organizations involved a dramatic change in the militants' images of their external world.

9

Leaving Clandestinity?

Reversing Mechanisms of Engagement

Although political violence in Italy as a whole covered a long period, the history of individual underground groups was usually very short. Only the Red Brigades survived, albeit in a state of organizational crisis, for more than a decade. The other long-standing organization, the Front Line, existed (under various names) for seven years, although it represented an effective threat for only four years. The history of the Nuclei Armati Proletari (NAP) spanned three short years between its creation in 1974 and its dissolution in 1976. Few of the other groups survived beyond their first year: the Unità Comuniste Combattenti (UCC) only lasted from 1976 to 1977; the Formazioni Comuniste Combattenti (FCC), created in the summer of 1977, ceased to exist in February 1979; the Reparti Comunisti Armati (RCA) and the Movimento Comunista Rivoluzionario (MCR) were active between 1979 and the beginning of 1981; the Guerriglia Rossa, created at the beginning of 1979, had already changed its name by March of the same year and disappeared entirely in the summer of 1980; the Nuclei carried out their first action in June 1981 and their last in November 1982; the Proletari Armati per il Comunismo (PAC) operated between 1978 and 1979; the actions of Per il Comunismo were carried out between December 1979 and January 1980; and the Brigata Lo Muscio barely lasted ten months, from January to October 1980.

Generally speaking, the immediate reason behind the disappearance of these groups was the arrests or deaths of their activists. Seven members of the NAP died in gun battles with police or accidental explosions, whereas many others were arrested. The FCC crisis was closely linked to the arrest of its founder, Corrado Alunni, in October 1978. The PAC ceased to exist a few months after the group's creation, by which time most of its supporters were already in prison. Similarly, Nuclei disappeared in 1983 after the arrests of all its members. The immediate reasons behind the defeat of the Guerriglia Rossa and the Brigata Lo Muscio were similar: between the summer and autumn of 1980, confessions by their respective leaders led to the arrest and sentencing of all their followers. In the end, the organizational development of the different strands of the BR was also decisively marked by the results of police and judicial investigations. As early as the beginning of the 1970s, the infiltration of police agents and cross-checks at the land registry office had led to the discovery of various militant dens and the arrests of many activists: only one member of the first executive committee escaped arrest, and most of the founders were in prison by the end of 1976. Even though the BR re-emerged through an intense recruitment effort over the following years, from 1980 onward confessions by various members of the organization led to arrests of a large number of activists at all levels. The PL broke down after a long series of arrests that hit the organization in 1979 and 1980.

The short lifespan of the Italian clandestine groups is not exceptional: according to some statistics (Rapoport 1992: 1067), 90 percent of underground groups are active for less than a year, and an additional 5 percent survive for less than a decade. The discussion in the previous chapters of some causal mechanisms that drive the process of radicalization in the underground is not meant to give the impression of a permanent threat or unavoidable evolution. Agency can be found in the escalation and also de-escalation processes. Although I do not expect to provide an exhaustive list, in this last part I reflect on the reasons why the aforementioned mechanisms of radicalization were inverted and thus de-escalation ensued. Although political violence might cover long periods, the history of individual underground groups was usually quite short. As aforementioned, the immediate reason behind the disappearance of these groups was the arrests or deaths of their activists. But what were the reasons behind these setbacks? Why were these organizations not able to integrate new recruits into groups decimated by arrests? Research on the (societal, organizational, and individual) departure from political violence has been very limited – as is the case with criminology in general, which has been criticized for devoting "more attention to why individuals and groups offend than why they stop offending" (LaFree and Miller 2008: 203).

The phenomena variously defined as abandonment, defection, decline, or defeat have also been little explored in sociological literature. In his recent work on activist disengagement, Olivier Fillieule (2005) singled out a few trends that, essentially incidentally, touched on themes linked to this topic: works within the sociology of religion have looked at conversion; the sociology of family, at divorce; labor sociology, at professional mobility; and political sociology, at cycles of public commitment.

One problem lies within the very conceptualization of the process of leaving political violence. First, leaving could be conceptualized at the societal level, as the end of critical levels of violence; at the organizational level, as the demise of clandestine groups; or at the individual level, as the departure of militants from the underground. In addition, abandonment can be either voluntary or forced, depending on whether an individual or organization makes a choice or is constrained to adopt certain behavior (Bjørgo and Horgan 2009). Arrest and, more rarely, death or dismissal from political activism organizations

(Klandermans 2005; Labbé and Croisat 1992) are all causes of forced departure. At the organizational level, as Audrey Cronin synthesized,

> there are at least seven broader explanations or critical elements in the decline and ending of terrorist groups in the modern era: (1) the capture or killing of the leader, (2) failure to transition to the next generation, (3) achievement of the group's aims, (4) transition to a legitimate political process, (5) undermining of popular support, (6) repression, and (7) transitioning from terrorism to other forms of violence. (2009a: 55)

Individual and organizational processes do of course affect the level of violence that is widespread at the societal level, but organizational demise and individual redemption do not automatically bring about the end of critical phases of violence in specific societies, as other splinter radical groups might emerge and other individuals may become involved in militant activities.

At all levels, the abandonment path can be fairly long and difficult. Stages of departure have been identified at the individual level, with a period of incoherency as regards identity tending to precede a real and proper exit (Pudal 2005: 168). At the organizational level as well, all of the paths singled out previously involve experimentations with various strategies, often featuring splits between those who favor increasing militarization and those who opt instead for moderation. Leaving clandestine violence can occur either individually or collectively and can involve a variety of people from the same group. Leaving terrorism behind can mean either renouncing the use of weapons or abandoning the organization – two events that rarely coincide. The first, often linked to arrest, does not in itself mean giving up membership within an organization. Moreover, the different positions taken as regards a specific organization and armed struggle need to be distinguished: in the context of frequent sectarianism and isolation, departure from one group does not necessarily precede moving away from the armed struggle as a whole, but rather may involve recruitment to or creation of another underground organization.

At the theoretical level, these conceptual ambiguities are reflected in weak theorization. On the one hand, the more traditional, instrumental approach to crime stresses deterrence through increased costs and risks. As LaFree, Dugan, and Korte observed,

> the belief that credible threats of apprehension and punishment deter crime is as old as criminal law itself and it has broad appeal to both policy makers and the public. Deterrence models generally assume that human beings are rational, self-interested actors who seek to minimize personal cost while maximizing personal gain.... Indeed, deterrence-based thinking has dominated counterterrorist policies in most countries since the origins of modern terrorism in the late 1960s. (2009: 18)

In general, "the threat and/or imposition of punishment does not always deter future acts of violence and may increase violence in some cases" (ibid.).

In fact, the limited research on the effects of counterterrorism policies based on increasing punishment has yielded inconsistent results. In some cases, deterrence effects prevailed, leading to a reduction of violence; in others, there was instead a backlash effect, leading to an increase in violence. As "threats from out-groups generally increase the cohesion of in-groups as well as the pressure on in-group deviants to conform and support in-group leaders," clandestine groups "frequently rely on the response of governments to mobilize the sympathies of would-be supporters. The extent to which government-based counter-terrorist strategies outrage participants or energize a base of potential supporters may increase the likelihood of more terrorist strikes" (LaFree, Dugan, and Korte 2009: 21).[1]

In fact, criminologists theorize that the results of repression are influenced by the legitimacy of the sanctions among the offenders and their groups of reference. The size of the clandestine group and the support it enjoys in the population also influence the balance of deterrence versus backlash effects (LaFree and Miller 2008; Ross and Gurr 1989). A particular problem when looking at the process of leaving violence is the lack of integrated theoretical reflections on the individual, organizational, and societal processes of de-radicalization.

Forms of abandonment have often been linked to types of previous commitment, with regard to both an individual's position and the characteristics of a group. In general, the greater the price of admission, the greater the price, be it material and/or psychological, of defection (Kanter 1972). Participation levels in underground groups certainly vary, as do the psychological and material price and the intensity of commitment. For many, support for underground groups was less binding – from both a material and a psychological point of view – than many stereotypes of "professional terrorists" lead one to believe. In the case of left-wing violence in Italy, for example, only 11 percent (129 individuals) of the more than 1,000 activists I studied during earlier research were in hiding (della Porta 1990). Moreover, a good 66.8 percent of activists had never participated in action against people, and 40 percent had never been involved in any armed action. Only 6 percent had been members of "fire groups," that is, they had been employed prevailingly for military-style action, whereas 44 percent had carried out exclusively logistical or administrative duties. Moreover, the duration of each individual's political activism within an underground group was usually short.

In what follows, I address these questions, looking at how the mechanisms of radicalization studied in the previous chapters might be reversed. Given the large amount of information, as well as the advanced stage of the de-escalation process, my observation is mainly based on the Italian case, but some references to the other cases are also provided.

---

[1] For instance, in Northern Ireland, the deterrent effects of repressive policies were limited, as "erroneous arrests of nonterrorists during the implementation of the internment policy seriously undermined the legitimacy of the operation. Additionally, the policy of internment without trial represented an obvious departure from widespread norms of rule by law, which is deeply ingrained in western liberal democracies" (LaFree, Dugan, and Korte 2009: 36).

SOCIETAL DE-ESCALATION

As aforementioned, counterinsurgency can indeed produce either an increase or a decrease in violence. Similarly, reforms do not always bring about deradicalization, as "organizational and psychological pressures may explain why changes in the political conditions that made terrorism seem appropriate or even necessary at the outset of a conflict may not reduce conflict" (Crenshaw 1996: 259). To understand the contradictory effects of counterterrorist policies, in an influential piece comparing the United States and Canada, Ross and Gurr (1989) built a typology by crossing two dimensions of organizational resources: military or political and internal or external. Military capacity, they suggested, is reduced if protection of the target is increased (*preemption*) or if there is an increase in the risks and costs of using violent repertoires (*deterrence*). As for political capacity, demise is facilitated by the loss of commitment by members (*burnout*) or the external constituency (*backlash*). Because the military strength of clandestine groups is usually limited, their political strength is most important in determining survival or demise: in both the United States and Canada, in fact, the defeat of the Weather Underground and the Front de Libération National du Quebec (FLNQ), respectively, derived from political changes such as the end of the Vietnam War in 1975, which reduced the potential support for the Weathermen, and the outrage produced in the FLNQ's potential constituency by the 1970 kidnapping and assassination of Quebec's minister of immigration and labor, Pierre Laporte. Indeed, Martha Crenshaw (1991) stressed the importance, together with state policies, of the strategic mistakes made by the clandestine groups themselves.

Suggesting a more dynamic perspective, Clark McCauley (2008: 286) observed that the response to terrorism is

a long-term game with many players, as identified earlier under Actors. Each government response to terrorism, as identified under Actions, should be considered in relation to its likely interpretation by each actor, including not only the terrorists and their sympathizers and supporters but also the government's competitors and supporters, both domestic and foreign. Second, given the projected effect on each actor, the capacities and intentions of each actor should be considered in order to predict what, if any, response each actor is likely to make to their interpretation of the government tactic.

In this section, we observe the effects on clandestine political violence of both state policies and transformation in the organizations' potential base of support.

Protest Moderation

As aforementioned (in Chapter 3, in particular), research on protest cycles has linked radicalization to the decline of mobilization. Although some forms of violence increase when mobilization declines, violence also tends to have its own cycle, with ups and then downs, whose dynamic is in fact related with the twin processes of radicalization and moderation. When social movement activists recognize, through their own experience or historical memories, the negative effects of violence on mobilization, the room for radical repertoires shrinks. Although clandestine groups are, to a certain extent at least, "strategic actors that usually deliberate about their targets and calculate the effects of attacks on their constituent populations, ... they can also undermine their own cause if they miscalculate, resulting in plummeting popular support and even the demise of the group. They generally cannot survive without either active or passive support from a surrounding population" (Cronin 2009a: 61). In particular, support is often lost when the clandestine groups' attacks start to produce revulsion among their potential supporters.

As research on youth gangs indicated, in the short term the ensuing isolation can have the effect of increased stigmatization of the deviants, making it more difficult for them to reintegrate into society (Bjørgo and Horgan 2009). In the long term, however, protest moderation means failure of clandestine groups to find new recruits as well as sympathizers, which facilitates de-radicalization. Evidence of failure increases the perception of what John Horgan defined as "the crushing disparity between the fantasies that moulded their initial search for a place in the movement, with the subsequent reality of involvement" (2009: 22).

Competitive escalation develops when the use of violence seems to provide a competitive advantage in the internal competition within the social movement family and sector. However, when those strategies appear as useless or even damaging to most social movement activists, and when nonviolence spreads, we may observe a *competitive de-escalation*. As Albert Hirschman observed in *Shifting Involvements* (1982), public commitment tends to fluctuate in cycles. Research on social movements has also observed the presence of cycles of protest with dynamics of emergence, peak, and decline, and they in turn are sometimes interwoven with cycles of political violence (della Porta 1995; della Porta and Tarrow 1986; Tarrow 1989). The end of armed struggle is also actually motivated by the realization on the part of activists in underground organizations that a protest cycle had ended.

At the end of the protest cycle in Italy, member exit was facilitated by widespread doubts over the effectiveness of armed struggle. Significantly, during the Moro trial in October 1982, a group of prisoners read a document stating that "a generational cycle is closing, ending, a cycle in which ... the enrichment of social change and the long marches, the social democracy of assemblies and the Jacobin fascination with the steel party, went into a spin. The push forward of the October Revolution and the Welfare State is being halted now by events" (quoted in Morucci 2004: 234). This process was facilitated when legal exit options for those who wanted to quit the underground were opened (see the subsequent discussion). According to former BR militant Gallinari,

it is certainly not new but it is not badly thought of either, the power strategy. Diverging treatment and prospects tear open the prison environment and subsequently encourage crises among political prisoners. Many comrades were already assailed with doubts and questions. The Ministry's prison policy required clear political horizons and impartial ethical motivations if it were to be handled with the necessary strength and patience. But this itself was increasingly lacking. (2006: 302)

Given that activists in armed groups preserve a political purpose, they also look in their surroundings for confirmation of their own choices. Notwithstanding cognitive closure, signs of defeat also filter through to the closed environment of underground organizations sooner or later. In many accounts by activists, the act of leaving the underground is linked to a perception of the inefficacy of armed struggle. A few immediate signs were noticeable in defeat, described in the accounts as "friends who started to drink," "heroin that penetrated the environment of the revolutionary left," and "increasingly frequent defections" (della Porta 1990: chap. 4).

The declining cycle also meant reduced support. One former PL militant declared, with regard to the progressive reduction of the network of external sympathizers available to offer logistical help,

When this sort of character who, despite appearances, holds the life of the organisation in his hands, starts to break away, you sense it, even if you dismiss it ideologically, you sense that people are quitting in the background, and in practice all the apparatus starts to stiffen up, so you end up with a large number of peoples in hiding and you don't know where to keep them, you have to start multiplying funding activities and by multiplying those you start to multiply incidents, deaths, injuries, arrests. (Life History no. 12: 38)

According to some interpretations, widespread justification of the use of violence spread in Italy in the 1970s because of the prevalence in the social movement sector of a particular type of culture. The myth of imminent revolution, the definition of democracy as a mask hiding exploitation, scorn for human life, ideas on the supremacy of ideology over theory, and an emphasis on the sacrifice of the individual for the common good have been considered to be cultural preconditions for the emergence of clandestine political violence. The debate on violence accelerated criticism of this sort of culture through closer examination of several main themes, some of which were already evident during the protest movements of the late 1960s: the wrongs of bureaucratic centralism, the mistakes of the Leninist theory of the state, the negative consequences of an end-justifies-the-means philosophy, and a re-evaluation of the needs of the individual. These new elements of the emerging culture reduced the propensity for political violence, which was increasingly considered as illegitimate and had no appeal in emerging social movement organizations that were characterized by nontotalitarian activism, possessed little organizational structure, and were prevailingly nonviolent in nature. Attempts by residual factions of the BR to infiltrate the peace movement did not end positively for them. The same can be said for the most recent movement for global justice that claims to support nonviolent ideals (della Porta 2007).

The perception that armed struggle had been defeated was also at the basis of individual departure in the case of the ETA. In a letter written in 2004, six ETA leaders in prison claimed that the "political-military strategy has been defeated by enemy repression," recognizing that "never in the history of this organization have we been on such a bad way" (cited in Alonso 2009: 95). Even in nationalist environments, protest emerged against ETA violence. For example, the main umbrella social movement organization against violence since the late 1990s, Gesto por la Paz, is made up of 160 groups and about 1,500 activists, with up to 40,000 supporters. It has a pluralistic membership in terms of political positions, and a large proportion of young activists, especially in the cities. When someone is kidnapped, members meet once a week and stand in silence, holding a banner requesting that the hostage be freed. Another organization, Elkarri (among all of us), is composed of 107 local chapters with a total of about 1,200 members, mainly intellectuals, who are oriented to developing conflict resolution solutions. It mainly recruits members from the nationalist Left, and even former ETA supporters (Funes 1998).

In the case of Islamist violence in Egypt, the demise of al-Jamaa and the Egyptian Islamic Jihad is linked to the acknowledgment, by most of their leaders in prison, of the failure of armed struggle. In particular, on July 1997, six of the historical leaders of the two organizations issued a statement in which they declared an end to all combat operations. This statement "marked the beginning of an active profound process of reassessment and revision, begun by Gama'a al-Islamiya and followed by the Jihad" (Rashwan 2009: 121). Various documents addressed a self-critique based on new readings of religious texts, as well as signs of increasing isolation. In fact, "using the jurisprudence of utility versus injury, the Gama'a al-Islamiya reconsidered its past violent practices, concluding that they did not achieve the desired benefit but only increased the injuries to the organization, individual Muslims and Islamic state and society" (ibid.: 127). Indeed, this phenomenon has been linked to the historical moderation of socio-political Islamist movements in the last fourteen centuries. A prison policy that facilitated encounters between the leaders and the militant base allowed for the nonviolent narrative to spread.

During this process of organizational weakening, the Luxor attack represented an attempt by radical splinter groups to resist the organizational disbandment by pushing the state to overreact, thus producing a process of growing solidarity within the community. According to McCauley's analysis,

the Luxor attack was a bid for leadership by members of the Islamic Group still at large (terrorist leadership/strategy/tactics competitors). It represented a major escalation of the level of violence and a shift in targeting to focus on foreign tourists (terrorist actions – violence up and different targets). The proximate goal was to cut tourism and its hard currency support for the Egyptian government (decrease foreign support for government). But a further goal was to provoke a heavy government response against political Islam that would sideline the imprisoned leaders and develop new support for violence by Islamic radicals (increase sympathy and support for terrorists;

decrease sympathy and support for government).... Instead the immediate reaction of Luxor citizens was outrage at the terrorists who had killed "their" tourists and "their" income (decrease sympathy and support for terrorists; increase sympathy and support for government). The Egyptian government took the outrage and built on it. The government did not launch a broad increase in repression, did not shut down its connection to the Islamic Group leaders in prison. Instead the government initiated a new security regime that was relatively discriminating in attacking only extremists and their sympathizers, and launched a mass media campaign to reinforce nationwide the outrage of the citizens of Luxor who chased the terrorists into the hills (government actions – political initiatives aimed).... Religious leaders joined political leaders in a broad Egyptian consensus condemning the Luxor attack, a consensus that came to include condemning terrorist violence as a tactic. (2008: 289–90)

DE-ESCALATING POLICING AND EXIT OPTIONS

If escalating policing fuels radicalization, the development of more inclusive, negotiated, and *de-escalated policing* helps to diffuse conflicts. As mentioned in Chapter 2, protest policing had perverse effects, especially when harsh and diffuse repression increases support for opponents. This also happened with antiterrorist strategies, as "the true irony of retaliation and military force as a tool of counterterrorism is that in the one moment it is a child of, and a father to, the cycle of vengeance and common human desire for revenge and retribution" (Silke 2012: 352).

Decisions to leave the underground are certainly affected by the efficiency of repression, but they are also influenced by the offering of conversion opportunities (Sommier 2005: 177). As Bjørgo and Horgan concluded, "with no exit option but death or life in prison, terrorists may continue even if they realize that their struggle is lost" (2009: 249).

In Italy, the defeat of clandestine organizations was made easier by policy measures that facilitated breaking the associative pact by reducing the psychological costs of leaving – from creating homogeneous areas for prisoners serving sentences for terrorist offences to extending some reductions in sentences to all those who publicly declared that they would leave armed struggle (della Porta 1993).

Crisis in underground organizations was in fact accelerated by some award measures provided by the 1980 antiterrorism law, which varied from nonpunishment to reduction of sentences by half and nonapplication of aggravating circumstances for members of terrorist organizations who had chosen to collaborate with the investigating authorities. It was, at least on the surface, particularly thanks to these confessions that the state machinery managed to achieve its first consistent victories in the fight against terrorism.

Many members of armed groups benefited from the possibilities offered by these legislative measures, thereby breaking the pact of allegiance to the organization. According to data provided by the Ministry of Justice, on expiration of the terms fixed in the law on *dissociazione* (which was scheduled to last 120 days and then extended by another 120), 389 people had benefited from it: 78 as

"great repenters," 134 as "repenters," and 177 as "*dissociati.*" With few exceptions, activists of underground left-wing groups in prison successively and in
various ways publicly declared the end of armed struggle in Italy. The beginning
of the 1990s saw a moving away from terrorism by Prima Linea activists (who
disbanded their organization) and those involved in the so-called investigations
of 7 April (who published *The Manifesto*, also known as the Document of the
51). Shortly afterward came the statement by the founders of the Red Brigades,
Franceschini and Ognibene, who, after a December 1983 hunger strike to
protest conditions in special prisons, declared that the historical phase of
armed struggle was over. This decision was echoed by other activists from the
historical nucleus, including Curcio, who, in January 1987, issued a statement
claiming that "the social battle of the 1970s is historically exhausted" and
requesting a "political and social way out of the cycle of violence of the
1970s" (quoted in Gallinari 2006: 329). Lamenting political errors and admitting defeat, another nucleus of the BR announced, "Today, October 1988, the
Red Brigades overlap *de facto* with the political prisoners of the Red Brigades"
(ibid.: 340).

   This dissolution process was encouraged by the creation of homogeneous
areas in prisons, that is, areas where prisoners from underground organizations
who publicly distanced themselves from the armed struggle could assemble with
those with whom they considered themselves ideologically (or emotionally)
close, thus resulting in more favorable detention conditions. The project began
in San Vittore Prison in Milan at the request of a group of "political prisoners
who – according to one of them – no longer have anything to do with the armed
organizations, not even in individual cases, and are therefore all 'exes'; these
people are united by favorable conditions for remembering" (Life History no. 3:
75). Shortly afterward, in the Roman prison of Rebibbia, prisoners in the
homogeneous areas issued the Document of the 51 (according to one activist,
"the first document of political *dissociazione* in Italy" [ibid.: 281]). One of the
founders of the BR, Prospero Gallinari, had this to say about the granting of
homogeneous areas:

In prison, this campaign had devastating effects. Not least because it came up against
what the *Partito Guerriglia* were encouraging – they preached a head-on collision ...
doubts spread. Many friends disappeared overnight, headed for the homogeneous areas
quickly put at their disposal by the Ministry to foster defections. This situation quickly led
to dialectic madness and internal contradictions. It was enough just to have given the
judge something, a minimum, not glorious certainly but all things considered only a small
concession, to be declared enemies. (2006: 279)

   Exit options can have different results according to the support for violence in
the surrounding environment. In the case of the ETA, for instance, various
attempts at negotiation and temporary ceasefires were cut short because of a
lack of reciprocal trust, as well as, on the side of the ETA leaders, the perception
that a basis of support for armed struggle still existed. Half a dozen attempts to

negotiate, often accompanied by ceasefires, developed inconsistently and eventually failed. In 1978, the ETA military (ETA-M) declared its willingness to cease fire, but only under the five conditions designated in the KAS platform, which was set up by radical nationalist actors. Some first negotiations between the ETA-M and socialist governments took place during the Algiers talks, between 1986 and 1989, but they collapsed, notwithstanding a ceasefire declared by the ETA (and then broken off). Another short ceasefire was proclaimed by the ETA-M in 1992, after most political parties had agreed on anti-ETA pacts and after Herri Batasuna (HB), a party similar to the ETA, had expressed self-criticism of its reliance on a military solution. Between 1996 and 2004, the center-right governments led by José Maria Aznar took a confrontational stand, not only against the ETA but also against the Basque ethnic movement in general. Starting in 1997, twenty-three members of the HB leadership were arrested. The prisoners' rights association Gestora Pro-Amnistia and the youth *abertzale* (patriotic) organization Jarrai were criminalized, along with the KAS, whereas two newspapers (*Egin* and *Egunkaria*) were outlawed (Muro 2008: 168). In 1998, the pact of Lizarra, signed by the PNV, HB, and other Basque organizations, pushed the ETA to declare a ceasefire, which was intended to give those groups space to maneuver to achieve more autonomy.

The ensuing Zurich negotiations in 1999 were again immediately broken off, and the ETA resumed its violent activities in 2000. In 2002, the Organic Law of Political Parties was voted in, causing the HB to be suspended by the Supreme Court (only to reappear under another name at the next election). Opportunities for negotiation reopened under the socialist government led by José Luis Rodriguez Zapatero. A peace process was initiated in 2005, when the Congress of Deputies voted to allow the government to open talks with the ETA, with the condition that it renounce the use of violence. In 2006, the ETA proclaimed a unilateral ceasefire. Negotiations reopened but were broken off again; in December, the ETA had already resumed violent action with an attack against the Madrid airport. New negotiations started and a new ceasefire was declared in 2011, but no final agreement has been reached.

As regards the strategy of offering exit options to those who leave the underground, attempts have been made in Yemen and Saudi Arabia, among other countries, to develop a dialogue between arrested Islamist leaders and religious leaders, sheiks, and scholars, often involving family members as mediators. Yemen's Committee for Dialogue was launched in 2002 as a way to address "the need to engage in dialogue with young men from Afghanistan and other Islamists because they held violent beliefs which could translate into violent extremism" (Boucek, Beg, and Horgan 2009: 184). Even suspected leaders of al-Qaeda engaged in a dialogue with ulemas on the Qur'an and the Sunnah. Eventually, 364 prisoners were released after they had participated in the program and renounced their previous beliefs. In Saudi Arabia, the Counselling Program involves prisoners (who are considered only marginally involved in clandestine activities) in a sort of reeducation through discussions with an

274 Clandestine Political Violence

advisory committee that range from short, two-hour sessions to "long study sessions" of up to six weeks (Boucek 2009). Theological dialogue has also been used as a rehabilitation instrument in Malaysia, Singapore, and Indonesia (Abuza 2009). The efficacy of these programs is, however, still being debated, especially as they were often combined with harsh repression that thwarted the development of relations of trust.

ORGANIZATIONAL DISBANDMENT

Generally speaking, it has been observed that organizational characteristics and paths can provoke forceful abandonment: an organization may disband, split, or expel some members. Particularly dramatic or rapid organizational changes can lead to the defection of those who were most strongly identified with the original model. For example, an old activist linked the crisis of the French Communist Party in a mining basin with the entry of new activists: "Young people who want to change everything, who have destroyed everything, discipline, class struggle, who wanted to teach us about activism, us, with all we went through" (Leclercq 2005: 149). In the Dutch peace movement, some defections were related to the very success of mobilizations against the deployment of the NATO nuclear missile, which had led activists from other movements with different practices and motivations from those of the original nucleus to join the group (Klandermans 2005). Radical Right activists have also mentioned disillusionment with group life as a motivating factor for defection (Bjørgo 2009). Generally speaking, where there are internal conflicts, defections are often motivated by an ideological disagreement over the right direction to take and by deteriorating relations and worsening internal sociality generally, which are seen by supporters to be the end of harmony (Leclerqu 2005, on the French Communist Party).

In fact, at some point in their history underground organizations often either disband or resurface. This tends to happen through critiques of the mechanisms of organizational compartmentalization, action militarization, and ideological encapsulation that we have observed. In particular, many activists in underground organizations refer to their disappointment in perceiving that their group was changing from its form under the original project. In the words of a former leader of the BR: "It's as if the organisation followed an independent path of laws that are not its own and become at that moment the laws of defeat and are therefore also determined by rivals" (Life History no. 27: 4). Alfredo Buonavita, one of the founders of the BR, who was imprisoned in 1974, spoke of his "disgust as regards a practice that was no longer suitable for me in simple human terms," noting that "a part always continues to want to break with this thing and yet there is an inability and impossibility to reach an agreement" (Life History no. 5: 148–9).

There was in fact a perception of failure of the compartmentalized model. The organization's image was being transformed, while arrests were making relationships with other members increasingly impersonal:

This organisation that is tearing itself apart for not providing solutions to problems and that can't find a way out of this impasse.... Nearly all the people I knew were in prison, that is the people I had started out with were no longer there, there were no more links, there was nothing, everyone ended up in prison ... at that moment I understood what had happened – the fact that really we had nothing to present, nothing to propose. (Life History no. 27: 56)

As the armed groups evolved, the increasing brutality of their actions ended up disgusting their own activists. Latent tensions exploded in the face of precipitating events.[2] Former supporters of the Italian clandestine groups recalled episodes they considered particularly cruel. Valerio Morucci, leader of the Roman column of the BR, claimed that his crisis began with the killing of Aldo Moro[3] and subsequently of the worker and trade unionist Guido Rossa, who was accused of denouncing a BR activist – "the BR meanwhile were pursuing their path. And, obviously, I no longer shared it. The last straw was the killing of Guido Rossa.... I wrote that the murder of Guido Rossa had been a serious mistake. All of us in the BR thought so – except the people who killed him." The BR "just continued killing and we couldn't take it anymore" (2004: 203).

Similarly, repeated experiences with the death of comrades lead to emotional shocks. Thus a former activist for an underground organization recalls his "immense pain" and "indescribable loss" over the death of two of his comrades during a robbery:

A month passed before I was arrested and in that month the only clear memory that I have is that there was a lot to correct. The doubts I had before exploded. The impact between motivations and reality produced a severe, decisive crisis that I live alone and communicate to the group. The group, in inverted commas obviously, unravelled and dispersed and my crisis was very obvious. (Life History no. 9: 279)

Among the organizational developments presented as being the most difficult to justify are internal vendettas and murders. Former BR member Valerio Morucci, speaking of "massacre," wrote, "When the Revolution goes to wrack and ruin, gangs appear whose initial political characteristics are surpassed by individual resentments or even, if you look more closely, individual neuroses" (Morucci 2004: 218). The massacre of which Morucci spoke happened in prisons, including the killing of Giorgio Soldati and Ennio Di Rocco, one at Cuneo Prison and the other at Trani Prison, by their comrades: "All young, all kids. Killed by those who should have been their brothers. They were boys that few or no one knew.... Yes, this is the darkest day" (2004: 219). A former PL supporter recalled the killing of a presumed informer as "the

---

[2] As Bert Klandermans observed when comparing abandonment paths in union and peace movements, "insufficient gratifications, combined with declining commitment, are translated into a growing intention to defect. It is at this point that a critical event influences the balance and produces the exiting" (Klandermans 2005: 95).

[3] Morucci had participated in Moro's kidnapping before unsuccessfully opposing his murder: "A prisoner couldn't be killed. It was an abomination" (Morucci 2004: 145).

element that makes me say I don't even see them anymore" (Life History no. 3: 73). Similarly, Gallinari commented on the killing of two sworn guards during a robbery by the Brigate Rosse Partito Guerriglia, a killing carried out to highlight news of a presumed betrayal of one of their supporters: "21 October 1982, the news that came over the radio is totally absurd ... it is totally shocking. Doubts about the political position and combative practices of the *Partito Guerriglia* had only increased amongst us in the last few months. But such an implosion had never entered our heads" (2006: 281).

Similarly, in the ETA as well as in religious fundamentalist groups, organizational splits were motivated by disagreements on levels and forms of violence. In the ETA, as aforementioned (see Chapter 5), the factions nearer to a class discourse and mass intervention in the factory tended to be more pragmatic. Similarly, in the case of religious groups, splits occurred as some groups rejected increases in violence. As Horgan recalls, "a tactical issue, in combination with tension in the relationship with the leaders, lay at the heart of the high-profile disengagement of Mohammed Nassir Bin Abbas from Jemaah Islamiyah" (2009: 23). Bin Abbas, the chief of the military training section, disagreed with the targeting of noncombatant civilians.

INDIVIDUAL DE-ENCAPSULATION

Not only are the histories of clandestine groups short, but individual histories in the underground also tend to be limited to a few months or years and also tend to vary enormously in terms of degree of commitment – only a small percentage of members commit crimes against people. We can observe, in fact, mechanisms of *individual de-encapsulation*. Research on paths taken to abandoning political participation has to take into account the structure of social relationships in which an individual acts. As McCauley observed, "crime is increased by weak connections with conventional others and by strong connections with criminal others. Conversely, increasing connections with conventional others and decreasing connections with criminal others should reduce the likelihood that individuals will turn to crime, or increase the likelihood of desistance for current offenders" (2008: 287). Research on the American peace movement (Downton and Wehr 1997), on solidarity with the southern hemisphere in Switzerland (Passy 2005), or on youth gangs (Bjørgo and Horgan 2009) has linked long-term commitment with not only socialization toward some values but also connections among the three main spheres of life: family, professional, and political. Persistent activists are those who manage to interweave into their life projects commitment to a movement, an emotional life, and a professional career. Activist identities are also connected to emotional support. Vice versa, defection is more likely when the three spheres of politics, family, and work become more distant from one another or, as research on youth gangs indicated, when an individual finds suitable affective substitutes for his or her closest friends that belong to those gangs. On an individual level, exit is facilitated by the development of new circles of support that are sympathetic toward possible signs of abandonment.

The difficulty of leaving is connected to the intensity of previous commitment. Many activists describe the experience of ending their political support as being particularly painful. One activist from the Italian *autonomia* recalls that "it was a devastating experience, to go back home, to give up, when at the same time some of our comrades, who were recognized as the most generous, the most available ones, they were instead imprisoned, or they were killing other people" (quoted in Sommier 2005: 178). A sense of solidarity certainly slows down the process of moving away from an organization, especially as long as the only possible option is to choose between "repentance" – and denouncing comrades – or unshakable loyalty to the organization. In the words of one former activist, "you knew that these weren't your BR anymore but this is disappointing and admitting disappointment is always hard if you've dedicated your life to something.... It's a very difficult individual decision. I thought about killing myself twice" (Life History no. 7: 10–11). In fact, for a long time the widespread perception in Italy was that

putting yourself in the hands of the state means two things: either being there as a poor lonely, isolated devil leading a horrible life forever because you're isolated from the other detainees – and the guards get their revenge for what happened to them before because you didn't have a very nice past. Or, instead you decide to send people to prison, to collaborate, to "repent" in inverted commas and then indeed you find a place where you can live and where you're protected.... So however many splits there were, on the one hand there's a solidarity and friendship that binds you together and the necessity to face things together to live in prison, and on the other hand the impossibility of a political departure from the organization. (Life History no. 5: 120)

As it does in keeping commitments, solidarity toward a small group of comrades from the organization also influences the process of separation from armed struggle in prison. Many interviewees said that "you don't leave alone," claiming that "they waited for the others" so as not to "tear apart internal relations with the other detainees" and that they "waited for a process of collective maturity" to "reduce the weight of recognising mistakes" (quoted in della Porta 1990: 279–83). With regard to his initial position of refusing all self-criticism, one PL supporter declared,

It was very hard because substantially I thought that what was left of this element of cohesion and solidarity should hold firm.... I felt, yes, that I had to save this collective movement at all costs, had to save these relationships at all costs.... For me, they were relationships from '72 and '73, I mean, it was a life we had lived together, in all our choices. (Life History no. 26: 31–3 passim)

As Morucci wrote, his departure from the underground organization was delayed by the fact that "I couldn't yet leave the BR without also leaving behind my revolutionary faith.... And this is not an easy journey for a communist. Precisely because, going beyond the ideology, it has been a faith" (2004: 193).

In this regard, it is worth noting that, despite reaching a critical position on armed struggle and a significant reflection on the past, many of the interviewees expressed an overall positive final judgment of their experience. This also allowed self-respect to be maintained and avoided an identity crisis. Let us cite just a few examples of a common position expressed in most of the life histories collected: "I believe that it would be very bad if, having reached this point, one simply said 'I've done a lot of stupid things, I've always been wide of the mark, look how stupid I've been, now that's enough, turn the page, I don't want to hear any more about it'" (Life History no. 28: 98). "Despite thousands of mistakes and contradictions, I disown absolutely nothing of those years; they were and are part and parcel of my life as a woman, I who has never succeeded in accepting things as they were but who has tried, through mistakes too, to contribute to changing them" (Life History no. 24: 54).

In this sense, abandonment paths are thwarted by different attitudes toward failure. According to Pizzorno, in the event of failure in the pursuit of collective objectives, reactions vary from denial of defeat to recognition of weakness and simultaneously an exploitation of the sociality between members of the group. In other cases, "some members of the group, who don't believe or don't accept weakness, continue to conceive life itself as dedicated to the same ideas as those of the original movement, and make it the demonstration of an individual morality. We call this, the testimony case" (Pizzorno 2007).

Militant enclosure could, however, be reversed in *militant disclosure*. The beginning of awareness of the weakness of the armed struggle project leads to a transformation of the meaning of formerly accepted behavior. The use of violence "became more serious when it became useless, and it therefore became a useless scattering of blood while before it was part of a context that justified it" (Life History no. 19: 74), or, in the words of another, "when the revolutionary programme loses credibility, the dead are still murdered dead" (Life History no. 24: 60). Following arrest, the prospect of a long prison sentence becomes much more dramatic when a person admits the weakness of his own life project and, consequently, ends the illusion that liberation can come from the outside: "It is impossible for a person who was ready to undergo a long prison sentence or even death to construct a communist society, and when he realises that an irreversible reverse process is happening, i.e. when the political defeat is confirmed by the facts, to pay such a high price so easily" (Life History no. 24: 59–60). Thus, slowly, the perception of breaking the bonds of solidarity due to growing, if limited, "repentance" is added to the growing awareness of crisis in the underground organization, which is accentuated by the impossibility of resisting arrests and recruiting from new social movements.

Scholars have also studied emotional characteristics to explain abandonment because of so-called burnout, which is linked to the stress of a commitment that is too demanding in terms of time or emotional investment. Not surprisingly, this reason for abandoning an organization was noted in groups working in the field of AIDS and especially among those who were motivated by personal experience with the illness (Fillieule and Broqua 2005: 206ff.), as well as in the radical Right (Bjørgo 2009). Supporters of underground organizations also mentioned burnout. They repeatedly noted the amount of energy dedicated to the organization on a daily basis, not least as an impediment to critical reflection on one's own choice – the "impossibility not only for me but also I believe of the situation of being able to stop for a moment and say no" (Life History no. 21: 43). Another Italian activist recalls "incredible tiredness; at that time I injured my leg, I was hurt, I was in bed for two months and I seemed to see things clearly.... I really had this impression that I could stop and look in from the outside ... this self-nurturing mechanism" (Life History no. 29: 45). However, burnout can also speed up the process of separation. Two Italian activists recall in very similar words a sense of almost relief over the arrest that interrupted an activity that had been too intense:

We woke up at 5 o'clock ... to do reconnaissance [obtaining information on a possible target] ... then I couldn't go home, I had to meet people, so I had to be in Rome all day; then I went home in the evening, we had to do documents, type, do a load of other things, then we went to bed at about midnight. At that time, I was also having a relationship with the person living with me, we would chat a bit, do other things, this and that, it was one o'clock, at five I had to be up again. I got between three and four hours sleep a night ... when they knocked on my door that morning, my first thought was "I knew it"; the second was "thank goodness, more sleep." (Life History no. 1: 75–6)

I dedicated all my free time to the organisation, I worked eight hours a day, at the end of the day I got the car, I went to Torino, kept going until 3 o'clock in the morning.... In fact, during the first few days in prison, I actually thought "ah, finally I can rest." (Life History no. 17: 31)

In conclusion, legislation oriented to favor the abandoning of underground organizations is only effective if it takes into account these bonds that change depending on the level of individual commitment and the type of motivation (instrumental, emotional, or ideological). The different stages of departure are influenced by emotional intensity, the level and type of benefits, multiplicity of roles, and potential conflicts (Ebaugh 1988). These elements can favor departure when they allow an activist to keep some aspects of his or her initial point of view and therefore leave room for approval within the individual's circle.

LEAVING CLANDESTINITY: CONCLUSIONS

For underground organizations, as for other organizations, political or non-political, the exit process is complex, containing as it does a change in both the life project itself and perceptions of surrounding reality.

By focusing on the process of abandoning commitment to left-wing underground organizations active in Italy during 1970s and halfway through the following decade, I have suggested an interpretive model that takes into account the reversal of the causal mechanisms I have singled out as causing escalation. As regards environmental conditions, explanations for departure from terrorism dwell prevailingly on the efficiency of repressive policies. However, many studies on radicalization processes have indicated that hard repression can produce perverse effects by reinforcing individuals' choices and increasing solidarity in the outside community. In the Italian case, repressive so-called emergency policies were interwoven with the apparently more effective policies of facilitating departure through reduction of prison sentences and through the creation of homogeneous areas in prisons. Whereas repressive policies operate with a view to increasing the price of staying committed, rewarding the open abandonment of armed struggle reduces the price of leaving (especially the emotional and cognitive costs), allowing collective paths toward changes in solidarity and identification. Again from the environmental point of view, I have also observed the effects stemming from a change in forms of collective action, resulting in a growing stigmatization of the most violent forms. Defeats and isolation also fuel tactical disagreements and therefore create stress and tensions for the militants.

This interpretation underlines the political dimension of violence and therefore the persistent (if reduced) ability of activists to assess the effects (both military and nonmilitary) of their actions. As Horgan observed, "factors contributing to psychological disengagement include ... disillusionment arising from the incongruence between the initial ideals and fantasies that shaped a person's initial involvement and their subsequent experiences of what is entailed by involvement – in other words, the mismatch between the fantasy and the reality" (2009: 21–2). For al-Qaeda or IRA members, as for those of the Italian underground, evidence of criminal behavior or lies among fellow members of the underground group produced signs, both small and large, of psychological uneasiness.

Environmental conditions interact with organizational evolution. Choosing to go underground implies progressive isolation and the militarization of armed organizations, involving increasingly bloody action and elitist, closed ideologies. At the same time, their activists tend to dismiss perceptions of defeat, reducing the impact of outside information sources and strengthening emotional investment in the armed group. However, such dismissal does not appear to be complete. In particular, growing fractionalization and sectarianism in underground groups created crises in emotional relationships and reciprocal solidarity. Some events (from the killing of presumed informers to the most brutal terrorist attacks) often act as precipitating factors on already-existing paths toward change.

Individual perceptions and motivations therefore filter the effects of the environmental and organizational changes on activist careers. Because they often entered underground organizations at a very young age, after being socialized into politics in phases of profound radicalization of social conflict, Italian militants (of the Left and also of the Right) often reported burnout processes, especially during periods when they were on the run. Above all, however, exit paths from underground organizations appear to be influenced by the social relationships of individuals.

Departure is facilitated if there is a wide circle of support, and activism in underground groups normally restricts these circles. Joining racist groups implies "inclusion and socialization into a new and stigmatized community, and severance of ties to the normal community outside" (Bjørgo 2009: 33). As research on the radical Right indicated, the more stigmatized the groups, the fewer the opportunities to find a way out through reconstituting alternative affective circles, even though the perceived costs of participation are also higher (ibid.). As a radical Right activist declared, "as soon as it was known to others that I was with the nationalist groups, I was branded" (ibid.: 35).

However, leaving the underground becomes easier when collective paths of exiting are created. Additionally, new affective relations might then help in breaking cognitive closure, pushing the militants to change their construction of external reality as well as their assessment of the morality or immorality of their actions.

10

Clandestine Political Violence

Conclusions

Research on political violence, which has bloomed in recent years, has offered numerous explanations of the structural preconditions for, organizational characteristics of, and individual predispositions toward the development of clandestine political violence. In particular, literature on terrorism has linked it to a broad list of pathologies. Although rich in case studies, which are sometimes of good quality, terrorism studies as a field has been strongly criticized for the inadequacy of its sources of information, as well as its lack of theorization and predominant orientation toward counterterrorism. Social movement studies, which instead offers concepts and theories for the study of the evolution of repertoires of protest, has only rarely addressed violence, especially in its more radical forms. This volume aimed at filling this gap by focusing on what I have defined as clandestine political violence. In this conclusion, I first synthesize my empirical results and then discuss some potential extensions of these results.

In considering clandestine political violence as an extreme form of violence perpetrated by political groups active in the underground, I have looked at the field of social movements for inspiration. Following that literature, I have considered the evolution of violence as embedded in social and political conflicts, influenced by the political opportunities available for elites and challengers as well as the material and cognitive resources available to contenders. Building on some important innovations in the area, I suggested that violence could not be satisfactorily explained by looking exclusively at structural conditions. Clandestine forms of violence, in particular, are embraced by tiny minorities that react with radicalization to conditions that lead others toward moderation.

Without claiming to explain clandestine political violence, I singled out some causal mechanisms that I found at work in the different cases, linking macro, meso, and micro levels of action. Rather than emphasizing teleological or behavioral explanations, I have built on what Charles Tilly (2003) called a *relational* perspective. In all my cases, radicalization processes happened during

the interactions of various collective actors, including social movement organizations as well as state institutions. These actors engaged in changing relations
of cooperation and competition.

I have also emphasized the *constructed* nature of the process, as contextual
conditions are filtered through the perceptions of such conditions – the "attribution of opportunities" in McAdam, Tarrow, and Tilly's (2001) language. In
all my cases, I noted how clandestine groups perceived that the spaces for
peaceful protest were closing down and also that conditions conducive to violent
action were opening up.

Moreover, I have stressed that violence developed during long-lasting processes: conditions were not only preexisting but also formed in action. In this
sense, violence is an *emergent* phenomenon, reproducing in action the conditions for its very development. Transformative events feed escalation through
the constitution of radical identities, as well as by forcing actors to take positions
(Sewell 1996).

My attempt at global comparisons – which I defined as based on a small-N
comparison of critical cases, chosen on the basis of a most-different research
design – brought me to the search not for root causes but for causal mechanisms,
as chains of interactions during which structural conditions are filtered and
produce effects but are also themselves transformed. No doubt, the degree of
economic development, democratic qualities, and national cultures vary broadly
among the historical cases I have analyzed, which include illustrations of left-
wing, right-wing, ethnonationalist, and religious types of clandestine political
violence. However, my analysis has also shown some similarities in the mechanisms that underlie the radicalization of political conflicts and sustain clandestine political violence. I have defined these mechanisms as competitive
escalation, escalating policing, organizational compartmentalization, action
militarization, ideological encapsulation, networking into clandestinity, and
militant enclosure, and I have devoted a chapter to each concept.

Escalating policing is the first mechanism I singled out. Protest, as a challenge
to public order, normally brings about interactions between protestors with
police, who are charged with defending the public order. Strategies of protest
policing, however, vary broadly. The police can privilege the right to demonstrate over disturbances to public order and thus tolerate minor violations, or
they can strictly enforce law and order. They can rely on softer or harder tactics
when they intervene, using persuasion or force. Their intervention can be not
only more or less brutal but also more or less selective. As Tilly (1978) suggested,
regimes are distinguished by a variable mix of facilitation of some groups and
forms of participation and repression of others.

In all of the cases studied, in a process of double diffusion (della Porta and
Tarrow 2012), the radicalization of the forms of protest interacted with repressive styles that were not only brutal but also often diffuse, hitting not only violent
militants but also nonviolent ones. Tactical interactions developed through
reciprocal adaptation to innovative turns, such that each party's choices were

influenced by those of the adversary (McAdam 1983). Violence spread when the state was perceived to have overreacted to the emergence of protest – as was the case in Italy, when the student movement and the labor movement protest signaled a growing intensity of conflicts; this process was even more evident in Franco's Spain, when labor protests met ethnic revival, and in the authoritarian regimes in the Middle East, which reacted strongly to the so-called religious awakening.

In all of the cases, in fact, everyday experiences of physical confrontation with police brought about an image of an unfair state that was ready to use brutal force against its citizens. The more the repression was perceived as indiscriminate, the greater the people's solidarity with – or at least the tolerance of – the militant groups: this was the case, in particular, in Franco's Spain and under the authoritarian regime of Mubarak in Egypt or the Israeli occupation in Palestine. These types of police actions delegitimized not only the police but also the state, which the police claimed to serve. Moreover, perceptions of injustice increased when the state was seen as taking sides, repressing some groups' violent behaviors but tolerating the violence of others – as was the case in Italy, where the state was seen as supporting the radical Right. In action, repression created subcultures sympathetic to violence, often resuscitating old myths; thus violence itself started to be perceived as a resource in the internal competition within the social movement family. Escalation was facilitated by not only indiscriminate but also inconsistent repression. For the Italian right-wingers as well as for the Islamists in Saudi Arabia, feelings of disconcert were created by what was considered as a betrayal by a state that had been seen as somewhat supportive. In all cases, repression was perceived as unjust (Gamson, Fireman, and Rytina 1982).

In fact, repression produced transformative events (Beissinger 2002; della Porta 2008b; Sewell 1996). Left-wing, right-wing, ethnonationalist, and religious militants alike recalled brutal charges of demonstrators or the killing of comrades as fueling intense emotions of identification with a community of fighters and the designation of the state as an enemy. Repression created and recreated martyrs and myths, which justified violence as defense and/or revenge. Read within a broader narrative of oppression and resistance, heavy repression was framed as an indicator that there was no other way out. This led to, at the same time, mistrust in peaceful means of protest and also confidence in the effectiveness of violence.

Furthermore, the interactions in the streets were then embedded in broader relations that involved various actors: from political parties to interest groups, and from social movement organizations to opinion makers. Protesting and policing became bones of contention, resulting in intense debates on the limits on protest rights and on forms of police repression. In short, those debates addressed the metaquestion of the meaning of democracy, in particular the development of civil rights versus law-and-order coalitions (della Porta 1995). These conflicts often led to legitimation of some forms of protest and stigmatization of violent ones.

However, the process of depolarization had different timings, twists, and turns in different cases; the differences were related not so much to the class, ethnic, or religious identities of the violent actors but rather to the characteristics of the political regimes they addressed. In fact, the escalation of violence went much farther in nondemocratic countries. In authoritarian Franco's Spain and in the Middle East, hard repression was usually unable – at least in the short term – to demobilize protests, contributing instead to a radicalization that was all the more challenging because it went along with increasing popular support, which often included a sort of temporary territorial control of some areas by the rebels. However, as the Spanish case indicates, violence can develop as opportunities are opening up, within a process of liberalization and transition, as a means of negotiation and/or as a reaction to the perceived frustration of hopes for a quicker and deeper democratization process.

I also focused on the mechanism of competitive escalation. Social movement studies have linked radicalization to the development of protest cycles. Whereas waves of protest often bring about a normalization of once-unconventional forms of protest, as well as a civilization of its form, an immediate outcome is often the development of some violent forms of action. These tend to change along the cycle: primarily occasional and defensive in the beginning, they become increasingly organized and ritualized. Toward the end of the cycle, although the number and size of protest events decline, clandestine forms of violence develop. One of the reasons I identified for this escalation is organizational competition within dense milieus of social movements, social movement families (made up of social movements that share some general orientations and are often allied), and also broader social movement sectors involving a plurality of social movement families.

The protest cycles from which the clandestine organizations examined grew originated not only from within existing collective actors but also through internal contestation: the PCI for the Italian left-wing groups, the MSI for their right-wing counterparts, the PNV for the ETA, and the MBs for the Islamist groups were such original actors, which the emergent social movements contested as too tame, if not traitorous.

Although protest cycles bring about the emergence of large numbers of social movement organizations that tend to cooperate with one another during the peak of protest, the decline of mobilization produces conflicts about the best strategies and tactics to be used to overcome the perceived crises. On the left as on the right and in the case of the ETA and Islamist fundamentalism, we saw internal strategic struggles, which ended with the more or less rapid and intense radicalization of one part of the group in question and the moderation of another. Additionally, cycles of protest stimulated the emergence of counter-movements, often involving physical conflicts between militants of different fronts.

In all of the covered cases, experimentation with violent tactics emerged from attempts to outbid the other groups – attracting the residual militants – and through small everyday adaptations to the tactics of adversaries. Organizational competition influenced the radicalization processes. The choice to use radical forms and action was a sort of "slight product differentiation (offering marginally different goals) and, especially, tactical differentiation" (McCarthy and Zald 1973: 6). Addressing different constituencies, various movement organizations targeted their strategic choices to make themselves more attractive to their audience. Especially during the declining phases of mobilization, violence became a trademark, designed to attract attention in the radicalized movement groups.

In these adaptations of practices, activists were slowly socialized to violence, while at the same time the organizations adapted their structures – for instance, through the creation of marshal bodies, devoted first to defense but later to attack. In all cases, structures that specialized in violent repertoires developed slowly, during fights with political adversaries and the police, until occasions of violence or repression, in particular, pushed their members underground. Whereas in the Italian case street fights involved left- against right-wingers, in the Basque Country ethnonationalists competed (although not necessarily physically) with a class definition of the conflicts, and in the case of the Islamists, harsh (sometimes physical) struggles pitted left-wing social movement organizations against nationalist and religious ones.

The activation of militant networks is another mechanism I have singled out. Rather than psychological characteristics and beyond heterogeneous social background, what militants who joined clandestine organizations had in common was their belonging to networks of friends-comrades. Social science literature on social movements (and other subjects as well) has time and again stressed the role of social networks for recruitment in contentious politics. The cases examined fit well in Doug McAdam's model of recruitment to high-risk and high-cost activism (1986: especially 68–71). According to this model, families or other socialization agencies play a role in making individuals receptive to certain political ideas; when individuals who have thus become politically sensitive encounter political activists, they are then motivated to become involved in an initial low-cost and low-risk activism. Under conditions of "biographical availability" – that is, for instance, for young people – "these 'safe' forays into activism may have longer-range consequences ... for they place the new recruit 'at risk' of being drawn into more costly forms of participation through the cyclical process of integration and resocialization" (McAdam 1986: 69). For the activists in the groups discussed herein, as for the Freedom Summer activists McAdam studied, this process involved an increasing integration into activist networks that formed a "culture of solidarities," as "a cultural expression that arises within the wider culture, yet which is emergent in its embodiment of oppositional practices and meanings" (Fantasia 1988: 17). Cultures of solidarity emerge "in those moments when the customary practices of daily life are suspended and crisis requires a new repertoire of behavior, associational ties, and valuations" (ibid.: 14). For the activists, the reality of everyday life – the "reality par excellence," in which "the tension of consciousness is highest" (Berger and Luckmann 1966: 21) – created the conditions for a gradual acceptance of violence as a political means.

If networks are important for most types of activities, the challenge is to specify which networks are conducive to commitment in clandestine organizations. In this text, the four types of clandestine violence differ in terms of the relevance of the specific movement milieus – leftist, rightist, ethnonationalist, and religious, respectively – from which they derived their recruits.

However, there were also similarities. In all cases, the organizations recruited in groups that had already undergone a process of radicalization, and blocs of recruits often came from a process of splitting within the most radical wings of a social movement family. Intensive affective relations were typical of these nets. In all cases, networks were not only exploited but also produced by the radical groups. As Elisabeth Wood (2003) observed on different forms of political commitments, social networks are created in action. This also explains why, in all four types of clandestine organizations, I found two (or even more) generations.

The first generation grew inside long-standing social movement traditions, nurtured in the red subculture of the Left, in nostalgic milieus in the case of neofascists, in nationalist communities in the case of the ETA, and in specific religious enclaves in the case of Islamic fundamentalists. Family ties were particularly relevant, sometimes materially but more often symbolically. Recruitment or, better, the foundation of clandestine organizations proceeded mainly within the political environments in which the militants had been socialized at a very young age.

Militant networks developed in small and radical groupings in which political commitment and friendship mutually strengthened each other. Relays were constituted in action and influenced the perceptions of the activists as well as intensifying their emotional attachment, and therefore the peer-group pressure. Grievance and greed were not (predominant) preexisting predispositions; rather, they increased in action.

Once active, the clandestine organizations themselves contributed to the constitution of radicalized milieus, from which they then recruited a second generation of activists. When the founders were arrested or forced into exile, new and more radical recruits took over their roles. They grew during the escalation to which clandestine organizations contributed and were socialized to violence very early on, almost skipping nonviolent forms of politics. These second generations were described as more violence prone.

Once underground, clandestine organizations underwent a process of implosion, in which interactions with the outside were reduced. To illustrate this process, I singled out mechanisms of organizational compartmentalization, action radicalization, and ideological encapsulation.

In terms of organizational compartmentalization, the organizational structures of the four types of clandestine groups showed some differences as well as some similarities. Clandestine organizations of each type took inspiration from the organizational repertoires (Clemens 1996) that characterized their social movement families, adapting them to a hostile context. This produced a different balance of hierarchical and network structures, as well as different functional internal divisions that reflected, for example, the importance of the factory for the left-wing groups or of religious issues for the Islamists. In this sense, ideas and interests interacted in decision making. In addition, collective structures tended to reflect the organization's size in terms of members and resources.

However, the groups exhibited a similar cross-type evolution toward compartmentalized structures. Faced with rising repression and declining support, the clandestine organizations became more hierarchical, giving up on attempts to host large meetings and increasing the (formal) power of a few leaders. Like in organized crime, however, the aspiration to effective centralization and hierarchical control met with a reality that was more centrifugal. To begin with, clandestinity imposed a reduction of the role of organizational structures open to sympathizers and of the role of legal (rather than clandestine) militants, while the various cells became increasingly independent from one another and also difficult to control from above. In this process, the very difficulty of intervening in social conflicts increased the relevance of the military over the political organizational bodies. But being military oriented did not mean being obedient: in fact, in all of the cases factions formed from and fought against one another, in a never-ending process of splitting into ever-tinier units and, sometimes, bloody internal purges.

Similar remarks apply to the analysis of the next mechanism: action militarization. In this case as well, the comparative analysis has shown that, when choosing targets and forms of action, clandestine organizations followed some normative preferences. Action strategies were indeed not only assessed instrumentally but also constrained by group norms. The shift from actions against property to actions against people, and then from wounding to killing, produced tensions among the left-wing radicals. In the radical Right, massacres of randomly selected people were stigmatized by a new generation of militants. In the ETA, this was the case with bombings in public places, especially when issued warnings did not succeed in avoiding victims. For the Islamist groups as well, the killing of civilians, particularly fellow Muslims, raised opposition. In all groups, creating victims among people considered as innocent (or at least noncommitted) led to internal criticism – as did violence used internally, to punish withdrawal or "betrayal." Suicide missions, even if they might have been effective, were in fact used by only a few groups in extremely radicalized conflicts; for most groups, such tactics were not even in the realm of possibility.

However, I also noted a process of growing detachment from action aimed at propaganda and an increasing tendency toward action oriented to mere organizational survival. As repression increased organizational isolation, as well as the acceptance of violence, the so-called repressive apparatuses (police, army, judges, and so on) became the main targets of clandestine action. The logic of action became increasingly military and decreasingly political. In fact, the normative constraints against the most brutal forms of action were overcome as a result of the militants' search for a certain type of reputation as soldiers and heroes. In a vicious circle, however, this reputation started to damage rather than advantage the clandestine groups. Often (in the case of the ETA and especially in Egypt), territorial control meant attempting to force the population into certain types of behavior, as well as at extracting resources, and this in turn reduced support. As they became increasingly isolated, the clandestine organizations tended to target the very social and political groups they had previously tried to attract: the Left, the Right, the Basques, and Muslims, respectively. The pace of the process interacted with the degree of radicalization of existing conflicts and its cultural effects in terms of tolerance for violence.

These developments also interacted with still another mechanism: ideological encapsulation. As aforementioned, political violence was normatively justified, as radical beliefs were at the same time preconditions and, especially, effects of violent actions. In general, all narratives described a path from a glorious past, to a long decadence, and then to a rebirth. Dichotomous visions, a sense of moral superiority, and essentializing thinking all developed in action. Justification follows escalation, which is only to a certain extent strategically planned. Rather than emerging from preexisting ideologies, violence developed with repression and competition.

As for the previous phenomena, we noted some differences in the narratives initially adopted by the clandestine organizations as they embedded their discourses in the broader cultures of the social movements they wanted to address. So the Italian Left stressed resistance and revolution; the Right revived the fascist spirit; the ETA built on the Basque mythology; and the Islamist groups went back to specific trends in the interpretation of religious texts. All types of clandestine organizations, however, shared a certain path toward a narrative that became less resonant with those of the social movements they wanted to influence. Adapting their discourse to the organizational compartmentalization and action militarization, they changed their definition of themselves from (effective) soldiers to (defeated) martyrs. In all four types, the self-justification became ever more elitist, depicting an image of heroic – if not successful – fighters. And to justify ever more cruel forms of action, clandestine organizations constructed an image of an absolute evil, whose cognitive borders grew ever broader.

In a vicious circle, the more isolated the organizations became, the more they withdrew from attempts at bridging their frames with those of activists in potentially sympathetic environments, developing instead a self-contained and self-referential narrative. Whereas it was initially justified instrumentally as the only way out against a powerful adversary, violence then increasingly became an existential response to a hostile environment – from consequentialism there was a move to deontological justification. Therefore the Marxist-Leninist, neofascist, exclusive nationalist, or Islamist fundamentalist ideologies – which had been available for ages – were not the direct causes of the waves of clandestine violence. Rather, they were twisted and transformed through the process. Even the language changed, becoming less understandable from outside.

Similarly, once the groups went underground, members' commitments were kept through mechanisms of militant enclosure. In some cases, the group slowly transformed from a source of support to a prison: "Participants in some social movements find an oppressive and stifling side to close-knit personal relationships. So-called cultural free spaces sometimes become prisons from which some participants would like to escape but cannot because they lack the courage to defy the group censure and ostracism that would follow" (Gamson 1992: 64). A sort of affective enclosure followed the everyday experiences of the militants in their environment. Political socialization in clandestine organizations involved in fact "a transformation in the reference system, that is, a gradual process of individual exit from the majoritarian culture and integration in a political counterculture with divergent norms, values and loyalties, and a particularly rigid pressure to conform" (Jäger and Böllinger 1981: 232). It has been observed that the clandestine organization

provides back-up when other support is eradicated. Within the group several psychological variables become essential: solidarity, complicity, and reality perception. Group membership means obligatory acceptance of a certain system of values and norms; deviations from these are punished. The group dynamics of complicity catalyze actions that any one member would hardly have been able to accomplish alone and that he has difficulty understanding later on. He acts within a set of mutual expectations and role assignments. Being forced into the underground, the group lives in isolation and, [its members] working in close cooperation, evolves new models for the interpretation of reality that acquire a binding character for the group members. (Rasch 1979: 82)

Affective ties among friends-comrades in the underground are notable for their intensity,[1] as participation requires broad changes in the individual's value system and behavior, or, in other words, alterations that

resemble primary socialization, because they have radically to reassign reality accents and, consequently, must replicate to a considerable degree the strongly affective identification with the socializing personnel that was characteristic of childhood. They are different from primary socialization because they do not start *ex nihilo*, and as a result they must cope with a problem of dismantling, disintegrating the preceding nomic structure of subjective reality. (Berger and Luckmann 1966: 157)

Thus "people and ideas that are discrepant with the new definitions of reality are systematically avoided" (ibid.: 159).

In addition, group identification increased with level of risk. McAdam's Freedom Summer participants described their experiences as a sort of "ecstasy," a "sense of liberation," a feeling of being "finally at home," and a "transcendent experience": "These people were me and I was them" (McAdam 1988: 71). Similarly, for militants of the underground, as for those in other high-risk secret

---

[1] Movements are said to differ from one another in terms of "the emotional tenor, presence, affective climate, or demeanor enacted and communicated by movement organizations" (Lofland 1985: 219).

societies (Erikson 1981), the excitement of shared risks strengthens friendships. In fact, the need for secrecy tends to become the most important determinant of the organization's structure and strategy (ibid.).

Although at the beginning of their careers militants recruited in the underground were embedded in broader networks, affective and cognitive dynamics interacted to produce a progressive encapsulation of the small circles of friends-comrades. From the affective point of view, identification with a group of "heroic" peers increased at the same pace as the severing of other ties outside the group. For individuals in the underground, the comrades active in their own organizations became their only source of material and emotional support. This does not means that life in the underground was only rosy, funny, and exciting: small-group dynamics also brought tensions and breaks, increasing stress in not only political but also everyday life. The experience was certainly intense, leaving little space for other relations – which were in fact actively discouraged.

From the cognitive point of view, the (increasingly tinier) groups became the only trusted source of information for their members. Justifications for violence were built on not only emotional identification with dead or imprisoned comrades but also the construction of a special vision of external reality. At the individual level, this reflected the increasing encapsulation of the organizational narrative that I have already described. Within totalitarian types of institutions, as in clandestine ones, cognitive closure produced an increasing detachment from shared visions as the pressure of cognitive coherence deterred members from opening up alternative channels of communication.

These mechanisms developed in part as reactions to external challenges (see J. H. Jackson and Morgan 1978), but in progressively hostile environments, strategic choices were limited. In fact, perverse effects, neither planned nor foreseen, strongly influenced the evolution of these organizations, whose decline was often related to the very choice of clandestinity. The unanticipated results of this and subsequent choices, addressing different problems of survival, reduced the range of options available to the group. In general, tactical transformation required adaptation in the organizational structure as well as symbolic changes, which in turn had unpredictable effects that required new adaptations. As I had observed with reference to the Italian and German left-wing radical groups,

unable to avoid arrest and alienation from the external reality, they were drawn deeper and deeper into a sort of spiral in which each successive turn further reduced their strategic options. The very condition of clandestinity drew the organization into a kind of vicious circle in which each attempt to face problems at one level produced new difficulties at another. As a result, the organizations had to abandon externally oriented aims for a "private war" with the state apparatuses. That is, operating illegally as they did, the militants of the armed struggle could not appear at the site of social conflicts, and this physical distance led to a kind of psychic distance as well. It reduced the terrorists' capacity to pursue effective propaganda strategies. Abandoning their propaganda efforts, they concentrated their energies on their struggle with the state and became increasingly involved in their private war, an obsession that isolated them still further. And the more isolated they became, the weaker was their capacity to escape repression. (della Porta 1995: 135)

These internal dynamics became increasingly relevant once the radical groups went underground. Even if they continued to try to adapt their strategies to the changing external reality, the moves they had made to clandestinity drastically reduced their range of possible choices and further weakened the group's sense of reality. In fact, the very choice of clandestinity forced them into a losing military conflict with the much more powerful state apparatuses. Clandestinity by definition entails material and psychological isolation, and the distinctive spiraling pattern of radicalization and isolation characteristic of semi-illegal groups only accelerated when the groups went underground. As their action became increasingly brutal, most radical groups lost the (large or small) external support they had received when they were first organized. Each successive turn in this spiral reduced the groups' strategic options, making them a prisoner of their own version of reality. Entrepreneurs of violence thus unleashed a force they could not control: embracing violence, they cultivated the source of their own dissolution.

Whereas environmental conditions were relevant at the onset, however, there was also an agency power of radical organizations, which themselves reproduced the resources for their survival. In a vicious circle, as groups adapted to radical resources in their environment, they helped to perpetuate them. The process developed through trials and errors, advances and retreats, in which groups experimented with different forms of action and organizational formats and then justified them through frames of amplification. In addition, as skills for violence were gradually formed, those who possessed those skills then played a role in spreading them.

Radicalization can in fact be seen as a good example of the evolution of "absurd" chance processes or vicious circles, characterized by spirals of negative feedback that produce different effects from what was planned. In these processes, participants operate based on a self-constructed image of reality, gambling on the results of the choices made (Neidhardt 1981: 245, 251–2). The final outcome of their actions results from a chain of actions and reactions, based on miscalculations of the moves of the different actors: "This circle of actions and reactions forms a routine until a more or less chance event ruptures the pattern and produces a qualitative jump, the group debates its possible choices, and in this crisis some members decide to go underground" (della Porta 1995: 111). In vicious circles, negative feedback loops can actually produce results that are the opposite of those expected (see, for instance, Masuch 1985: 14–5; see also Merton 1957). The choice of clandestinity evolved gradually and during long processes; it was only in part premeditated, and not irreversible. Radicalization was therefore the result of not only strategic choices but also unplanned internal dynamics. It showed not only attempts at strategic action but also their limits. Collective choices also emerged as short-sighted, featuring some short-term advantages but also disastrous consequences in the medium and long term. Semimilitary units were created to organize violent practices, but they then privileged military action and split from the main organization. Choosing clandestinity, they avoided immediate repression but also reduced their capacity to speak to their constituency, increasingly reducing their contacts with the outside. For these specific organizations, the tendency toward moderation was hindered by reliance on ideological incentive and strong group solidarity (Zald and Ash 1966).

The timing of this trend toward dissolution was influenced by the environmental conditions that influenced the degree of isolation of the underground groups. The higher the support for the use of violence in the environment, the slower the process of implosion tended to be. At the same time, however, the presence of resources for violence in the environment – sometimes including a territorial control over some areas – pushes clandestine organizations toward the use of brutal forms of violence.

Throughout the presentation of these various mechanisms, I have noted similarities as well as some differences. Although I stated that I am not interested in lawlike statements, some caveats must be mentioned if one is to move beyond the internal validity of the description of the selected cases to address the study's external validity – that is, its potential generalization to other cases within a broader geographical and historical range.

First, although I tried to make the most of my past fieldwork on several of the cases covered, the research design is a cross-national historical comparison, based in good part on published materials. As such, it inherits all the richness and challenges of historical sociology, as I have mixed (various amounts of) firsthand empirical evidence with secondary analysis of the literature. Even though I tried to cover as many studies as I could, I encountered obvious difficulties in obtaining complete information on all of my cases. More focused empirical fieldwork in the future can enrich the analysis of each of the mechanisms I singled out.

Second, although I have selected crucial cases of left-wing, right-wing, ethnonationalist, and religious types of clandestine political violence, their representativeness is certainly questionable. In particular, most of my cases are European, and, although they address different waves of protest, they still cover no more than a half century. In the course of the volume, I have systematically compared the Italian and German left-wing clandestine groups but barely mentioned the Weather Underground in the United States or the Japanese Red Army, which seem to share some of their characteristics (Zwerman, Steinhoff, and della Porta 2000). I have also introduced occasional references to works on the American radical Right (Wright 2007), the Irish ethnonationalist conflict (Bosi 2006; Waldmann 1998; White 1993), and the Algerian conflicts, all of which appear to confirm the presence of some of the mentioned mechanisms. However, more systematic comparison is clearly needed before one can claim too much about the generalizability of my results.

Third, the research focused on cases of conflict radicalization that ended in clandestine political violence. Future research that compares positive cases, in which clandestine violence developed, to negative cases, in which clandestine violence did not develop, notwithstanding the presence of some escalation, would represent a further step in our knowledge. As observed by McAdam, Tarrow, and Tilly (2001: chap. 7), many revolutionary situations do not actually develop into revolutions. In parallel, of the many self-determination movements, only a few escalate into violent forms (for example, in 2006, 28 out of 168 such movements escalated, according to data from the Center for International Development and Conflict Management, reported in Hewitt, Wilkenfeld, and Gurr 2007). And there are many situations in which harsh repression of intense cycles of protest and organizational competition help the spread of some violent repertoires, but events stop short of the foundation of clandestine organizations. Among the cases I have studied, the contestation over the use of locally unwanted land in Italy in the 2000s (della Porta and Piazza 2008); the transnational protests in the early 2000s (della Porta 2007); the French riots of the past decades (della Porta and Gbikpi 2011); the activities of the radical Right in Italy, Germany, and the United States (Caiani, della Porta, and Wagemann 2011); or the politicization of religious conflicts in Italy in the 2000s (Bosi and della Porta 2010) could be good candidates for a systematic comparison of a universe of positive and negative cases.

Rather than exhausting the study of clandestine political violence, I hope in fact that my work can stimulate it. In particular, during a time in which every new wave of clandestine political violence is presented as peculiarly evil and irrational, I believe that my analysis has provided enough evidence on the existence of similar mechanisms to stimulate comparative analysis among different types of violence.

Primary Sources

Life Histories

All of the Life Histories listed herein are available at the Istituto Carlo Cattaneo, Bologna, as unpublished manuscripts.

1: Former militant of the PL in Campania; collected by Giuseppe de Lutiis, 1987.
2: Former militant of the PL in Naples; collected by Giuseppe de Lutiis, 1987 ("Raffaele" in Catanzaro and Manconi 1995: 365–408).
3: Former militant of a clandestine group similar to the group Senza Tregua in Milan; collected by Luigi Manconi, 1987 ("Enrico Baglioni" in Catanzaro and Manconi 1995: 21–79).
4: Former militant of the FCC in Turin; collected by Giuseppe de Lutiis, 1987.
5: Former militant of the BR in Milan; collected by Luisa Passerini, 1987 ("Alfredo Buonavita" in Catanzaro and Manconi 1995: 79–162).
6: Former militant of the Nuclei Comunisti Rivoluzionari in Turin; collected by Domenico Nigro, 1987.
7: Former militant of the BR from Reggio Emilia; collected by Donatella della Porta, 1987.
8: Former militant of the PL in Turin; collected by Domenico Nigro, 1987.
9: Former militant of the Movimento Comunista Rivoluzionario in Rome; collected by Luigi Manconi, 1987 ("Piero" in Catanzaro and Manconi 1995: 221–82).
10: Former militant of the PL in Turin; collected by Donatella della Porta, 1987.
11: Former militant of the BR in Liguria; collected by Giuseppe de Lutiis, 1987.
12: Former militant of the PL in Milan; collected by Donatella della Porta, 1987 ("Marco" in Catanzaro and Manconi 1995: 317–64).
13: Former militant of the PL in Turin; collected by Domenico Nigro, 1987.
14: Former militant of the PL in Turin; collected by Claudio Novaro, 1987.
15: Former militant of the PL in Milan; collected by Donatella della Porta, 1987.
16: Former militant of the UCC in Rome; collected by Luigi Manconi, 1987 ("Paolo Lapponi" in Catanzaro and Manconi 1995: 163–220).
17: Former militant of the PL in Turin; collected by Claudio Novaro, 1987.
18: Former militant of the PL in Turin; collected by Claudio Novaro, 1987.

19: Former militant of the BR in Rome; collected by Giuseppe de Lutiis, 1987.

20: Nonmilitant of a clandestine organization; collected by Domenico Nigro, 1987.

21: Former militant of the PL in Florence; collected by Donatella della Porta, 1987 ("Claudia" in Catanzaro and Manconi 1995: 283–315).

22: Former militant of a clandestine group related to the journal *Linea di Condotta*; collected by Luigi Manconi, 1987.

23: Former militant of the PL in Rome; collected by Donatella della Porta, 1987.

24: Former sympathizer of the BR in Rome; collected by Giuseppe de Lutiis, 1987.

25: Former militant of Nuclei Comunisti Territoriali in Turin; collected by Domenico Nigro, 1987.

26: Former militant of the PL in Turin; collected by Patrizia Guerra, 1987.

27: Former militant of the BR in Rome; collected by Giuseppe de Lutiis, 1987 ("Antonio Savasta" in Catanzaro and Manconi 1995: 409–72).

28: Former militant of the PL in Turin; collected by Domenico Nigro, 1987.

29: Former militant of the PL in Turin; collected by Donatella della Porta, 1987.

Clandestine Group Documents

AQ, "Declaration of War against the Americans Occupying the Land of the Two Holy Places," 1996.

Azzam, Sheykh Abdullah, *Martyrs: The Building Blocks of Nations*. http://www.religioscope. com/info/doc/jihad/azzam_martyrs.htm, accessed 17 November 2012.

Bewegung 2 Juni, *Die Entführung aus unsere Sicht*, 1975.

Bin Laden, Osama, "Declaration of Jihad," *Al Islah* (London), 2 September 1996.

Brigate Rosse, *Brigate rosse*, September 1971.

Brigate Rosse, *Organizziamo un grande processo popolare*, 1971.

Brigate Rosse, *Alcune questioni per la discussione sull'organizzazione*, 1972.

Brigate Rosse, *La crisi è lo strumento usato dalla reazione . . .*, December 1973.

Brigate Rosse, *Contro il neogollismo . . .*, April 1974.

Brigate Rosse, *Risoluzione della direzione strategica*, April 1975.

Brigate Rosse, *Risoluzione della direzione strategica*, 1979.

Brigate Rosse, *Risoluzione della direzione strategica*, February 1978.

Brigate Rosse, *Portare l'attacco al cuore dello stato imperialista delle multinazionali . . .*, October 1978.

Detenuti del Carcere di Brescia, *Documento*, 1981.

ETA, *José Luis Zabilde's Insurreccion en Euskadi*, 1964

Formazioni Comuniste Combattenti, *Statuto*, 1978.

Prima Linea, "Court of Turin: Investigative Magistrate's Bill of Indictment and Public Persecutors Charge." In *Judicial Proceeding JP* 321/80, 1980.

Revolutionäre Zelle, *Revolutionärer Zorn: Zeitung der Revolutionäre Zelle*, no. 1, May 1975.

Revolutionäre Zelle, *Revolutionärer Zorn: Zeitung der Revolutionäre Zelle*, no. 4, January 1978.

Rote Armee Fraktion, *Die Aktion des Schwarzen September in München: Zur Strategie des antiimperialistischen Kampfes*, November 1972.

Bibliographical References

Abbas, Tahir. 2007. "Muslim Minorities in Britain: Integration, Multiculturalism and Radicalism in the Post-7/7 Period." *Journal of Intercultural Studies* 28 (3): 287–300.

Abuza, Zachary. 2009. "The Re-Habilitation of Jemaah Islamiyah Detenees in South East Asia: A Preliminary Assessment." In Tore Bjørgo and John Horgan, eds., *Leaving Terrorism Behind*. London: Routledge, pp. 193–211.

Ahmed, Isham H. 2005. "Palestinian Resistance and 'Suicide Bombers.'" In Tore Bjørgo, ed., *Root Causes of Terrorism: Myths, Reality and Ways Forward*. London: Routledge, pp. 87–102.

Al-Berry, Khaled. 2002. *La terre est plus belle que le paradis*. Paris: JC Lattes.

Alimi, Eitan Y. 2007. *Israeli Politics and the First Palestinian Intifada*. London: Routledge.

Alimi, Eitan Y. 2011. "Relational Dynamics in Factional Adoption of Terrorist Tactics: A Comparative Perspective." *Theory and Society* 40: 95–118.

Alonso, Rogelio. 2007. *The IRA and Armed Struggle*. New York and London: Routledge.

Alonso, Rogelio. 2009. "Leaving Terrorism Behind in Northern Ireland and the Basque County." In Tore Bjørgo and John Horgan, eds., *Leaving Terrorism Behind*. London: Routledge, pp. 88–112.

Aminzade, Ron, and Doug McAdam. 2001. "Emotions and Contentious Politics." In Ronald Aminzade, Jack Goldstone, Doug McAdam, Elizabeth Perry, William H. Sewell, Jr., Sidney Tarrow, and Charles Tilly, eds., *Silence and Voice in the Study of Contentious Politics*. Cambridge: Cambridge University Press, pp. 51–88.

Aminzade, Ronald R., and Elizabeth J. Perry. 2001. "The Sacred, Religious and Secular in Contentious Politics: Blurring the Boundaries." In Ronald Aminzade, Jack Goldstone, Doug McAdam, Elizabeth Perry, William H. Sewell, Jr., Sidney Tarrow, and Charles Tilly, eds., *Silence and Voice in the Study of Contentious Politics*. Cambridge: Cambridge University Press, pp. 155–78.

APSA, Task Force Report on Political Violence and Terrorism. 2007. *How Political Violence Ends: Paths to Conflict Deescalation and Termination*. Prepared for presentation at the 2007 meeting of the American Political Science Association, Chicago, IL.

Apter, David. 1997. "Political Violence in an Analytical Perspective." In David E. Apter, ed., *The Legitimation of Violence*. Basingstoke: Macmillan, pp. 1–32.

Ardica, Giuseppe. 2008. *Io, l'uomo nero. Intervista a Pierluigi Concutelli*. Venice: Marsilio.

Arquilla, John, and David Rondfelt. 2001. *Networks and Netwars: The Future of Terror, Crime, and Militancy*. Santa Monica, CA: RAND.

Asal, Victor, and R. Karl Rethemeyer. 2008. "The Nature of the Beast: Organizational Structures and the Lethality of Terrorist Attacks." *Journal of Politics* 70: 437–49.

Atran, Scott. 2006. *Global Network Terrorism: Sacred Values and Radicalization*. National Science Foundation Briefing, White House, Washington, DC.

Aust, Stefan. 1985. *Der Baader-Meinhof Komplex*. Hamburg: Hoffmann und Campe.

Bakker, Edwin. 2006. "Jihadi Terrorists in Europe." Clingendael Security Paper No. 2, Netherlands Institute of International Relations.

Bakker, Edwin, and Leen Boer. 2007. *The Evolution of Al-Qaedism*. Clingedael: Netherlands Institute of International Relations.

Baum, Gerhard, and Horst Mahler. 1979. "Wir brauchen mehr Gelllssenheit." *Der Spiegel* 53: 34–49.

Baumann, Michael. 1976. *Tupamaros Berlin-Ouest*. Paris: Les Presses d'aujourd'hui.

Beck, Jan Mansvelt. 1999. "The Continuity of Basque Political Violence: A Geographical Perspective on the Legitimisation of Violence." *GeoJournal* 48: 109–121.

Becker, Howard S. 1970. "Practitioners of Vice and Crime." In Robert Habenstein, ed., *Pathways to Data*. Chicago: Aldine, pp. 30–49.

Beissinger, Mark R. 2002. *Nationalist Mobilization and the Collapse of the Soviet State*. Cambridge: Cambridge University Press.

Berger, Peter, and Thomas Luckmann. 1966. *The Social Construction of Reality: A Treatise in the Sociology of Knowledge*. Garden City, NY: Doubleday, Anchor Books.

Berman, Eli. 2009. *Radical, Religious, and Violent: The New Economy of Terrorism*. Cambridge, MA: MIT Press.

Bianconi, Giovanni. 1992. *A mano armata: Vita violenta di Giusva Fioravanti*. Milan: Baldini e Castoldi.

Bittner, Egon. 1967. "The Police Skid-Row." *American Sociological Review* 32: 699–715.

Bjørgo, Tore. 2004. "Justifying Violence: Extreme Nationalist and Racist Discourses in Scandinavia." In Angelica Fenner and Eric Weitz, eds., *Fascism and Neofascism: Critical Writings on the Radical Right in Europe*. Houndmills, Basingstoke: Palgrave Macmillan, pp. 207–18.

Bjørgo, Tore. 2005. *Root Causes of Terrorism: Myths, Reality and Ways Forward*. London and New York: Routledge.

Bjørgo, Tore. 2009. "Processes of Disengagement from Violent Groups of the Extreme Right." In Tore Bjørgo and John Horgan, eds., *Leaving Terrorism Behind*. London: Routledge, pp. 30–48.

Bjørgo, Tore, and John Horgan. 2009. "Introduction." In Tore Bjørgo and John Horgan, eds., *Leaving Terrorism Behind*. London: Routledge, pp. 1–14.

Blanchard, Christopher M. 2007. *Al Quaeda: Statements and Evolving Ideology. CRS Report for Congress*. Washington, DC: Congressional Research Center.

Blomberg, S. Brock, Gregory D. Hess, and Akila Weerapana. 2004. "Economic Conditions and Terrorism." *European Journal of Political Economy* 20: 463–78.

Bobbio, Luigi. 1988. *Storia di Lotta Continua*. Milan: Feltrinelli.

Böllinger, Lorenz. 1981. "Die Entwicklung zu terroristischem Randeln als psychosoziale Prozess." In Herbert Jäger, Gerhard Schmidtchen, and Liselotte Sueillwold, eds., *Lebenslaufanalysen*. Opladen: Westdeutscher Verlag, pp. 175–231.

Boock, Peter. 1981. "Im Schtutzengraben fuer die falsche Sache." *Der Spiegel* 9: 110–15.

Booth, Ken. 1991. "Security and Emancipation." *Review of International Studies* 17: 313–26.

Borum, Randy, and Michael Gelles. 2005. "Al Quaeda's Operational Evolution: Behavioral and Organizational Perspectives." *Behavioral Sciences and the Law*, 23: 467–83.

Bosi, Lorenzo. 2006. "The Dynamics of Social Movement Development: Northern Ireland's Civil Rights Movement in the 1960s." *Mobilization*: 81–100.

Bosi, Lorenzo, and Donatella della Porta. 2010. "*Ideology, Instrumentality and Solidarity: Explaining Micro-Mobilization Paths into Political Violence.*" Paper presented at the Conference on Political Violence, Florence, EUI.

Bosi, Lorenzo, and Donatella della Porta. 2012. "Micro-Mobilization into Armed Groups: Ideological, Instrumental and Solidaristic Paths." *Qualitative Sociology*, 35: 361–83.

Boucek, Christopher. 2009. "Extremist Re-Education and Rehabilitation in Saudi Arabia." In Tore Bjørgo and John Horgan, eds., *Leaving Terrorism Behind*. London: Routledge, pp. 212–23.

Boucek, Christopher, Shaazadi Beg, and John Horgan. 2009. "Opening up the Jihadi Debate: Yemen's Committee for Dialogue." In Tore Bjørgo and John Horgan, eds., *Leaving Terrorism Behind*. London: Routledge, pp. 181–92.

Boudreau, Vincent. 2004. *Resisting Dictatorship: Repression and Protest in Southeast Asia*. Cambridge: Cambridge University Press.

Breen Smyth, Marie. 2007. "A Critical Research Agenda for the Study of Political Terror." *European Political Science* 6: 260–7.

Brubaker, Rogers, and David Laitin. 1998. "Ethnic and Nationalist Violence." *Annual Review of Sociology* 4: 423–52.

Buijs, F. J. 2001. "Political Violence, Threat and Challenge." *Netherlands Journal of Social Science* 37 (1): 7–23.

Burris, Val, Emory Smith, and Ann Strahm. 2000. "White Supremacist Networks on the Internet." *Sociological Focus* 33: 215–34.

Busch, Heiner, Albrecht Funk, Kau B. Udo, Wolf Dieter Narr, and Falco Werkentin. 1988. *Die Polizei in die Bundesrepublik Deutschland*. Frankfurt am Main: Campus.

Buzan, Barry, Ole Wæver, and Jaap de Wilde. 1998. *Security: A New Framework for Analysis*. Boulder, CO: Rienner.

Byman, Daniel. 2003. "Al-Qaeda as an Adversary: Do We Understand Our Enemy?" *World Politics* 56: 139–63.

Caiani, Manuela, Donatella Della Porta, and Claudius Wagemann. 2011. *Mobilizing on the Extreme Right*. Oxford: Oxford University Press.

Calleja, José Maria, and Ignacio Sánchez-Cuenca. 2006. *La derrota de ETA*. Madrid: Adhara Publicaciones.

Canosa, Romano. 1976. *La polizia in Italia dal 1945 ad oggi*. Bologna: Il Mulino.

Caselli, Giancarlo, and Donatella della Porta. 1984. "La storia delle Brigate Rosse: Strutture organizzative e strategie d'azione." In Donatella della Porta, ed., *Terrorismi in Italia*. Bologna: Il Mulino, pp. 153–221.

Casquette, Jesus. 2003. "From Imagination to Visualization: Protest Rituals in the Basque Country." WZB unpublished paper.

Catanzaro, Raimondo. 1990. "Il sentito e il vissuto. La violenza nel racconto dei protagonisti." In Raimondo Catanzaro, ed., *Ideologia, Movimenti, Terrorismi*. Bologna: Il Mulino, pp. 203–44.

Catanzaro, Raimondo, and Luigi Manconi. 1995. *Storie di lotta armata*. Bologna: Il Mulino.

Cavanaugh, William T. 2009. *The Myth of Religious Violence.* Oxford: Oxford University Press.

Cento Bull, Anna. 2007. *Italian Neofascism: The Strategy of Tension and the Politics of Nonreconciliation.* Oxford: Berghahn Books.

Chhabra, Sandeep S. 2010. "Adapt-Qaeda: Analyzing the Relationship between Organizational Transformation and the Exploitation of Information Technology." *Critique: A Worldwide Journal of Politics:* 1–16.

Chiarini, Roberto. 1995. "The Italian Far Right: The Search for Legitimacy." In Luciano Cheles, Ronnier Ferguson, and Michalina Vaughan, eds., *The Far Right in Western and Eastern Europe.* London: Longman, pp. 5–35.

Clark, Robert P. 1984. *The Basque Insurgents: ETA, 1952–1980.* Madison: University of Wisconsin Press.

Clemens, Elisabeth S. 1996. "Organizational Form as Frame: Collective Identity and Political Strategy in the American Labor Movement." In Doug McAdam, John D. McCarthy, and Mayer N. Zald, eds., *Comparative Perspectives on Social Movements: Political Opportunities, Mobilizing Structures, and Cultural Framings.* Cambridge/New York: Cambridge University Press, pp. 205–26.

Clemens, Elisabeth S., and Debra C. Minkoff. 2004. "Beyond the Iron Law: Rethinking the Place of Organizations in Social Movement Research." In David A. Snow, Sarah A. Soule, and Hanspeter Kriesi, eds., *The Blackwell Companion to Social Movement Research.* Oxford: Blackwell, pp. 155–70.

Coleman, James S. 1986. "Social Theory, Social Research and a Theory of Action." *American Journal of Sociology* 91: 1309–35.

Collier, Paul, and Anke Hoeffler. 2004. "Greed and Grievance in Civil War." *Oxford Economic Paper* 56: 563–95.

Collier, Paul, and Nicholas Sambanis. 2002. "Understanding Civil War – A New Agenda." *Journal of Conflict Resolution* 46: 3–12.

Conversi, Daniele. 1997. *The Basques, the Catalans and Spain: Alternative Routes to Nationalist Mobilization.* Reno: University of Nevada Press.

Coolsaet, Rik. 2005. *Radicalisation and Europe's Counter-Terrorism Strategy.* Royal Institute for International Relations (Brussels) & Ghent University, The Transatlantic Dialogue on Terrorism CSIS/Clingendael, The Hague, 8–9 December.

Corso, Guido. 1979. *L'ordine pubblico.* Bologna: Il Mulino.

Cragin, Kim. 2007. "Understanding Terrorist Ideology." Testimony presented before the Senate Select Committee on Intelligence.

Crenshaw, Martha. 1981. "The Causes of Terrorism." *Comparative Politics* 13: 379–99.

Crenshaw, Martha. 1991. "How Terrorism Declines." *Terrorism and Political Violence* 3: 69–87.

Crenshaw, Martha. 1996. "Why Violence Is Rejected or Renounced: A Case Study of Oppositional Terrorism." In Thomas Gregor, ed., *A Natural History of Peace.* Nashville, TN: Vanderbilt University Press, pp. 249–72.

Crenshaw, Martha. 2009. "Hearing on Reassessing the Evolving al-Qa'ida Threat to the Homeland." Unpublished paper.

Crenshaw, Martha. 2011. *Explaining Terrorism: Causes, Processes and Consequences.* London: Routledge.

Critcher, Chas, and David Waddington, eds. 1996. *Policing Public Order: Theoretical and Practical Issues.* Aldershot: Ashgate.

Croft, Stuart. 2006. *Culture, Crisis and America's War on Terrorism*. Cambridge: Cambridge University Press.

Cronin, Audrey Kurth. 2009a. "How Terrorist Campaigns End." In Tore Bjørgo and John Horgan, eds., *Leaving Terrorism Behind*. London: Routledge, pp. 49–65.

Cronin, Audry Kurth. 2009b. *How Terrorism Ends: Understanding the Decline and Demise of Terrorist Campaigns*. Princeton, NJ: Princeton University Press.

Davenport, Christian. 1995. "Multi-Dimensional Threat Perception and State Repression: An Inquiry into Why States Apply Negative Sanctions." *American Journal of Political Science* 39: 683–713.

Davenport, Christian. 2000. *Paths to State Repression: Human Rights Violations and Contentious Politics*. Boulder, CO: Rowman & Littlefield.

Davenport, Christian. 2005. "Introduction. Repression and Mobilization: Insights from Political Science and Sociology." In Christian Davenport, Hank Johnston, and Carol Mueller, eds., *Repression and Mobilization*. Minneapolis: University of Minnesota Press, pp. vii–xli.

De la Calle, Luis. n.d. "Fighting for the Local Control: The Street Violence in the Basque Country." Unpublished manuscript, working paper.

De la Calle, Luis, and Ignacio Sánchez-Cuenca. 2004. "La selección de víctimas en ETA." *Revista Española de Ciencia Política* 10: 53–79.

De la Calle, Luis, and Ignacio Sánchez-Cuenca. 2006. "The Production of Terrorist Violence: Analyzing Target Selection within the IRA and ETA." Working Paper 2006/230. Madrid: Juan March Institute.

De la Calle, Luis, and Ignacio Sánchez-Cuenca. 2012. "Rebels without a Territory: An Analysis of Nonterritorial Conflicts in the World, 1970–1977." *Journal of Conflict Resolution*. Online preprint version.

De la Calle Robles, Luis. 2009. *Accounting for Nationalist Violence in Affluent Countries*. PhD Thesis, European University Institute.

De la Corte Ibanez, Luis. 2006. *La Logica del Terrorismo*. Madrid: Alianza editorial.

Del Boca, Angelo, and Mario Giovana. 1965. *I figli del sole*. Milan: Feltrinelli.

Della Porta, Donatella. 1988. "Recruitment Processes in Clandestine Political Organizations." In Bert Klandermans, Hanspeter Kriesi, and Sidney Tarrow, eds., *New Social Movements in Western Europe and the United States*. Greenwich, CT: JAI Press, pp. 155–69.

Della Porta, Donatella. 1990. *Il terrorismo di sinistra*. Bologna: Il Mulino.

Della Porta, Donatella. 1993. "State Responses to Terrorism: The Italian Case." In Ronald D. Crelinston and Alex P. Schmidt, eds., *Western Responses to Terrorism*. London: Frank Cass, pp. 151–70.

Della Porta, Donatella. 1995. *Social Movements, Political Violence and the State*. Cambridge: Cambridge University Press.

Della Porta, Donatella. 1998. "The Political Discourse on Protest Policing." In Marco Giugni, Doug McAdam, and Charles Tilly, eds., *How Movements Matter*. Minneapolis: University of Minnesota Press, pp. 66–96.

Della Porta, Donatella. 2002. "Gewalt und die neue Linke." In Wilhelm Heitmeyer and John Hagan, eds., *Internationales Handbuch der Gewaltforschung*. Wiesbaden: Westdeutscher, pp. 479–500.

Della Porta, Donatella. 2007. *The Global Justice Movement: Cross National and Transnational Perspectives*. Boulder, CO: Paradigm.

Della Porta, Donatella. 2008a. "Comparative Analysis: Case-Oriented versus Variable-Oriented Research." In Donatella della Porta and Michael Keating, eds., *Approaches and Methodologies in the Social Sciences: A Pluralist Perspective*. Cambridge: Cambridge University Press, pp. 198–222.

Della Porta, Donatella. 2008b. "Eventful Protests, Global Conflicts." *Distinktion. Scandinavian Journal of Social Theory* 17: 27–56.

Della Porta, Donatella. 2008c. "Leaving Left-Wing Terrorism in Italy: A Sociological Analysis." In Tore Bjørgo and John Horgan, eds., *Leaving Terrorism Behind*. London: Routledge, pp. 49–65.

Della Porta, Donatella. 2008d. "Research on Social Movements and Political Violence." *Qualitative Sociology* 31 (3): 221–30.

Della Porta, Donatella. 2010. *L'intervista qualitativa*. Bari-Rome: Laterza.

Della Porta, Donatella, and Mario Diani. 2006. *Social Movements: An Introduction*. Oxford: Blackwell.

Della Porta, Donatella, and Olivier Fillieule. 2004. "Policing Social Movements." In David A. Snow, Sarah A. Soule, and Hanspeter Kriesi, eds., *The Blackwell Companion to Social Movements*. Oxford: Blackwell, pp. 217–41.

Della Porta, Donatella, and Bernard Gbikpi. 2011. "Riots: A Dynamic View." In Seraphim Sepheriadis and Hank Johnston, eds., *Political Violence*. Aldershot: Ashgate, pp. 87–102.

Della Porta, Donatella, and Michael Keating. 2008. *Approaches and Methodologies in the Social Sciences: A Pluralist Perspective*. Cambridge: Cambridge University Press.

Della Porta, Donatella, and Lasse Lindekilde. 2012. "European Counter-Terrorist Policies 10 Years After, Editors' Introduction." Special issue. *European Journal on Criminal Policy and Research* 18(4): 307–10.

Della Porta, Donatella, and Liborio Mattina. 1985. "I movimenti politici a base etnica: il caso basco in prospettiva comparata." *Rivista italiana di scienza politica* 15 (1): 35–67.

Della Porta, Donatella, Abby Peterson, and Herbert Reiter. 2006. *The Policing of Transnational Protest*. Aldershot: Ashgate.

Della Porta, Donatella, and Gianni Piazza. 2008. *Voices of the Valley, Voices of the Straits: How Protest Creates Communities*. Oxford: Berghahn Books.

Della Porta, Donatella, and Herbert Reiter. 1998a. "The Policing of Protest in Western Democracies." In Donatella della Porta and Herbert Reiter, eds., *Policing Protest: The Control of Mass Demonstrations in Western Democracies*. Minneapolis: University of Minnesota Press, pp. 1–32.

Della Porta, Donatella, and Herbert Reiter. 1998b. *Policing Protest: The Control of Mass Demonstrations in Western Democracies*. Minneapolis: University of Minnesota Press.

Della Porta, Donatella, and Herbert Reiter. 2004. *Polizia e Protesta*. Bologna: Il Mulino.

Della Porta, Donatella, and Maurizio Rossi. 1984. *Cifre crudeli: Bilancio dei terrorismi italiani*. Bologna: Istituto Cattaneo.

Della Porta, Donatella, and Dieter Rucht. 1995. "Left-Libertarian Movements in Context: Comparing Italy and West Germany, 1965–1990." In J. C. Jenkins and B. Klandermans, eds., *The Politics of Social Protest: Comparative Perspectives on States and Social Movements*. Minneapolis: University of Minnesota Press, pp. 229–72.

Della Porta, Donatella, and Sidney Tarrow. 1986. "Unwanted Children: Political Violence and the Cycle of Protest in Italy, 1966–1973." *European Journal of Political Research* 14: 607–32.

Della Porta, Donatella, and Sidney Tarrow. 2012. "Double Diffusion: Police and Protestors in Transnational Contention." *Comparative Political Studies* 20: 1–34.

Della Porta, Donatella, and Claudius Wagemann. 2005. "Patterns of Radicalization in Political Activism: Research Design." Veto Project Report, Florence EUI.

Demetriou, Chares. 2007. "Political Violence and Legitimation: The Episode of Colonial Cyprus." *Qualitative Sociology* 30: 171–93.

DeNardo, James. 1985. *Power in Numbers: The Political Strategy of Protest and Rebellion*. Princeton, NJ: Princeton University Press.

DiMaggio, Paul J., and Walter W. Powell. 1991. "Introduction." In Paul Powell and Walter DiMaggio, eds., *The New Institutionalism in Organizational Analysis*. Chicago/London: University of Chicago Press, pp. 1–38.

Dominguez Iribarren, Florencio. 1998. *ETA: Estrategia Organizativa y Actuaciones. 1978–1992*. Bilbao: Universidad Pais Vasco, Servicio Editorial.

Downton, James V., and Paul Wehr. 1997. *Persistent Activists: How Peace Commitment Develops and Survives*. Boulder, CO: Westview Press.

Duyvesteyn, Isabelle. 2012. "How New Is the New Terrorism?" In John Horgan and Kurt Braddock, eds., *Terrorism Studies: A Reader*. London: Routledge, pp. 27–40.

Earl, Jennifer. 2003. "Tanks, Tear Gas and Taxes." *Sociological Theory* 21: 44–68.

Earl, Jennifer, Sarah A. Soule, and John McCarthy. 2003. "Protest under Fire? Explaining Protest Policing." *American Sociological Review* 69: 581–606.

Ebaugh, Helen R. 1988. *Becoming an Ex: The Process of Role Exit*. Chicago: University of Chicago Press.

Edelman, Murray. 1971. *Politics as a Symbolic Action*. Chicago: Markham.

Egerton, Frazer. 2011. *Jihad in the West: The Rise of Militant Salafism*. Cambridge: Cambridge University Press.

Eilstrup-Sangiovanni, Mette, and Calvert Jones. 2008. "Assessing the Dangers of Illicit Networks: Why al-Qaida May Be Less Threatening Than Many Think." *International Security* 33: 7–44.

Elbadawi, Ibrahim, and Paul Sambanis. 2002. "How Much War Will We See? Explaining the Prevalence of Civil War." *Journal of Conflict Resolution* 46 (3): 307–34.

Eliasoph, Nina. 1998. *Avoiding Politics: How Americans Produce Apathy in Everyday Life*. New York: Cambridge University Press.

Engene, Jan Oscar. 2004. *Terrorism in Western Europe*. Cheltenham: Edward Elgar.

English, Richard. 2009. *Terrorism: How to Respond*. Oxford: Oxford University Press.

Erikson, Bonnie H. 1981. "Secret Societies and Social Structures." *Social Forces* 60: 188–210.

Esposito, John L. 2002. *Unholy War: Terror in the Name of Islam*. New York: Oxford University Press.

Esposito, John L. 2006. "Terrorism and the Rise of Political Islam." In Louise Richardson, ed., *The Roots of Terrorism*. London: Routledge, pp. 145–58.

Esposito, John L. 2011. *What Everyone Needs to Know About Islam*. Oxford: Oxford University Press, 2nd ed.

European Commission. 2005. *Communication from the Commission to the European Parliament and the Council Concerning Terrorist Recruitment – Addressing the Factors Contributing to Violent Radicalisation*. COM/2005/0313 final.

Expert Group on Violent Radicalisation. 2008. *Radicalisation Processes Leading to Acts of Terrorism*. Report to the European Commission, unpublished. http://www.gsdrc.org/go/display&type=Document&id=3447, accessed 26 October 2012.

Eyerman, Ron. 2005. "How Social Movements Move: Emotions and Social Movements." In Helena Flam and Debra King, eds., *Emotions and Social Movements*. London: Routledge, pp. 41–57.

Fanon, Frantz. 1961. *Les Damnés de la terre*. Paris: Editions Maspero.

Fantasia, Rick. 1988. *Cultures of Solidarity: Consciousness, Action, and Contemporary American Workers*. Berkeley: University of California Press.

Fasanella, Giovanni, and Alberto Franceschini. 2004. *Che cosa sono le BR*. Milan: Bur.

Fearon, James D., and David D. Laitin. 2003. "Ethnicity, Insurgency, and Civil War." *American Political Science Review* 97: 75–90.

Fernandez, Luis A. 2008. *Policing Dissent: Social Control and the Anti-Globalization Movement*. London: Rutgers.

Ferraresi, Franco. 1984. "La destra eversiva." In Donatella della Porta, ed., *Terrorismi in Italia*. Bologna: Il Mulino, pp. 227–89.

Ferraresi, Franco. 1994. "La parabola della destra radicale." *Democrazia e Diritto* 1: 135–52.

Ferraresi, Franco. 1995. *Minacce alla democrazia: La Destra radicale e la strategia della tensione nell'Italia nel dopoguerra*. Milan: Feltrinelli.

Fetscher, Iring, Herfried Munkler, and Hannelore Ludwig. 1981. "Ideologien der Terroristen in der Bundesrepublik Deutschland." In Iring Fetscher and Günther Rohrmoser, eds., *Ideologien und Strategien*. Opladen: Westdeutscher Verlag, pp. 15–71.

Fiasco, Maurizio. 1990. "La simbiosi ambigua: Il neofascismo, i movimenti e la strategia delle stragi." In Raimondo Catanzaro, ed., *Ideologia, movimenti, terrorismi*. Bologna: Il Mulino, pp. 153–89.

Fillieule, Olivier. 2005. "Temps biographique, temps sociale et variabilité des retributions." In Olivier Fillieule, ed., *Le désengagement militant*. Paris: Belin, pp. 17–48.

Fillieule, Olivier, and Christophe Broqua. 2005. "La défection dans deux associations de lutte contre le sida: Act up et Aides." In Olivier Fillieule, ed., *Le désengagement militant*. Paris: Belin, pp. 189–228.

Fillieule, Olivier, and Fabien Jobard. 1998. "The Policing of Protest in France: Towards a Model of Protest Policing." In Donatella della Porta and Herbert Reiter, eds., *Policing Protest: The Control of Mass Demonstrations in Western Democracies*. Minneapolis: University of Minnesota Press, pp. 70–90.

Fishman, Robert M. 1990. *Working-Class Organization and the Return to Democracy in Spain*. Ithaca, NY: Cornell University Press.

Flam, Helena. 1994. "Political Responses to the Anti-Nuclear Challenge." In Helena Flam, ed., *States and Antinuclear Movements*. Edinburgh: Edinburgh University Press, pp. 329–54.

Flam, Helena. 2005. "Emotions' Map: A Research Agenda." In Helena Flam and Debra King, eds., *Emotions and Social Movements*. London: Routledge, pp. 19–41.

Forndran, Erhard. 1991. Religion und Politik – Eine einführende Problemanzeige. In Erhard Forndran, ed., *Religion und Politik in einer säkularisierten Welt*. Baden-Baden: Nomos, pp. 9–64.

Franceschini, Enrico (with Pietro Buffa and Franco Giustolisi). 1988. *Mara, Renato e io: Storia dei fondatori delle Brigate Rosse*. Milan: Mondadori.

Francisco, Ronald A. 1996. "Coercion and Protest: An Empirical Test in Two Democratic States." *American Journal of Political Science* 40: 1179–1204.

Francisco, Ronald A. 2005. "The Dictator's Dilemma." In Christian Davenport, Hank Johnston, and Carol Mueller, eds., *Repression and Mobilization*. Minneapolis: University of Minnesota Press, pp. 58–83.

Franks, Jason. 2006. *Rethinking the Roots of Terrorism*. Basingstock: Palgrave.

Franzinelli, Mimmo. 2008. *La sottile Linea Nera. Neofascismo e Servizi Segreti. Da Piazza Fontana a Piazza della Loggia.* Milan: Rizzoli.

Fuller, Graham E. 2002. *The Future of Political Islam.* New York: Palgrave Macmillan.

Funes, Maria. 1998. "Social Responses to Political Violence in the Basque Country: Peace Movements and Their Audience." *Journal of Conflict Resolution* 42: 493–510.

Galante, Severino. 1981. "Alle origini del partito armato." *Il Mulino* 275: 44–7.

Galfré, Monica. 2012. "La lotta armata: Forme, tempi, geografie." In Simone Neri Serneri, ed., *Verso la lotta armata.* Bologna: Il Mulino, pp. 63–92.

Galleni, Mauro. 1981. *Rapporto sul terrorismo: Le stragi, gli agguati, i sequestri, le sigle. 1969–1980.* Milan: Rizzoli.

Gallinari, Prospero. 2006. *Un contadino nella metropolis: Ricordi di un militante delle Brigate Rosse.* Milan: Bompiani.

Gambetta, Diego, ed. 2005. *Making Sense of Suicide Missions.* Oxford: Oxford University Press.

Gamson, William A. 1975. *The Strategy of Social Protest.* Belmont, CA: Wadsworth.

Gamson, William A. 1992. "The Social Psychology of Collective Action." In Aldon D. Morris and Carol McClurg Mueller, eds., *Frontiers in Social Movement Theory.* New Haven, CT: Yale University Press, pp. 53–76.

Gamson, William A., Bruce Fireman, and Steven Rytina. 1982. *Encounters with Unjust Authorities.* Homewood, IL: Dorsey Press.

Gamson, William, and David S. Meyer. 1996. "Framing Political Opportunity." In D. McAdam, J. D. McCarthy, and M. N. Zald, eds., *Opportunities, Mobilizing Structures, and Framing.* Cambridge: Cambridge University Press, pp. 275–90.

Garner, Roberta, and Mayer N. Zald. 1985. "The Political Economy of Social Movement Sectors." In Gerard D. Suttles and Mayer N. Zald, eds., *The Challenge of Social Control.* Norwood, NJ: Ablex, pp. 119–45.

Garrison, Arthur H. 2004. "Defining Terrorism: Philosophy of the Bomb, Propaganda by Deed and Change through Fear and Violence." *Criminal Justice Studies* 17 (3): 259–79.

George, Alexander. 1991. "The Discipline of Terrorology." In Alexander George, ed., *Western State Terrorism.* Cambridge: Polity Press, pp. 76–101.

Gerges, Fawaz A. 2005. *The Far Enemy: Why the Jihad Went Global.* Cambridge: Cambridge University Press.

Gerring, John. 2007. "The Mechanismic Worldview: Thinking inside the Box." *British Journal of Political Science* 38: 161–79.

Gillespie, Richard. 1982. *Soldiers of Peron: Argentina's Montoneros.* New York: Oxford University Press.

Goldstone, Jack A. 1991. *Revolution and Rebellion in the Early Modern World.* Berkeley and Los Angeles: University of California Press.

Goodwin, Jeff. 1997. *No Other Way Out.* Cambridge: Cambridge University Press.

Goodwin, Jeff. 2004. "Review Essays: What Must We Explain to Explain Terrorism?" *Social Movement Studies* 3: 259–65.

Goodwin, Jeff, James Jaspers, and Francesca Polletta. 2001. *Passionate Politics: Emotions and Social Movements.* Chicago: University of Chicago Press.

Graham, H. D., and Ted Gurr. 1969. "Editor's Introduction." In H. D. Graham and Ted Gurr, eds., *Violence in America.* New York: Praeger, pp. xxviii–xxxiv.

Grässle-Münschen, Josef. 1991. *Kriminelle Vereinigung. Von den Burschenschaften bis zur RAF.* Hamburg: Europeiische Verlagsanstalt.

Greenberg, Karen. 2005. *Al Qaeda Now: Understanding Today's Terrorists.* New York: Cambridge University Press.

Grevi, Vittorio. 1984. "Sistema penale e leggi dell'emergenza." In Gianfranco Pasquino, ed., *La prova delle armi.* Bologna: Il Mulino, pp. 17–75.

Griffin, Roger. 2003. "Shattering Crystals: The Role of 'Dream Time' in Extreme Right-Wing Political Violence." *Terrorism and Political Violence* 15: 57–95.

Grispigni, Marco. 2012. "La strage è di stato: Gli anni Settanta, la violenza politica e il caso italiano." In Simone Neri Serneri, ed., *Verso la lotta armata.* Bologna: Il Mulino, pp. 93–116.

Guelke, Adrian. 2006. *Terrorism and Global Disorder.* London: I.B. Tauris.

Guerrieri, Loredana. 2008. "Le strategie di destabilizzazione viste nella pubblicistica dell'estrema destra: 'La rivoluzione, si sa, è come il vento ... non la si può fermare, le si può solo far perdere tempo!'" In Mirco Dondi, ed., *I neri e i rossi: Terrorismo, violenza e informazione negli anni Settanta.* Nardò, LE: Edizioni Controluce.

Guerrieri, Loredana. 2010. "Un'autonoma via rivoluzionaria nei gruppi dell'estrema destra italiana: dalla strategia della tensione allo spontaneismo armato." *Storia e problemi contemporanei* 23: 55–78.

Gunaratna, Rohan. 2003. *Inside Al Qaeda: Global Network of Terror.* New York: Berkley Trade, Rei Sub Edition.

Gunaratna, Rohan. 2005. "Ideology in Terrorism and Counter Terrorism: Lessons from Combating Al Qaeda and Al Jemaah Al Islamiyah in Southeast Asia." Unpublished paper, CSRC discussion paper 05/42.

Gunning, Jeroen. 2007. *Hamas in Politics: Democracy, Religion, Violence.* London: Hurst.

Gunning, Jeroen. 2009. "Social Movement Theory and the Study of Terrorism." In Richard Jackson, Marie Breen Smyth, and Jeroen Gunning, eds., *Critical Terrorism Studies: A New Research Agenda.* London: Routledge, pp. 156–77.

Gupta, Dipak K., Harinder Singh, and Tom Sprague. 1993. "Government Coercion of Dissidents: Deterrence or Provocation?" *Journal of Conflict Resolution* 37: 301–39.

Gurr, Ted R. 1970. *Why Men Rebel.* Princeton, NJ: Princeton University Press.

Gurr, Ted. 2000. "Ethnic Warfare on the Wane." *Foreign Affairs* 79: 52–64.

Gurr, Ted. 2006. "Economic Factors." In Louise Richardson, ed., *The Roots of Terrorism.* New York: Routledge, pp. 85–101.

Hafez, Mohammed M. 2004. "From Marginalization to Massacres: A Political Process Explanation." In Quintan Wiktorowicz, ed., *Islamic Activism: A Social Movement Theory Approach.* Bloomington: Indiana University Press, pp. 37–60.

Hafez, Mohammed. 2006. "Political Repression and Violent Rebellion in the Muslim World." In J. Forest, ed., *The Making of a Terrorist: Recruitment, Training and Root Causes.* Westport, CT/London: Praeger Security International, Vol. 3, pp. 74–91.

Hafez, Mohammed. 2007. *Suicide Bombers in Iraq: The Strategy and Ideology of Martyrdom.* Washington, DC: USIP Press.

Hafez, Mohammed M., and Quintan Wiktorowicz. 2004. "Violence as Contention in the Egyptian Islamic Movement." In Quintan Wiktorowicz, ed., *Islamic Activism: A Social Movement Theory Approach.* Bloomington: Indiana University Press, pp. 61–88.

Hall, Peter A. 2003. "Aligning Ontology and Methodology in Comparative Research." In James Mahoney and Dietrich Rueschemeyer, eds., *Comparative Historical Research.* Cambridge: Cambridge University Press, pp. 373–404.

Hasenclever, Andreas, and Volker Rittberger. 2000. "Does Religion Make a Difference? Theoretical Approaches to the Impact of Faith on Political Conflict." *Millennium: Journal of International Studies* 29: 641–74.

Hassan, Muhammad H. B. 2006. "Key Considerations in Counterideological Work against Terrorist Ideology." *Studies in Conflict & Terrorism* 29: 531–58.

Hedström, Peter, and Peter Bearman. 2009. "What Is Analytic Sociology All About? An Introductory Essay." In Peter Hedström and Peter Bearman, *The Oxford Handbook of Analytic Sociology*. Oxford: Oxford University Press, pp. 3–15.

Hedström, Peter, and Richard Swedberg. 1998. *Social Mechanisms: An Analytical Approach to Social Theory*. Cambridge: Cambridge University Press.

Hegghammer, Thomas. 2010. *Jihad in Saudi Arabia, Violence and Pan-Islamism since 1979*. Cambridge: Cambridge University Press.

Heitmeyer, Wilhelm. 2005. "Right-Wing Terrorism." In Tore Bjørgo, ed., *Root Causes of Terrorism: Myths, Reality and Ways Forward*. London: Routledge, pp. 141–53.

Hewitt, Joseph, Jonathan Wilkenfeld, and Ted Robert Gurr. 2007. *Peace and Conflict*. Boulder, CO: Paradigm.

Higgins, Rosalyn. 1997. "The General International Law of Terrorism." In Rosalyn Higgins and Maurice Flory, eds., *Terrorism and International Law*. London: Routledge, pp. 13–30.

Hirschman, Albert O. 1982. *Shifting Involvements: Private Interests and Public Action*. Princeton, NJ: Princeton University Press.

Hobsbawm, Eric J. 1959. *The Primitive Rebels*. Manchester: University of Manchester Press.

Hoffman, Bruce. 1999. "Terrorism Trends and Prospects." In Ian Lesser, ed., *Countering the New Terrorism*. Santa Monica, CA: RAND, pp. 7–38.

Holmes, Stephen. 2005. "Al Qaeda, September 11, 2001." In Diego Gambetta, ed., *Making Sense of Suicide Missions*. Oxford: Oxford University Press, pp. 131–72.

Horgan, John. 2003. "The Search for the Terrorist Personality." In Andrew Silke, ed., *Terrorists, Victims and Society: Psychological Perspectives on Terrorism and Its Consequences*. West Sussex: John Wiley & Sons, pp. 3–28.

Horgan, John. 2005a. *Psychology of Terrorism*. London: Routledge.

Horgan, John. 2005b. "The Social and Psychological Characteristics of Terrorism and Terrorists." In Tore Bjørgo, ed., *Root Causes of Terrorism: Myths, Reality and Ways Forward*. London: Routledge, pp. 44–53.

Horgan, John. 2008. "Understanding Terrorism: Old Assumption, New Assertions and Challenges for Research." In J. Victoroff and A. Kruglanski, eds., *Psychology of Terrorism*. London: Psychology Press.

Horgan, John. 2009. "Individual Disengagement from Violent Groups of the Extreme Right." In Tore Bjørgo and John Horgan, eds., *Leaving Terrorism Behind*. London: Routledge, pp. 17–29.

Horn, Michael. 1982. *Sozialpsychologie des Terrorismus*. Frankfurt am Main: Campus.

Hübner, Klaus. 1979. "Erfahrungen mit Einsatzkonzeptionen in Berlin." *Die Polizei* 7: 10–12.

Huntington, Samuel P. 1968. *Political Order in Changing Society*. New Haven, CT: Yale University Press.

Huntington, Samuel P. 1996. *The Clash of Civilization and the Remaking of the World Order*. New York: Simon and Shuster.

Huq, Aziz Z. 2010. "*Modelling Terrorist Radicalization.*" University of Chicago, Public Law and Legal Theory Working Paper no. 301.

Ibarra, Pedro. 1989. *La evolucion estrategica de Eta.* Donostia: Kriselu.

Ignazi, Piero. 1994. *L'estrema destra in Europa.* Bologna: Il Mulino.

Ignazi, Piero. 2002. "The Extreme Right: Defining the Object and Assessing the Causes." In Martin Schain, Aristide Zolberg, and Patrick Hossay, eds., *Shadows over Europe: The Development and Impact of the Extreme Right in Western Europe.* New York and Houndmills, Basingstoke: Palgrave Macmillan, pp. 21–37.

Itcaina, Xabier. 2007. *Les virtuoses de l'identité: Religion et politique en Pays Basque.* Rennes: Presses Universitaire de Rennes.

Jackson, John H., and Cyril P. Morgan. 1978. *Organizational Theory: A Macroperspective for Management.* Englewood Cliffs, NJ: Prentice-Hall.

Jackson, Richard. 2007a. "The Core Commitments of Critical Terrorism Studies." *European Political Studies* 6 (3): 244–51.

Jackson, Richard. 2007b. "Language, Policy and the Construction of a Torture Culture in the War on Terrorism." *Review of International Studies* 33: 353–71.

Jackson, Richard. 2009. "Knowledge, Power and Politics in the Study of Political Terrorism." In Richard Jackson, Marie Breen Smyth, and Jeroen Gunning, eds., *Critical Terrorism Studies: A New Research Agenda.* London: Routledge, pp. 66–83.

Jackson, Richard, Marie Breen Smyth, and Jeroen Gunning. 2009. "Introduction: The Case for Critical Terrorism Studies." In Richard Jackson, Marie Breen Smyth, and Jeroen Gunning, eds., *Critical Terrorism Studies: A New Research Agenda.* London: Routledge, pp. 1–9.

Jäger, Herbert. 1981. "Die individuelle Dimension terroristischen Handelns." In Herbert Jäger, Gerhard Schmidtchen, and Liselotte Süllwold, eds., *Lebenslaufanalysen.* Opladen: Westdeutscher Verlag, pp. 120–74.

Jäger, Herbert, and Lorenz Böllinger. 1981. "Thesen zur weiteren Diskussion des Terrorismus." In Herbert Jäger, Gerhard Schmidtchen, and Liselotte Süllwold, eds., *Lebenslaufanalysen.* Opladen: Westdeutscher Verlag, pp. 232–42.

Jaime-Jiménez, Oscar, and Fernando Reinares. 1998. "The Policing of Mass Demonstrations in Spain." In Donatella della Porta and Herbert Reiter, eds., *The Policing of Mass Demonstrations in Contemporary Democracies.* Minneapolis: University of Minnesota Press, pp. 166–87.

Jamieson, Allison. 1989. *The Heart Attacked.* New York: Marion Boyars.

Jasper, James M. 2004. "A Strategic Approach to Collective Action: Looking for Agency in Social Movement Choices." *Mobilization: An International Journal* 9: 1–16.

Jasper, James M. 2006. *Getting Your Way: Using Strategy in Everyday Life.* Chicago: University of Chicago Press.

Jauregui Bereciartu, Gurutz. 1981. *Ideologia y estrategia politica de ETA: Analisis de su evolucion entre 1959 y 1968.* Madrid: Siglo XXI.

Jauregui Bereciartu, Gurutz. 1986. "National Identity and Political Violence in the Basque Country." *European Journal of Political Research* 14: 587–605.

Jenkins, Brian. 1975. "International Terrorism: A New Mode of Conflict." In David Carlton and Carlo Schaerf, eds., *International Terrorism and World Security.* London: Croom Helm.

Jenkins, Brian 2006. *The New Age of Terrorism.* Santa Monica, CA: RAND.

Jenkins, Brian. 2007. "Building an Army of Believers: Jihadist Radicalisation and Recruitment." Testimony presented before the House Homeland Security

Committee, Subcommittee on Intelligence, Information Sharing and Terrorism Risk Assessment.

Juergensmeyer, Mark. 2000. *Terror in the Name of God: The Global Rise of Religious Violence*. Berkeley: University of California Press.

Jünschke, Klaus. 1988. *Spaetlese: Texte zu Raf und Knast*. Frankfurt am Main: Neue Kritik.

Kalyvas, Stathis. 1999. "Wanton and Senseless? The Logic of Massacres in Algeria." *Rationality and Society* 11: 243–85.

Kalyvas, Stathis. 2006. *The Logic of Violence in Civil Wars*. Cambridge: Cambridge University Press.

Kanter, Rosabeth M. 1968. "Commitment and Social Organization: A Study of Commitment Mechanisms in Utopian Communities." *American Sociological Review* 13: 499–517.

Kanter, Rosabeth M. 1972. *Commitment and Community: Communes and Utopias in Sociological Perspective*. Cambridge, MA: Harvard University Press.

Karagiannis, Immanuel. 2011. *Political Islam in Central Asia: The Challenge of Itzb Ut-Tahrir*. London: Routledge.

Karagiannis, Immanuel, and Clark McCauley. 2006. "Hizb ut-Tahrir al-Islami: Evaluating the Threat Posed by a Radical Islamic Group That Remains Nonviolent." *Terrorism and Political Violence* 18: 315–34.

Kasmir, Sharryn. 2002. "'More Basque than You!': Class, Youth, and Identity in an Industrial Basque Town." *Identities* 9: 39–68.

Katzman, Kenneth. 2005. *Al Qaeda: Profile and Threat Assessment*. CRS report for Congress, Congressional Research Service: The Library of Congress.

Kaufmann, Eric, and Daniel Conversi. 2007. "Ethnic and Nationalist Mobilization." In Jean Tournon and Adrian Guelke, eds., *Ethnic Groups and Politics: Recent Analytical Developments*. Berlin: VS-Verlag.

Kepel, Gilles. 1985. *Muslim Extremism in Egypt: The Prophet and Pharaoh*. London: Saqi.

Kepel, Gilles. 2002. *Jihad: The Trail of Political Islam*. Cambridge, MA: Belknap Press of Harvard University Press.

Kepel, Gilles. 2005. *The Roots of the Radical Islam*. London: Saqi.

Kepel, Gilles, and Jean-Pierre Milelli. 2008. *Al Qaeda in Its Own Words*. Cambridge, MA: Harvard University Press.

Khalidi, Rashid. 1997. *Palestinian Identity: The Construction of Modern National Consciousness*. New York: Columbia University Press.

Khosrokhavar, Farad. 2006. *Quand al-Quaïda parle*. Paris: Grasset.

Kitschelt, Herbert. 1985. "New Social Movements in West Germany and the United States." *Political Power and Social Theory* 5: 273–342.

Kitschelt, Herbert. 1986. "Political Opportunity Structures and Political Protest: Anti-Nuclear Movements in Four Democracies." *British Journal of Political Science* 16: 57–85.

Klandermans, Bert. 2004. "The Demand and Supply of Participation: Social-Psychological Correlates of Participation in Social Movements." In David Snow, Sarah Soule, and Hanspeter Kriesi, eds., *The Blackwell Companion to Social Movements*. Oxford: Blackwell, pp. 360–79.

Klandermans, Bert. 2005. "Une psychologie sociale de l'exit." In Olivier Fillieule, ed., *Le désengagement militant*. Paris: Belin, pp. 95–110.

Klein, Hans-Joachim. 1980. *La mort mercenaire: Temoignage d'un ancient terroriste*. Paris: Seuil.

Kohlmann, Evan. 2004. *Al Qaida's Jihad in Europe: The Afghan-Bosnian Network.* Oxford: Berg.

Koopmans, Ruud. 1995. *Democracy from Below: New Social Movements and the Political System in West Germany.* Boulder, CO: Westview Press.

Koschade, Stuart A. 2006. "The Developing Jihad: The Ideological Consistency of Jihadi Doctrine from Al-Qaeda to the Revolutionary Fundamentalist Movement." In Carly Hall and Chanel Hopkinson, eds., *Social Change in the 21st Century.* Carseldine: Brisbane.

Kriesi, Hanspeter. 1996. "The Political Opportunity Structure of New Social Movements: Its Impact on Their Mobilization." In Craig Jenkins and Bert Klandermans, eds., *The Politics of Social Protest.* Minneapolis, MN/London: University of Minnesota Press/UCL Press, pp. 167–98.

Kriesi, Hanspeter, Ruud Koopmans, Jan-Willem Duyvendak, and Marco Giugni. 1995. *New Social Movements in Western Europe.* Minneapolis: University of Minnesota Press/UCL Press.

Krueger, Alan B., and Jitka Malečková. 2003. "Education, Poverty and Terrorism: Is There a Causal Connection?" *Journal of Economic Perspectives* 17: 119–44.

Krutwig, Federico [pseud.]. 1973. *Vasconia: Estudio Dialectico de una Nacionalidad.* Buenos Aires: Ediciones Norbati.

Kurzman, Charles. 2004. "Conclusion: Social Movement Theory and Islamic Studies." In Quintan Wiktorowicz, ed., *Islamic Activism: A Social Movement Theory Approach.* Bloomington: Indiana University Press, pp. 289–304.

Labbé, D., and M. Croisat. 1992. *La fin de syndicats?* Paris: L'Harmattan.

LaFree, Gary, Laura Dugan, and Raven Korte. 2009. "The Impact of British Counterterrorist Strategies on Political Violence in Northern Ireland: Comparing Deterrence and Backlash Models." *Criminology* 47: 17–45.

LaFree, Gary, and Erin Miller. 2008. "Desistance from Terrorism: What Can We Learn from Criminology?" *Dynamics of Asymmetric Conflict* 1: 203–30.

Laqueur, Walter. 2001. "Left, Right, and Beyond: The Changing Face of Terror." In James F. Hoge, Jr. and Gideon Rose, eds., *How Did This Happen? Terrorism and the New War.* New York: Public Affairs, pp. 71–82.

Laqueur, Walter. 2003. *No End to War: Terrorism in the Twenty-First Century.* New York: Continuum.

Laurenzano, Marco. 2000. *ETA: Il nazionalismo radicale basco. 1973–1980.* Rome: Semar.

Lawson, Fred H. 2004. "Repertoires of Contention in Contemporary Bahrain." In Quintan Wiktorowicz, ed., *Islamic Activism: A Social Movement Theory Approach.* Bloomington: Indiana University Press, pp. 89–111.

Leclercq, Catherine. 2005. "'Raisons de sortir': Les militants du Partie communiste francais." In Olivier Fillieule, ed., *Le désengagement militant.* Paris: Belin, pp. 131–54.

Lichbach, Mark Irving. 1987. "Deterrence or Escalation? The Puzzle of Aggregate Studies of Repression and Dissent." *Journal of Conflict Resolution* 31: 266–97.

Lipsky, Michael. 1965. *Protest and City Politics.* Chicago: Rand McNally.

Lofland, John. 1985. "Social Movement Culture." In John Lofland, ed., *Protest: Studies of Collective Behavior and Social Movements.* New Brunswick, NJ: Transaction, pp. 219–39.

Lofland, John. 1996. *Social Movement Organizations: Guide to Research on Insurgent Realities.* Hawthorne, NY: Aldine Transaction.

Mahler, Horst. 1977. "Ausbruch aus einem Missverständnis." *Kursbuch* 48: 77–100.

Mahler, Horst. 1980. *Per la critica del terrorismo*. Bari: De Donato.

Mahoney, James. 2003. *Tentative Answers to Questions about Causal Mechanisms*. Philadelphia: APSA.

Mahoney, James, and Gary Goertz. 2006. "A Tale of Two Cultures: Contrasting Quantitative and Qualitative Research." *Political Analysis* 14: 227–49.

Maleckova, Jitka. 2005. "Impoverished Terrorists: Stereotypes or Reality?" In Tore Bjørgo, ed., *Root Causes of Terrorism: Myths, Reality and Ways Forward*. London: Routledge, pp. 33–41.

Malpricht, Gunter. 1984. *Interaktionsprozesse bei Demonstrationen*. Heidelberg: Kriminalistik Verlag.

Malthaner, Stefan. 2011. *Mobilizing the Faithful*. Frankfurt am Main: Campus Verlag.

Manconi, Luigi. 1990. "Il nemico assoluto. Antifascismo e contropotere nella fase aurorale del terrorismo di sinistra." In Raimondo Catanzaro, ed., *Ideologia, movimenti e terrorismo*. Bologna: Il Mulino.

Mandaville, Peter. 2007. *Global Political Islam*. New York: Routledge.

March, James G. 1988. *Decisions and Organizations*. Oxford: Blackwell.

Marchi, Valerio. 1994. "Gioventù, territorio, rancore: il modello bonehead." *Democrazia e diritto* 34 (1): 53–178.

Masuch, Michael. 1985. "Vicious Circles in Organizations." *Administrative Science Quarterly* 30: 14–33.

Mayntz, Renate. 2004. "Organizational Forms of Terrorism: Hierarchy, Network, or a Type sui generis?" MPIfG Discussion Paper 04/4, Max Planck Institute for the Study of Societies, Cologne.

McAdam, Doug. 1982. *Political Process and the Development of Black Insurgency. 1930–1970*. Chicago: University of Chicago Press.

McAdam, Doug. 1983. "Tactical Innovation and the Pace of Insurgency." *American Sociological Review* 48: 735–54.

McAdam, Doug. 1986. "Recruitment to High-Risk Activism: The Case of Freedom Summer." *American Journal of Sociology* 92: 64–90.

McAdam, Doug. 1988. *Freedom Summer*. Oxford: Oxford University Press.

McAdam, Doug, Sidney Tarrow, and Charles Tilly. 2001. *Dynamics of Contention*. Cambridge: Cambridge University Press.

McAuly, Denis. 2006. "The Ideology of Osama Bin Laden: Nation, Tribe and World Economy." *Journal of Political Ideologies* 10: 269–87.

McCarthy, John D., and Mayer N. Zald. 1973. *The Trend of Social Movements*. Morrilltown, NJ: General Learning Press.

McCarthy, John D., and Mayer N. Zald. 1977. "Resource Mobilization and Social Movements: A Partial Theory." *American Journal of Sociology* 82: 1212–41.

McCauley, Clark. 2008. "Group Desistance from Terrorism: A Dynamic Perspective." *Dynamics of Asymmetric Conflict* 1: 269–93

McCauley, Clark, and Sophia Moskalenko. 2011. *Friction: How Radicalization Happens to Them and Us*. Oxford: Oxford University Press.

McCormick, Gordon. 2003. "Terrorist Decision Making." *Annual Review of Political Science* 6: 473–507.

McPhail, Clark, David Schweingruber, and John McCarthy. 1998. "Policing Protest in the United States." In Donatella Della Porta and Herbert Reiter, eds., *Policing Protest: The Control of Mass Demonstrations in Western Democracies*. Minneapolis: University of Minnesota Press, pp. 49–69.

McPhillips, Patricia E. 2010. *Toward Greater Understanding: The Jihadist Ideology of Al Qaeda*. Fort Leavenworth, KS: US Army Command and General Staff College.

Merari, Ariel. 2005. "Social, Organizational and Psychological Factors in Suicide Terrorism." In Tore Bjørgo, ed., *Root Causes of Terrorism: Myths, Reality and Ways Forward*. London: Routledge, pp. 70–87.

Merkl, Peter H. 1986. *Political Violence and Terror: Motifs and Motivations*. Berkeley: University of California Press.

Merkl, Peter H. 1997. "Why Are They So Strong Now? Comparative Reflections on the Revival of the Radical Right in Europe." In Peter H. Merkl and Leonard Weinberg, eds., *The Revival of Right-Wing Extremism in the Nineties*. London: Frank Cass, pp. 17–46.

Merton, Robert K. 1957. *Social Theory and Social Structure*. New York: Free Press.

Minkenberg, Michael. 1998. *Die neue radikale Rechte im Vergleich*. Opladen: Westdeutscher Verlag.

Minna, Rosario. 1984. "Il terrorismo di destra." In Donatella della Porta, ed., *Terrorismi in Italia*. Bologna: Il Mulino, pp. 21–72.

Mishal, Sahul, and Maoz Rosenthal. 2005. "Al Qaeda as a Dune Organization: Toward a Typology of Islamic Terrorist Organizations." *Studies in Conflict & Terrorism* 28: 275–93.

Moghaddam, Fathali. 2005. "The Staircase to Terrorism: A Psychological Exploration." *American Psychologist* 60: 161–9.

Moore, Will H. 1998. "Repression and Dissent: Substitution, Context and Timing." *American Journal of Political Science* 42: 851–73.

Morf, Gustave. 1970. *Terror in Quebec*. Toronto: Clark, Irwin.

Morgan, Jane. 1987. *Conflict and Order: The Police and Labour Disputes in England and Wales. 1900–1939*. Oxford: Clarendon Press.

Morgan, M. J. 2004. "The Origins of the New Terrorism." *Parameters* 34 (Spring): 29–43.

Morucci, Valerio. 2004. *La peggio gioventù: Una vita nella lotta armata*. Milan: Bompiani.

Moyano, Maria J. 1995. *Argentina's Lost Patrol: Armed Struggle, 1969–1979*. New Haven, CT: Yale University Press.

Muñoz Alonso, Alejandro. 1982. *El terrorismo en España: El terror frente a la convivencia pluralista en libertad*. Barcelona: Planeta.

Muro, Diego. 2008. *Ethnicity and Violence: The Case of Radical Basque Nationalism*. New York: Routledge.

Neidhardt, Friedhelm. 1981. "Über Zufall, Eigendynamik und Institutionalisierbarkeit absurder Prozesse: Notizen am Bespiel der Entstehung und Einrichtung einer terroristischen Gruppe." In Heinz von Alemann and Hans Peter Thurn, eds., *Soziologie in weltbürgerlicher Absicht*. Opladen: Westdeutscher, pp. 243–57.

Neidhardt, Friedhelm. 1982. "Soziale Bedingungen terroristischen Handelns: Das Beispiel der 'Baader-Meinhof-Gruppe' (RAF)." In Wanda von Baeyer-Katte, Dieter Claessens, Hubert Feger, and Friedhelm Neidhardt, eds., *Gruppenprozesse*. Opladen: Westdeutscher Verlag, pp. 318–91.

Nesser, Peter. 2006a. "Jihad in Europe: Recruitment for Terrorist Cells in Europe." In *Path to Global Jihad: Radicalisation and Recruitment to Terror Networks*. Proceedings from a FFI seminar, Oslo, 15 March, www.ffi.no/TERRA, accessed 26 October 2012.

Nesser, Peter. 2006b. "Jihadism in Western Europe after the Invasion of Iraq: Tracing Motivational Influences from the Iraq War on Jihadist Terrorism in Western Europe." *Studies in Conflict and Terrorism* 29 (4): 323–42.

Neuhauser, Peter. 1978. "The Mind of a Terrorist: Interview with Michael 'Bommi' Baumann." *Encounter* 51: 84.

Neumann, Peter, and Brooke Rogers. 2007. "Recruitment and Mobilisation for the Islamist Militant Movement in Europe." European Commission, Directorate General for Justice.

Noakes, John, and Patrick F. Gillham. 2006. "Aspects of the 'New Penology' in the Police Response to Major Political Protests in the United States, 1999–2000." In Donatella della Porta, Abby Peterson, and Herbert Reiter, eds., *Policing Transnational Protest: In the Aftermath of the "Battle of Seattle."* Aldershot: Ashgate, pp. 97–116.

Norris, Pippa. 2002. *Democratic Phoenix: Reinventing Political Activism.* New York: Cambridge University Press.

Novelli, Diego, and Nicola Tranfaglia. 1988. *Vite sospese: Le generazioni del terrorismo.* Milan: Garzanti.

O'Boyle, G. 2002. "Theories of Justification and Political Violence: Examples from Four Groups." *Terrorism and Political Violence* 14: 23–46.

Opp, Karl-Dieter, and Wolfgang Roehl. 1990. "Repression, Micromobilization, and Political Protest." *Social Forces* 69: 521–47.

Pantazis, Christina, and Simon Pemberton. 2009. "From the 'Old' to the 'New' Suspect Community." *British Journal of Criminology* 49: 646–66.

Panvini, Guido. 2009. *Ordine nero, Guerriglia rossa: La violenza politica nell'Italia degli anni Sessanta e Settanta (1966–1975).* Torino: Einaudi.

Pape, Robert A. 2005. *Dying to Win: The Strategic Logic of Suicide Terrorism.* New York: Random House.

Passy, Florence. 2005. "Interactions sociales et imbrications des sphères de vie." In Olivier Fillieule, ed., *Le désengagement militant.* Paris: Belin, pp. 111–30.

Pérez-Agote, Alfonso. 1984. *La reproduccion del nazionalismo: El caso vasco.* Madrid: Cis-Siglo XXI.

Pérez-Agote, Alfonso. 2006. *The Social Roots of Basque Nationalism.* Reno: University of Nevada Press.

Pisetta, Enrico. 1990. "Militanza partitica e scelte eversive nei terroristi neofascisti." In Raimondo Catanzaro, ed., *Ideologia, movimenti, terrorismi.* Bologna: Il Mulino, pp. 191–210.

Piven, Frances F., and Cloward, Richard. 1977. *Poor People's Movements.* New York: Pantheon.

Pizzorno, Alessandro. 1978. "Political Exchange and Collective Identity in Industrial Conflict." In Colin Crouch and Alessandro Pizzorno, eds., *The Resurgence of Class Conflict in Western Europe.* New York: Holmes & Meier, pp. 277–98.

Pizzorno, Alessandro. 1993. *Le radici della politica assoluta.* Milan: Feltrinelli.

Pizzorno, Alessandro. 2007. *Il velo della diversità.* Milan: Feltrinelli.

Poe, Steven, and C. Neal Tate. 1994. "Repression of Human-Rights to Personal Integrity in the 1980s – A Global Analysis." *American Political Science Review* 88: 853–72.

Poe, Steven C., C. Neal Tate, and Linda Camp Keith. 1999. "Repression of the Human Rights to Personal Integrity Revised: A Global Cross-National Study Covering the Years 1976–1993." *International Study Quarterly* 43: 291–313.

Post, Jerrold M. 2005. "The Sociocultural Underpinnings of Terrorist Psychology." In Tore Bjørgo, ed., *Root Causes of Terrorism: Myths, Reality and Ways Forward.* London: Routledge, pp. 54–69.

Poynting, Scott, and Victoria Mason. 2006. "Tolerance, Freedom, Justice and Peace? Britain, Australia and Anti-Muslim Racism since 11 September 2011." *Journal of Intercultural Studies* 27: 365–91.

Proll, Astrid. 1978. "Zu viele Graber sind auf meinem Weg." *Stern* 48: 20–30.

Prowe, Diethelm. 2004. "The Fascist Phantom and Anti-Immigrant Violence: The Power of (False) Equation." In Eric Weitz and Angelica Fenner, eds., *Fascism and Neofascism*. New York and Houndmills, Basingstoke: Palgrave Macmillan, pp. 125–40.

Pudal, Bernard. 2005. "Gérard Belloin, de l'engagement communiste à l' 'auto-analyse.'" In Olivier Fillieule, ed., *Le désengagement militant*. Paris: Belin, pp. 155–7.

Ranstorp, Magnus. 2009. "Mapping Terrorism Studies after 9/11." In Richard Jackson, Marie Breen Smyth, and Jeroen Gunning, eds., *Critical Terrorism Studies: A New Research Agenda*. London: Routledge, pp. 13–33.

Raphael, Sam. 2009. "In the Service of Power: Terrorism Studies and US Intervention in the Global South." In Richard Jackson, Marie Breen Smyth, and Jeroen Gunning, eds., *Critical Terrorism Studies: A New Research Agenda*. London: Routledge, pp. 49–65.

Rapoport, David C. 1992. "Terrorism." In Mary Hawkesworth and Maurice Kogan, eds., *Routledge Encyclopedia of Government and Politics*. London: Routledge, Vol. 2.

Rapoport, David C. 2012. "Fear and Trembling: Terrorism in Three Religious Traditions." In John Horgan and Kurt Braddock, eds., *Terrorism Studies: A Reader*. London: Routledge, pp. 3–26.

Rasch, Winfried. 1979. "Psychological Dimensions of Political Terrorism in the Federal Republic of Germany." *International Journal of Law and Psychiatry* 2: 79–85.

Rashwan, Diaa. 2009. "The Renounciation of Violence by Egyptian Jihadi Organizations." In Tore Bjørgo and John Horgan, eds., *Leaving Terrorism Behind*. London: Routledge, pp. 113–32.

Reinares, Fernando. 2001. *Patriotas de la muerte: Quiénes han militado en ETA y por qué?* Madrid: Taurus.

Reinares, Fernando. 2005. "Nationalist Separatism and Terrorism in Comparative Perspective." In Tore Bjørgo, ed., *Root Causes of Terrorism: Myths, Reality and Ways Forward*. London: Routledge, pp. 119–30.

Reinares, Fernando, and Werner Herzog. 1993. "Baskenland: 'Es hat uns unvorbereitet getroffen.'" In Peter Waldmann, ed., *Beruf: Terrorist*. Munich: Beck, pp. 16–41.

Reiter, Herbert. 1998. "Police and Public Order in Italy, 1944–1948: The Case of Florence." In Donatella della Porta and Herbert Reiter, eds., *Policing Protest: The Control of Mass Demonstrations in Western Democracies*. Minneapolis: University of Minnesota Press, pp. 143–65.

Richards, Michael A. 1998. *A Time of Silence: Civil War and the Culture of Repression in Franco's Spain*. Cambridge: Cambridge University Press.

Richardson, Louise. 2006a. *The Roots of Terrorism*. New York: Routledge.

Richardson, Louise. 2006b. *What Terrorists Want*. New York: Random House.

Ricolfi, Luca. 2005. "Palestinians, 1981–2003." In Diego Gambetta, ed., *Making Sense of Suicide Missions*. Oxford: Oxford University Press, pp. 76–129.

Ritter, Daniel. 2010. *Why the Iranian Revolution Was Non-Violent: Internationalized Social Change and the Iron Cage of Liberalism*. PhD Thesis, University of Texas at Austin.

Rochon, Thomas R. 1998. *Culture Moves: Ideas, Activism, and Changing Values*. Princeton, NJ: Princeton University Press.

Rohrmoser, Günter. 1981. "Ideologische Ursachen des Terrorismus." In Iring Fetscher and Günter Rohrmoser, eds., *Ideologien und Strategies*. Opladen: Westdeutscher, pp. 274–339.

Rosefsky Wickham, Carrie. 2004. "Interests, Ideas, and Islamist Outreach in Egypt." In Quintan Wiktorowicz, ed., *Islamic Activism: A Social Movement Theory Approach.* Bloomington: Indiana University Press, pp. 231–49.

Ross, Jeff I., and Ted R. Gurr. 1989. "Why Terrorism Subsides: A Comparative Study of Canada and the United States." *Comparative Politics* 21: 405–26.

Roy, Olivier. 2004. *Globalised Islam: The Search for a New Ummah.* London: Hurst.

Roy, Olivier. 2008. "Al Qaeda in the West as a Youth Movement: The Power of a Narrative." University of Sussex, Micron Policy Working Paper 2.

Rubinstein, Jonathan. 1980. "Cops' Rules." In R. J. Landman, ed., *Police Behavior.* New York: Oxford University Press.

Rucht, Dieter. 1994. *Modernisierung und Soziale Bewegungen.* Frankfurt am Main: Campus.

Russel, Charles A., and Bowman H. Miller. 1983. "Profile of a Terrorist." In L. Z. Ian and Yonas Alexander, eds., *Perspectives on Terrorism.* Wilmington, RI: Scholarly Resources, pp. 45–59.

Sack, Fritz. 1984. "Die Reaktion von Gesellschaft: Politik und Staat auf die Studenten Bewegung." In Fritz Sack and Heinz Steiner, eds., *Protest und Reaktion.* Opladen: Westdeutscher Verlag, pp. 107–227.

Sadowski, Yahya. 2006. "Political Islam: Asking the Wrong Questions?" *Annual Review of Political Science* 9: 215–40.

Sageman, Marc. 2004. *Understanding Terror Networks.* Philadelphia: University of Pennsylvania Press.

Sageman, Marc, 2008. *Leaderless Jihad.* Philadelphia: University of Pennsylvania Press.

Salierno, Giuliano. 1976. *Autobiografia di un picchiatore fascista.* Torino: Einaudi.

Sambanis, Paul. 2000. "Partition as a Solution to Ethnic War: An Empirical Critique of the Theoretical Literature." *World Politics* 52: 437–83.

Sambanis, Paul. 2005. "Using Case Studies to Refine and Expand the Theory of Civil War." In Paul Collier and Nicholas Sambanis, eds., *Understanding Civil War: Evidence and Analysis.* Washington, DC: World Bank.

Sánchez-Cuenca, Ignacio. 2001. *Eta contra el Estado: Las estrategias del terrorismo.* Barcellona: Tusquetz Editores.

Sánchez-Cuenca, Ignacio. 2009. "Explaining Temporal Variation in the Lethality of ETA." Paper, Juan March Institute and Complutense University (Madrid).

Sánchez-Cuenca, Ignacio, and Paloma Aguillar. 2009. "Terrorist Violence and Popular Mobilization: The Case of Spanish Transition to Democracy." Juan March Institute, unpublished manuscript.

Scavino, Marco. 2012. "La piazza e la forza: I percorsi verso la lotta armata dal sessantotto alla metà degli anni Settanta." In Simone Neri Serneri, ed., *Verso la lotta armata.* Bologna: Il Mulino, pp. 117–206.

Schiffauer, Werner. 2008. "Suspect Subjects: Muslim Migrants and the Security Agencies in Germany." In Julia M. Eckert, ed., *The Social Life of Anti-Terrorism Laws.* Bielefeld: Transcript, pp. 55–77.

Schmid, Alex P., and Albert J. Jongman. 1988. *Political Terrorism.* New Brunswick, NJ: Transaction.

Schmid, Alex, and Albert Jongman. 2005. *Political Terrorism*. Piscataway, NJ: Transaction.

Scott, W. Richard. 1983. "The Organization of Environments: Networks, Cultural, and Historical Elements." In J. W. Meyer and W. R. Scott, eds., *Organizational Environments: Ritual and Rationality*. Beverly Hills, CA: Sage, pp. 155–75.

Serafino, Davide. 2012. "Genova: La lotta armata in una città operaia." In Simone Neri Serneri, ed., *Verso la lotta armata*. Bologna: Il Mulino, pp. 367–90.

Seufert, Michael. 1978. "Schleyer was ein richtig Ziel." *Stern* 22.

Sewell, William H. 1996. "Three Temporalities: Toward an Eventful Sociology." In Terence J. McDonald, ed., *The Historic Turn in the Human Sciences*. Ann Arbor: University of Michigan Press, pp. 245–80.

Sheptycki, James W. E. 2005. "Policing Protest When Politics Go Global: Comparing Public Order Policing in Canada and Bolivia." *Policing and Society* 15: 327–52.

Silke, Andrew. 2003. "The Psychology of Suicidal Terrorism." In Andrew Silke, ed., *Terrorist, Victims, and Society: Psychological Perspectives on Terrorism and Its Consequence*. London: John Wiley, pp. 93–108.

Silke, Andrew. 2004. "An Introduction to Terrorism Research." In Andrew Silke, ed., *Research on Terrorism: Trends, Achievements, and Failures*. London: Frank Cass, pp. 1–29.

Silke, Andrew. 2006. "The Impact of 9/11 on Research on Terrorism." In M. Ranstorp, ed., *Mapping Terrorism Research: State of the Art. Gaps and Future Direction*. London: Routledge, pp. 175–93.

Silke, Andrew. 2009. "Contemporary Terrorist Studies, Issues in Research." In Richard Jackson, Marie Breen Smyth, and Jeroen Gunning, eds., *Critical Terrorism Studies: A New Research Agenda*. London: Routledge, pp. 34–48.

Silke, Andrew. 2012. "Fire of Iolaus: The Role of State Countermeasures in Causing Terrorism and What Needs to Be Done." In John Horgan and Kurt Braddock, eds., *Terrorism Studies: A Reader*. London: Routledge, pp. 345–57.

Simon, Steven, and Daniel Benjamin. 2000. "America and the New Terrorism." *Survival* 42: 59–75.

Singerman, Diana. 2004. "The Networked World of Islamist Social Movements." In Quintan Wiktorowicz, ed., *Islamic Activism: A Social Movement Theory Approach*. Bloomington: Indiana University Press, pp. 143–63.

Skolnick, Jerome H. 1966. *Justice without Trial: Law Enforcement in Democratic Society*. New York: John Wiley and Sons.

Smelser, Neil J. 2007. *The Faces of Terrorism: Social and Psychological Dimensions*. Princeton, NJ: Princeton University Press.

Snow, David A., and Scott C. Byrd. 2007. "Ideology, Framing Processes and Islamic Terrorist Movements." *Mobilization* 12: 119–36.

Snow, David A., Burke E. Rochford, Steven Worden, and Robert Benford. 1986. "Frame Alignment Processes, Micromobilization, and Movement Participation." *American Sociological Review* 51: 464–81.

Snow, David A., Louis A. Zurcher, and Sheldon Ekland-Olson. 1980. "Social Networks and Social Movements: A Microstructural Approach to Differential Recruitment." *American Sociological Review* 45: 787–801.

Sobek, David, and Alex Braithwaite. 2004. "Unspoken Reciprocity: The Effects of Major Shifts in Israeli Policy on International Terrorism." Paper presented at the annual meeting of the International Studies Association.

Soccorso Rosso. 1976. *Brigate Rosse*. Milan: Feltrinelli.

Sommier, Isabelle. 2005. "Une expérience 'incommunicable'? Les ex-militants d'extreme-gauche francais et italiens." In Olivier Fillieule, ed., *Le désengagement militant*. Paris: Belin, pp. 171–88.

Spalek, Basia. 2010. "Community Policing, Trust, and Muslim Communities in Relation to 'New Terrorism.'" *Politics & Policy* 38: 789–815.

Spalek, Basia, and Robert Lambert. 2008. "Muslim Communities, Counter-Terrorism and Counter-Radicalisation: A Critically Reflective Approach to Engagement." *International Journal of Law, Crime and Justice* 36: 257–70.

Speitel, Volker. 1980a. "Wir wollten alles und gleichzeitig nichts. I." *Der Spiegel* 31: 36–49.

Speitel, Volker. 1980b. "Wir wollten alles und gleichzeitig nichts. II." *Der Spiegel* 32: 30–9.

Speitel, Volker. 1980c. "Wir wollten alles und gleichzeitig nichts. III." *Der Spiegel* 33: 33–6.

Sprinzak, Ehud. 1995. "Right-Wing Terrorism in a Comparative Perspective: The Case of Split Delegitimization." In Tore Bjørgo, ed., *Terror from the Extreme Right*. London: Frank Cass.

Steiner, Anne, and Lois Debray. 1987. *La Fraktion Armée Rouge*. Paris: Meridiens.

Taarnby, M. 2005. "Recruitment of Islamist Terrorists in Europe: Trends and Perspectives." Research report funded by the Danish Ministry of Justice.

Taggart, Paul. 2002. "Populism and the Pathology of Representative Politics." In Yves Mény and Yves Surel, eds., *Democracies and the Populist Challenge*. New York: Palgrave.

Tarchi, Marco. 1995. *Cinquant'anni di nostalgia: Intervista di Antonio Carioti*. Milan: Rizzoli.

Tarrow, Sidney. 1989. *Democracy and Disorder: Protest and Politics in Italy, 1965–1975*. Oxford/New York: Oxford University Press.

Tarrow, Sidney. 1994. *Power in Movement: Social Movements, Collective Action and Politics*. New York/Cambridge: Cambridge University Press.

Tarrow, Sidney. 2010. "The Strategy of Paired Comparison: Towards a Theory of Practice." *Comparative Political Studies* 43: 230–59.

Tarrow, Sidney. 2011. *Power in Movement: Social Movements, Collective Action and Politics*. New York/Cambridge: Cambridge University Press, 3rd expanded ed.

Taylor, Max, and John Horgan. 2012. "A Conceptual Framework for Addressing Psychological Process in the Development of the Terrorists." In John Horgan and Kurt Braddock, eds., *Terrorism Studies: A Reader*. London: Routledge, pp. 130–44.

Taylor, Verta, and Nella van Dyke. 2004. "'Get up. Stand up': Tactical Repertoires of Social Movements." In David A. Snow, Sarah A. Soule, and Hanspeter Kriesi, eds., *The Blackwell Companion to Social Movements*. Oxford: Blackwell, pp. 262–93.

Tejerina, Benjamin. 2001. "Protest Cycle, Political Violence and Social Movements in the Basque Country." *Nations and Nationalism* 7: 39–57.

Tilly, Charles. 1978. *From Mobilization to Revolution*. Reading, MA: Addison Wesley.

Tilly, Charles. 1986. *The Contentious French*. Cambridge, MA: Harvard University Press.

Tilly, Charles. 2001. "Mechanisms in Political Science." *Annual Review of Political Science* 4: 21–41.

Tilly, Charles. 2003. *The Politics of Collective Violence*. Cambridge: Cambridge University Press.

Tilly, Charles. 2004. *Contention and Democracy in Europe: 1650–2000*. Cambridge: Cambridge University Press.

Tololyan, Khachig. 1987. "Culture Narrative and the Motivation of the Terrorist." *Journal of Strategic Studies* 10: 217–33.

Transnational Terrorism, Security and the Rule of Law. 2008a. "Causal Factors of Radicalization." WP4, April. www.transnationalterrorism.eu, accessed 1 August 2011.

Transnational Terrorism, Security and the Rule of Law. 2008b. "Defining Terrorism." WP3, October. www.transnationalterrorism.eu, accessed 1 August 2011.

Transnational Terrorism, Security and the Rule of Law. 2008c. "Exploring Root and Trigger Causes of Terrorism." WP3, April. www.transnationalterrorism.eu, accessed 1 August 2011.

Transnational Terrorism, Security and the Rule of Law. 2008d. "The 'Hofstadgroep,' Working Group." www.transnationalterrorism.eu, accessed 1 August 2011.

Unzueta, Patxo. 1988. *Los Nietos de la Ira: Nacionalismo y violencia en el Pais Vasco.* Madrid: El Pais/Aguillar.

Uysal, Ayshen. 2005. "Organisation du maintien de l'ordre et répression policière en Turquie." In Donatella della Porta and Olivier Fillieule, eds., *Maintien de l'ordre et police des foules.* Paris: Presses de Science Po.

Van Den Broek, Hanspeter. 2004. "BORROKA – The Legitimation of Street Violence in the Political Discourse of Radical Basque Nationalists." *Terrorism and Political Violence* 16: 714–36.

Varon, Jeremy. 2004. *Bringing the War Home: The Weather Underground, the Red Army Faction, and Revolutionary Violence in the Sixties and Seventies.* London: University of California Press.

Vasilenko, V. I. 2004. "The Concept and Typology of Terrorism." *Statutes and Decisions: The Laws of the USSR and Its Successor States* 40: 46–56.

Ventura, Angelo. 1980. "Il problema storico del terrorismo italiano." *Rivista storica italiana* 92: 125–51.

Vertigans, Stephen. 2010. "British Muslims and the UK Government's 'War on Terror' within: Evidence of a Clash of Civilizations or Emergent De-Civilizing Processes?" *British Journal of Sociology* 61 (1): 26–44.

Veugelers, John. 2011. "Dissenting Families and Social Movement Abeyance: The Transmission of Neo-Fascist Frames in Postwar Italy." *British Journal of Sociology* 62: 241–61.

Victoroff, Jeff. 2005. "The Mind of the Terrorist: A Review and Critique of Psychological Approaches." *Journal of Conflict Resolution* 49: 3–42.

Viterna, Jocelyn. 2006. "Pulled, Pushed, and Persuaded: Explaining Women's Mobilization into Salvadoran Guerrilla Army." *American Journal of Sociology* 112: 1–45.

Waddington, David, and Colin Critcher. 2000. "Policing Pit Closures, 1984–1992." In R. Bessel and C. Emsley, eds., *Patterns of Provocation: Police and Public Disorder.* Oxford: Berghahn Books.

Waddington, P. A. J. 1994. *Liberty and Order: Public Order Policing in a Capital City.* London: UCL Press.

Waldmann, Peter. 1992. "Ethnic and Sociorevolutionary Terrorism: A Comparison of Structures." In Donatella della Porta, ed., *Social Movements and Violence: Participation in Underground Organizations.* Greenwich, CT: JAI Press, pp. 237–57.

Waldmann, Peter. 1998. *Ethnischer Radikalismus: Ursachen und Folgen Gewaltsamer Minderheitenkonflikte.* Opladen: Westdeutscher Verlag.

Wasmund, Klaus. 1986. "The Political Socialization of West German Terrorists." In Peter H. Merkl, ed., *Political Violence and Terror: Motifs and Motivations.* Berkeley: University of California Press, pp. 191–226.

Weinberg, Leonard. 2005. "Democracy and Terrorism." In Louise Richardson, ed., *The Roots of Terrorism*. New York: Routledge, pp. 45–56.

Weinberg, Leonard, and William Lee Eubank. 1987. *The Rise and Fall of Italian Terrorism*. Boulder, CO: Westview Press.

Weinberg, Leonard, and William Lee Eubank. 1988. "Neo-Fascist and Far Left Terrorists in Italy: Some Biographical Observations." *British Journal of Political Science* 18 (4): 531–49.

Weinberg, L., A. Pedahzur, and S. Hirsch-Hoefler. 2004. "The Challenges of Conceptualising Terrorism." *Terrorism and Political Violence* 16: 777–94.

Weinstein, Jeremy M. 2007. *Inside Rebellion, the Politics of Insurgent Violence*. Cambridge: Cambridge University Press.

White, Robert W. 1993. *Provisional Irish Republicans: An Oral and Interpretative History*. Westport, CT: Greenwood Press.

Wieviorka, Michel. 1988. *Société et terrorisme*. Paris: Fayard.

Wieviorka, Michel. 1993. *The Making of Terrorism*. Chicago: University of Chicago Press.

Wiktorowicz, Quintan. 2001. *The Management of Islamic Activism*. Albany: State University of New York Press.

Wiktorowicz, Q. 2004. Islamic Activism in Social Movement Theory. In Q. Wiktorowicz, ed., *Islamic Activism: A Social Movement Theory Approach*. Bloomington: Indiana University Press, pp. 1–33.

Wiktorowicz, Quintan. 2005. *Radical Islam Rising: Muslim Extremism in the West*. Lanham, MD: Rowman & Littlefield.

Wilson, John. 1973. *Introduction to Social Movements*. New York: Basic Books.

Winter, Martin. 1998. "Police Philosophy and Protest Policing in the Federal Republic of Germany (1960–1990)." In Donatella della Porta and Herbert Reiter, eds., *Policing Protest: The Control of Mass Demonstrations in Western Democracies*. Minneapolis: University of Minnesota Press, pp. 188–212.

Wood, Elisabeth Jean. 2003. *Insurgent Collective Action and Civil War in El Salvador*. Cambridge: Cambridge University Press.

Wright, Stuart A. 2007. *Patriots, Politics and the Oklahoma City Bombing*. Cambridge: Cambridge University Press.

Yavuz, M. Hakan. 2004. "Opportunity Spaces, Identity and Islamic Meaning in Turkey." In Quintan Wiktorowicz, ed., *Islamic Activism: A Social Movement Theory Approach*. Bloomington: Indiana University Press, pp. 270–88.

Zald, Mayer N., and Roberta Ash. 1966. "Social Movement Organizations: Growth, Decay, and Change." *Social Forces* 44: 327–41.

Zald, Mayer N., and John McCarthy. 1987. *Social Movements in an Organizational Society*. New Brunswick, NJ: Transaction.

Zald, Mayer N., and Bert Useem. 1987. "Movement and Countermovement Interaction: Mobilization, Tactics, and State Involvement." In M. N. Zald and J. D. McCarthy, eds., *Social Movements in an Organizational Society*. New Brunswick, NJ: Transaction Books, pp. 247–72.

Zirakzadeh, Cyrus Ernesto. 2002. "From Revolutionary Dreams to Organizational Fragmentation: Disputes over Violence within ETA and Sendero Luminoso." *Terrorism and Political Violence* 14: 66–92.

Zwerman, Gilda, Patricia G. Steinhoff, and Donatella della Porta. 2000. "Disappearing Social Movements: Clandestinity in the Cycle of New Left Protest in the US, Japan, Germany and Italy." *Mobilization* 5: 83–100.

Index

Acca Larentia attack, 44, 68, 88
action militarization, 201–03, 288–89
    definition, 175–76
affective focusing, 191, 243–52
    definition, 243, 261
al-Aqsa Martyrs Brigades. *See* Aqsa
    Martyrs Brigades, al-
al-Jamaa al-Islamiyya. *See* Jamaa
    al-Islamiyya, al-
al-Jihad. *See* Jihad, al-
al-Qaeda. *See* Qaeda, al-
al-Qaeda in the Arabic Peninsula. *See*
    Qaeda in the Arabic Peninsula, al-
al-Qaeda Iraq. *See* Qaeda Iraq, al-
al-Zawahir, Ayman. *See* Zawahir,
    Ayman, al-
AN. *See* Avanguardia Nazionale (National
    Vanguard)
antiterrorism, 4, 12, 66, 215, 265, 271,
    282. *See also* antiterrorist laws;
    curfews
    in the EU, 205
    profiling, 241–42
antiterrorist laws
    in Germany, 46
    in Italy, 271–72
    in Spain, 53
AQ. *See* Qaeda, al-
AQAP. *See* Qaeda in the Arabic
    Peninsula, al-
Aqsa Martyrs Brigades, al-, 62
Atta, Mohamed, 143
autonomia. See autonomous collectives
autonomous collectives, 81–83, 85, 123,
    209, 221

Avanguardia Nazionale (National
    Vanguard), 40, 43–44, 86–87, 225
    actions, 186
    ideology, 214–15, 216
    organizational structures, 158–59
Azzam, Abdullah, 110, 167, 226–27,
    231, 251

B2J. *See* Bewegung 2 Juni (June 2nd
    Movement)
Basque language, 51, 53–54, 91,
    132–35
    repression of its use, 50, 135
Battisti, Cesare, 2
Bewegung 2 Juni (June 2nd Movement),
    124
    forms, 184
    ideology, 209–13
    organizational structures, 155–56
    targets, 179
Bin Laden, Osama, 64–65, 98, 104, 110,
    138, 167–69, 171, 204, 226–30,
    231–32, 235–36, 251–52
Bouyeri, Muhammad, 142
BR. *See* Brigate Rosse (Red Brigades)
Brigate Rosse (Red Brigades), 83–84,
    118–20, 122–23, 263–64, 269, 271,
    272, 274–75, 277
    forms, 184–85
    ideology, 147, 208–13, 215
    organizational structures, 153–55, 157,
    161, 201
    targets, 179–83
Burgos trial, 49–50, 55, 93, 135, 190
burnout, 279

For EU product safety concerns, contact us at Calle de José Abascal, 56–1°,
28003 Madrid, Spain or eugpsr@cambridge.org.

www.ingramcontent.com/pod-product-compliance
Ingram Content Group UK Ltd.
Pitfield, Milton Keynes, MK11 3LW, UK
UKHW010731190625
459647UK00030B/1210